WHEN THE
AIRLINES
WENT TO
WAR

WHEN THE AIRLINES WENT TO WAR

Robert J. Serling

Kensington Books
http://www.kensingtonbooks.com

KENSINGTON BOOKS are published by

Kensington Publishing Corp.
850 Third Avenue
New York, NY 10022

Library of Congress Card Catalog Number: 97-072810
ISBN 1-57566-246-9

First Kensington Hardcover Printing: November, 1997
10 9 8 7 6 5 4 3 2 1

Printed in the United States of America

This book is dedicated to someone from aviation's
past, and to someone I hope will be part of
aviation's future:

To the memory of Edgar Staley Gorrell, first president
of the Air Transport Association of America and
architect of global airlift.
And to my grandson, Caleb Rodman Serling.

Contents

Prologue

In the half century that has elapsed since World War II ended with total victory over the Axis, millions of words have been written about the men, the machines, and the weapons deserving major credit for achieving that victory.

All justified, with the names of Churchill and Roosevelt obviously heading the wartime honor roll. Theirs and the roster of brilliant military leaders, combat planes like the Spitfire, Dauntless dive bomber, and B-17, the heroic sagas of such battles as Midway and the Normandy invasion, and the incredible technological developments that included radar and proximity fuses, already have filled history's pages. Yet comparatively little attention has been accorded another important—and in many ways vital—contributor to winning the war.

It's understandable, inasmuch as this particular contributor never officially fired a shot, downed an enemy plane, sank an enemy ship, blew up an enemy tank, dropped a single bomb on an enemy city, nor killed even one enemy soldier. For a long time, the bulk of its personnel consisted of civilians who had problems following military protocol, wore improvised uniforms with all the sartorial splendor of unmade beds, and compiled a record that included almost as many extracurricular shennanigans as exploits.

But the latter involved two magic words . . .

Global airlift.

For the first time in the history of warfare, the airplane became an integral part of military supply lines—and in some instances, the *only* supply line. It didn't win the war, yet the war couldn't have been won without it. Airlift almost single-handedly kept China from collapsing, helped prevent Rommel from overrunning North Africa, and on more than one occasion provided the thin margin that spelled victory instead of defeat. It also saved lives; one out of every five American servicemen wounded in WW II was airlifted back to the United States for extended medical treatment.

By the time the war ended, this global airlift had accumulated 28 million miles, flown by more than 25,000 pilots in some 3000 aircraft maintained by 60,000 ground crewmen. Admittedly, when the airlift reached its peak in 1944, the overwhelming majority of the personnel serving in its two operating units—the Army's Air Transport Command (ATC) and the Naval Air Transport Service (NATS)—was strictly military, composed of commissioned officers and enlisted men.

But they had inherited much from the experiences of the civilians who preceded them. From airline pilots they had learned techniques that enabled them to survive under the worst flying conditions; from airline ground crews they had learned the sheer art of improvisation in the most adverse kinds of environment—whether jungle, desert, or frozen ice cap. For when the airlift began, in the dark, defeat-ridden days that followed Pearl Harbor, the military was forced to call on the only source of manpower and aircraft available: the U.S. airline industry.

That it was available at all was due largely to one man. He was a feisty little ex–Army pilot who had served under General John J. "Black Jack" Pershing in the latter's campaign against Mexican rebel leader Pancho Villa. His name was Edgar Staley Gorrell, and in 1936 he had become the first president of the Air Transport Association (ATA), a trade group organized that year to represent the nation's loosely allied commercial air carriers.

One of his first acts as ATA president was to draw up a detailed plan that put the airlines, their planes, pilots, mechanics, and technical experts at the military's disposal in the event of war. By December 7, 1941, he already had the plan updated for instant and full implementation, needing only White House approval to put it into effect.

A few days after Pearl Harbor, Gorrell went to 1600 Pennsylvania Avenue seeking that approval, with two strikes against him.

Strike One: Franklin D. Roosevelt already had signed, with

almost gleeful alacrity, an executive order nationalizing the entire airline industry for the duration; the order was on the president's desk when Gorrell was ushered into the Oval Office.

Strike Two: FDR had no reason to love the airlines; he had feuded with them since 1934, when he was talked into canceling all private air mail contracts and letting the Army fly the mail—a decision which cost the lives of a dozen Army pilots and brought the wrath of press and public down on Roosevelt's head.

But when Gorrell finally walked out of the Oval Office that cold December day, the executive order had been torn up before his eyes—and in that dramatic heartbeat of history, the concept of global airlift was truly born.

$$\star \quad \star \quad \textbf{1} \quad \star \quad \star$$

The Little Colonel

Feisty, as defined in a standard dictionary, runs the gamut from "lively, energetic, exuberant" to "quarrelsome, aggressive, belligerent."

All six adjectives applied to Edgar Gorrell, yet his complex personality included a curious anomaly; on certain occasions, particularly social, he could be rather shy. Not really surprising, however, for social occasions were a distraction to a man intensely focused on whatever problem, mission, or project he happened to be interested in.

If at times Gorrell appeared to be afflicted with tunnel vision, it was vision with tremendous range—a kind of uncanny, omniscient foresight capable of predicting future obstacles and crises. That he also could be abrasively blunt in making such predictions didn't win him many friends. That Gorrell didn't really give a damn about finishing first in popularity contests also happened to be his greatest asset. What he really cared about was U.S. aviation—military and civilian—finishing first. For such was the nature of this diminutive man who helped father global airlift.

It was typical of Edgar Staley Gorrell that his decision to enroll at West Point apparently was reached at the ripely mature age of four. At least that was how old he was when his mother found him strutting around their Baltimore home—heels together, toes angled slightly out, and knees pumping like tiny pistons. He resembled a miniaturized Buckingham Palace guard parading in front of a sentry box, and his mother naturally asked why.

"This is the way I'm going to walk when I'm a general," he explained solemnly.

Gorrell never did achieve such exalted military status, but he did go to West Point (barely meeting the Academy's minimum height requirement), and eventually attained the rank of colonel. Even after he left the Army, he liked being called "Colonel," which happened to be vastly preferable to the nicknames he acquired in his plebe year at West Point: "Napoleon" or "Little Corporal." Achieving the rank of cadet corporal was an accomplishment in itself; how he managed the feat is one of West Point's legends. In his yearling (second) year, he gained admission to the commandant's sacrosanct office with a complaint.

"Sir," he inquired, "how do I get to be a corporal around here? I've been a private long enough."

By the time he graduated in 1912, Gorrell had risen to company captain, ranking in the upper third of his class. He applied for assignment to the aviation section of the Signal Corps but first had to serve the requisite two years of line service as an infantry second lieutenant. He was posted to Fort Seward, Alaska, marking the start of a lifelong love affair with what was then still a territory. Not until 1915 was his transfer to aviation approved, at which point he learned how to fly at the Signal Corps' flight training facility at Coronado, California. After winning his wings—only the thirty-ninth man in the United States to become a licensed pilot—he joined the 1st Aero Squadron and was in that unit when it became part of the campaign against Mexican rebel Pancho Villa in 1916.

Commander of the American punitive expedition was General John J. "Black Jack" Pershing, whose first awareness of an undersized flight lieutenant named Eddie Gorrell came in a report on his miraculous survival after a forced landing in the Mexican desert.

He had with him one pint of water, a single concentrated meal ration, and a pistol. Completely lost, he wandered around the desert for four days, exhibiting life-saving willpower by resisting the temptation to drink the water in his small canteen; when thirst became too great, he rinsed out his mouth with a swig and spit the water back into the canteen. On the fifth day, he stumbled into a U.S. cavalry patrol, which mistook this emaciated scarecrow for a rebel bandit and arrested him. Not until Gorrell feebly removed his flight overalls to reveal his pilot's wings was he released and rushed to medical aid.

This happened to have been his second forced landing in Mexico; after the first one, caused by a fuel leak, a relatively easy three-mile hike had taken him to a friendly village where he was able to procure gas. But the two experiences, combined with similar incidents involving fellow pilots, left him angry and disillusioned. And once again, his name came before Pershing—this time a report implying gross insubordination on the part of several pilots, Gorrell included.

Assigned to the 1st Aero Squadron as a war correspondent was a young United Press reporter named Webb Miller. After interviewing a number of the squadron's pilots, Miller wrote a scathing, widely published story to the effect that the Army was operating flying death traps.

It took very little time for the War Department's inspector general to come thundering down on the squadron's collective head, demanding the names of those who had given Miller so many damning quotes—especially one which had described the planes in Pershing's tiny eight-airplane fleet (virtually the nation's entire aerial combat force at the time) as "junk." One by one, each pilot denied having talked to the reporter, until the inspector general came to Lieutenant Gorrell.

"Yes, sir, I said it," Gorrell snapped. "And it's all true. The planes are rotten, the engines fall apart, the propellers split, and it's dangerous to leave the ground in one of those bunches of junk. The U.S. Army is in danger of killing off the handful of trained pilots it has right now, when it looks as though we're heading into bigger troubles."

It was a small miracle that he wasn't court-martialed. It was a slightly larger miracle that instead of even being reprimanded, the War Department shipped the brash lieutenant to the prestigious Massachusetts Institute of Technology. He completed a one-year aeronautical engineering course in six months, earning a Master of Science degree just before the U.S. entered World War I. One month after the U.S. declared war on Germany, Gorrell celebrated his promotion to captain by going to Europe as a member of the Aircraft Production Board, a group of Army and Navy officers and civilian industrial engineers whose mission was to evaluate

European airplane production, and apply any lessons learned to American aircraft manufacturing.

Gorrell's busy mind wasn't satisfied with such mundane matters as building warplanes; how best to use them *after* they were built absorbed his interest even more. Among the voluminous reports he dumped on the desks of War Department superiors was a detailed plan for defending U.S. territory against submarine and air attacks, and another outlining a program for strategic bombing so advanced that it could have been a preliminary blueprint for World War II bombing missions.

Black Jack Pershing must have remembered the spunky little maverick who had braved the wrath of the inspector general, for at the general's request Gorrell was assigned to the American Expeditionary Force (AEF), first as chief engineering officer, and then assistant chief of staff. By the end of the war, Gorrell was the A.E.F.'s air chief of staff, holding the rank of colonel and serving as General William "Billy" Mitchell's second-in-command.

His first postwar assignment was to write a history of American aviation's role in the conflict. The Army would have been happy with a publishable 700-page manuscript; Gorrell's opus, which included thousands of photographs, charts, diagrams, and statistical tables, filled 280 *volumes*. But out of this massive job of research and writing had come an extremely controversial conclusion: Gorrell was convinced that air power alone never could win a major war.

It was a publicly expressed opinion that put him at odds with Billy Mitchell, the highly visible proponent of a separate, completely independent air force, and also at odds with virtually all Army pilots, who worshipped Mitchell. The outspoken Gorrell suddenly found himself persona non grata among the majority of his fellow airmen.

In 1920, he unexpectedly resigned his commission and took a $25-a-week job as a junior engineer at the Marmon Motor Company. To his dying day, Gorrell never confided the reason he left military service so abruptly and prematurely. It may have been his facing up to the inevitable postwar cutbacks emasculating the armed forces, the infant air service being an especially easy target in an era when most Americans still regarded the airplane as more of a dangerous toy than a true weapon or instrument of commerce. But Gorrell's realization that his opposition to an independent air force had made him a pariah among his brother airmen also may have been a factor.

He prospered, at least temporarily, in the automobile business, becoming vice president of Marmon only four years after joining the company. In 1925 the Stutz Motor Car Company hired him as vice president and general manager; in that position he was instrumental in developing the Stutz Blackhawk, companion to the famed Bearcat, and he also designed the braking system of the Stutz Super Bearcat. The company elected him president in 1929, a promotion akin to being named captain of the *Titanic* just before her maiden voyage; Stutz fell victim to the Great Depression that followed the 1929 stock market crash and folded.

But it was during his tenure at Stutz that Gorrell got another shot at his true love: aviation. The Army Air Corps' disappointing performance in carrying the mail after the 1934 cancellation of private contracts had prompted formation of a special investigating committee known as the Baker Board—after its chairman, former Secretary of War Newton D. Baker. Its members, both civilian and military, included such famous fliers as Jimmy Doolittle and Clarence Chamberlin. Gorrell was asked to serve on the board, an invitation he accepted quickly, and its final report was a model of constructive criticism. It pointed out serious shortcomings in training and equipment that in large measure were due to a parsimonious Congress feeding the Air Corps on a starvation diet; skimpy funding, for example, limited Army pilots to only 175 flight hours a year, a pitifully short time in which to hone skills and gain essential experience.

After Stutz went under, Gorrell started a small investment company, unaware that his contributions to the Baker Board had attracted some unexpected attention from an unanticipated source:

Namely, the fractious, divided U.S. airline industry, still reeling and bloody from the so-called air mail scandal.

It was more politics than scandal, more smoke than fire, and it all dated back to 1930, when President Hoover's postmaster general, a rather stuffy Harvard-educated lawyer named Walter Folger Brown, decided to reform the airline industry. His intentions were good; at that point in time, there were forty-four airlines trying to survive primarily on mail pay, with little interest in developing passenger traffic. Brown sincerely believed that civil air transportation would never come of age if its future depended on this spaghetti bowl of carriers, most of them small, inadequately financed, inefficiently operated, and overreliant on mail revenues.

Brown's solution was draconian, and the weapon he wielded was the McNary-Watres Act of 1930, a loosely written piece of legislation ostensibly aimed at lowering mail rates. But it contained one provision that Brown himself had authored, giving the PMG authority to extend or consolidate mail routes "when in his judgment the public interest will be promoted thereof." Those eleven words were Brown's blank check, and only two weeks after Hoover signed McNary-Watres into law, the postmaster general filled it in.

He summoned the top executives of the major airlines to Washington to discuss major revisions in the nation's air route system. The meeting, which eventually would become known as the infamous Spoils Conference, was by no means secret, as was later charged; the smaller carriers simply weren't invited. For twelve raucous days, the participants loudly and heatedly argued, while the wily Brown sat back and watched the unruly proceedings with the sly smile of a Cheshire cat. He knew this gang of rugged individualists couldn't have agreed on the time of day, and when the conferees finally ran out of arguments, protests and temper tantrums, Brown stepped forward with his own plan to rewrite the nation's tangled, uncoordinated airways map.

His solution involved (1) a merger of Transcontinental Air Transport and Western Air Express which would become Transcontinental and Western Air, initialized to TWA; (2) the addition of two transcontinental routes to the northern route already flown by United: American would operate a southern route, and TWA a central one. And, having completed this massive restructuring, Brown took another step aimed at putting inefficient smaller carriers out of the airmail competition: he put all mail routes up for rebidding, without mentioning that he was determined to award contracts on the basis of financial stability, operating experience, and overall efficiency; a low bid did not rank high in priority.

The major route restructuring actually proved to be the best thing that could have happened to civil aviation. It matured the airline industry and, as Brown had intended, pruned the inefficient, weaker carriers down to a shorter "survival of the fittest" list. What wrecked Brown's reputation and led to the alleged scandal—in retrospect unfairly—was his rebidding process. Three years after the Spoils Conference, an enterprising Hearst reporter named Fulton Lewis Jr. uncovered evidence that the new mail contracts had seldom gone to the lowest bidder, with larger carriers winning over small airlines even though the latter had submitted lower bids.

Lewis turned his evidence over to Senator Hugo Black of Alabama, who convinced President Roosevelt that the mail contracts had been won by fraud and thus called for punitive action. Not that Roosevelt needed much convincing, inasmuch as he saw a chance to further humiliate the already discredited Hoover administration. Against the advice of his own postmaster general, Jim Farley, FDR canceled all existing contracts and ordered the Army to fly the mail.

Out of the subsequent debacle in which twelve Army pilots died trying to fly the mail through severe winter storms, came Hugo Black's (and FDR's) face-saving revenge for having to return air mail service to the airlines—under new rules that were more like criminal indictments. Although Senate hearings had failed to produce any evidence that Brown had acted illegally, Black introduced legislation as draconian as anything Walter Brown ever perpetrated: the Air Mail Act of 1934, which banned any carrier that had attended the Spoils Conference from bidding on a mail contract, made it illegal for any aircraft or engine manufacturer to have any connection with an airline, and forbid any airline executive who had attended Brown's meeting ever to hold office in a carrier possessing a mail contract. The final spanking was a provision—probably unconstitutional, but never challenged in the courts by the demoralized, disorganized carriers—limiting the annual salary of airline officers to a maximum of $17,500.

In historical perspective, Black did the industry at least a partial favor; requiring the airlines to sever all relations with manufacturers gave them more freedom in equipment decisions. But a platoon of able airline executives lost their jobs, and stripping major carriers of their mail route authorizations threatened to turn the nation's air transportation system into a chaotic shambles. It was Jim Farley who prevented this from happening, by secretly advising the affected airlines merely to change their corporate names.

Thus, for example, American Airways became American Airlines; Eastern Air Transport switched to Eastern Air Lines; United Air Lines replaced United Aircraft and Transport; Western created a dummy corporation named General Air Lines in which it held all the stock, and TWA merely added "Incorporated" to its initials.

The loophole Farley had suggested saved the industry from collapse, but the whole unhappy experience had taught some of its more far-sighted leaders a valuable lesson—the hotly competitive airlines lacked a unified voice in its relations with Washington. Throughout the entire air mail crisis, only once had the airlines displayed any semblance of real unity; on February 18, 1934, TWA's Jack Frye and Eastern's Eddie Rickenbacker took off in the new Douglas DC-1, prototype of the DC-2 transport, and flew the last load of privately contracted mail from Burbank to Newark, setting a new transcontinental speed record of thirteen hours and four minutes in the process.

The flight, which was Frye's idea, symbolized industry's belief that the airlines were better equipped to fly the mail than inexperienced military pilots. As a dramatic gesture of defiance it looked even better in light of the tragic aftermath, but it also was a temporary, one-shot demonstration of unity almost forgotten when Hugo Black's vindictive crusade became law.

Significantly, Frye was among the handful of airline executives determined to give the industry a unified voice in the form of its own trade organization, named the Air Transport Association of America. Frye and three fellow executives—United's William "Pat" Patterson, crusty Eddie Rickenbacker of Eastern, and American's new president, C.R. Smith—formed a committee to select the man who would head the new ATA. On January 14, 1936, meeting in Chicago where the ATA would be headquartered, they announced its creation and the name of its first president.

It was Edgar Gorrell.

The four-man committee left no written record of who else was considered for the post, if anyone, and Gorrell may well have been the only serious candidate—his track record in both the military and industry was outstanding. Considering the personalities of the selection quartet, four powerful men heading the nation's four largest domestic airlines, some historians have voiced the natural suspicion that all four thought they were getting someone they could control.

It should be remembered that in the mid 1930s and well into the jet age, the biggest and most successful carriers often were mirror images of exceptionally strong, domineering leaders. In some cases, and Rickenbacker was a classic example, they were benevolent despots ruling with iron fist and iron will. Many were aeronautical buccaneers who had started their airline careers at a time when passengers sat on mail sacks in open-air biplanes; they were individualistic, suspicious, territorially jealous, stubborn, sometimes ruthless and uncompromising—patriarchs whose words, opinions, and decisions were seldom questioned. Yet these were not necessarily evil qualities; their realm was an industry on the verge of growing into long pants in an era when the average American would have preferred facing a hungry tiger to traveling by air. When the typical passenger bragged, "I flew to New York last week" in the same tone as "I went three rounds with Jack Dempsey the other day."

If it was true that the industry deliberately sought an easy-to-manipulate patsy, a weak yes-man, it could have stemmed from Gorrell's own conflicting personality. Reportedly, when the four-man committee interviewed him, the colonel seemed modest and diffident, even shy. His own physical appearance may have contributed to this impression; nearly 45 years old when he was picked, Gorrell already was almost totally bald, and with his small stature did not cut much of an imposing figure. What undoubtedly impressed the selection committee was his technical knowledge, especially in aviation matters, plus the fact that he knew his way around Washington.

It took very little time for the airlines to discover the true caliber of ATA's first president. He had been in office only a month when he began telling them what was wrong with the industry—starting with that seldom-mentioned-in-public word: Safety. Gorrell's conception of ATA went far beyond what some airline heads had intended: a typical trade association whose chief functions were lobbying and public relations. He accepted those functions, but he also turned the Association into what it is to this day—a clearinghouse for technological developments and operational methods that would enhance safety. He added two technical experts to ATA's small staff that originally consisted of Gorrell and three secretaries—they were called stenographers in those days. He began prodding the woefully lethargic federal government into adopting some of the industry's own suggestions, and he was not afraid to do battle with the airline executives who were his nominal bosses. If two or more of them started arguing at an ATA meeting, Gorrell would cut off the debate with a cold "let's get back to business, gentlemen." He was supposed to have been hired to listen; they often wound up listening to him.

He hadn't been in office very long when a minor crisis arose. Warner Brothers had released *Ceiling Zero,* a 1936 aviation film starring James Cagney and Pat O'Brien with an inordinate number of scenes depicting flaming crashes in fog and storms. Inasmuch as the airlines' 1936 safety record was nothing to brag about to begin with, the movie was guaranteed to steer any travel-bound viewer toward the nearest bus or train station.

Gorrell, at the frantic urging of several carriers, protested to movie industry czar Will Hays, arguing that the film portrayed civil aviation unfairly. Hays got Warners to add a disclaimer in the form of the following prologue, reportedly composed by Gorrell himself:

"This picture depicts pioneer days in air travel. As a result of these heroic events, we have arrived at today's safety."

ATA's first headquarters consisted of a three-room suite on the twelfth floor of the Field Building, 135 S. LaSalle St., Chicago. But Gorrell spent almost as much time in Washington as in Chicago, fighting for legislation that would help an industry still suffering from the continuing aftershocks of the Black-generated earthquake. When Gorrell took office, the airlines were being regulated by no fewer than three separate federal agencies, each with its own interests, policies, and purpose. The Post Office Department supervised mail contracts and routes; the Interstate Commerce Commission controlled mail rates and passenger/freight tariffs; the Department of Commerce, through its subordinate Bureau of Air Commerce, was responsible for safety rules, pilot/aircraft licensing, and airways. (Until 1936, the airlines had operated their own air traffic control system, developed originally by an American Airlines dispatcher/radio operator.)

When ATA was first formed, Gorrell had hired a smart young Washington lawyer named Howard Westwood to serve as the new organization's counsel. That he even picked Westwood raised enough eyebrows to generate a stiff breeze; in his youth, the attorney was a far-to-the-left liberal who had once campaigned for socialist Norman Thomas. The youngest partner in the very proper, extremely conservative Washington law firm of Convington and

Burling, Westwood used to walk down its staid corridors defiantly whistling the communist anthem, the "Internationale."

It was the brilliant if eccentric Westwood to whom Gorrell turned in his crusade to lift the airline industry out of the morass of divided regulatory authority. The lawyer, with Gorrell's help, fashioned legislation known as the Civil Aeronautics Act which became law in 1938. It created an independent, five-member Civil Aeronautics Authority with jurisdiction over every phase of civil aviation except accident investigation; this was turned over to a three-man safety board. (It also included a Gorrell-authored provision eliminating the $17,500 cap on airline presidential salaries.)

Once Gorrell got several legislators to sponsor this industry Magna Carta in both the House and Senate, he lobbied tirelessly for its passage; he may have been shy at social functions, but he was at his best testifying before a congressional committee. At one hearing, he produced a huge map of the United States (it took two men standing on chairs to hold it upright) on which were a number of black crosses, each with an adjacent red marking.

"The black crosses mark the sites of recent airline crashes," Gorrell explained laconically. "The red symbols indicate the lack of weather reporting facilities that might have prevented the accidents."

Another of his effective testifying aids was a 100-pound case containing more than a thousand color-coded index cards: blue for weather stations, buff indicating radio ranges, yellow showing landing fields, and pink displaying teletype facilities. The cards, organized by state, type of facility, and airline route, were tabbed to pinpoint where improvements were needed.

He went far beyond the industry's immediate needs in successfully lobbying key congressmen to vote higher fiscal 1937/1938 appropriations for additional weather stations and air navigation aids. His lobbying efforts included, with almost incredible foresight, funds for installation of airports and weather services at a number of Pacific islands, Alaska, the Aleutians, and the Caribbean—locations that less than four years later would become links in the global airlift system. Significantly, many of his own ATA members—in effect his superiors—objected to his fighting for projects that at the time seemed to benefit a single airline: Pan American, then the nation's only international carrier. Gorrell brushed off such criticism with the gruff bluntness he displayed during his entire

ATA career; there were times when he force-fed the industry, like a stern parent holding the nose of a protesting child while feeding it castor oil.

His entire career was studded with examples of prescience. Almost two years before Pearl Harbor, he sent an employee to a public library with instructions to copy down anything the aide could find on Ascension Island—the same island that would become a mid-Atlantic refueling and maintenance base for the Air Transport Command's South Atlantic route. Long before the airlines went to war, Gorrell urged them to train their domestic pilots in celestial navigation, foreseeing the day when many would be flying ocean routes. In 1940, he commissioned creation of a projection map that displayed north-polar routes and mileages between major U.S. cities and various destinations in Europe, Asia, and Africa; the Air Transport Command would fly many of the same routes during the war.

Inevitably, the Little Colonel ruffled not a few feathers within the airlines themselves, especially when he delivered sermons on the subject of safety. Eddie Rickenbacker, for example—although he was one of the four airline presidents who had picked Gorrell— was never an unqualified fan either of ATA or of its leader. When the Association was first founded, its board of directors debated whether to give salaried ATA officers like Gorrell free air transportation on member carriers. Only Rickenbacker objected. "I don't want them riding around free on Eastern," he grumbled to C.R. Smith.

Smith, who loved to needle EAL's president (he would infuriate Rickenbacker by calling him "Eddie" instead of "Captain"), just smiled. "Don't worry, Eddie," he said gently. "They'll only try Eastern once."

Except for a distinct discrepancy in height, C.R. actually had a lot in common with Edgar Gorrell—including baldness. Smith, too, was simultaneously shy and forceful, rather inept at small talk but overpowering when it came to decision-time, and just as far-sighted. It was C.R., along with United's Patterson and TWA's Frye, who led support for a plan Gorrell had put before the industry shortly after he took office in 1936.

The ATA president proposed that the airlines mobilize their resources in the event of a national emergency, including war, and a blueprint for what in effect would be the nation's first civil reserve air fleet was circulated throughout the industry. Not a few airline executives questioned the need for such a drastic step, although Gorrell kept insisting, "if we don't have our own plan, the government's going to shove one down our throats." At any rate, no one paid much attention to the idea until two years later, when the airlines actually had a chance to stage what amounted to a dress rehearsal under dramatic circumstances.

On September 30, 1938, a killer hurricane roared out of the Caribbean and smashed into New England. In a matter of hours, almost the entire area was devastated, with hundreds injured and thousands made homeless. New England was virtually cut off from the rest of the nation; highways and railroads were under water and the area's transportation system was at a standstill.

With one exception: the air.

At the time, American was the only carrier operating a New York to Boston route. C.R. assigned every available DC-3 in the airline's fleet to fly mercy missions, shuttling back and forth between the two cities carrying medical supplies and emergency personnel. Within twenty-four hours, Smith knew American couldn't do the job alone. Normally the airline carried about 200 passengers a day over the route; on the first day after the hurricane, more than 1000 people were clamoring for seats and the demand multiplied with the need for emergency construction and utility crews.

C.R. called Gorrell. "We need help and fast," he informed the ATA president.

Gorrell phoned Frye, Patterson, and Rickenbacker, whose airlines, like C.R.'s, were operating the new twenty-one-passenger Douglas DC-3s, the biggest transport aircraft available. "I want you to divert as many aircraft as possible to New England," he told them. His next step was to obtain from Washington temporary authorization for TWA, United, and Eastern to operate flights over American's franchised New York to Boston route.

For seven days, this four-airline armada operated an unprecedented airlift in and out of Boston, flying in 60,000 tons of emergency supplies. Their planes also carried more than a thousand rescue and construction workers into New England and took some 1500 stranded refugees out of the ravaged area. There weren't enough DC-3s available, so American and TWA threw their older DC-2s into the airlift.

One TWA pilot arrived in Newark from Kansas City and confronted an American captain.

"I've never flown the east coast before," he admitted. "How the hell do I get to Boston?"

"Just get back in your airplane and follow us," was the reply.

By the time weary ground and flight crews from the four carriers had returned to their regular jobs and schedules, they had shown Edgar Gorrell and the entire industry the tremendous potential of air transportation in a major crisis. It was a lesson Gorrell and his ATA members were not to forget when the war clouds gathered, and it strengthened the colonel's conviction that the airlines had to be ready if war ever came.

Nor did Gorrell forget C.R. Smith's initiative not only in launching the airlift, but swiftly recognizing the need for unselfish interairline cooperation when the New England crisis strained the resources of a single carrier. If Gorrell was close to any airline president, it had to have been the big Texan who was one of the few industry executives in favor of mentioning safety out loud.

C.R., in fact, had stunned the whole industry in 1937 with a controversial advertisement that in bold type asked: "AFRAID TO FLY?" Under this, in slightly smaller letters, was the line, "Why Dodge This Question?"

The third sentence in the text of the ad declared, "As regrettable as it is, the records show there have been accidents and fatalities in every form of transportation." The ad went on to point out that people are afraid of things they know little or nothing about, pointed out that they'd be afraid of trains if they had never ridden on one, and declared that flying was safer than most Americans realized.

Just to mention safety was heresy, let alone admitting that airplanes sometimes crash. But the advertisement was right down Edgar Gorrell's tell-it-like-it-is alley; although he diplomatically refrained from endorsing it publicly, he privately complimented C.R. for his courage in facing up to the issue of public confidence in air travel.

One of the difficulties of heading an organization like ATA was the inherent hazard of trying to serve too many masters, each with his own agenda, priorities, and ideas on what industry policy should be. Gorrell's blunt preaching and scolding was done within the confines of closed ATA meetings; pragmatically, he knew he was a spokesman for all the airlines. The greatest satisfaction he derived from the hurricane airlift was the knowledge that this fiercely independent gang of buccaneers actually could unite when the chips were down, thanks to leaders like Patterson, Frye, and Smith.

It was C.R. on whom Gorrell naturally relied in 1940, almost a year before Pearl Harbor, when the ATA president realized his emergency mobilization plan needed major updating. The obvious menace of a conquering Adolf Hitler and the rising truculence of Japan convinced Gorrell that the U.S. was heading for war.

"Our most recent emergency plan is almost three years old," he told Smith. "Do you have anyone at American who can help us?"

C.R. put M.P. "Rosie" Stallter, one of his airline's top operations experts, at Gorrell's disposal. Stallter took five assistants into the basement den of his home and five weeks later they emerged with a precise, detailed study of what the airlines could provide the military in a national emergency.

Their study, when typed and turned over to the War Department, was an inch thick. A copy of this mobilization blueprint was in Gorrell's hands when the first bombs fell on the Pacific fleet, and it was very much in his mind when he was summoned to the White House to face the skeptical Franklin Delano Roosevelt. On FDR's desk, dated December 13, 1941 and already bearing his signature, was the executive order issued "pursuant to Title 10, U.S.C., sec. 1361, authorizing the President through the Secretary of War to take possession or assume control of any transportation system or part thereof."

In other words, nationalization of the airline industry.

Fortunately for the ATA president, he had a powerful, influential ally sitting in the same room—General H.H. "Hap" Arnold, chief of the Army Air Corps, who had accompanied him to the White House. As soon as they sat down, Roosevelt announced that he had signed the executive order and handed it to Gorrell to read.

Gorrell, not only stunned but angry, gave it to Arnold, who studied it impassively and waited for the ATA president to comment. As politely as possible, Gorrell reminded the chief executive that the War Department at that very moment was putting ATA's civil reserve air fleet plan into effect, with airline planes and their crews being diverted to emergency military missions. If the Army itself even then was implementing the plan that Rosie Stallter and his five associates had forged, Gorrell argued, then what purpose would it serve to nationalize an industry fully prepared to go all-out in the war effort?

FDR asked Arnold what he thought, and Gorrell held his breath—even generals don't like to contradict the President of the United States. He needn't have worried. Arnold bluntly told Roosevelt that Gorrell was absolutely right. Only the airlines, he pointed out, had the equipment and skilled manpower to run a global air transportation system, as a civil adjunct to the military, but under military orders. He had studied the ATA plan, he added, and noted that it included immediate requisitioning of a sizable proportion of airline flight equipment by the military, to be flown by civilian crews as military aircraft until the Air Corps got more of its own transports. The whole civil reserve air fleet plan, Arnold emphasized, offered solid proof of the industry's good faith and capability.

Curiously, in his 626-page postwar autobiography *Global Mission,* Arnold made no mention of Gorrell whatsoever, nor the White House meeting so crucial to the airlines and their future war role. It was a puzzling omission, for in Hap Arnold the airlines had as a friend a man who firmly believed that air transportation is a vital component of air power. At one time, Arnold had told Donald Douglas he should be building only fighters and bombers for the Army. But when the aircraft industry began gearing up for war production in earnest, Arnold had a change of heart and personally blocked a proposal that America's airplane factories manufacture combat planes exclusively. Furthermore, he not only shared Gorrell's exceptional visionary qualities, but also his streak of stubborn independence—the same willingness to challenge the military establishment. Arnold was one of several young officers who received official reprimands for testifying in Billy Mitchell's defense at the latter's 1925 insubordination court-martial.

The Air Corps chief definitely was not the type of man to let that executive order intimidate him. And Gorrell, encouraged by Arnold's support, interjected the rather sly observation that the first World War had provided an excellent example of why any transportation system suffered under nationalization. In 1917 America's railroads were taken over by the government and almost collapsed under the weight of bureaucratic inefficiency and red tape. FDR, who had served as assistant secretary of the Navy in that war, remembered the railroad mess only too well and had the grace to smile ruefully.

Then he picked up the executive order, still smiling, and tore it up.

Saved from total seizure by Gorrell's impassioned plea and Arnold's stalwart support, yet knowing that under its own plan it was going to lose at least half of its aircraft and hundreds of trained personnel, the airline industry was in the war—from the giants like American, United, TWA, Eastern, and Pan Am, right down to such tiny carriers as Continental, Pennsylvania Central, and Northeast.

"We'll take at least half—but first paint 'em olive drab."

It may not have been put in exactly those words, but essentially that was what the War Department told the airlines when representatives of ATA's nineteen member carriers met in Washington four and a half months after Pearl Harbor to officially swallow a bitter if voluntary pill: finalizing what portion of its fleet each must turn over to the military.

They had already given up some planes, and had a pretty good idea of what else they were going to lose under the emergency mobilization plan outlined by Rosie Stallter. He had warned Edgar Gorrell that the airlines should expect to surrender about half their flight equipment, and a corresponding number of flight and ground personnel to man and maintain the airline aircraft that had been drafted. As of the day of this meeting, May 15, 1942, the civil transport fleet operated by the certificated domestic carriers totaled 359 aircraft—this has been the most widely accepted figure although no official total was ever established, because the exact size changed almost daily as new aircraft were delivered and older ones were discarded. The total did not include planes operated by Pan American, Panagra, and Hawaiian Airlines, nor the hodge-podge, generally obsolete aircraft of the numerous then-tiny Alaskan carriers—virtually all still run by the enterprising bush pilots who had founded them.

Hawaiian gave up far more than airplanes—it literally lost its independence as a civil carrier. Hawaiian, at the time serving strictly interisland routes, found itself embroiled in the middle of a real war zone when Pearl Harbor was bombed. One of its DC-3s, in fact, was the first U.S. civilian airliner to be attacked by Japanese fighters, during the December 7 raid.

The Hawaiian plane, Aircraft Number 9, was about to take off on a routine interisland flight with twenty-four passengers aboard when a Japanese Zero strafed the airport. A stray bullet set fire to the cockpit fire extinguisher which promptly discharged and doused the blaze—a one-in-a-million shot that actually made Ripley's "Believe It or Not" syndicated feature. Nearly two decades later, the sequel to this unusual incident achieved the ultimate in irony. The airline sold Number 9, which crews had labeled "Old Patches," to North Japan Airlines, which complained about the metal patches on the fuselage.

Hawaiian spent the rest of the war with its employees and entire fleet of DC-3s operating under strict Army supervision. When the War Shipping Administration took over all island steamers, Hawaiian's DC-3s provided the only means of interisland transportation. Not until after V-J Day did Hawaiian regain full status as a civilian airline, gradually expanding into a formidable long-range carrier not only serving interisland points—competing with Aloha—but with transpacific routes that stretched eastward to California, as far west as Australia, and a modern big-jet fleet that progressed from Douglas DC-8s to wide-body Lockheed L-1011s and eventually a fleet of McDonnell Douglas DC-10s.

The bulk of the domestic fleet consisted of relatively new twenty-one-passenger DC-3s, easily converted to an all-cargo configuration, but still too short-ranged for extensive transocean operations even with extra fuel tanks. The rest was a mixed bag of older Douglas DC-2s, four-engine Boeing Stratoliners and twin-engine Boeing 247s, two-engine Lockheed L-14 Super Electras, and the larger L-18 Lodestars. These were all land-based airplanes; the Navy naturally was interested in Pan American's big four-engine Boeing, Martin, and Sikorsky flying boats.

These seaplanes—especially the giant Boeing 314s—and the eight Stratoliners (TWA operated five and Pan Am three) were the figurative picks of the litter. They were the only civil transports then capable of long-range ocean flying, and there was no doubt they were the most immediately coveted, even ahead of the superb but limited-range DC-3s that had dominated domestic civil air travel since their introduction in 1936. The four-engine Douglas DC-4 was just over the horizon, but full-scale production was just beginning.

The military already had acquired a number of airplanes via outright sale or lease even before Pearl Harbor. In mid 1940, the government's new Priorities Board had placed restrictions on the delivery of commercial transports to the airlines, and carrier after carrier saw its fleet expansion plans demolished. TWA, for instance, had ordered fifteen new DC-3s and received only four. But the final fleet emasculation revealed at the May 15 meeting, presided over by the War Department's Military Director of Civil Aviation, amounted to major surgery: he announced that the Army was requisitioning 193 transports out of the 359-plane domestic fleet—overall, nearly three out of every five aircraft.

United, for example, lost thirty-six of its sixty-nine DC-3s. American, which operated seventy-nine, gave up thirty-eight, and Eastern also surrendered slightly more than half of its "Great Silver Fleet." (Repainted in Army olive drab, which was more of a dull khaki, its planes were quickly if unofficially dubbed, "The Great Chocolate Fleet.")

TWA in one respect took a harder blow than anyone else. A year before Pearl Harbor, President Jack Frye had agreed that in the event of war, he'd turn his airline's five Stratoliners—the world's first pressurized airliners—over to the Army, but with the stipulation that those five big aircraft would be considered the equivalent of ten DC-3s. The Army, desperate for any transport possessing two wings and engines, reneged and still grabbed more than half of TWA's DC-3s, plus the Stratoliners.

But the larger carriers were still left with fleets large enough to provide at least some flexibility with which to rejigger schedules and routes. This wasn't true of the smaller ones, to whom a fifty percent slash in fleet size was like asking a one-legged man to sprint. Typical was Western, which in mid 1941 was operating seven DC-3s and five ten-passenger Boeing 247s over a 1400-mile route system that stretched from California to Montana and southwestern Canada.

A few months before Pearl Harbor, WAL agreed to lease two of its 247s to the Army; when the War Department lowered the boom under the Stallter plan, it commandeered the remaining 247s plus four DC-3s, leaving Western with only three DC-3s to serve 1400 miles of airways from San Diego and Burbank all the way to Great

Falls, Montana, and Lethbridge, Canada. It picked up a surplus fourteen-passenger Lockheed Lodestar which helped a little, and there was one incident involving the Army's takeover that produced sly smiles instead of general concern.

An officious, rather smug young Air Corps lieutenant arrived at Burbank one day to inspect one of the Western 247s destined for military service. The pompous shavetail had never been inside a Boeing 247 in his life, and had no idea that the massive center wing spar ran right through the cabin, hidden by a small, carpet-covered metal step. He was striding briskly through the passenger compartment on the way to the cockpit when he tripped over the spar-hiding step and fell flat on his face.

He got to his feet, cursing as he brushed himself off. "The first thing you gotta do," he announced loudly, "is get rid of that goddamned step!"

But Western wasn't the only sufferer. Continental, which hadn't been able to afford the $125,000 price a new DC-3 carried, was serving a number of cities in Colorado, Kansas, and Texas with six heavily mortgaged Lodestars. Only three months before Pearl Harbor, Continental's fiery founder and president, Bob Six, had confidently informed the airline's stockholders:

> *"Your management is pleased to report that . . . it has not been called upon by the United States government to give up any of its equipment. In addition, we have been fortunate in retaining our trained personnel and have not been asked to surrender them for national defense needs."*

It was a classic case of false optimism, for the Army grabbed three of CAL's six Lodestars—and eventually, Bob Six himself. Continental, which had to slash schedules and drop some routes entirely, was so crippled that its credit standing evaporated virtually overnight. The airline came so close to bankruptcy that for weeks all purchases were delivered C.O.D.

Before they won military cargo and/or aircraft modification contracts, some of the smaller carriers survived by resorting to old-fashioned horse-trading within the industry, and Northeast provided one case in point. In May of 1941, it had taken delivery on three brand-new DC-3s, only to run into a severe cash shortage. The airline's president, Sam Solomon, was forced to swap the three new planes to TWA for $202,000 cash and five of TWA's "modern-ized" DC-2s, known to airline people as "DC-TWEE's"; they were fourteen-passenger DC-2s equipped with DC-3 wings to give them greater range. Then along came the Army's requisitioning axe and Northeast had to give up all five hybrids. The desperate Solomon finally managed to scrounge a pair of older DC-3s from American so Northeast could continue operating its major routes.

(If a DC-2 flying with DC-3 wings seems not only far-fetched but aerodynamically implausible, consider the bizarre but true saga of a DC-3 flown by China National Aviation Corporation, more familiarly known as CNAC. It was attacked on the ground by Japa-nese fighters who shot the fuselage full of holes and blew off the right wing. There wasn't a spare DC-3 right wing available in the entire country, but American mechanics working for CNAC—the airline was partially owned by Pan Am and staffed mostly by Yanks—bolted a DC-2 right wing to the stub of the missing DC-3 wing. The improvised right wing was several feet shorter than the left, but the repaired airplane, from then on known as the DC-2 and 1/2, proved airworthy except for minor difficulties in trimming the airplane.)

Route abandonment was another means of survival. Northwest, for example, saw half its DC-3 fleet acquire military garb and drastic service cuts resulted, such as reducing the busy Twin Cities-Chicago route from seven daily flights to only three, and dropping several routes entirely.

Delta, at the time of Pearl Harbor a relatively small carrier, was in the middle of major route expansion when war broke out. Paternalistic C.E. Woolman's one-time tiny crop dusting company was operating five DC-3s and four L-14 Super Electras, but had just ordered six additional DC-3s to replace the Electras. The Army grabbed all four Lockheeds plus one DC-3, and Delta was told to cancel its six-aircraft order with Douglas.

The script was the same for all the others, including Pennsylvania Central, which gave up two-thirds of its DC-3s, and tiny Colonial which lost six out of its eight planes. Braniff's fleet of a dozen DC-2s and five spanking-new DC-3s was sliced to seven DC-2s. Equally sharp axes fell on Mid-Continent, National, Chicago and Southern, Inland, All-American (today's US Airways), and mighty Pan Ameri-can Airways.

The latter, however, was a very special case; the nation's only true international carrier (it controlled Panagra) was operating not only transatlantic and transpacific routes, but serving Latin and South America as well. It was the sole U.S. carrier flying smack into the fringes of the European war zone with its New York–Southampton service, and it also served numerous potential trouble spots in the Far East, including the Philippines and Hong Kong. When the bombs began falling on Pearl Harbor, most of its predominantly long-range seaplane fleet instantly became uninsurable, exposed to unacceptable wartime risks. The airline did have a few new DC-3s to serve some of its South and Latin America destinations, but the queens of its fleet were the big seaplanes.

The heart of Pan Am's four-engined flying boat armada consisted of nine giant Boeing 314s, a pair of slightly smaller Martin 130s, and several even smaller Sikorsky S-42s. The airline originally had contracted for a dozen Boeings, but at President Roosevelt's request—and as a favor to Winston Churchill—Pan Am relinquished three of them to British Overseas Airways Corporation (BOAC). One of the Pan Am Sikorskys was destroyed in a Japanese air raid on Hong Kong December 8, 1941; two weeks after Pearl Harbor, the airline sold its nine 314s to the War Department— they became C-98s—and then leased them back for the duration. It was the only way Pan Am could operate uninsurable aircraft.

Pan Am also sold both of its big Martins outright to the Navy, which insisted on operating its own wartime airlift as the Naval Air Transport Service (NATS). And all three Stratoliners, along with their five TWA sisters, went into the military acquisition maw. But losing airplanes didn't bother Pan American's chieftain, Juan Trippe, nearly as much as a development he considered even worse. He took a decidedly dim view of ambitious, expansion-minded domestic airlines like TWA—or *any* domestic carrier, for that matter—acquiring wartime overseas operational experience. That same experience was sure to be cited in the inevitable postwar applications for international routes.

Trippe was as patriotic as any of his fellow airline tycoons, but what he feared most was losing Pan Am's monopoly on international service when the war ended. It was a case of possessiveness mixed with pride: Pan Am had pioneered its international routes, spent millions establishing bases for its great seaplanes, and compared to the kind of service it offered on its flying boats, most domestic air travel was like going steerage. Trippe knew his potential future competitors possessed a weapon that PAA lacked: domestic routes that could be tied into new international routes. Pan Am's Achilles' heel in that event would be its total lack of domestic authority. It may have been a combination of honest conviction mixed with ulterior motives, but he never wavered from his frequently expressed belief that only Pan Am had the experience and technical expertise to operate internationally.

Ironically, as it turned out, a number of Pan Am seaplane pilots had to take some unexpected flying lessons from their domestic brethern, airmen some Pan Am crews previously had regarded with a kind of amused, almost haughty tolerance that bordered on disdain. No U.S. airline captain carried more dignified authority than a typical four-striper from Pan Am's flying boat fleet—from his white naval officer's cap to his polished black shoes, he *looked* like a ship's captain and often acted like one. An industry gag at the time ran, "You can always tell a senior Pan Am captain, but you can't tell him a hell of a lot."

These veteran pilots, boasting thousands of logged flying hours, faced an unusual handicap: Except in extremely rare cases, Pan Am simply did not want its flying boats to take off or land in the dark, because there was too much chance of colliding with a half-submerged log or a poorly lit small craft. The inevitable consequence was a lack of experience in night flying, which would be a serious deficiency in the far greater demands of a round-the-clock military airlift. And there also was the necessity of transitioning many seaplane pilots to the land-based aircraft Pan Am was sure to be operating as its war role spread.

So one of Eastern's earliest wartime assignments was giving additional training to certain groups of Pan Am's airmen. As retired EAL Capt. Ernie Burton, who had been one of those special tutors, recalled years later:

"The Pan Am guys were damn good, but few of them had done much night flying—nothing was more dangerous than moving a seaplane in water at night. For that very reason, they hadn't had a great deal of instrument experience. When the war came and Pan Am began operating its own military missions with land planes, we had to teach their crews a few things in operational areas with which they were unfamiliar. It was no reflection on them or Pan Am, just a fact of life they had to face."

Months before the U.S. entered the war, the airlines had been secretly handling priority military cargo, such as an emergency shipment of tires for P-40 fighters being flown by the famed Flying Tigers against the Japanese in China. American Airlines blocked off space on a number of scheduled passenger flights so it could rush 20,000 pounds of new tires from New York to the West Coast. Virtually every carrier fielded such assignments, even if it meant dumping revenue passengers because of weight restrictions. For many weeks United loaded the cargo bins of its DC-3s with special materials and blueprints for the new defense plants mushrooming all over America's industrial landscapes.

The airlines also supplied flight and maintenance personnel to the Army's Air Ferrying Command, actually the forerunner to the wartime Air Transport Command. In June of 1941, TWA opened a training center in Albuquerque, New Mexico, for U.S. and British pilots delivering lend-lease bombers to England, a project undertaken at the personal request of General Hap Arnold; he had told Jack Frye both the Ferrying Command and the Royal Air Force Ferry Command were losing too many planes flown by too many inexperienced airmen over the dangerous, so often storm-plagued Atlantic.

The center was appropriately named "Eagle's Nest." Its curriculum included instrument flight training and also transitional instruction for pilots and flight engineers who would be delivering four-engine equipment like the Boeing B-17 and Consolidated B-24 bombers to hard-pressed Britain. Eagle's Nest eventually hatched hundreds of fine birdmen, including Royal Air Force personnel, but in its early months the school had more problems with its faculty than with its students. Teaching was a whole new ballgame to most of the veteran airline pilots serving as instructors, and they encountered great difficultites communicating with their eager but pea-green charges.

TWA Captain Otis Bryan, who had picked Albuquerque over New Orleans as the site and organized the school itself, spent one week observing his "professors" conducting classes in an atmosphere of general futility, and decided desperation measures were called for. He hired a public speaking expert to teach the teachers.

"Like most pilots in those days," Bryan explained, "all they knew was how to fly an airplane, and this was true for about ninety-nine out of a hundred of them. They didn't have the slightest idea how to teach, how to relate to students. So I contacted my old college speech professor, and got him out to Albuquerque to give a crash course to our instructors."

Bryan's "hired gun" proved successful, although there were a few dissenters among the rugged individualists to whom he was trying to impart elocutionary skills. His final "pass-or-fail-the-course" examination required each pilot to stand up in front of the speech class and talk extemporaneously for five minutes. On any list of unpleasant experiences, this was an ordeal some of them ranked only slightly lower than structural failure at 20,000 feet. Complained one senior captain:

"Well, we've sailed across the Atlantic, we've flown across the Atlantic, and now we're gonna talk our damn way across."

The Navy inserted another hurdle to surmount by objecting to any airline pilot holding a reserve naval commission being used as an instructor. And some airlines were reluctant to release experienced pilots to Eagle's Nest. The Army's Ferrying Command resolved both problems: it politely told the Navy Department that the school's needs held a higher priority, at least temporarily, than the Navy's call on its reserve officers. And recalcitrant carriers were informed that if they didn't provide instructors, the Army would get them anyway by calling Air Corps reserve pilots to active duty as Eagle's Nest instructors.

Graduates who were American citizens and assigned to the RAF Ferrying Command created another thorny issue: pay scales, which were traditionally lower in the RAF. It was finally agreed that each man, regardless of nationality, would get $10 a day while in school. Graduates qualifying as captains would make $500 per round-trip with a monthly guarantee of a thousand dollars. Copilots would earn $400 per round-trip and navigators $300.

This prewar school, and later even bigger airline-operated training facilities, were badly needed. A full year before Eagle's Nest opened, President Roosevelt announced his startling goal of producing 50,000 military airplanes annually—a figure derided by many "experts" including Germany's Hermann Goering, many congressmen and, of all people, Charles Lindbergh. They were wrong; in 1943 alone, the U.S. aircraft industry was to build more than 90,000 planes. Wartime production, in fact, was a gargantuan achievement that required a matching effort in crew training.

This meant making airmen out of hundreds of thousands of raw civilians, most of them knowing absolutely nothing about airplanes, whether it meant flying, fixing, or navigating them. At Eagle's Nest, for example, a TWA captain/instructor took some student flight engineers on a B-24 training flight. After they landed, he casually asked one of the trainees, "How's it going, son?"

The young student, who didn't look old enough to shave, shrugged. "I don't know, sir."

"Well, are you getting along okay?"

"I think so, sir."

"You think so? Dammit, don't you know?"

"Sir," the trainee confessed, "that was my first airplane ride."

Eagle's Nest was an important early project, but on nowhere near the scale of Pan Am's prewar involvement with defense matters, dictated largely by the very nature of its global route system. It was no secret that Juan Trippe usually acted as his own State Department when it came to negotiating for landing rights in countries he wanted to serve, and some of the deals he had masterminded proved advantageous to the U.S. when war came.

Trippe was particularly influential throughout Latin and South America, a status partially due to the widespread belief (stemming from his first name) that he was part Hispanic. Trippe never claimed Spanish ancestry, although he did absolutely nothing to discourage this erroneous assumption. Actually, he came from an old New England seafaring family and was about as Hispanic as clam chowder, but his parents chose to christen him "Juan" in honor of a favorite aunt named Juanita. From that supposedly inconsequential parental whim sprang the seeds for Pan Am's domination of the southern hemisphere.

And it was a domination that paid defense dividends. After Hitler came to power in the mid 1930s, Germany had begun steady economic and political infiltration throughout South America, and this was achieved largely by owning or partially controlling airlines in six countries: Brazil (Varig, Condor, and LATI), Ecuador (SEDTA), Bolivia (LAB), Argentina (Corporacion Sudamericana), Peru (Deutche Lufthansa Sucursal en Peru), and Colombia (SCADTA). Those eight carriers employed many German pilots and technical personnel, and there was a sizable percentage of Germans in their management ranks.

Following Hitler's invasion of Poland in 1939, a special U.S. War Department commission quietly began investigating the extent of German penetration of our Latin American neighbors, and its

potential threat to the United States. The commission's report to
Secretary of War Henry Stimson not only warned that a very real
threat existed, but singled out the Colombian airline SCADTA
(Sociedad Colombo-Alemana de Transportes Aereos) as especially
menacing. One of America's biggest military concerns was the safety
of the Panama Canal, so vitally needed to shift U.S. Navy warships
back and forth between the Pacific and Atlantic, and considered
dangerously vulnerable to a sneak attack or sabotage in the event
of war. By plane, the report noted, Colombia was only two hours
away from the Canal Zone and SCADTA's routes took its planes
right over Panama.

In addition, the commission expressed alarm at the number of
first- and second-generation Germans living in South America: an
estimated two million compared to only 23,000 Americans. While
Italy hadn't yet entered the war at the time the report was in
preparation, it also noted that Italy was an Axis partner, and that
there were even more Italians living in South America than Germans.

The alarm bells really went off when France surrendered in June
1940. A large portion of the supposedly neutralized French fleet
was based at Dakar, on the West Coast of Africa. American defense
planners were concerned that if the Germans ever grabbed control
of both the fleet and that well-equipped naval base, they would be
a slim 1900 miles from Brazil's east coast city of Natal—a truncated
transatlantic stretch known as the Dakar-Natal bulge. The War
Department took the possibility of Germany invading thinly
defended Brazil via a foothold at Natal very seriously, and Colombia's proximity to the Panama Canal equally so.

It came as a surprise and distinct shock to both the War and
State Departments when they learned that since 1931, Pan Am had
owned a whopping eighty-five percent of SCADTA, its German-
dominated personnel and Austrian-born president, Peter von
Bauer, notwithstanding. Trippe had made an oblique reference to
the $1.1 million takeover in his 1931 annual report to Pan Am
stockholders, but carefully phrased it as acquiring "a substantial
interest" without bothering to reveal that he had grabbed majority
control of the airline.

Trippe also claimed that the Post Office Department, which
controlled international mail rates, had been duly and properly
informed in writing, but somehow this letter was never sent and it

was eight years later that the State Department finally got around to asking Trippe: exactly what did "substantial interest" mean?

Nor had Trippe, with his penchant for making secret deals, ever informed the Colombian government itself that Pan Am actually owned majority stock in the country's proud national airline. When the extent of the acquisition was exposed to the furious Colombians, he mollified their outrage by upgrading SCADTA's service with new DC-3s, but then had to face the State Department's wrath—he was ordered to rid the airline of all German influence. At first Trippe refused, pointing out that von Bauer and many of his German colleagues had become naturalized and presumably very loyal Colombian citizens who posed no threat to the U.S., an argument which fell on deaf ears. Trippe finally pried $250,000 out of his board of directors which he used as severance pay to "clean house" of unwanted employees. And in 1941, SCADTA became Aerovias Nacionales de Colombia.

Subsidiaries and alliances were the cornerstones of Pan Am's far-flung empire, and U.S. defense officials began taking full advantage of them in the prewar years. A good example was Panagra, based in Lima, Peru, and born out of a partnership between Pan Am and the Grace Steamship Company; under War Department prodding, the airline led a purge of German-supported carriers that by the fall of 1941 had virtually eliminated German influence along the entire west coast of South America—including strategic Natal.

Another Latin American carrier with strong Pan Am connections was TACA (Transportes Aereos Centros Americanos) of Honduras, originally owned by a colorful soldier of fortune from New Zealand named Lowell Yerex, with routes serving Guatemala, Costa Rica, Mexico, and Nicaragua. He was about to sell the airline to American Export Airlines when Trippe sneaked in through the back door, and in a series of not-too-kosher maneuvers—including cutthroat fare wars—wound up controlling TACA.

In the Far East, as previously noted, there were Pan Am's holdings in CNAC. And PAA went into Africa, too, at the request of the British government. An aircraft-ferrying subsidiary called Atlantic Airways, owned jointly by PAA and BOAC, was established in the summer of 1941 to keep an African air supply route open to the hard-pressed British forces trying to maintain a foothold in North

Africa. BOAC had been trying valiantly to do the job alone but lacked sufficient resources.

Atlantic Airways, whose name was changed later to Pan American Air Ferries reflecting its increased role in ferrying combat planes across the South Atlantic, served a route that stretched from Miami to Africa via Trinidad and the Brazilian cities of Belem and Natal. The latter, however, also happened to be the terminus of Italy's air mail service to Brazil, and the Pan Am subsidiary got early and uncomfortable confirmation of fears that Mussolini's minions in South America could cause trouble.

An Atlantic Airways Lockheed Lodestar took off from Natal late one afternoon, its crew unaware that Italians, who had a lot of freedom around the airport, had sabotaged the plane by loosening the spark plugs on one engine and crippling the landing gear. The flight was 300 miles out of Natal when the affected engine quit. The pilot decided to return, but as he approached Natal and tried to lower the landing gear, only one wheel came down.

By now it was dark and the field itself was pitch-black; the Italians had informed the tower that no more planes were expected until morning and that neither runway lighting nor radio communications were needed for the rest of the night. The Lodestar pilot, with only his wing lights to guide him, made five attempts to land—on one wheel—and finally made it safely on the sixth try with only minor damage to the airplane.

Pan American Airways–Africa, Ltd. (PAA-Africa) was another prewar subsidiary serving numerous points within Africa, again at Britain's request. In the eleven months preceding Pearl Harbor, Pan Am's African operations added more than 25,000 miles to its octopus-shaped route structure. But the airline's most significant contribution in these pre–Pearl Harbor months was the establishment of strategically located Western Hemisphere airfield facilities, a network that extended from Canada southward throughout the Caribbean, and the west coasts of Central and South America.

This massive air base plan had a built-in obstacle: officially, the United States had no right to build bases in neutral nations anxious to stay out of any global conflict. But a privately owned airline could, and thus entered Pan Am, so solidly entrenched in many of these critical areas, and already operating out of a number of existing airport facilities—many of them planned and constructed by PAA itself as part of landing rights agreements. The War Department, much against the advice of several high-ranking State Department officials who detested Trippe, made the obvious and necessary choice: in November 1940, it signed a secret contract with a new PAA subsidiary, Pan American Airports Corporation, which would operate an "Airport Development Program" ostensibly intended for the improvement of commercial airport facilities, but in reality mostly aimed at building airfields designed primarily for military use. Included were longer runways for heavy bombers and transports, weather stations, better communications facilities, traffic control towers, and fuel storage depots.

Juan Trippe wasn't being entirely altruistic or patriotic in accepting the job; America was still at peace, and initially he regarded it as a glorious opportunity to improve and expand the airline's Western Hemisphere facilities without having to spend one dime of corporate money. Building new runways for land planes, for instance, was a decided bonus; Pan Am already was reequipping its fleet with such airliners, for Trippe knew the reign of the luxurious but slow seaplane was coming to a close. In fact, at first he picked new sites that were better fitted for commercial than military use, and he had to be reminded of priorities: namely, that the carefully camouflaged Airport Development Program was created for defense purposes.

The contract had to be amended ten times over the next four years as new projects were added to the original thirty-four (the War Department had asked for twenty-five land airports and nine seaplane bases in fourteen countries); the total eventually reached fifty-two, employing nearly a thousand Americans along with 25,000 foreign nationals, and cost four times the initial estimate, but the investment paid dividends.

It is true that the Brazilian invasion fears and the threat to the Panama Canal proved unfounded, even exaggerated; historians agree that Germany, and Italy even more so, lacked sufficient air and naval muscle to support a successful invasion of South America. But from 1939 and well into 1942, the danger seemed real enough to justify that network of air bases as protection against the worst scenario, however implausible the script appeared. And when war did come, many of those same bases became part of the airlift network.

Seven days after Pearl Harbor, even as black smoke from oil-fed fires still shrouded the ravaged battleships of the Pacific fleet, the full airline industry mobilization plan—massive in concept, swift in execution, and awesome in its eventual scope—was launched officially and operationally with a mission involving fifteen American Airlines DC-3s flown by pilots under secret orders.

Their final destination: Natal, Brazil.

Fifteen DC-3s whose routine trips were suddenly interrupted added up to thirty mystified airline pilots and a few hundred equally mystified passengers. All fifteen flights were en route to regularly scheduled destinations when terse messages began crackling over cockpit radios: "Land at the nearest airport, disembark your passengers, and you'll receive further instructions."

The instructions were hammer-blunt: refuel and ferry their now-empty planes to Fort Lauderdale, Florida. American made other travel arrangements for the suddenly "disenfranchised" passengers, most of them important businessmen (business travel constituted about ninety-five per cent of airline traffic in those days). Reportedly one of those bumped off at Phoenix from a California-bound flight was a very angry, loudly protesting famous movie star, but unfortunately his or her identity has been lost in antiquity—there is no mention of the name in American's historical files.

The widely scattered fifteen-plane armada proceeded to Fort Lauderdale, where the aircraft were stripped of all unnecessary weight and new passengers boarded. There were no movie stars nor busnessmen among them, for all fifteen DC-3s were jammed with some 300 Signal Corps communications specialists who would man the air base at Natal. Fresh crews flew the DC-3s to Brazil in what was the first actual wartime mission for an airline, and significantly one that was a specific cog in Rosie Stallter's planning machine. American's dispatchers knew exactly what had to be done the minute the War Department told the airline to execute the Signal Corps airlift.

Thanks to his organizational skills and Edgar Gorrell's foresight, key officials at every carrier knew more about their initial war assignments than merely the number of airplanes they were losing. This applied both to military cargo and personnel flights within the United States, and those airlift operations that took airline crews straight into the war zones. It was Gorrell who talked the War Department into surveying the cargo requirements of the understaffed, inadequately equipped Air Service Command, responsible for transporting men and materials between domestic supply depots and air bases.

Stallter was sent on a five-day tour of ASC depots in six states—Pennsylvania, California, Utah, Ohio, Alabama, and Texas. The survey showed him one salient fact: ASC couldn't do the job on its own. So he quickly created a detailed plan for a domestic Army cargo service operated by the airlines under military contracts, with the carriers providing their own maintenance. In general, he geared cargo assignments to the location of a carrier's principal maintenance facility. And in establishing overseas airlift responsibilities when war came, the same principal was applied—such as eventually assigning United to the Pacific because of UAL's big maintenance base in San Francisco, and giving Miami-based Eastern missions involving operations to and out of the Caribbean and South America.

For domestic operations, under a format Stallter updated as late as January of 1942, the nation was divided into five sectors: United was assigned the west coast, American the east coast, Northwest appropriately drew the northwest, Eastern took responsibility for the southeastern area, and Braniff got the southwest.

So successful was the domestic cargo system, even before the new sector assignments went into effect, that the Army Air Corps shared with the airline industry and the ATA the 1941 Collier Trophy, a coveted honor awarded annually for major aviation achievements. But both Gorrell and his members wisely stayed out of a bitter intraservice jurisdictional feud that developed within the Air Corps, the brawling principals being the Air Service Command and the Ferrying Command, which shortly after Pearl Harbor changed its name to the Air Transport Command.

The Ferrying Command itself was created six months before Pearl Harbor, under Colonel Robert Olds, a dedicated, hard-working Air Corps veteran whose initial staff consisted of six officers and a civilian clerk. In March of 1942, the exhausted Olds, who suffered from arthritis, collapsed at his desk and was ordered to take emergency sick leave. His replacement was Colonel Harold Lee George, and it was under his regime that the Ferrying Command became ATC.

When war came, ASC insisted that it should continue its domestic operations while ATC confined itself to flying overseas. George wanted all airlift operations combined under one tent—that of

ATC—and the dispute ended up on Hap Arnold's desk. Arnold at first refused to play referee and did what came naturally in bureaucratic Washington: he turned the controvery over to a Pentagon committee to study the matter. The committee also did what came naturally to all committees: it proposed a compromise. It recommended that the Air Service Command take over all air transportation within the Western Hemisphere, leaving the Air Transport Command to handle everything outside that hemisphere.

George's military specialty was strategic bombardment, and he frankly admitted he didn't know beans about transportation—he hadn't wanted Bob Olds's job to begin with. Yet he knew enough about the hazards of divided command authority to tell Hap Arnold the committee's compromise would be a disaster.

"If confusion and inefficiency were the objectives to be attained, no plan could have been proposed that would better accomplish it," he was to comment later.

Arnold, although furious at his own committee, considered himself technically bound by its decision. So he went straight to Chief of Staff George Marshall and came out with a directive giving the Air Transport Command sole responsibility for air transportation both within the United States and to all war zones. And having won an intramural scrap that made him boss of what literally would become the biggest airline in the world, Hal George turned for counsel and advice to the kind of man who knew something about running an airline.

His name was Cyrus Rowlett Smith.

C.R. was George's first and only choice to be ATC's deputy commander, although there was one other belated and self-nominated candidate: Juan Trippe. He met with Hap Arnold in Washington shortly after Wake and Guam fell to the Japanese, still fuming over American Export Airlines being awarded a Naval Air Transport Service contract to fly the Atlantic, and blithely suggested that Arnold turn all military transport operations over to the one carrier capable of running a global airlift: Pan Am, naturally.

Trippe predicted dire consequences if domestic airlines, inexperienced both in operating four-engine equipment and in overseas navigation, tried to fly the oceans on any kind of large scale. Too many carriers in ATC meant too much inefficiency, he argued, so just let the domestic airlines carry cargo and personnel within the U.S. and give the bulk of the air transportation job to the only experienced international carrier. Even if Arnold had bought this transparently self-serving plan, so obviously aimed at preserving Pan Am's monopoly even in the middle of a bloody world war, Trippe really shot himself in the foot by adding that the military would have no management role whatsoever in the operation.

When Arnold's eyebrows shot up to full staff at this stipulation, Trippe condescendingly added that naturally the Air Corps Chief of Staff, the Chief of Naval Operations, and the Undersecretary of State would be invited to attend meetings involving the airlift. Trippe, insisting that he was merely trying to further the war effort by assuring greater efficiency, offered to serve as head of the whole shebang—but only if Arnold agreed to adopt his plan in its entirety.

Which Arnold, of course, rejected as fast as he could propel, "I'm sorry, but—" out of his mouth. A few months later, he offered to make Trippe a brigadier general in the Air Transport Command but Trippe began the discussion by criticizing the way ATC was being run and repeating his proposal to turn all ATC overseas operations over to Pan Am. Arnold lost his temper and ordered him out of his office.

Even some of his greatest admirers felt that Trippe may have been his own worst enemy with his almost blind obsession to protect Pan Am from any competition, even in wartime. Rightly or wrongly, it was an attitude that made him persona non grata in official Washington, and there is no doubt he got on the wrong side of too many top government officials—including the White House and Civil Aeronautics Board—to such an extent that it hurt his own airline. The chickens came home to roost after the war when he lost his battle to keep other U.S. carriers out of the international market, and then, in a perfectly understandable effort to level the playing field, he filed for domestic authority, only to have every application rejected.

It is ironic that so many historians remember this brilliant pioneer of oceanic air travel more for his Machiavellian maneuvering than for his enormous contributions to civil aviation. For that matter, to judge Pan Am on Juan Trippe alone would be a disservice to his own airline, and to the loyal people of Pan Am. They were the ones who helped build those vital air bases, who flew and maintained Juan Trippe's beloved Clippers—many of them wearing the drab sea-gray of the Naval Air Transport Service—as part of an unprecedented airlift to the far corners of a war-torn planet.

It would have been poetic justice if Hal George had asked TWA's Jack Frye to serve as his ATC deputy; Trippe feared TWA's potential as a future international competitor more than any other airline, especially with Howard Hughes bankrolling TWA's finances. But George never considered anyone but C.R. Smith. They met for the first time in Washington at Hap Arnold's suggestion, after George had tried to get out of replacing Olds. He had expected overseas duty commanding a heavy bomber group, and begged Arnold to give the transport job to someone else.

"General, I realize the importance of air transportation," George pleaded. "But with due respect, sir, I know absolutely nothing about the problems of creating a worldwide air transport system—and I don't think there's anyone in the Ferrying Command itself with that kind of knowledge."

Arnold said nothing for a moment, then asked, "Do you know C.R. Smith?"

"I know he's president of American Airlines. I don't know him personally."

"Well, I do. I'll call him and have him fly down here tomorrow (American's corporate headquarters at the time were in New York). You meet him, and if you two can get along together, I'll make him a colonel."

George, still a colonel himself at that point, gave Arnold a quizzical look that said "I'm only a colonel myself" and Hap added with a grin, "Oh, by the way, I'm recommending you for brigadier general."

Hal George and C.R. met in a Washington hotel room the next morning. As Arnold suspected, they hit it off immediately, although the Air Corps officer learned quickly that Smith never went around end when going through center was faster. Over coffee, George told C.R. he figured the first thing his new command needed more than anything else was a cadre of experienced airline executives and managers capable of setting up and then running a global system.

Smith nodded, took out a fountain pen, and on a piece of hotel stationery wrote down about twenty names. He showed George the list.

"I don't know any of them," George confessed.

"I do, and they're the best in the industry," C.R. assured him. "We'll send telegrams to the presidents of their airlines telling them that these people are absolutely essential to the war effort and that they must be released for military service."

Smith composed the telegram text himself, and showed the draft to George who shook his head worriedly.

"C.R., I'm afraid it's phrased so strongly that only General Arnold could sign that kind of message and have it mean anything to a guy who's top boss of an airline."

"You're right," Smith agreed. "We'll just sign his name to every telegram and send 'em out."

"Wait a minute," George protested. "We can't put Hap Arnold's name on those wires without his approval."

"The hell we can't," C.R. argued. "He can't shoot you for doing it."

No, George thought, although I could get court-martialed. But the unauthorized telegrams went out that afternoon, ostensibly and very illegally signed by "General H.H. Arnold, chief of staff, United States Army Air Corps." Nervously, George confessed to Arnold what they had done.

"You might be getting some telephone calls from a few unhappy airline presidents," he added.

The general laughed. "I'll handle 'em, Hal. They've got to realize this country's at war. By the way, if you and C.R. can work together, take him down to the Adjutant General's office and have him sworn in as a colonel."

It was typical of C.R. Smith that he did not try to staff ATC with familiar and trusted men from his own airline, which would have been the easiest recruiting course to take. But C.R.—fiercely loyal to American Airlines though he was—went for top talent regardless of what carrier it came from. The initial twenty-man roster he had scribbled down for George eventually was expanded manyfold as ATC and NATS grew into a pair of globe-spanning giants; the mention of only one individual will suffice because his donning a uniform was so appropriate—Rosie Stallter, who a full month after Pearl Harbor was still keeping the mobilization plan up-to-date, eventually went into ATC as a colonel.

And that was how a soft-spoken bomber pilot from New England and an airline executive from Texas launched their wartime partnership, one that was to produce logistical miracles and prove that not only this war, but wars yet to come, would need air transport to assure victory.

They were sharing command of an air transportation armada that in a four-year period carried nearly three million passengers and cargo tonnage that can only be guessed at, because so many planes took off with loads far heavier than were listed on weight and balance manifests—and often with loads the planes weren't even designed to haul. ATC personnel alone on V-J Day numbered some 200,000; combined with NATS, the global airlift involved more than 300,000 men and women—the numerical equivalent of twelve infantry divisions—while its aircraft roamed the world's skies routinely.

But it wasn't that way at the beginning, when ATC and NATS went to war with a handful of transports mostly designed for peace-time flying—and only a handful of men who knew how to fly them.

★ ★ 3 ★ ★
Of Planes and "Professors"

After the end of World War II, General Dwight Eisenhower listed four pieces of equipment that he and his senior commanders, in his own words, considered "among the most vital to our success in Africa and Europe."

Not one was a military weapon. The first three were the bulldozer, the jeep, and the two-and-a-half-ton truck. The fourth was the C-47.

The accolade was well deserved, although the fame this legendary transport plane earned has tended to obscure the impressive war roles of other great if occasionally maligned airplanes, including one workhorse—the Curtiss C-46 Commando—that was rushed into service before there was time to flush out all its bugs.

With one exception—the four-engine Consolidated B-24 Liberator bomber that became the C-87 transport—the major land-based planes serving ATC and NATS were designed originally for airline passenger service, and that included the C-47, which began life as the DC-3. This one fact makes their accomplishments even more remarkable; just as the crucible of war turned ordinary civilians into fighting men, so did these machines of peace become important tools of war.

It is equally interesting and significant to note that none of the Axis powers ever developed a real air transport system that provided long-range logistical support to combat zones, certainly nowhere near the scale of the Allied effort. Germany came the closest with her large fleet of Junkers Ju-52 trimotors, a sturdy all-metal airliner slightly larger than the well-known Ford "Tin Goose" (which copied the Junkers' corrugated fuselage). Used mostly as a troop and parachutist carrier, the Ju-52 quickly became obsolete and Germany never developed—at least in sufficiently large numbers—a more modern replacement for this fine but overaged airplane. It was the Ju-52 that through no fault of its own failed in its one true airlift effort: supplying the besieged Sixth Army at Stalingrad, a task far beyond its capabilities.

Germany did produce a pair of excellent four-engine transports in the Focke-Wulf Condor and Junkers Ju-90. But the former was used almost exclusively as a long-range patrol bomber, particularly against shipping, and while the Ju-90 did serve as a military transport and glider tow plane, Junkers was allowed to build only fourteen of them. It was an excellent example of why military historians have regarded Hitler's indifference to the value of long-range airplanes as one of his frequent major strategic mistakes.

Italy, whose military operations were confined largely to the Mediterranean theater, didn't really need much of an airlift. Its most modern airliner, the high-wing Savoia Marchetti SM 74, carried only twenty-four passengers despite its four engines, and was used only sporadically as a military transport. So were the Savoia Marchetti trimotor SM 83, civil version of the Regia Aeronautica's standard bomber (the SM 79 Sparvieo), and the Savoia Marchetti SM 73—another trimotor closely resembling the Ju-52 but not nearly as rugged.

Japan, trying to protect bases and conquered territories thousands of miles from her homeland, needed long-range airlift capability more than either Germany or Italy. But Japan simply lacked adequate transport aircraft, relying mostly on converted twin-engine bombers for noncombat tasks. Japan did develop two prewar commercial airliners—the eight-passenger Nakajima AT-2 and eleven-passenger Mitsubishi MC-20, both twin-engine airplanes—but they were too small for anything but minor wartime transport duties.

Ironically, Japanese civil aviation before the war relied heavily on an American-designed airliner, the Lockheed L-14 Super Electra, buying more than 100 of them and building a few under license. They saw mostly commercial use, however, while the L-14 and

Lockheed's other prewar airliner—the Model 18 Lodestar—became the only U.S. civil transports to be converted into combat aircraft, serving as twin-engine medium bombers. Neither carried enough of a bomb load to be truly effective in a rather miscast role, but both performed valiantly in other military tasks.

Until bigger and faster transports entered ATC service, two "Ancient Pelicans" filled in temporarily unmanned gaps and deserve mention as well as praise. Boeing's pace-setting 247, America's first all-metal, twin-engine airliner, was one of the first civil transports drafted into the Army, mostly from smaller carriers, and took part in flying priority domestic cargo. Effectiveness was limited not only by its small size but lack of numbers—Boeing built only seventy-five, the first sixty going to United, which was stuck with an obsolete fleet as soon as the bigger, faster DC-2 was introduced.

Yet the sturdy 247 also played an inadvertent wartime role. Lufthansa, the German airline, purchased two of them before the war but neither saw much passenger service. Both airplanes were appropriated by the military, which had them dismantled in order to study their internal construction. During the war, the British captured a Heinkel 111 twin-engine bomber intact and shipped it to Seattle so Boeing engineers could examine how it was built. They found the Heinkel's tail and much of the internal structure identical to that of the 247.

The venerable DC-2 also flew a lot of stateside military cargo. A number of the some 200 that were produced, however, served overseas as well, especially in the Far East, including the hazardous China-Burma-India (CBI) theater, where they shouldered much of the air transport burden until bigger and more modern cargo aircraft took over. The commercial DC-2 was like an older child totally eclipsed by the arrival of a far more brilliant younger brother, a genius who outshines him in almost every respect. In a sense, the DC-3 did to the DC-2 what the latter did to the 247, assigning it to a premature obsolescence.

Aside from these two veterans, there were six different airplanes that can be classed as the principal land-based aircraft that operated America's wartime airlift. And each warrants a more detailed look . . .

Lockheed's Twins

The L-14 first won fame in 1938, when Howard Hughes flew one around the world in the then-record time of three days and nineteen hours; he was going to use Douglas's DC-1 prototype, but chose the L-14 because it was faster. Like many airliners of that era, the L-14 had a relatively small cargo capacity, which limited its usefulness as a military transport. But Lockheed modified the Electra into the widely used Hudson bomber, identical to the civilian model except for a fuselage that was two feet shorter; the RAF operated hundreds of them, especially in its Coastal Command, which successfully employed Hudsons on countless antisubmarine patrol missions.

Many L-14s that flew in the Pacific theater saw the kind of combat action for which they were never really designed. One of World War II's almost unbelievable air war stories involved a Hudson bomber that tangled with Japan's leading fighter ace, Saburo Sakai, and five other pilots all flying fast, maneuverable Zeros. The L-14 had just blown up an enemy supply dump when Sakai's patrol intercepted it. Instead of fleeing, the Hudson waded into the Japanese formation and engaged the six Zeros in a wild dogfight—including a maneuver Sakai said later he had never dreamed any bomber was capable of performing.

It was a full snap roll, "the fastest I had ever seen for a twin-engined plane," Sakai marveled. For more than ten minutes, those six deadly fighters failed to score a single hit on a bomber that was being flown like an acrobatic plane. Then a burst finally caught the Lockheed's top gunner, and it was all over.

The versatile, more powerful Lodestar was just a bigger L-14, and ranked as the fastest commercial transport in the world until four-engine planes made their appearance. The L-18 cruised at well over 220 miles per hour, compared to the DC-3's modest 180 mph. Although popular as an airliner, the Lodestar's cargo space limitations kept it from being a successful military cargo aircraft. But after Lockheed stretched the fuselage a few feet, the L-18 was turned into the Ventura bomber, flown by all three branches of the U.S. armed forces in a variety of tasks: as a bomber, troop and personnel carrier and hospital transport, as well as assignments to antisubmarine patrols, reconnaissance flights, and glider-towing missions. It was a Navy Ventura on a patrol mission that first sighted survivors of the torpedoed cruiser *Indianapolis*. Of the 624 Lodestars Lockheed built, 480 were operated by the Air Corps, Navy, and Marines.

The Stratoliner—the Unsuccessful Revolution

As a technological development, Boeing's Model 307 was a huge step forward, but one that went several steps backward commercially. Only ten were built—six ordered by TWA and four by Pan Am—but only eight ever went into airline service. The Stratoliner being used for test purposes, one of the four PAA had ordered, crashed during a test flight and the accident gave the 307 a black eye from which it never recovered; Pan Am even refused to accept a replacement and took delivery on only three airplanes. Then Howard Hughes grabbed one of TWA's Stratoliners as his personal airplane and never relinquished it.

Yet the Stratoliner, the world's first pressurized airliner capable of cruising comfortably above most weather, was a truly revolutionary transport that deserved a better fate. It was typical of Boeing transport designs of that era, a hybrid that borrowed heavily from Boeing's great bombers. The 307's wings, Wright Cyclone engines, and initial tail surfaces were identical to those of the early model B-17 bombers.

Tommy Tomlinson, a former Navy pilot who became a key figure in TWA's engineering department, had pioneeered much of the high-altitude test work that went into development of the 307's pressurization system—literally a means of compressing the thin air of the upper atmosphere into heavier, breathable air as it enters the cabin. He went back into the Navy after Pearl Harbor, not too happy over the Army's weight-saving decision to operate the Stratoliners without pressurization.

The 307 entered airline service in mid 1940, and while it proved operationally successful and popular (knocking two hours off the DC-3's best transcontinental time), it stood no chance of competing against the DC-4 either as an airliner or a military transport. The blunt truth was that Boeing enjoyed an exemplary reputation for designing heavy bombers, but Douglas ruled the commercial transport world and it would be an uncontested reign until the dawn of the jet age.

The Stratoliners were pressed into the Air Transport Command as C-75s, all flown by ex-TWA and Pan Am crews, and did what they did best: long-range transocean flights carrying priority cargo and personnel, and doing the work of at least twice their actual number. Sadly, only one still exists today: Pan Am's former *Clipper Flying Cloud,* which the Pima Air and Space Museum in Tucson, Arizona, turned over to Boeing volunteers in Seattle to restore for museum display. It is the lone survivor of those revolutionary airliners that waranted the label of pioneer.

The C-46—Love It or Hate It

The fat-bellied C-46 Commando, one of the largest twin-engine piston transports ever built, enjoyed far more success during the war than when peace came and it tried to resume the role for which it originally was intended: a pressurized, thirty-eight-passenger commercial airliner called the CW-20. The prototype first flew early in 1940, and Curtiss-Wright hoped to sell it as a direct competitor to the DC-3. In that capacity it was considered a compete failure— no major airline operated the passenger version, although after the war several flew C-46s as freighters. At one time there were more than 600 of them flying freight in and out of South America, and as late as 1985 about sixty C-46s were still being flown as cargo planes.

Carrying cargo was the airplane's forte—12,000 pounds in the earliest models, increasing to a whopping 16,000 pounds in the later C-46D. An eight-ton load was about double the advertised maximum capacity of a C-47, and the C-46 usually carried even heavier loads under the most adverse conditions encountered by any wartime transport aircraft. Many of the rugged Commandos were employed in the China-Burma-India (CBI) theater of operations over a route known as the "Hump," and there was no more treacherous airway in the world than what crews faced tackling this towering Himalayan mountain terrain. The C-46, which had better high-altitude capability than the C-47/DC-3, was the best available transport for the job.

The Army didn't share the airlines' lack of interest in the commercial CW-20. In mid 1940 the Air Corps ordered forty of the big planes for about $350,000 each, specifying that they be unpressurized, and by the time the war ended, Curtiss-Wright had produced more than 3300, all for the military. But the Commando had several faults that didn't endear it to pilots. It was not the easiest airplane to fly, and the earlier versions were underpowered. The original engines were 1700-hp Wright Cyclones, which proved insufficient for a twin-engine airplane that weighed fifteen tons empty; lose an engine and a pilot was flying an iron bathtub. Lose one on takeoff in hot weather with a load exceeding allowable maximums—an almost inevitable situation with C-46 flights—and the crew might as well start singing hymns. One pilot painted MOAN on his port engine nacelle and GROAN on the starboard nacelle. Actually it was an exceptionally stable airplane with good single-engine performance when carrying normal loads—which in wartime wasn't very often.

Later C-46 models were equipped with 2000-hp Pratt & Whitney Double Wasp engines—powerful 18-cylinder monsters, more reliable but not easy to maintain. The Commando's size and weight also begged for a tricycle landing gear, which would have given pilots the greater ease of nose wheel steering, but Curtiss-Wright opted for the same kind of tailwheel gear as the DC-3/C-47, and this made the C-46 almost as hard to maneuver on the ground as in the air. There was a kind of love-hate relationship between the C-46 and its crews, for pilots groused and grumbled constantly about the big transport's flying idiosyncrasies even as they appreciated its brute strength.

"You'd start trimming the damn thing and nothing would happen," one ATC captain recounted. "Then all of a sudden the hydraulics would kick in and you'd be standing on your nose or tail."

Unhealthy Hybrid—the C-87

That same love-hate relationship infected the airmen who flew the Consolidated C-87s, which basically were modified B-24 bombers stripped of all armament and beefed up to carry huge cargo loads and, occasionally, about twenty passengers. If so many airliners were cast in unfamiliar wartime roles, the C-87 was a case in reverse—an airplane designed as a bomber that turned out to be a badly needed if somewhat flawed transport.

The airplane literally was drafted into ATC and NATS as the only immediately available long-range, four-engine combat aircraft that could be converted into a transport with a minimum of effort, time and expense. The B-24 itself was a very fine airplane, a bomber that actually carried a heavier payload farther, faster, and higher than the B-17, and its considerably wider fuselage was nicely adaptable to airlift purposes. So the ATC version became the C-87, Consolidated producing 276 for the Air Corps, five for the Navy, which designated them as RY-2s, and twenty-four for the RAF, where they were called C.VIIs.

A later model—the C-87A—was turned into a VIP transport equipped with ten sleeper berths; the ATC operated six of them and the Navy three. A tenth C-87A, officially Aircraft 159 and carrying the serial number 124159, was a rather special airplane. This particular converted bomber had a truly deluxe interior with Pullman-style berths, a private suite, and a large galley that included a Tappan electric range. It was christened *Guess Where II,* and the reason for such plushness (and the name) was the fact that the airplane was intended for White House use—*Guess Where II* technically was the ancestor of the future Presidential transports that would be known as Air Force One.

"Technically" is the key word; although A/C 124159 was supposed to be the first "Flying White House," the Secret Service refused to let President Roosevelt fly in it. One of the C-87's drawbacks was a nasty reputation of being prone to in-flight fires believed to have been the cause of a number of unexplained aircraft disappearances while on ATC missions over the Atlantic. And there was some evidence to support the Secret Service's concerns, even though the average B-24 pilot loved the plane's steady flying qualities and durability; perhaps significantly, the bomber was blessed with more defenders than the transport version, which had more than a few vociferous critics among the airline pilots flying for ATC.

It was, even to its staunchest defenders, a rather ugly aircraft, of such unaesthetic quality that both the B-24 and C-87 inspired several uncomplimentary descriptions. Examples: (1) they looked like the crates in which B-17s were shipped, and (2) they closely resembled a beached harpooned whale. One of aviation's oldest axioms is that an airplane flies like it looks; the C-87 in particular seemed to bear out that saying, being especially vulnerable to icing.

Pilot/author Ernie Gann once remarked that the C-87 wing "would not carry enough ice to chill a bucket of champagne."

TWA crews flew a lot of C-87s for ATC and some pilots were frankly afraid of the the big plane because of the fire hazard. The transport version's fuel transfer system was located on the internal rear wing spar, plainly visible from the cockpit, with a little gutter that was supposed to dump any fuel overflow safely. But right on top of that same wing section was all the radio equipment, and a single spark could ignite spilled fuel.

"If you lit a cigarette at the wrong time," one captain remembered, "the plane could blow up."

Otis Bryan, who went into ATC after he got Eagle's Nest off and running, agreed that the C-87's propensity to catch fire was its chief flaw.

"Throw a rock at one and you could set it on fire," he reminisced. And he wasn't kidding. The fuel gauges on the cockpit instrument panel were also tiny windows through which the pilots could actually see the gas level. If something broke the glass, and it could be as accidental as inadvertently hitting a gauge with a foot, fuel would spray all over the flight deck—and if someone was smoking at the time . . .

A C-87 manned by a TWA crew vanished on a flight between Natal and Ascension Island; no trace of either the airplane or the crew was ever found, and there were several similar unsolved disappearances involving C-87s. Yet there were a lot of positives about the airplane as well as negatives, such as the ruggedness it inherited from its bomber genes. There also was the undisputed fact that except for those eight Stratoliners, C-87s were ATC's only long-range transport until Douglas began full C-54 production. The Air Corps needed C-87s so badly that a number of planes in ATC's C-87 fleet consisted of worn-out or combat-damaged B-24s hastily repaired, converted into transports, and equipped with new engines. Some of these war-weary veterans were assigned to difficult, dangerous Hump flights. Consolidated did turn out an airplane that was a better bomber than a transport, but any beat-up aircraft that could operate successfully in the CBI theater couldn't have been all bad.

Thoroughbred—the C-54

The C-54 didn't really replace any transport, including the C-87; it was in a league of its own, perfectly suited for military airlift tasks even though it was a prewar airliner whose first flight dated back to 1938. The airplane was born as the DC-4E (E for Experimental), the first and only commercial transport in history whose development costs were partially subsidized by airlines who would be eventual customers.

This unusual partnership was the brainchild of United's William A. "Pat" Patterson, who sounded out top officials at TWA, American, Eastern, and Pan American and convinced them that (1) they all needed a four-engine airliner vastly superior to anything else flying, and (2) the costs of designing such a huge airplane were too much for Douglas to swallow alone. Patterson pledged $60,000 from United and talked the other members of the so-called "Big Five" into matching United's contribution; that added up to the $300,000 Douglas estimated it needed to help cover what wound up as a total $1.6 million eventually spent to design and build the prototype.

It may boggle the mind that the renowned Douglas Aircraft Co. needed a $300,000 helping hand from this unprecedented alliance before it could launch the DC-4 project. Yet in those days, spending more than $1.6 million to develop what would be the biggest land-based airliner in the world represented an enormous technological and financial gamble. (As a yardstick for comparing the cost of aeronautical progress in today's world of commercial aviation, exactly fifty years later Boeing was to commit $4 billion for development of the 777.)

Luxurious peacetime air travel on a scale that promised to equal that of Pan Am's great flying boats was the goal of Douglas and its five contributors. The advance publicity on the DC-4E was sprinkled with some forgivable hyperbole, forgivable because the airplane went to war before it could carry a single passenger—and in postwar airline service the by-then outdated DC-4 became a very prosaic, conventional airliner.

But in those halcyon days of 1938, Douglas press releases referred to the new giant as "The Grand Hotel with wings," featuring such amenities as separate washrooms for men and women, a ladies lounge and men's dressing room, a private "Bridal Suite" compartment, a full kitchen with all-electric appliances located admidships to facilitate meal service (United's idea), electric shavers for male passengers and curling irons for the distaff side. Of less interest to passengers but of vast importance to flight crews was the DC-4E's tricycle landing gear, making it the first American-built transport that was a dream even to taxi as well as fly.

The DC-4E was designed to carry forty-two passengers by day and thirty on sleeper flights. The prototype was equipped with huge lounge-type chairs, twenty on each side of the aisle, fifteen of them arranged like those in a Pullman car so they could be transformed into berths. Out of the lavatory faucets came hot and cold running water. Cabin comfort was assured by air-conditioning and steam heat; Douglas originally planned to build an unpressurized airplane to save weight, but with two of the Big Five—TWA and Pan Am—already operating pressurized Boeing Stratoliners, United, Eastern, and American insisted that the DC-4 should be pressurized, too. The five sponsors ordered a total of sixty airplanes.

The DC-4E, like virtually every transport prototype ever built, required a lot of modifications before it became the production DC-4. One mistake was equipping it with a triple tail, much like the later Lockheed Constellation. It was a feature aimed at facilitating access to hangars with low entrances, but test flights revealed that a single large tail provided more stability and Douglas switched to the single tail on the production airplane. The major problem with the DC-4E was excessive weight, a common affliction with airliner prototypes, and test flights prompted engineers to reduce wing span from 145 feet to 117 feet, a surgical procedure that not only slashed unwanted weight but improved handling.

Consistent docility was one of the DC-4/C-54 series' finest virtues. The production DC-4 turned out to be a true pilot's airplane, one that could cruise safely on two engines. Hydraulically boosted controls made what was then considered a huge aircraft as responsive as a DC-3, although the DC-4 was almost three times bigger; the DC-4's gross weight of 65,000 pounds was twenty tons more than a fully loaded DC-3. Another plus was structural strength; like its smaller sister, the airplane could take a lot of punishment. There is one case on record in which a DC-4 exceeded 300 miles an hour in an inverted dive, encountering such stresses that when the plane landed, the wings were twisted out of line with the fuselage.

One of the DC-4's greatest admirers was famed author-pilot Ernie

Gann, an American Airlines captain who flew the big transport for ATC during the war. In his book *Ernest K. Gann's Flying Circus,* this veteran airman expressed his unabashed praise in words that could come only from a pilot who looked on airplanes almost as living creatures:

"[They were] of such sturdy and reliable temperament many pilots developed a DC-4 yawn. As an instrument aircraft they were so docile even low-time pilots could shoot a near-perfect approach. If one engine failed even at takeoff the effect was nicely manageable and if two succumbed during cruise the aircraft remained very airkindly while producing a minimum of perspiration on crew brows. With nose wheel steering governed by a large hand wheel just above the captain's knee, taxiing was easy and crosswind takeoffs firmly begun. Ordinary takeoffs were nearly automatic with the DC-4's seemingly anxious tendency to become airborne."

There were some ATC pilots who claimed no two C-54s flew exactly alike, but they were in a decided minority. Nobody, however, complained about the airplane's load-carrying muscle; the C-54's official payload of 32,000 pounds doubled the C-46's, and in actual service the airplane's cargo capability seemed almost limitless. During the Korean War, the crew of a C-54 complained that the airplane had handled sluggishly on a flight from California to Tokyo. It turned out that thanks to a mistake by the loadmasters (cargo handlers), it was carrying twice the C-54's authorized load.

The DC-4 became the C-54 following a pair of visits to the Douglas plant in 1940. The first DC-4s had begun rolling down the assembly line when Air Corps chief Hap Arnold came to Santa Monica to look at the new airplanes. As soon as he returned to Washington, he sent a teletype to Donald Douglas ordering him to stop work on the transport and concentrate on building combat planes like the twin-engine Havoc bombers going to the RAF, and Dauntless dive bombers for the U.S. Navy. Douglas, furious, replied that DC-4 production could continue on schedule without affecting military output.

There then arrived in Santa Monica a second visitor—Assistant Secretary of War Robert A. Lovett, who took one look at the new DC-4 and promptly informed Arnold that Douglas was building the perfect airplane to meet all military logistical airlift requirements. But if Donald Douglas thought he could turn out civilian DC-4s and military C-54s simultaneously, he never got the chance;

not only Hap Arnold but the White House persuaded United and American, holding the first DC-4 delivery positions, to cancel their orders so Douglas could concentrate exclusively on the military version.

So the DC-4 became the C-54 Skymaster, like all wartime military transports unpressurized to save weight and increase payload. Full production began early in 1942 and by war's end Douglas had built more than a thousand—only one-tenth of C-47 production but still a Herculean total considering that one C-54 could do the work of almost three C-47s. The Navy's NATS operated the airplane as the R5-D and there were two ATC hospital plane versions: the C-54A, which carried twenty-four litters, and the C-54B, which had twenty-eight—the airplane's large cabin made it an ideal transport for medical evacuation missions. A specially modified C-54 became the first Air Force One, although presidential aircraft didn't carry that impressive sobriquet until after the war. The C-54 would serve as the chief workhorse in the 1948 Berlin Airlift. And the basic C-54 was to remain in active military transport service almost into the 1970s, the ultimate tribute to its sound design.

As an aeronautical success story, the history of this great Douglas transport is marred only by the ignimonious fate of the DC-4E prototype. Long before Pearl Harbor, Douglas sold the triple-tailed airplane to Japan, where an inexperienced Japanese crew attempted a full-flap landing with one engine out and dove the plane into Tokyo Bay.

Legend—the C-47

Dwight Eisenhower was not quite on target. Yes, the ubiquitous C-47 did contribute almost as much to victory as any fighter plane or bomber, but not merely in Europe and Africa. It performed the mundane and the miraculous in *every* theater of war, its wings casting shadows over the world's oceans, jungles, deserts, and mountains.

To use biblical phraseology, the DC-1 begat the DC-2, which begat the DST (Douglas Sleeper Transport), which begat the DC-3, which begat the C-47. But it was none other than C.R. Smith who was largely responsible for commercial aviation's most beloved airplane being built in the first place. He wasn't entirely happy with American's DC-2s, a fourteen-passenger airliner he considered too small to be truly profitable, and possessing too many idiosyncra-sies—such as vulnerability to icing and a noisy cabin heater that produced more decibels than a boilerplate factory. So he talked Donald Douglas into building an airplane he didn't want to build: an improved, twenty-one-passenger version of the DC-2 equipped with fourteen berths for night flights—namely, the DST.

They argued on the phone for well over two hours, a long-distance debate that cost C.R. $335.50. Douglas kept resisting until Smith promised to buy twenty DSTs sight unseen, with options for another twenty, and even then the manufacturer privately thought C.R. was crazy.

"Who in the hell is gonna buy a sleeper plane anyway?" he grumbled to one of his engineers. "Night flying is about as popular as silent movies." Later, Douglas almost had apoplexy when the first DST went on display in the cavernous Los Angeles Auditorium. What he saw as soon as he walked in was a large sign in front of the gleaming silver airliner:

21 SEATS—14 BIRTHS

Actually, Douglas wasn't that far off base in his opinion of sleeper flight popularity. Passengers had to be awakened before every land-ing to prevent eardrum discomfort, and the airlines had to levy a surcharge to compensate for the loss of seven revenue seats on sleeper flights; when American turned over half its fleet to the Army, the first airplanes to go were its DSTs. And it was the basic twenty-one-passenger DC-3 that literally revolutionized air travel with its reputation for safety and reliability. Thanks to this single airplane, for the first time in aviation history flight insurance (25 cents for $5000 coverage) became available to the public in 1937, only a year after the DC-3 went into airline service. It also freed the airline industry from almost total reliance on mail subsidies; C.R. called it the first airplane that could make money just by carrying people. And it was a pilot's airplane from the day it first flew—exceptionally rugged, reliable, and relatively free of the annoying "bugs" that inevitably plague new transports. The biggest complaint pilots had about the DC-3 was the tendency of the cockpit windshield to leak in the rain; some crews actually wore raincoats in the cockpit and one of aviation's most enduring legends is the en route weather report one captain radioed: "Light precipitation outside, heavy inside."

The Army's interest in the DC-3 as a military transport came naturally. As a matter of fact, in 1939 the Air Corps' Tenth Air Transport Group based at Wright-Patterson Field in Dayton began supply flights to Army depots throughout the U.S. using C-33s— these were DC-2s equipped with a larger tail and a cargo door. The C-33 was later modified into the C-39, a hybrid that combined the DC-2 fuselage with a DC-3 tail.

The C-47 itself carried an alphabet soup of designations. The C-47B, for example, had modified engines for high altitude flying. Various versions went all the way up to the C-47D, and there were C-49s, 50s and 53s—the C-49 series alone eventually reached the C-49K level. Navy C-47s were R-4Ds, and in the Royal Air Force the airplane was called the Dakota. In addition to C-47s acquired via lend-lease, the Russians built about 2000 under license as the IL-2 (although the Soviets never acknowledged that the lend-lease C-47s were manufactured in America, and always claimed the IL-2 itself was Russian-designed).

The official Air Corps moniker for the C-47 was Skytrain, or Skytrooper for aircraft assigned to paratroop operations. But to every American pilot who ever flew one, however, the C-47 was known as the "Gooney Bird." The derivation of that nickname is generally attributed to the real-life Gooney Bird, a large species of seagull that inhabits small South Pacific atolls like Wake Island. But there are at least two other theories as to the cognomen's origin.

An Air Corps colonel once wrote Douglas that "Gooney Bird" was never derived from a bird, but instead comes from the word "goon," which the dictionary defines as "a stupid person."

"We called them Gooney Birds because these planes were just stupid," he added. "They didn't know they could do the things they did."

His story has tongue-in-cheek characteristics, yet another theory holds that "Gooney" actually predated the war and was the nickname pilots of the Tenth Transport Group, for unknown reasons, bestowed on the C-39. Douglas itself has never taken sides on any explanation because its own historical files can't confirm the exact origin; it seems to have been one of those natural nicknames that sprang into existence from nowhere, its author or authors to remain forever anonymous.

The first C-47 built to military specifications was identical in external appearance to the DC-3 except for the addition of a large cargo door and a Plexiglas navigator's dome on top of the fuselage just behind the cockpit. But internally there were important differences; the cabin floor was strengthened, military cargo weighing a lot more than twenty-one passengers and their luggage. Also beefed up were bulkheads, longerons, and other key structural components. Most prewar DC-3s used Wright Cyclones, but the majority of C-47s were powered by Pratt & Whitney Twin Wasps.

It should be emphasized that brand-new C-47s were airplanes built specifically for a gamut of military assignments: cargo, personnel, medical evacuation, paratroop operations, and glider towing, to name a few. In the early stages of the war, there just weren't enough of them for either ATC or NATS to operate effectively— and this necessitated heavy reliance on the initial airline DC-3s that the Army had appropriated.

Only a minimum of modification work was possible; time was of the essence for airplanes needed in a hurry. When the Army or Navy got eager hands on a civilian DC-3, its interior was stripped clean, often down to the bare metal, and what went into the denuded cabin depended on the military's plans for the plane's employment. Extra fuel tanks were a frequent addition, and so were bench or so-called bucket seats and tie-down equipment for securing cargo. Whatever changes were made, the purpose was to reduce unnecessary weight in order to increase payload and range.

(The eight Boeing Stratoliners taken over by the military went back into postwar airline service without their pressurization systems, nor was any civilian DC-4 ever operated with a pressurized cabin.)

The DC-3's superb aerodynamics and rugged structure were such that even an unaltered airplane was capable of prodigious feats. After Jimmy Doolittle led the raid on Tokyo in 1942, he found his way to Burma, where he was invited to board a standard CNAC DC-3 and fly to safety before the advancing Japanese army reached the airfield. Doolittle, one of the last to board, took one look at who else was getting on the airplane and shook his head in disbelief. This particular DC-3, he told himself, was never going to get off the ground.

The total passenger count set a record for the daunty Douglas airliner: a whopping seventy-five human beings, including twenty-two children who sat on laps, fourteen adults who stood in the aisle, and ten more adults who rode in the waist cargo bin and forward mail compartment. Doolittle gaped at the boarding mob and muttered to the captain, "If I had any sense, I'd walk home."

This exploit was almost equalled by an ATC C-47 flown by a lieutenant named Harold Donohue, who was assigned a mission involving the evacuation of sixty-one children from an enemy-threatened airfield. The runway was only 1800 feet long, with a mountain at one end, and Donohue had to take off in the direction of the mountain. He crammed all sixty-one children and eleven adults into the cabin; counting himself and his copilot that made seventy-four. The Gooney Bird's Pratt & Whitney engines never missed a beat as he climbed to a safe altitude. Yet this wasn't quite as hairy as the experience of a young Russian pilot who started to take off in a heavily loaded lend-lease C-47, realized he was almost out of runway, and in desperation retracted the landing gear while the wheels were still on the ground. When the gear came up, the laboring C-47 staggered into the air.

Such incidents, of course, usually represented overloading out of sheer necessity. When cargo was crammed into C-47s or virtually any ATC or NATS airplane, both the ground and flight crews simply ignored the strict weight-and-balance rules that governed civilian flights—such as assuring that every load must maintain the correct center of gravity, or CG. The only wartime concession to that inviolate CG requirement was the more careful placement of heavy spare engines; otherwise the loading process, as Ernie Gann laconically observed, consisted of shoving "everything as far foward as it will go."

The kind of punishment a C-47 could absorb rivaled the storybook toughness of Boeing's B-17 bombers. A C-47 once collided with an attacking Japanese Zero, the impact severing all but a foot and a half of the transport's tail section. The fighter crashed but the C-47 made it back to its base safely—and became the only C-47 unofficially credited with downing a Zero. Another Gooney Bird slammed into a violent Pacific thunderhead at 12,000 feet, flipped over on its back, went into an 8000-foot dive and then a complete inside loop before the pilot regained control. When the airplane landed at the closest available base in Australia, a Douglas service engineer found the entire skin on both wings and the horizontal stabilizers twisted with wrinkles, and a wing rib hanging by a single rivet.

The pilot wanted to know if the airplane could be flown safely to its original destination—which happened to be 600 miles away, mostly over water.

"I'd advise against it," the Douglas representative said wryly.

The pilot went anyway—and made it.

There is one authenticated case of a C-47 that collided with a Hudson bomber and landed safely after losing almost an entire wing. A C-47 operating in the CBI theater was strafed on the ground by Japanese fighters that put an estimated 1000 holes into the fuselage and wings—the crew stopped counting at around 600. There were no maintenance facilities, so Chinese coolies covered the punctures with pieces of canvas cut from an awning and the plane took off for India carrying sixty-one refugees. En route, it flew into a monsoon that ripped off most of the patches, and when the C-47 finally approached its base in India, personnel at the field could hear its banshee whistles and screams long before it came into sight. The aircraft was henceforth known as "Whistlin' Willie."

It was the C-47 that helped the U.S. Marines cling to their precarious foothold on Guadalcanal. Japanese bombers had blown up a Navy supply ship carrying gas for the American fighters at Henderson Field. The fuel supply was so low that there wasn't enough to fill the tanks of even a single airplane. And it was at this critical point that fourteen C-47s of the Southwest Pacific Combat Air Transport Group—better known by its acronym SCAT—began flying in enough gas to keep Henderson's defending aircraft operational until the Navy could bring in other surface supply ships. By the time Guadalcanal was secured, SCAT's C-47s had flown almost 1000 trips into the island, hauling supplies in and wounded out.

Gooney Birds airlifted thousands of troops in time to save New Guinea's Port Moresby when Japanese invaders had pushed to within forty miles of this strategic base. More than 1000 C-47s were involved in the Normandy invasion, including flying 20,000 paratroopers into their assigned drop zones. Forty-four C-47s flew British paratroopers from the UK to Africa nonstop, a 1500-mile trip.

In 1944, a few hundred C-47s took off from England hauling 132 jeeps, seventy-three quarter-ton jeep trailers, thirty-two motorcycles, more than 3300 gallons of gasoline, some 60,000 pounds of rations, nearly 658,000 pounds of combat equipment, and 882 fully equipped fresh troops, and in three hours delivered the entire load to Holland, where the U.S. 82nd Airborne Division was battling to hold a strategic airfield.

In addition to combat-connected missions, where the C-47's performance was almost taken for granted, there were some ATC and NATS cargo flights that read like fiction. Captain John Mowatt was about to be rotated home after a long ATC tour flying the Hump, when he was ordered on another mission: carrying Christmas dinners to British troops fighting in the Burma jungle.

After Mowatt protested to no avail, he rationalized that helping weary soldiers celebrate Christmas with traditional holiday food was worth delaying his trip home. Then he was told what he'd be carrying in his C-47: eighty live sheep to be slaughtered into mutton, accompanied by sixteen Indian sheep herders each with some 200 pounds of personal baggage, plus miscellaneous equipment. The loadmasters assured Mowatt the C-47 wouldn't be carrying more than 4000 pounds. The pilot figured it was more like 11,000 pounds and the takeoff proved him right. The plane devoured 1000 feet of runway before he could even lift the tail wheel off the ground, let alone the main gear, and he finally got the struggling, overloaded C-47 airborne only a few feet from the end of the strip.

Some of the items listed on aircraft manifests would raise enough eyebrows to rustle a flag. Medical supplies, of course, filled many a C-47 cabin. But there also was one load of 100,000 dentures; beetles to devour a different species of beetles that were destroying war-valuable hemp crops in Honduras; Panama hats; a shipment of mining machinery; a few thousand sunglasses; a couple of top-priority passengers who turned out to be sheep herders being flown to an air base in Scotland, where sheep wandering onto runways were interfering with takeoffs and landings. A cow was once flown to an isolated air base on the coast of the Indian Ocean so the lonely GIs could have fresh milk.

The C-47 itself wore many strange trappings. A number of them served as flying post offices, their cabins equipped like railway mail cars. Several were converted into crop dusters, spraying insecticide on bug-infested Pacific jungles—to the grateful troops, the planes weren't Gooney Birds but "The Bug Killers." A pair of C-47s were used to drop napalm on deeply entranched Japanese troops—

forerunners of the ancient C-47 gunships that fought in the Vietnam war—and one Gooney Bird went on an impromptu raid against a Japanese airfield. The "bombs" the plane carried were as improvised as the homemade "jungle juice" the crew consumed before dreaming up the mission—they dropped gasoline-filled drums and then shot up the field with tommy guns, carbines, and hand grenades.

The war's most unique C-47 was the XCG-17 Glider, and that is not a misprint. The XCG-17 was an experimental glider, an engineless C-47 that could carry more than seven tons of payload. The C-47's aerodynamics were so good that the glider version had a powerless glide ratio of only fourteen to one, which meant it dropped only one foot for every fourteen feet it flew forward. This was even better than conventional gliders, whose best ratio was twelve to one. Only a single XCG-17 was built, but it led to the successful development of bigger military gliders, like the XCG-10A, which was so huge that fully loaded it required two Gooney Birds to get it off the ground before it could be towed by one.

There also were C-47s that became flying "wreckers," an idea dreamed up by Colonel Monty Wilson of the Air Corps. They carried complete repair facilities for fixing damaged combat aircraft. Called "Flying Depots," they hauled instrument test stands, drill presses, air compressors, lathes, welding equipment, and generators for powering machine tools. If one could land anywhere near a grounded fighter or bomber, its crew could get it combat-ready in less than three days instead of the more than two weeks it normally took.

A Douglas service engineer named Harry Booth devised a special rig that enabled a C-47 to fit an entire airplane wing under the transport's belly and fly it into advanced air bases. The attachment gear was so strong that C-47s were lugging even huge B-24 and B-17 wings for crippled bombers. The Army equipped one C-47 as a propaganda airplane, with a printing press that turned out leaflets and newspapers the crew dropped on towns ahead of advancing Allied troops. And then there was the Gooney Bird christened "The Dirty Underwear Special"—this one had washing machines, dryers, and irons and paid regularly scheduled visits to remote air bases.

An even more welcome sight were the C-47 "chuck wagons," airplanes converted into flying canteens and equipped with complete field kitchens. There didn't seems to be any task, however unusual or weird, a C-47 couldn't handle—and do it while some 10,000 of them compiled a brilliant reliability and safety record. Case in point: the saga of "Old Miscellaneous," which happened to be the tenth C-47 hatched out of the Santa Monica plant.

The airplane was delivered to ATC in February 1942, and sent by freighter to Australia, where it began the first of more than 2000 Southwest Pacific missions, in the course of which the airplane wore out a dozen engines and required replacements for her wing tips, elevators, and rudders. "Old Miscellaneous" eventually was returned to the U.S. for a bond tour and then supposedly was heading for honorable retirement at Wright-Patterson when she was recruited for test flights with the XCG-17 Glider.

Throughout every war theater, the exploits of the C-47 gradually merged with the solid reputation of the DC-3 until the two airplanes became a single, indestructible legend. But no mere aerial machine, however beloved and incredibly efficient, can achieve legendary status without the help of the men who fly, navigate, and maintain it. And very few histories of World War II even mention the fact that the nation's airlines did far more than provide ATC and NATS with hundreds of pilots, planes, and mechanics in the first years of the war. By the time the war ended, the majority of military transport flight crews and ground personnel had been trained in airline-operated and airline-supervised schools that transformed thousands of raw neophytes into the world's best transport pilots, flight engineers, navigators, radio operators, air traffic controllers, mechanics, loadmasters, and meteorologists—all taught by "professors" from the airline industry.

In the sweltering heat of July 1942, less than two months after the airline industry saw half its airplanes drafted, the presidents of ATA's nineteen member carriers were summoned to Washington's Carlton Hotel for an off-the-record meeting with General Harold George.

It was quite an august audience the ATC chief was addressing, a veritable roll call of the world of civil aviation. ATA's Edgar Gorrell, of course, quiet but ever-observant and sitting next to pudgy, paternalistic Pat Patterson of United; Eastern's hawk-nosed Eddie Rickenbacker; Continental's towering Bob Six, whose granite, lantern-jawed countenance, someone once remarked, should have been the fifth head on Mount Rushmore. His commanding presence belied the fact that he headed one of ATA's smallest members; Six's own entry into military service was only a month away. Balding Croil Hunter of Northwest was there, and Delta's beloved C.E. Woolman, who ran his airline like a benign southern patriarch.

Heavy-jowled Tom Braniff represented the carrier that his brother Paul had founded. Behind a fat, dirigible-sized cigar and wearing a thin, almost cynical smile was the heavy visage of National's George Baker, the most notorious wheeler-dealer in the big conference room. C.R. Smith already had joined ATC, and with some curiousity Hal George noted the presence of Smith's hand-picked successor at American: Alexander Kemp, who had spent most of his adult life in the insurance business. He was a grandfatherly, pleasant-tempered gentleman who since 1941 had been a fairly junior member of American's board of directors. Hardly anyone present knew him, and why C.R. picked Kemp to run the airline during the war remains a mystery to this day.

Also present was Northeast's popular Sam Solomon, who had no idea of what was about to befall him. Northeast was a midget compared to the giants like United, Eastern, and American, and Solomon figured he was there to play follow-the-leader in whatever George said the industry could contribute to the war effort.

The contribution turned out to be more than anyone in the room expected. George began by praising the industry's past and present cooperation with the military, acknowledging that ATC operations would be hopelessly inadequate without the infusion of airline aircraft and personnel. But, he pointed out, the equipment situation was beginning to change—thousands of new C-47s, C-46s, and C-87s were beginning to pour off assembly lines, and soon ATC would be taking delivery of new C-54s.

Every day, he added, ATC's routes also were expanding throughout the world: over the North Atlantic to Scotland and England; across the mid-Atlantic via the Azores; from Brazil to North Africa over the South Atlantic; across Africa to India, Burma, and China; the ATC/NATS island-hopping airways spanning the vast Pacific to Australia. And accompanying all this expansion in both equipment and global commitment was a dwindling supply of trained manpower with which to operate the system.

George said Army and Navy schools could teach the basics in flight and ground skills, but these schools gave priority to combat assignments and not the advanced, highly specialized training a global air transportation system required. The talent coming out of the Civilian Pilot Training Program was drying up fast, and the airlines—whose pilots already were manning at least half of ATC's missions—could not be expected to contribute much more in the way of personnel. A facility like Eagle's Nest, for example, was too small and too specialized for the kind of mass training program that would encompass all key ground personnel as well as flight. The same was true of the other transportation schools a number of carriers had opened, and the many private aviation schools that offered courses for pilots and mechanics. No two schools taught the same way nor offered the same curriculum—they were all going off in too many different directions.

What the military critically needed, George concluded, was a special administrative body for the nation's widely scattered, unco-ordinated aviation schools, one that would be established under a nonprofit government contract—a literal ATC university offering extensive, standardized courses that embraced every ground and flight phase of military air transportation.

Not a real school with its own "campus," he emphasized, but rather a headquarters facility that would create the necessary courses and appropriate textbooks and distribute them to scores of training branches: airline-operated schools, including the ones already in existence, and qualified private aviation schools. The main headquarters would be administered by a joint central organization composed of airline officials and an ATC liaison group. This central organization, he added, should be headed by a top airline executive, and the choice was up to the men in that room.

After a moment's silence, while the nineteen airline chiefs digested George's remarks, Eastern's Eddie Rickenbacker rose.

"I can assure General George of the airlines' solid support," he announced. "As for the proposed central organization, it can only be as good as the man selected to head it. In my view, there's only one man outstandingly qualified for the job, and that's Sam Solomon of Northeast. His airline already has led the way in establishing airline training schools—the one Northeast started at Burlington [Vermont] is a fine example of the high professional standards ATC needs. So I nominate Sam."

Solomon's jaw dropped like the hinged bow of a beached landing craft unloading marines. He was among the several airline presidents with whom Rickenbacker had feuded bitterly on more than one occasion (Juan Trippe and George Baker topped the list)— and Captain Eddie was known to hold a grudge longer than a camel retains water. Someone seconded the nomination and it was approved unanimously by voice vote.

Sam stood up, visibly affected. "I'm flattered by your confidence," he said quietly, "and I'd like very much to accept this assignment. But I can't give you a yes or no at this moment. Let me sleep on it and I'll advise you tomorrow."

He talked it over with his wife Alma that same day and also contacted Northeast's directors for permission to take the job. Then he sought the counsel of a fellow airline executive whose opinion he not only respected but who already was in ATC itself: C.R. Smith. Late in the afternoon, Solomon went to C.R.'s office at ATC headquarters, then located on a Potomac River shoreline known as Gravelly Point, and adjacent to the new state-of-the-art Washington National Airport. Their meeting was well-described in Jim Haggarty's fine 1974 biography of Solomon, *Aviation's Uncle Sam.*

"I don't want this job unless I can be assured of solid backing from both the airlines and the ATC staff," he told Smith, who bluntly allowed that Solomon might expect to get more cooperation from the military than from some of his fellow airline executives.

"Sam, I want to remind you of one thing," Smith said. "Airline presidents individually are nice guys, but collectively they're a bunch of terrible people."

Solomon smiled. "You ought to know, C.R."

Smith returned the smile. "So should you—you're one of them."

But C.R. did assure him that he could count on ATC for full support—a promise that was kept to the letter—and Solomon went back to the Carlton the next morning and accepted the assignment, on the condition that every man in the room would pledge the same support C.R. had promised. He got such assurances and they were honored, with a few relatively minor exceptions and one major incident that resulted in the offending airline being booted out of the program.

The sinner was National, caught using trainees from its transport school on some of the airline's scheduled passenger flights. In vain did George Baker defend the practice on the grounds that this amounted to practical, on-the-job experience, and the ouster stuck—the only black mark on National's wartime service, flying domestic military cargo. Baker was considered something of an industry black sheep, but this may well have been a bum rap; many of the derogatory stories told about him, including one canard that he got his start in aviation by flying illegal liquor into the U.S. from Canada during Prohibition, were spread by the large roster of enemies he had made in the industry, including Eddie Rickenbacker, who absolutely despised him.

(Rickenbacker once angrily called him "a buccaneer," intending it as an insulting commentary on his business ethics, but instead of taking offense, Baker thought the word fit his little airline and its system perfectly. He adopted "Route of the Buccaneers" as National's slogan and a one-eyed pirate as its official logo. Baker actually had much in common with Bob Six, with his maverick reputation and fierce competitiveness; one of the better stories told about his career, perhaps apocryphal, is that he once recruited the entire chorus line of a musical comedy stranded in Pittsburgh and hired them as stewardesses.)

The confrontation with National was a minor item on Sam Solomon's worry list. His first task was to enlist the best assistant he could find, and he knew where to look. He wanted Jerome Lederer, chief of the Civil Aeronautics Board's Safety Bureau and the nation's top air accident investigator, to be his deputy. Diminutive in stature, but a giant in reputation, Jerry Lederer was "Mr. Air Safety" to everyone in civil aviation—he pioneered the basic procedures and techniques of crash investigation that are still in use today. Lederer enjoyed the respect of pilots and industry officials alike, and after the war he was to become the first president of the Flight Safety Foundation, an organization supported by all segments of industry, from the airlines and their pilot unions to the airframe and engine manufacturers. (In his nineties at this writing, he still serves as FSF's president emeritus.)

Solomon met with Lederer to outline the program's general goals. Jerry didn't wait for an official job offer—"I'll go back to the CAB and resign immediately," he declared.

"Wait a minute," Sam protested. "It's only tentative. We have no contract, no appropriation, no money to pay you or anyone else. Wait until the War Department and the airlines work out something definite. I'll get back to you."

Only a half hour after Lederer left, Solomon got an angry call from L. Welch Pogue, the CAB chairman.

"That was some dirty trick you pulled," he raged. "Jerry Lederer just came in and resigned. He said he was going to work for you."

"I just sounded him out," Sam explained. "I made no commitment."

Pogue sighed. "Well, that's Jerry. When he gets enthused about a new project, he has to start moving on it right away."

Which, Solomon thought happily, is exactly what was needed.

The Airlines War Training Institute (AWTI) was born August 11, 1942, only about a month after the Carlton Hotel meeting. Officially it was an unincorporated association composed of nineteen U.S. airlines, with Solomon as president and director of training, and Lederer as vice president. The school's main headquarters were established in Washington, for convenient liaison with ATC, but another office was opened in New York sharing space with ATC's Domestic Transportation Division, which was to oversee AWTI's operations.

This ATC Division was housed in a block-long building that fronted on both Pine and Wall Streets. The official postal address was 40 Wall Street, but ATC was forced to use 33 Pine Street because some nervous War Department public relations officer had a public image problem: he thought any Wall Street address implied that ATC was being run by a bunch of civilian stockbrokers.

After the New York facility opened, the War Department learned that Solomon had put "40 Wall Street" on all its letterheads. It was politely but firmly suggested that the New York address must be the same as the one ATC was using. It was with equal politenesss and firmness that Sam refused.

"I've been waiting all my life for an office on Wall Street," he argued, "and you're not gonna make me use the back door."

This burst of military static was mild compared to the blast of civilian lightning that hit Solomon almost as soon as he opened the Washington office. One day, in walked Orval "Red" Mosier, senior vice president of American Airlines, a bon vivant who was proud of the fact that he knew every maître d' in every top restaurant in New York City (and a few other cities as well) by his first name.

Mosier announced that American was going to tell Solomon and Lederer how to run AWTI, pointing out that his airline was one of the first to start a training school for transport pilots. Sam politely reminded him that while this was true, Northeast's own school was the first. Anyway, Solomon said firmly, no single airline was going to run AWTI. Mosier then threatened to pull American out of the Institute and Solomon, who suspected Red was acting strictly on his own, called his bluff.

"Okay," he agreed affably, "I'll call General George and inform him that American is withdrawing from the program." He reached for the phone and Mosier did a fast one-eighty.

"Wait a minute," he said hastily. "Let's talk this over."

American stayed in, of course, and Sam graciously refrained from telling C.R. about the incident—and also wisely for Mosier's sake, because Smith probably would have gone ballistic. One of Mosier's best friends at American heard the story later and remarked, "If C.R. knew what Mosier tried to pull, he would have kicked Red's ass across the Potomac farther than George Washington threw that damn silver dollar."

The AWTI staff in Washington numbered about forty-five people, whose work involved two primary responsibilities:

1. Serving as a liaison unit between ATC and the airlines, so the Command didn't have to deal with some 100 individual aviation schools. The liaison covered numerous areas, such as keeping track of ATC equipment changes which might affect the number of trainees needed for specific airplanes, or new equipment that required changes in training manuals. By working so closely with ATC, the Institute was able to advise the various schools as to current needs in housing, equipment, faculty staffing, and classroom space.

2. Assuring training uniformity and improved quality in textbooks and manuals. Before AWTI was created, the nation's hodgepodge of aviation schools, including those that were airline-operated, suffered from lack of consistency in training methods; Hal George wanted every school to teach the same courses using identical procedures and techniques, and it was Solomon himself who insisted on simpler, better-written textbooks, devoid of military or technical gobbledygook that youngsters fresh out of the nontechnical civilian world found hard to understand.

Both Solomon and Lederer spent much of their time inspecting the airline schools that were part of the AWTI program, making sure they were complying with all established standards and procedures. Sam's personal interest in supplying improved textbooks and manuals resulted in the Institute hiring Howard Morgan, TWA's chief of engineering, to oversee the preparation of new publications, not only easy and even fun to read, but illustrated with appropriate cartoons as learning aids. Morgan hired a few part-time writers from the airlines and aviation magazines and turned them loose.

"Howard was an absolute genius," Jerry Lederer recalled. "He was not only a brilliant engineer but a fine editor, and he gave us the first fifteen new textbooks in sixteen weeks."

Under Morgan's direction, AWTI produced a total of twenty-eight manuals in less than a year, and kept them updated. Thousands were distributed to the schools free and even veteran airline pilots, traditionally cynical about the literary ability of manual and textbook authors, praised their quality and practicality.

"If a man could read and digest all the material in these textbooks, he'd really know his stuff," one wrote. "I can't recall a more sane and efficient treatment of the problems that present themselves to a pilot."

ATC came up with a request for a survival manual, a guide for crews forced down in the ocean, arctic, jungle, or desert. Lederer started looking for an expert who also could write about the subject in plain English, and mentioned the problem one day to Roy Alexander, then *Time* magazine's top military writer, whom he knew casually.

"I've got just the person for you," Alexander said. "Our medical editor, Felice Swados."

Felice's subsequent manual, titled *Survival*, provided all the necessary information and advice on staying alive after a crash or forced landing, in exactly 116 tautly written, interesting pages whose preface set the tone of what was to follow: *"A Word to the Unwise* seems a more suitable title for this book . . ."

And the opening paragraph added another note of warning:

"The aim of this book is to get you out of a jam almost anywhere. But we can't help you if you don't help yourself."

The main thrust of the manual's message was simple: don't panic. To those forced down in the arctic, the manual advised: "Let your mind thaw out. Don't fight nature. Play around with her." Such as, Swados suggested, using a flashlight or a candle to lure rabbits close enough to club. On surviving the perils of the jungle, the manual pointed out that those perils were "largely a product of Hollywood imagination."

"Jungle beasts usually clear out of man's way before they see him coming," the handbook explained. "The real dangers of the jungle are not the animals or the natives but the tiny flies, ticks, parasites, and mosquitos which carry the germs of lingering diseases.''

A plethora of practical tips included this example: jungle-stranded airmen were cautioned not to eat a certain yellow or white Asiatic fruit that resembled an orange, because it contained heavy amounts of strychnine. And for those flying in desert regions, the handbook urged crews to always carry a plentiful supply of water and, in case of a crash, follow this inviolate rule: "Stick by your plane; do not budge, no matter how strong your impulse to get going. You may be ten minutes flying time from your base but on the ground this may mean a week's walk."

Lederer wrote one manual himself—it was more of a pamphlet—after learning that too many ATC crews flying into Africa made poor goodwill ambassadors because they openly poked fun at certain native customs. The title of his manual was as simple and as much to the point as the advice within the text: *Attitude.*

In AWTI's early days, there always seemed to be unexpected problems to solve. Solomon and Lederer were advised on one occasion that many Spanish-speaking trainees from New Mexico and Arizona needed special tutoring in English. One of Jerry's biggest headaches was selecting an experienced airline pilot to develop and direct a standardized transport pilot training program for all the schools. He finally went north for the right man; he contacted D.B. Collyer, founder of Air Canada, who had been Lederer's boss when both served in the U.S. Air Mail Service, and Collyer recommended retired Air Canada Captain William Straith, whom Lederer described later as "the ideal choice."

Perhaps the program's outstanding accomplishment was the drastic reduction in the length of training time without losing one iota of competency. Thanks to the Institute's standardized, smoothly streamlined instructional procedures, a course that once required a year or two to complete in peacetime could now be mastered in only sixty to ninety days. This compression of training time actually put AWTI out of business sooner than anyone expected. General George ordered it officially disbanded October 31, 1943, after the schools it governed, monitored, and advised had—in only fourteen months—produced more than 12,000 flight crew members and in excess of 35,000 ground personnel for both ATC and NATS.

After Solomon closed down both offices, he had the AWTI books audited and found a modest cash surplus which he donated to the Army Air Forces Aid Society. He also assigned publishing rights for the training manuals to the *Infantry Journal.*

Sam returned to Northeast, but in 1945, just as the war was ending, his ambitious postwar expansion plans for the airline ran into internal opposition and his own board of directors forced him to resign. He eventually tried to launch a low-cost carrier much like today's Southwest, but the CAB refused to approve the proposed fare structure. Solomon was seventy-eight years old when he died of a heart attack in 1977, five years after the airline he helped found was merged into Delta.

Few other than Northeast veterans remember this benign leader who could get more done with a smile than most executives achieve with barked orders. Nor is his a familiar name in the countless histories of World War II. Yet he left a giant legacy: the superbly trained men who operated the airlift army.

It was a somewhat unglamorous army, of course, one that earned few wartime headlines or medals and admittedly wasn't exposed to the kind of combat hazards that required so many pilot and aircraft replacements among fighter and bomber groups. This was a major factor in ATC's decision to terminate the Institute; with demand lessened, the schools were now capable of maintaining whatever supply of transport manpower was needed for the rest of the war.

But long before the Institute was preparing its graduates to man thousands of cockpits and nurse the innards of thousands of airplanes, it was the pilots and ground crews of America's airlines who wrote the first chapters of the victory to come.

And it is time to tell their story.

★ ★ 4 ★ ★
War Wings—Part I

They all went to war—the big, the medium, the small, one airline that wasn't really an airline, and another so tiny it flew nothing but mail in single-engine airplanes. Consolidated-Vultee Aircraft, builder of the B-24 bombers and C-87 transports, began flying priority military cargo and aircraft ferry personnel across the Pacific between San Diego and Australia in April of 1942, an operation unofficially known as the Consairway. So the "airline" was called Consairways, and this unusual choice of an airplane manufacturer to run an airlift had logic and precedent behind it. For several years, Consolidated's ferry pilots had acquired a lot of experience delivering airplanes to various points in the Pacific, starting with twin-engine bombers flown to Australia under a contract with the Netherlands government.

To bring the ferry crews back from Australia, Consolidated began using an earlier version of the C-87, the LB-30 which was just a converted B-24 with seats for passengers. Quite a few Consairways pilots liked this ad hoc version better than the later, more thoroughly modified C-87. And one thing the LB-30 proved right from the start was the superiority of a four-engine land plane over the big seaplanes. It was much faster, and taking off from a runway avoided the drag of a water takeoff, thus giving the land plane better range and assuring a heavier payload.

Consairways was a relatively small but important operation that contributed its own share of wartime stories. It was one of the first ATC carriers to fly USO entertainers into overseas bases, including one trip that could have ended in disaster. The big star aboard the C-87 was Gary Cooper, whose modesty and natural friendliness so impressed the crew that he was invited to sit in the copilot's seat during one leg of the Pacific flight. Also in the troupe were actresses Phyllis Brooks and Una Merkel, and when they landed at a remote island base to refuel, the girls got off to stretch their legs.

The Air Corps GI who was wielding the fuel hose hadn't seen a woman for months, let alone two attractive actresses, so he might be forgiven for what followed.

He stared. And stared. And stared. Until the wing tank he was filling overflowed and hundreds of gallons of flammable high-octane gas began spilling over the wing and onto the ground. Fortunately no one was smoking at the time.

A Consairways crew that had landed at a Pacific base was invited to witness a ceremony in which an Army captain who had single-handledly wiped out two Japanese machine gun nests received a battlefield promotion to major. He also received the even more welcome news that he was to fly back to the U.S. with Consairways and receive the Congressional Medal of Honor at the White House.

After the ceremony, the newly promoted hero boarded the C-87 along with other homeward-bound troops. The plane had just reached 9000 feet when the number one engine exploded, spewing hot oil over one side of the aircraft. The crew routinely feathered the stricken engine and was about to return to the island when they heard a commotion in the cabin. The flight engineer went back to check and discovered several soldiers restraining a panic-stricken fellow passenger who had gone berserk.

It was the brand-new major and Medal of Honor winner.

Consairways also became one of the several ATC airlines whose crews earned commendations for rescue work. A Consairways C-87 commanded by Captain Dick Probert had just left Tutuila Island in American Samoa en route from Australia to Hawaii when Probert's radio operator picked up a faint "Mayday" call from a C-47 in the process of ditching.

Probert went looking for the downed plane and finally spotted it just before it sank in a heavy sea, leaving its four survivors in a bobbing raft, frantically waving at the C-87 overhead. Probert radioed the Navy to send a PBY Catalina flying boat and kept circling the raft to keep it in sight.

The PBY arrived, landed, and picked up the four men but then ran into trouble of its own. A huge wave hit one propeller as the Catalina tried to take off; the prop flew off, smashed into the cockpit, killed the pilot and seriously injured the copilot. By now, Probert's plane was running low on fuel but he didn't dare leave. The Navy advised it was dispatching another PBY, but Probert warned it would only mean losing another Catalina—the waves were just too high.

"For God's sake, send a surface ship," he pleaded.

He agreed to keep circling until another aircraft could relieve him while a rescue vessel was rushed to the scene. Eventually an Army B-25 arrived and Probert flew back to Tutuila where he refueled. This exposure to fuel exhaustion while "standing guard" over life rafts from ditched aircraft was to be repeated by ATC and NATS crews many times during the war. The Army told Probert that if he and his crew weren't civilians they'd be getting Air Medals, which wasn't true, because quite a few ATC crews received Air Medals during the war. But Probert was promised they'd be receiving commendations. They never did, the necessary paperwork apparently getting lost in a bureaucratic shuffle.

Consolidated operated the Pacific service for several months without a contract, then continued the airlift for most of the war with nothing but a War Department letter of intent. For that matter, the airline industry did not, as some columnists charged after the war, reap huge profits from its participation in ATC and NATS. Some War Department or Navy contracts were on a cost-plus-fixed-fee basis, but in many cases the airlines received only their direct operating costs.

Contracts to fly military cargo and personnel had an additional benefit besides keeping some airlines in business: for cargo operations, the Army returned some of the airplanes it had commandeered, although they weren't the same ones originally appropriated, and more than a few were somewhat battered C-47s that had never seen airline service.

While the airlines generally were assigned specific operating areas, there were occasions—especially in the early months of the war—when an emergency situation called for a combined effort by a number of carriers. Such a crisis arose in June 1942, when the Japanese invaded the Aleutians, captured the small Alaskan islands of Attu and Kiska, and were threatening to seize the thinly held U.S. base at Dutch Harbor.

The interception of fifteen American Airlines flights right after Pearl Harbor was now repeated tenfold. The Army ordered flight superintendents and dispatchers at eleven carriers to divert every available airplane to Edmonton, Canada, a major railhead and the location of a huge U.S. Army supply depot. Aircraft in the process of completing normal passenger flights were told to land at the nearest airport, disembark all passengers, and head for the Canadian city. Planes leaving directly for Edmonton from stations with maintenance facilities were to carry mechanics.

The airlines involved in the emergency airlift were Pan Am, Eastern, Northwest, Western, TWA, American, United, Panagra, Pennsylvania Central, Chicago & Southern, and Braniff. So unexpected and hasty were the orders, transmitted on a Saturday shortly before 6 P.M. Pacific standard time, that some crews took off for Edmonton with just the uniforms they were wearing and nothing but pocket money. There was a flurry of quick improvising, American being one case in point.

At the airline's Burbank station, regional flight superintendent Ted Lewis got the mobilization call from his main operations office in New York and started phoning every AA base between Burbank and Fort Worth, mustering all the planes, pilots, and mechanics he could find. Then he suddenly realized nobody knew how long the mission would last, so he raced to American's Burbank ticket office and emptied the till which, unfortunately, contained only $300. He remembered that Sears's Burbank store stayed open Saturday nights, so he telephoned the manager, explaining his dilemma.

"Come right over," the manager invited.

From Sears, Lewis borrowed $6500 in cash and by Sunday morning he had sent nine DC-3s with eighteen pilots and half a dozen mechanics winging northward. These nine aircraft, plus two more American dispatched from New York, joined the "Minute Man Fleet" mobilized by the other ten airlines—nearly 100 airplanes that stopped in Edmonton just long enough to have the cabins filled with troops, ammunition, medical supplies, food, weapons, and other vital equipment. For the next month, each plane flew a daily round-trip between Edmonton and Dutch Harbor before the base was judged sufficiently reinforced.

The crew fraternalism that had marked the 1938 New England hurricane airlift was equally evident during this and subsequent Alaskan operations. At least ninety percent of the pilots, who had never flown to or in Alaska before, were suddenly introduced to an unfamiliar flight environment over thousands of miles of uncharted wilderness, and mountains more than 20,000 feet high. They weren't too proud to seek advice from some veterans of cold weather flying: Northwest crews who had cut their airmen's teeth on winter storms and the rugged terrain of the northwestern states. They also had been the first to fly contracted military cargo to Alaska and willingly taught their brethren how to stay out of trouble in a land where the scenery may be magnificent, but not when you have to make a forced landing in the middle of it. ATC pilots didn't get combat pay, but sometimes they deserved it, for nature could be as vicious and deadly an opponent as an armed enemy fighter.

The Northwest crews, in turn, had their own role models to follow: the veteran bush pilots of Alaska who had pioneered air transportation in this northernmost territory, a land where the airplane more often than not was the only means of getting from one place to another, and the aircraft themselves were usually of such ancient vintage that most prewar Alaskan airfields looked like scenes out of the first World War. Flying in the Aleutians was especially hazardous, for the island chain was home to a weather phenomenom known to native Alaskans as "willa-wahs"—violent horizontal and vertical wind gusts in excess of 100 mph and concentrated over a small area; they are akin to miniature hurricanes and are frighteningly similar to the wind shear menace that has destroyed more than one airliner.

A handful of the bush pilots started their own airlines, and no one typified the stubborn, laugh-at-adversity attitude of these rugged entrepreneurs more than Bob Reeve, who founded what is today Reeve Aleutian Airways. He was a charter member of the breed R.E.G. Davies portrayed so well in his history of U.S. airlines:

"They operated on a financial shoestring. The owner flew the aircraft, his wife kept the books. He sold tickets through friends and by the application of low cunning beat his rivals. His business ethics were born of the Klondike saloon and were hardly genteel. He would cheerfully risk his life and his assets (i.e., his aircraft) in a foolhardy gamble perhaps to make a quick dollar, perhaps to rescue a competitor in trouble . . . The men who contributed to the saga of Alaskan airline development belong to a distinguished company . . ."

Bob Reeve was both typical and unique in this "distinguished company"; calling him colorful would be like describing the Mona Lisa as a bland watercolor painted by a child. He had twenty-one forced landings in his years of Alaskan flying, yet only once did he damage an airplane beyond repair. The little airline he founded at Valdez, Alaska, as Reeve Airways greeted potential customers with a large sign painted on the side of the dilapidated shed that passed as a hangar:

ALWAYS USE REEVE AIRWAYS. SLOW UNRELIABLE UNFAIR AND CROOKED. SCARED UNLICENSED AND NUTS. REEVE AIRWAYS— THE BEST.

The only airline president ever to match his unconventional, irreverent, almost outlandish sense of humor came along some four decades later: Southwest's Herb Kelleher. Reeve drove to work in a Model T Ford on whose side he had painted AIRLINE OFFICIALS. During the war, he became a legend to virtually every ATC and airline crew that took part in the Alaskan airlift. He took part in it himself, using a 14-year-old, single-engine Fairchild monoplane and a Boeing 80-A trimotor biplane that dated back to 1928—the Model 80, in fact, was the first large transport plane Boeing ever built.

In those two ancient relics, either of which would have been at home in a museum, he flew in 1100 tons of cargo to help speed construction of a strategic airport at Northway, Alaska. He carried some 1000 troops between Alaskan bases and thousands of pounds of priority freight; he was the only bush pilot with an ATC contract, although the Army never could get him to follow military approach procedures at its Alaskan air bases.

The venerable Boeing, painted yellow, was known throughout Alaska as "The Yellow Peril." Reeve, however, bestowed his carefully rationed affection on the little Fairchild. He landed at an Army base during the war and was repairing a damaged tail wheel when a young Air Corps major stopped by to stare at the plane.

"What kind of airplane is it, old man?" he inquired.

"Fairchild," Reeve grunted.

"Fairchild, eh? What model?"

"Fairchild DGA," Reeve growled. "The DGA stands for Damn Good Airplane and if you call me 'old man' again, I'll take you over my knee."

The Aleutians were familiar territory to Reeve, which began an irregular service to the islands after the war and became a certificated carrier in 1948 with an authorized route from Anchorage to Attu. It also served the Pribilof Islands, making Reeve the only airline to operate a route that was based on the mating habits of seals. And fifty years after Bob Reeve delivered the first load of military freight to the Northway site, the little one-man company that became Reeve Aleutian Airways was one of the two Alaskan-born carriers participating in the modern Civil Reserve Air Fleet of the 1990s; Alaska Airlines was the other.

What Bob Reeve had started had come full circle.

The Alaskan airlift itself underlined the truth of an old airline adage, even more applicable to life in the ATC: "Flying is hours of boredom punctuated by moments of sheer terror."

Such was the experience of United Captain Bob Dawson two days after planes from a Japanese aircraft carrier bombed Dutch Harbor. The base was desperately short of ammunition and Dawson, with copilot M.W. Ashby, volunteered to fly fresh ammo from Edmonton to Cold Bay in the Aleutians, where it would be transferred to the base. Dawson accepted the assignment even after he was warned that the enemy carrier was reported to be still lurking in the area.

He took off from Edmonton at 9 P.M. and flew in the dark down the Aleutian chain, not daring to use any aircraft lights except those on his dimly lit instrument panel. Uncertain of their position at one point, he came down through the overcast to get his bearings. When he broke out, there was the Japanese carrier right under his wings. Luckily its lookouts must have been dozing, for they never saw him.

Dawson landed at Cold Bay in pitch darkness, only to learn that the night's work wasn't over yet. He immediately took off for Cordova and Ketchikan with another load of priority cargo. When they finally reached Ketchikan, they had logged forty-three consecutive hours of flight duty. It was an endurance ordeal that in peacetime airline flying would have sent both Dawson and Ashby straight to their union, the Air Line Pilots Association (ALPA), with a major grievance. But good ALPA members though the ATC airline pilots might be, there were few if any grievances filed in wartime; the airline crews willingly took as much of a physical beating as their airplanes.

The standard maximum of 100 flying hours per month written into most peacetime ALPA/airline contracts was blithely ignored by the ATC airmen. With both ATC and NATS, they were averaging 200 hours a month; 250 hours was not unusual, and one captain, who had just finished logging 275 hours in five weeks, volunteered to take the next flight out because the base was short of crews. Another ex-airline captain completed seven transocean trips in eleven days.

Airline pilots flying for ATC were issued military-style uniforms. On the left chest were wings carrying the initials ATC. No rank insignia was displayed except for sleeve stripes: ATC captains had three, copilots two, and flight engineers, navigators, and radio operators one. Unless you got close enough to an ATC flight crew member to read the insignia on his cap, it was easy to mistake him for a regular Air Corps officer (or Air Force—the Army Air Corps became the U.S. Army Air Forces during the war) and a lot of airline pilots drew illegal or at least unnecessary salutes that way. The same thing happened to NATS airline crews, who wore Navy-style officers' uniforms with NATS insignia.

It must be admitted, however, that it was rare to see an ATC crew member wearing his uniform anywhere except to a restaurant or officers' club. In the invariably cold cockpits, particularly on North Atlantic trips, the typical uniform of the day consisted of decrepit slacks and warm but shabby sweaters that would have been rejected by any self-respecting rummage sale. TWA had one ATC navigator who for reasons known only to himself refused to wear socks; the sight of him working at his navigation table in bare feet would have had Magellan revolving in his grave like a propeller. He finally was ordered to start wearing socks or face dismissal. The navigator solved this crisis by painting both feet black, a ruse he got away with for several more trips.

Another ATC sartorial rebel was Captain Jack Orwig, a former United pilot who joined Western during the war. Orwig, a tall, bulky man with an air of authority that would have done justice to a four-star general, evidently got tired of drawing salutes from green GIs who mistook the ATC uniform for the real McCoy. After one salute too many, he began reporting for duty in a double-peaked English hunting cap and smoking a curved Meerschaum pipe.

"He looks like an overweight Sherlock Holmes," one of his fellow pilots commented.

Western's wartime Alaskan assignment was rather unique in that ATC contract flying outside the continental United States usually was performed by much larger airlines. The smaller carriers' major contributions to the war effort more often involved aircraft modification centers—maintenance facilities that were transformed into miniature aircraft factories. Some were established even before the U.S. entered the war, preparing lend-lease aircraft for delivery to England and Russia.

The great advantage of modification centers was that assembly lines turning out military aircraft didn't have to be slowed or even shut down to incorporate changes dictated by actual combat experience, or to install improved or specialized equipment and systems. Airplanes completed at the regular factories and targeted for necessary modifications were flown to an appropriate center where the necessary work was performed and the aircraft released for military service. Some modifications depended on an airplane's intended operating environment or specific assignment—whether it would be assigned to a war theater in the desert or tropics, for instance, or needed to be configured for high-altitude photographic reconnaissance missions. The centers hung bomb racks on fighters, changed .30 caliber guns to more powerful .50 calibers, and gave bombers more defensive firepower by installing new "stinger" turrets in previously unarmed bellies, noses, and tails.

Most of the airlines opened modification centers, but for smaller carriers landing a modification contract or running an AWTI-administered school helped avoid bankruptcy. Typical was tiny Colonial, which percentagewise had suffered one of the heaviest fleet emasculation of any carrier by losing six of its eight airplanes. It also saw the majority of its skilled manpower enlist in the armed forces, but Colonial survived when it established two AWTI-approved schools: one for mechanics at the airline's La Guardia Field hangar, and a pilot's school in Albany, New York.

Bob Six's Denver-based Continental, down to only three Lode-stars for passenger service, had to serve some routes solely because of mail contract commitments—abandoning the routes would have voided the airline's mail authority. So Six bought an old single-engine Stinson Reliant and used it only to fly mail. He also bid for and won a contract for modifying bombers, mostly B-17s which were constantly undergoing changes to achieve greater defensive firepower and range.

Continental rented space in a United hangar at Denver for its initial modification jobs, but in 1943 the airline shifted all its work into two huge new $5 million hangars, each 600 feet long and 400 feet wide, erected on some ninety acres of concrete. Six also obtained a contract for flying ATC cargo transcontinentally, and sent some of CAL's pilots to the Army where they helped train Lockheed Hudson bomber pilots.

Modification centers often received orders to perform certain classified work, and Continental was no exception. While it was still using United's facilities, superintendent of maintenance Stan Shatto was ordered to fly to Wright-Patterson Field and to bring a sheet metal foreman with him. In Dayton, they were informed that fifty B-17s were being flown to Denver, and the Army would be grateful if the two Continental technicians could figure out how to install additional fuel tanks for greatly increased range, and complete the job on all fifty airplanes in not more than four days. Shatto and his foreman drew up some hasty plans and flew back to Denver.

The UAL hangar wasn't big enough to complete the work on fifty B-17s in that much of a hurry, so Shatto rented a large barn on a nearby chicken ranch for some of the necessary machine tooling. All fifty airplanes were modified in three and a half days, and not until later did Shatto learn where those bombers went after they left Denver: to the mid Pacific, where they took part in the battle of Midway.

Tennyson's "ours not to reason why" certainly applied to the modification centers, especially in the difficult early stages of the war when there wasn't time for anything except innovating, improvising, and experimenting. It was not unusual for an airline center to be assigned tasks for which no explanations nor instructions were offered. Mid-Continent mechanics, for example, were given the job of squeezing shapeless rubber gasoline tanks into the crawlways over the bomb bays of sixteen B-25 Mitchell bombers.

"Where the hell are the blueprints?" a maintenance foreman asked his supervisor.

"There aren't any," he was told. "We'll have to figure out something that'll work ourselves."

They did "figure out something," and learned later that the B-25s they had been working on were the Mitchell bombers Jimmy Doolittle had led in the first bombing of Tokyo.

That the centers could perform as well as they did, meeting demanding schedules on time for even the most difficult and challenging assignments, was a minor miracle in itself. By war's end, some 50,000 airplanes had gone through the airlines' modification facilities. Yet with thousands of skilled airline workers going into the armed services, the centers were heavily manned by men and women whose previous mechanical experience hadn't progressed much farther than hammering a few nails or changing light bulbs.

"Inexperienced" certainly described the majority of the Continental workers who installed those extra fuel tanks on the Midway B-17s; only three percent of them had ever worked in anything resembling a factory or airplane maintenance facility. Nor was Continental an exceptional case; the modification centers had to transform thousands of men and women from "unskilled" into "skilled"—yes, women, for not all Rosie the Riveters worked for the aircraft manufacturers.

Grasping the scope of airline contributions to victory may come easier if their accomplishments are viewed through individual close-ups, as we have just seen Continental's, rather than through a wide-angled lens. Let us therefore examine them on more of an individual basis, starting with a carrier who completed a special modification job that fit perfectly with its proud historical heritage.

Delta

The famed C-47 "Bug Killers" that dropped tons of insecticides on infested Pacfic islands and swamps were converted into "crop dusters" by none other than Delta, which also used single-engine "duster" biplanes for insect control at military bases throughout the south. Delta's crop dusting division, which at one time had been the company's biggest moneymaker, lasted almost into the 1970s before the company sold it for a modest $88,000.

"Dusting" rightfully being ranked close to the top of high-risk occupations, it is no wonder that Delta's operations contributed its share of colorful airmen to the war effort. This roster had to include the name of Captain Henry "Luke" Williamson, who acquired a reputation of flying so low he could have picked cotton with his landing gear. David Lewis, in the definitive story of Delta he coauthored with Wesley Newton (*Delta—The History of an Airline*), quotes one friend of Williamson who thought Luke seemed to be trying to plow fields instead of dusting them.

"Listen," he advised solemnly, "you can do a good job without flying so low. Three feet from the ground is low enough."

Williamson flew for Claire Chennault's Flying Tigers before the war, returned to Delta briefly, and after Pearl Harbor went back to China flying the Hump as a commissioned officer in ATC. Of less colorful hues but possessing equal abilities as an airman was Delta Captain Fritz Schwaemle, who also held an Army commission and flew for ATC until an eye infection grounded him; he eventually became the Command's chief of navigation.

Delta itself flew thousands of ATC cargo missions within the U.S., but in human terms the most important were the airline's many medical flights which transported not only supplies but wounded servicemen needing specialized treatment at selected hospitals. The domestic medical airlift began in May of 1942, utilizing litter-equipped aircraft modified in Delta's own shops, and flying daily schedules from Atlanta to hospitals in Dayton, Miami, and Oklahoma City. Frequent unscheduled trips were made to San Francisco, Seattle, and even to a hospital in Fort St. John, in northwestern Canada.

The airline played an indirect role in Alaskan airlift efforts, operating a feeder service from Atlanta to Wright-Patterson Field via Mobile and Memphis; in Dayton, military loads were transferred to United, which flew them to Alaska.

Delta, too, briefly operated one of the more specialized AWTI-approved schools, a facility that taught instrument flying to new graduates of Army flying schools. One of its instructors, Captain Edward Smith, invented a new kind of cockpit hood for teaching "blind" flying to C-47 crews. The device, which resembled a shuttered Venetian blind, was attached to the left side of a C-47's V-shaped windshield to block out most of the student's forward vision. To keep him from peeking out the instructor's right window, Smith simply hung a large cloth from the cockpit ceiling, so it dropped between the left and right seats.

The Delta modification center, like all the others, performed with unspectacular efficiency and its workers got the most satisfaction out of jobs everyone realized were of special importance. At the head of the list was the arrival in Atlanta of sixty P-51 North American Mustangs, generally regarded as World War II's finest fighter plane but, like all fighters, lacking enough range to accompany B-17s all the way to targets deep into Germany.

Unescorted B-17s had been taking a terrible beating on virtually every long-range bombing mission, Luftwaffe fighters jumping them as soon as the fuel-limited escorts turned to go home. Delta's center was the first to install newly designed long-range fuel tanks on the Mustangs, and these sixty modified P-51s, the first of many hundreds to be fitted with "seven-league boots," soon went into action over Germany and turned the air war around.

The Atlanta facility, in fact, won a reputation for work of such quality that it was one of the last the Army terminated as the war wound down; the Delta center closed in November of 1944, the last of what was an industry within an industry, each center—more often than not—symbolizing the American genius for ingenuity, imagination, and improvision.

Northeast

For its size, no airline contributed more to the war effort than tiny Northeast. It was aviation's equivalent of the supreme professional boxing accolade: "pound for pound, the best fighter in the world . . ."

Its operation of one of the first—and also one of the best—transport training schools already has been related. But the tiny airline, once known as Boston-Maine Airways because it was owned by the Boston and Maine Railroad, also was the smallest airline to fly the North Atlantic regularly for the Air Transport Command and, in fact, flew the first survey flight that actually established this crucial wartime route.

There was a considerable body of opinion within the Pentagon that the stormy North Atlantic was the last place in the world where anyone would want to operate an airlift, not when crews would be lucky if they got decent flying weather three months out of the year, and the refueling bases along the route were a collection of accident-inviting obstacle courses. The only thing a North Atlantic route had in its favor was distance—it was the shortest route between the U.S. and England. That was the argument American's C.R. Smith raised while he was still a civilian, and was trying to sell Hap

Arnold on the feasibility of operating a full-scale military transport airlift over the so-called Great Circle route.

Arnold didn't commit himself, but in January of 1942, Colonel Olds, in one of his last acts before leaving the Ferrying Command, phoned Sam Solomon and asked if Northeast could conduct a survey flight—basically inspecting airport facilities over the route to see whether a major North Atlantic operation was feasible.

Solomon instantly assured him Northeast could handle the job and Olds asked, "When can you leave?"

"Tomorrow," Solomon replied. Olds didn't know that "tomorrow" was Sam's standard answer to virtually every request, no matter how outlandishly difficult. In truth, the survey flight didn't leave for several days, one reason being that Northeast didn't have an airplane readily available and the Ferrying Command had to supply one: a beat-up Air Corps C-39, the hybrid DC-2 with a DC-3 tail, painted in olive drab. Its interior had been stripped for cargo except for folding aluminum seats along the cabin walls.

When the plane took off, with NEA chief Pilot Milt Anderson in command, it carried a full load of cargo, Solomon having signed the airlines' very first North Atlantic cargo contract with what was soon to become the Air Transport Command. The airplane also carried on its fuselage, in hastily drawn white-lettered script, the words NORTHEAST AIRLINES.

Anderson took the C-39 from Boston to Presque Isle, Maine, then to Gander, Newfoundland, via Moncton and Goose Bay in Labrador. The latter had a small airport occupied by the Royal Canadian Air Force, with a single runway carved out of a thick forest, and a radio beacon to guide incoming flights. Improved navigation aids and weather-reporting stations along the North Atlantic route were the most obvious needs, and many subsequent Northeast flights delivered new homing beacons to airfields lacking such equipment. The airline began using C-47s with extra fuel tanks in the cabin as the combined survey/cargo missions were gradually extended to Greenland, Iceland, and eventually to Scotland.

(Greenland actually was a Danish possession, but when the Nazis occupied Denmark the Danish government-in-exile asked the United States to act as Greenland's protector. The British occupied independent Iceland in 1940, also on invitation, as a means of preventing any German designs on the island.)

When Anderson flew the first Atlantic crossing to Scotland, Solomon not only insisted on going along but offered to perform any task Anderson assigned him.

"Okay," Milt said, "you're the steward." And Sam spent most of the flight delivering coffee and sandwiches to the rest of the crew. When Anderson tried to check the weather for the return flight, he was refused admittance to the Prestwick weather advisory station, operated by the Royal Air Force.

"This area is restricted to military personnel holding proper credentials," he was informed by a stern-faced RAF sentry.

Anderson, who was wearing some rather ancient-looking arctic flight gear, in desperation pulled out his old Boston and Maine air-rail-bus pass and barked out the pass number as if it were an official military authorization. The sentry stood aside and Anderson got his weather briefing.

But as an unpleasant experience, this encounter with the British military didn't come close to Anderson's first landing at Narsarsuak, Greenland, whose shoreline he approached in a heavy snowstorm with visibility of less than a mile. The sixty-mph surface winds did a 180-degree shift just as he was trying to locate the only fjord that led to the airport. He descended through the overcast guided only by a radio range signal leading him into a winding 8000-foot descent that was like driving down a narrow mountain road at night with no headlights.

Northeast's survey flights, and those conducted by American Airlines a few months later, proved to be lifesavers for the thousands of North Atlantic ATC pilots who had to land at some of the route's danger-studded airfields, as Anderson discovered when he made the first survey flight into Narsarsuak. Approaching Greenland from the air offers spectacular scenery—in clear weather, the ice cap is visible from 150 miles away. But Milt didn't make that first approach and landing in clear weather, nor did many subsequent wartime flights.

Every arriving aircraft would head for a radio station erected on a barren island located at the entrance to Tunugliarfik Fjord, the only fjord that led to the airport. The fjord itself was narrow, lined with perpendicular cliffs, and filled with a number of blind alleys that looked innocent but in reality invited disaster. If a pilot took any one of these false passageways, he'd suddenly find himself heading straight for some steep glacier with no time to climb out of danger and no room to turn around.

So finding that crucial fjord—Tunugliarfik—was imperative. Crews knew they were on the right course when they spotted a wrecked freighter about thirty miles from the fjord entrance; this welcome confirmation also told them the next turn had to be to the left, which took them safely to the airport's lone runway. But missing that turn would lead an airplane down another narrow blind alley with a towering glacier cliff waiting ominously at the other end. And navigating Tunugliarfik itself was no picnic. The freighter, so vital to navigation, could be hard to find if an airplane was groping its way through rain, fog, or snow. In clear weather, the fjord was wide enough to allow a one-hundred-eighty-degree turn; in poor visibility, a pilot would be playing Russian roulette if he tried to reverse course. It was no wonder that the airmen likened flying in the fjord in bad weather to flying in a tunnel.

Northeast's crews never knew from day to day what assignment they might draw. Very early in the war, when a major enemy raid on Iceland was rumored, they had to muster all available aircraft and transport combat troops between Reykjavík and Melgerdi. The raid never occurred, but that didn't detract from the efficiency of the operation. Just as Northwest's pilots profited from their long cold-weather flight experience, so did Northeast's veterans utilize their years of battling New England winters to keep them alive while shoehorning their way into frozen airports along the North Atlantic route.

One of them was Captain Ray Remick, who in March of 1944 volunteered to pick up an Air Force cook stricken with appendicitis at Hebron, a small Moravian mission on the northern coast of Labrador, where the Air Force maintained a small weather-observation station. The only place to land was on Hebron Fjord's snow-covered ice, but Remick was assured by radio that the snow was hard-packed enough for a safe landing. He took off with several passengers aboard—Air Force officers curious to see Hebron, because Charles and Anne Lindbergh had landed there several years ago on a survey flight for Pan Am.

When he landed his C-47 on the fjord, the wheels broke through the snow crust and sank so deep that the aircraft came to a stop with its belly resting on the snow. Now Remick had a double head-ache: He not only had to free his stuck airplane, but if he didn't take off soon, he knew he couldn't get the engines restarted in the bitter cold.

He radioed Goose Bay for an engine heater and was told the earliest that one could be sent was by boat—the following August. Remick took up a collection among his crew and passengers which came to $25. It was less than he hoped for, but he divided it up among some sympathetic Eskimos who with shovels, paddles, and bare hands helped the stranded Americans dig two trenches, each five feet wide and about 500 feet long, ahead of the mired wheels.

Remick frankly explained to his passengers their choices: try a takeoff now, or wait five months for the boat. It wasn't an easy decision, either, for fog was rolling in and it was getting dark. Furthermore, Remick admitted, they could take off only in one direction—toward a cliff. And that, according to copilot R.B. Hubbell's computations, gave them exactly forty-five seconds after getting airborne—if they got airborne—to turn and climb out safely.

They all voted to stay with the airplane, bundled the stricken cook into a seat, and Remick poured on the coal. The C-47 was doing less than sixty miles an hour when Remick, running out of both time and real estate, pulled the yoke back and yelled, "Gear up!"

"It's already up!" Hubbell yelled back.

Somehow, the staggering C-47 got airborne, but barely—it was only fifty feet off the ground, the visibility was zero in thick fog, and Hubbell announced that their forty-five-second safety margin had expired. Remick knew he didn't have enough altitude to turn yet, and the indicated airspeed was nudging only slightly above sixty mph, but he turned anyway—to a heading of ninety degrees. The C-47 began picking up speed and a few minutes later they were at a safe altitude and heading south to Goose Bay.

A year before the Remick/Hubbell rescue mission, Northeast Captain Alva V.R. Marsh volunteered for a mission that even some of his fellow pilots based at Presque Isle, Maine, and several American Airlines crews as well, flatly declined. The Air Force had a sick weather observer at one of its most remote stations: Arctic Bay, which was miles north of the north magnetic pole. More was involved than merely flying the patient out; the Air Force said that because of weather, no supply boat had been able to reach the station since the previous summer, and its thirteen months of provisions were just about exhausted.

Marsh had initial reservations about the flight, too, but he finally decided to go, and enlisted another veteran captain, Fran Chalifoux, who agreed to serve as his copilot. They rounded up three other volunteers—navigator Joe Sewall, flight engineer Winston Peacock, and radio operator Les Hughes, and left Presque Isle late in March. Sewall, knowing that their ordinary compasses would be useless flying so close to the north magnetic pole, brought along an astro-compass, an optical instrument that took bearings by the sun.

They not only brought in emergency supplies, picked up the ailing observer, and flew him to where he could get medical treatment, but went back to Arctic Bay with more supplies: a total of 2300 pounds in the two trips, that covered nearly 10,000 air miles in thirteen days. All five crew members were awarded Air Medals.

Fourteen years later, Al Marsh was in command of a Northeast DC-6A that crashed on Riker's Island shortly after taking off from La Guardia in a snowstorm. Of the ninety-five passengers aboard, twenty died when they failed to get out of the burning airplane in time—some were found with their seatbelts still fastened, and others sitting next to emergency exits they hadn't even tried to open, victims of what is known as "negative panic"—so frozen with fear they were unable to move.

The CAB said Marsh had failed to monitor essential flight instruments when he flew into a thick overcast almost as soon as the airplane got airborne. To anyone who knew this veteran of wartime ATC flying, it was a verdict that made no sense. His angry fellow pilots pointed accusing fingers at the airplane he was flying—this particular DC-6A was an ex–cargo plane Northeast had leased so it could start its new New York–Miami service on schedule; it was also an airplane that had compiled fifty-six separate reports of basic flight instrument malfunctions since Northeast had acquired it. But the pilot error judgment stood, Alva Marsh never flew again, and in a sense became the twenty-first victim of his last flight.

It was because of airmen like Al Marsh that Northeast compiled a perfect safety record in all the years it operated a North Atlantic airlift, even though the airline was the only one that had to use two-engine equipment throughout the war. Despite its size, Northeast shared with big American a position of dominance in the North Atlantic airlift. Other carriers flew the route from time to time, but Northeast was the only one not allotted four-engine C-87s and

C-54s. It did get some C-46s, dubbed "the Pregnant Whale" by irreverent crews, but the big Commando developed more ailments in cold weather flying than it did in warmer theaters. For several months, carburetor icing caused numerous flights to abort, and the streamlined contour of the C-46's cockpit windshield was not only difficult to deice but caused serious visibility problems in heavy rain.

Perhaps Northeast's most significant wartime contributions, however, were those first pathfinding survey flights that established the principal North Atlantic airway from Presque Isle to England. The Army used it before it was really ready for full-scale ATC operations; not long after the survey flights were completed, the Air Corps rushed fifty airplanes from six ATC contract carriers (American, TWA, United, Chicago & Southern, Pennsylvania Central, and Braniff) to Presque Isle where they were joined by another sixty transports of the Troop Carrier Command. Those 110 C-47s carried tons of supplies and hundreds of key personnel to the Newfoundland, Labrador, Greenland, and Iceland bases along the route, in preparation for the mass ferrying of bombers to Europe.

This was before the Airline War Training Institute got rolling, but it was a forerunner of how military transport pilots learned from their airline counterparts in ATC. The flying experience of most of the Army's C-47 pilots in this early North Atlantic airlift averaged only 300 hours, so each youngster flew his trip with a veteran airline pilot either serving as his captain or copilot.

And the North Atlantic, once deemed too dangerous to fly, was being tamed.

Western

Somewhat but not much larger than Sam Solomon's airline, Western shared Northeast's wartime reputation for getting a lot accomplished with a minimum of resources. It, too, was part of the AWTI "scholastic" network, operating one general transportation school in Fairfield, California, and a larger facility in Salt Lake City where fresh graduates from Air Corps schools, heading for the CBI theater and the Hump, received ninety days of C-46 training.

The Los Angeles–based airline got into the war on December 8, 1941, when on orders from the War Department it canceled all flights and used every airplane in its fleet to carry ammunition to the panicky West Coast which, in the aftermath of the Pearl Harbor disaster, was expecting at best Japanese air raids and at worst a Japanese invasion.

But Western's principal World War II role stemmed from a supposedly insignificant prewar route award from the Civil Aeronautics Board. It was just 170 miles long, a tiny spur that ran from Great Falls, Montana, to Lethbridge in southwestern Canada via Shelby and Cut Bank. During the war, however, that spur became the final link in an 11,250-mile intercontinental airway from Santiago, Chile to Nome, Alaska, and the spur was Western's ticket of admission to participate in the war's massive Alaskan airlift.

Northwest played the major role in flying priority cargo and personnel to America's northernmost territory, while Pan Am and United also were important participants in Alaskan ATC missions. But little Western wasn't any bit player; it operated a 2451-mile aerial supply line from Great Falls to Nome via Edmonton, White Horse (Canada), and Fairbanks, with a branch to Anchorage added later. To the WAL crews, it became known as Operation Sourdough.

Sourdough was headed by Captain Pat Carlson, a veteran who was a stickler for enforcing regulations without being a stiff-necked martinet. He set up headquarters at Edmonton in the summer of 1942 and the subsequent winter turned out to be Alaska's worst since 1898. Western's crews, many of them from the airline's balmy Los Angeles base, suffered cold-weather miseries and handicaps that their Northwest brethren had come to accept as almost routine—or at least to be expected.

Temperatures sank to 65 degrees below zero for weeks at a time. Rubber fittings crystallized to the point where the slightest touch would shatter them like fragile glass. Oil took on the consistency of thick mud, and grease simply froze in wheel bearings. Fuel hoses became so brittle they would snap in a modest wind. Altimeters, their air intakes often blocked by ice or heavy snow, could be a thousand feet off in either direction. Engine oil had to be diluted with gas to keep the oil cooler from rupturing if an airplane sat on the ground for any length of time in the freezing cold.

Airports, at least in the early stages of the war, were nothing but dirt strips, and for a long time radio navigation aids were virtually nonexistent. Compounding all these difficulties was the inadequacy of the Alaskan navigation charts, most of them the product of sheer guesswork. A Northwest captain once described to a new Sourdough crew the scientific technique he had developed for flying from Fairbanks to Anchorage:

"You just put your ship in a steep climb as soon as you take off," he lectured to his rapt audience. "Don't level off until your props are churning stardust. Then you hope you're at the spot in the Alaskan mountain range where Mount McKinley ain't."

Officially, Sourdough was operated as the Alaskan Division of Western Air Lines. Unofficially, it was operated by a collection of rugged individualists to whom improvision came as naturally as breathing, calculated risks were a daily occurrence to be taken for granted, and off-duty hours provided a time in which to play as hard as they worked. One of Pat Carlson's most frequent chores was to stave off, as diplomatically as possible, complaints from Alaskan hotel operators concerning pilot decorum—or lack of it. At various times the Sourdough flight crews stayed in three different Fairbanks hotels, forced to shift on a frequent basis because they had become personae non gratae at one or the other.

Of course, the wartime hotels weren't exactly havens of luxury. "At all the hotels, the plumbing was frozen half the time," Carlson recalled after the war. "The one I remember best was the old Nordale in Fairbanks. They never made the beds. When you'd sign in, they'd hand you your sheets and they were always wet. They had phones in each room but none of them had a bell—the bell box was on the wall. If it rang, you'd stumble out of bed half asleep and tear that damned box off the wall trying to find a receiver that wasn't there."

A few Sourdough pilots rented a small but comfortable cabin near Edmonton, and made friends with a black bear who came around regularly to wheedle food scraps. Came the day when a visiting pilot, who hadn't been briefed on the bear's free-loading status, shot it. He was promptly evicted from the premises with the bellows of an angry fellow airman blasting his eardrums:

"You stupid son of a bitch! You killed the only friend we have in Canada!"

Nearly 100 WAL employees were assigned to Sourdough, which began rather modestly, carrying ferry pilots from Fairbanks—where their airplanes had been flown for eventual delivery to the Soviet Union—back to Great Falls. But Sourdough quickly expanded into a major cargo operation, its C-47s and converted DC-3s hauling everything from priority lumber to heavy diesel machinery.

Military weight manifests could have won awards for great fiction writing—they were even less accurate than Alaskan aeronautical charts. Carlson once questioned the weight of a diesel engine being loaded on a C-47. The manifest listed it as slightly under 6000 pounds.

"If that thing weighs only six thousand pounds, it must be made of aluminum," Carlson snorted. "I want it weighed again before that plane takes off."

It weighed more than 10,000 pounds.

Snow and ice would accumulate on Alaskan airfields all winter, successfully defying all removal efforts. The supposedly welcome spring thaws didn't improve conditions much; ice would turn into heavy slush during the day and freeze over again at night. Warmer weather brought no respite because crews then had to battle ankle-deep mud. Nor was it always possible to build runways in line with prevailing winds. Western pilots became as adept as Northwest's in making crosswind landings that in civilian operations would have been illegal.

The main Alaskan food staple for ATC crews was steak—beef steak, bear steak, and moose steak; the latter was coarse, and some pilots thought it tasted like veal. Fresh vegetables were virtually unattainable, and the crews began yearning for greens with the same intensity an alcoholic craves liquor. Pat Carlson once willingly paid $1.75 for a lettuce sandwich, and one Western ATC captain walked into a Great Falls restaurant featuring the finest steaks in Montana and ordered every salad on the menu.

New arrivals to Sourdough would bring cases of fresh eggs with them, expecting rounds of grateful applause. What they got were some ungrateful grunts and such comments as, "What the hell do we need those for?" It seems the pilots and mechanics became so used to powdered eggs that they spurned the fresh.

All the vicissitudes, of necessity softened by occasional shenanigans, never obscured the fact that Sourdough was efficiently, even brilliantly executed. Western never lost a plane nor a man, an incredible safety record considering the technical handicaps under which it was achieved. Northwest's initial tutoring, offered so willingly because all ATC crews shared common dangers, certainly was partially responsible, but even the NWA airmen conceded that

Western's pilots learned their lessons fast and thoroughly. They had to, for the average Sourdough flight between any two points was 500 miles, and most of it had to be flown on instruments. Jack Orwig, he of the Sherlock Holmes headgear, flew one trip that took twenty-three hours, and he was in a solid overcast, flying entirely on instruments, for seventeen of them.

The Sourdough pilots had frequent reminders that they were as lucky as they were good. Often they joined search and rescue missions, for whenever a plane was reported missing or down, any flight coming into a Sourdough base was immediately unloaded and sent to join aircraft from Northwest and other ATC carriers in the search. They usually had to be fortunate to find anything, especially in the winter; a Northwest plane crashed very near a Sourdough airport, but it took almost a day to find the wreckage— buried in a snow-covered clump of trees so thick it was impossible to spot from the air.

When Sourdough ended in 1945, its planes had carried some 22 million tons of cargo ranging from mattresses to Soviet gold being shipped to the Denver mint. In terms of total Alaskan tonnage and personnel flown, it ran second to Northwest and while in overall ATC operations Western was dwarfed by the likes of TWA, American, United, Eastern, and Pan Am, it did it in major league style. Sourdough compiled the highest aircraft utilization rate in ATC's domestic operations—just under sixteen hours a day per airplane, compared to an industry average of less than twelve.

Northwest

When Northwest became part of the Air Transport Command, it was regarded mostly as a midsize carrier, yet one with more bad-weather flying experience than even the industry's giants could claim.

It was said that one could always spot a veteran NWA airman by the crow's feet around his eyes, telltale marks that come from squinting into a thousand stormy skies. Some claimed they could even get a rough idea of how long a senior Northwest captain had been flying by the size of those crow's feet, just as a tree's age can be determined by the number of its rings. It was even rumored (falsely) that the reason Northwest painted its aircraft tails a bright red was so that rescue planes could spot a downed NWA aircraft easier in the snow.

Northwest was one of the twelve pioneer airlines awarded the first privately contracted air mail routes in 1926, the year the U.S. airline industry was born. Then named Northwest Airways, it was assigned CAM 9 between the Twin Cities and Chicago, and by 1934—operating as Northwest Airlines—it had established a northern transcontinental route from Minnesota to Seattle, along with compiling thousands of hours of priceless winter flying experience over sparsely settled, desolate areas in such states as Montana, the Dakotas, and Idaho. The pilots didn't know it at the time, but it might as well have been a dress rehearsal for Alaska.

Just as Delta paid homage for so many years to its crop-dusting origins, so did Northwest honor the heritage of its air mail days. Even when the airline started flying jets, its airmen were the only ones whose uniform caps still carried their original 1926 insignia: wings with U.S. AIR MAIL lettering, an anachronism that was a sentimental tribute to a brave past.

Northwest's major wartime involvement began early in 1942, when it signed a contract with the War Department to fly priority military cargo and personnel from Fargo, North Dakota, to Fairbanks, Alaska, via several points in Canada, including the Edmonton railhead. The airline launched the airlift operation with admirable speed; the contract was signed late in February, and Northwest's crews began the first route-familiarization and base supply flights March 2.

NWA's Alaskan story was a carbon copy of Western's, albeit written on larger paper; in terms of cargo tonnage and passengers carried, as well as the number of aircraft and employees involved, Northwest's operation was at least twice as large as Sourdough. What the two airlifts had in common was cheerful adjustment to miserable living conditions, and usually even worse working conditions. Bitter cold was only one enemy; the crews found that the magnificent Northern Lights could be unpredictably deadly, by interfering with radio communications without warning. Yet the ATC Alaskan airlift was operated with an almost grim determination to complete every mission possible.

During the war, a fire swept through Nome's only hospital, totally destroying the building and all its contents. Within two days, a pair of Northwest C-47s that had started out with medical equipment loaded in St. Louis landed in Nome carrying what amounted to a complete replacement for the ravaged hospital: lumber for a new building, twenty-four new beds, a new X-ray machine, and all necessary items of medical supplies from vaccines and hypodermic needles to bedpans. For that matter, arranging to fly in a new hospital was nothing special for Tom Nolan, the airline's cargo superintendent in Edmonton—his loadmaster crews routinely shipped outsize cargo throughout the war: heavy steel matting for runways, road-building equipment, trucks, airplane fuel tanks, tons of ammunition, and even 55,000-gallon fuel storage tanks that had to be cut into sections before they could be loaded, then welded together when they reached Alaska.

NWA Captain Bill Wallace drew an assignment one day to fly a C-47 to remote, snow-covered Fort St. John deep in northwestern Canada, and asked what cargo he'd be carrying.

"Lumber," the dispatcher told him.

Wallace frowned. "Lumber? You think a load of wood is a high-priority item in the middle of a war?"

The dispatcher gave him an "orders are orders" shrug, and Wallace took off, still disgusted. He would have vastly preferred a more rewarding, important mission, like one of Northwest's lend-lease aircraft ferry flights to the Soviet Union through Alaska and Siberia. He landed at Fort St. John, where he was surprised to be greeted like an arriving savior, and no wonder. The wood was for the base's stoves, which had been out of fuel for five days.

After the U.S. recaptured Attu and Kiska, Northwest established a regular cargo service to Attu, at the far end of the Aleutian Islands chain, and virtually every mile of the 1600-mile route had to be flown on instruments—something the Air Transport Command originally had considered impossible. This eventually developed into three daily round-trips between Minneapolis and Attu, and later Northwest operated an ATC route from Seattle to Anchorage.

One of the airline's most unusual wartime assignments involved a special project aimed at circumventing the icing conditions ATC planes encountered so frequently in Alaska and over the North Atlantic. Icing was almost as hazardous to an airman's health as poor visibility; once an airplane began to ice up, the crews either had to seek the warmer air of lower altitudes, often dangerously close to the ground or ocean, or attempt to fly above the weather in unpressurized aircraft. The NWA experimental flights began in 1942, and the project wasn't terminated until 1947.

Northwest also established training and aircraft modification facilities, including a school at Billings, Montana that specialized in transitioning Army transport pilots into C-46 equipment, and also turned out radio technicians. An aircraft modification and flight test center was opened at Vandalia, Ohio, near Wright-Patterson Field, but the airline's major modification efforts came from a mammoth facility at Holman Field in St. Paul, where some 5000 employees sent more than 3000 modified bombers overseas. Its first assignment was modifying B-25 bombers earmarked for the Royal Air Force, and the center subsequently concentrated on B-24s.

The Holman work force included participants in an unusual experiment: The airline hired totally blind persons to recover and sort the numerous nuts, washers, and screws that were always getting lost, causing small but annoying delays. Northwest discovered that blind people, with their acute sense of touch, could do the job faster than someone with normal eyesight.

(Boeing once hired and trained five totally deaf men as riveters in a program aimed at easing the problem of riveting noise on the assembly line, so workers with no hearing impairment could be shifted to quieter jobs. Unfortunately, it was discovered that riveting vibrations disturbed the deaf as much as noise bothered the regular workers.)

The Northwest ATC planes which carved that airway to Attu, coming within 2000 miles of Tokyo, were casting shadows of the airline's peacetime future. After the war, it would invade Juan Trippe's hitherto sacrosanct Pacific territory as Northwest Orient Airlines.

They Also Served

"Banana Run" was the nickname bestowed on Braniff's chief wartime responsibility. It was assigned an ATC route from San Antonio to Guatemala and Albrook Field in the Panama Canal Zone, the first flight taking off April 13, 1942. By the time the Banana Run ended early in 1944, Braniff's ATC crews had flown more than 2300 accident-free trips carrying 6.5 million pounds of cargo and nearly 17,000 high-priority military passengers.

The Banana Run also served key bases in Mexico and Central America, and for a few crucial months—while German submarines were raising havoc with surface shipping in the Gulf of Mexico and the Caribbean—Braniff's planes were the major source of supply. The Banana Run was a two-way airlift; many of the return flights to Texas carried crude rubber.

Pennsylvania Central signed the first domestic military cargo contract with the Air Service Command shortly after losing two-thirds of its "Capitaliner" fleet to the Army early in 1942.

The initial contract called for flying cargo and personnel between the nation's capital and Chicago. But PCA, traditionally known as "a pilot's airline," spread its ATC wings all over the United States and even into Alaska and Greenland on special missions. And in the same year it began domestic cargo flights, the Army turned over to PCA all flight operations of the Ferrying Command's headquarters staff. It was an assignment that put the staff's twenty-three airplanes in charge of some of the airline's most senior pilots; the Army specified that no one with less than 4000 logged hours of airline experience could fly headquarters officers.

PCA had plenty of such veterans, men who had been weaned flying the airline's early routes over the rugged Allegheny Mountains. So PCA also was a natural choice to operate two AWTI schools, the largest one established in Roanoke, Virginia, where PCA instructors taught transport flying to Navy pilots going into NATS service. The second training facility was in a hangar at Washington National Airport and graduated hundreds of ATC pilots, flight engineers, navigators, radio operators, meteorologists, and mechanics.

After the war, PCA became Capital Airlines, the nation's fifth largest carrier, and eventually was merged into United. Like such sister airlines as Mid-Continent and Chicago & Southern (which merged with Braniff and Delta respectively after the war), PCA's postwar extinction made its wartime role pass into history almost unnoticed and virtually forgotten.

Also unappreciated, for no airline, large or small, served the armed forces with more skill and dedication than Pennsylvania Central.

*   *   *

All-American Aviation was the nation's tiniest air domestic carrier—an airline that flew only mail, carried no passengers, operated nothing but outmoded single-engine airplanes, yet improbably is credited with one of the war's most important military contributions.

All-American didn't even land at the small communities it provided with air mail service, towns isolated from the nation's civil airways. Its pilots would deliver incoming mail by dropping it in sacks; outgoing mail would be picked up via an ingenious system developed by an inventor named Lytle Adams, and financed by none other than Richard du Pont of the Wilmington du Ponts.

The technique was daring, and even in the immediate prewar years seemed oddly anachronistic. AAA's pilots would make low, frequently dangerous approaches to an airport and head for two poles which had the outgoing mailbag suspended between them. They'd catch the bag on a hook at the end of a cable attached to the aircraft's belly, a process that required the kind of skilled flying even the crop dusters might envy.

Richard du Pont himself, after reading about the Germans' employment of gliders in the 1941 invasion of the Low Countries and again in the capture of Crete, conceived the idea of adopting All-American's mail pickup system to glider operations. He arranged a series of tests at Wilmington, with an engineless Piper Cub playing the role of a glider, and one of the airline's Stinsons as the pickup plane; du Pont himself sat in the Cub's cockpit. The towline kept breaking, so du Pont substituted a far stronger, more elastic line fashioned from undrawn nylon.

After subsequent successful tests before Army officials at Wright-Patterson Field, du Pont developed an attachment rig strong enough to lift a 1500-pound glider off the ground. Even stronger attachments were designed, installed on test C-47s, and what had once been a primitive method of picking up air mail became a major component in airborne warfare.

The glider launching system wasn't All-American's only wartime involvement. The airline won a military cargo contract and its seven puddle-jumping Stinsons, painted olive drab although they were decidedly unmilitary, joined the C-47s, C-46s, C-87s, and C-54s of the ATC fleet. Flying seven days a week for more than two years, they delivered nearly 2.5 million pounds of war materials from North Carolina to Maine.

All-American's revenues for operating ATC cargo flights provided impressive evidence that the airlines weren't gouging the government. The initial Army cost-plus-fixed-fee contract guaranteed AAA a $10 profit per airplane daily. This was later increased to $21.25, which still added up to less than $150 total daily profit on all seven airplanes. The black ink was so pale that the airline's board of directors had difficulty borrowing money for additional aircraft with which to operate the mail routes.

AAA augmented the cargo flights by operating two AWTI schools, a pilot training facility at Harrisburg and a school for mechanics in Wilmington. The disadvantage of being a carrier with only single-engine pilots was eliminated by sending a number of All-American flight crews through transitional training that qualified them to fly twin-engine Lockheeds. This was a look into the postwar future: du Pont knew the airline was going to have to start flying passengers when the war ended.

When peace did arrive, little All-American Aviation changed its name to Allegheny Airlines. Then, after absorbing via a succession of mergers Lake Central, Mohawk, Pacific Southwest, and Piedmont, Allegheny became today's US Airways (formerly USAir) — an international carrier larger, in fact, than any of the "Big Five" that also fought the airlift war of 1942 to 1945.

★ ★ 5 ★ ★
War Wings—Part II

Pan American . . . TWA . . . American . . . Eastern . . . United.

They entered the war in 1941 as the "Big Five" of U.S. commercial aviation—large airlines, even huge by the standards of that era; acknowledged leaders in every aspect of civil aviation, from technology to route development; pacesetters in safety improvements; instigators and motivators of new transport designs; innovators in passenger service.

This quintet of carriers had taken America's air transportation system out of diapers and into long pants. Yes, other airlines contributed their own share of progress, and a few were pioneers in their own right. But all of them combined couldn't equal the overall impact of either the achievements or the influence of these five on commercial aviation.

But the winds of fate and the tides of history flow in unpredictable directions. Eastern, one of those five airlines who provided the main initial nucleus of America's mighty wartime airlift, no longer exists. Pan Am also folded, then managed to rise from the ashes of bankruptcy, resuming operations under its proud old name but as a smaller airline starting with an eleven-plane fleet of Airbus A-300s. TWA has stayed alive but has shrunk in both size and route structure, no longer one of the world's largest, truly dominant international carriers.

American and United, of course, are still industry giants—UAL being the nation's largest employee-owned company. But the rest of the industry has gone through some convulsive changes since Edgar Gorrell's obstreperous family united as one to help win the war. Delta and Northwest have become major air transportation players, both domestically and internationally, while little All-American Aviation eventually sprouted into today's US Airways. Continental is healthy again after surviving some rough times following Bob Six's retirement and subsequent death. Hawaiian, like Continental, suffered through a Chapter 11 bankruptcy filing before financial reorganization sent it flying straight and high once more. Alaska Airlines, founded in 1937 as Star Air Lines and a midget in the war years, grew into the forty-ninth state's biggest airline and, with Reeve Aleutian, Alaska's only wartime contributors still alive and prospering.

But the majority of the so-called "trunk" or major carriers that participated so wholeheartedly and brilliantly in the industry's wartime efforts became only pages in aviation's history books. In most cases, mergers that were really acquisitions caused their demises. Western was absorbed by Delta, which already had taken over Northeast and Chicago & Southern. Capital, formerly Pennsylvania Central, merged with United; Braniff did likewise with Mid-Continent, eventually went bankrupt, and so did Eastern. National, which in addition to its AWTI school also flew ATC cargo between Miami and Houston via New Orleans, became part of Pan Am—Juan Trippe, through this merger, finally got the domestic routes he had been seeking for years.

Too late, as it turned out, for this great pioneering airline eventually crashed into bankruptcy itself. Considering what its people and its planes did before and during the war, perhaps the fate of the most powerful pacesetting and influential international air carrier in aviation history was the most tragic story of them all . . .

Pan American Airways

Pan Am was one of the first U.S. airlines to come face to face with the grim realities of war:

Six hours after the Pearl Harbor attack, Japanese planes bombed Hong Kong, where the *Hong Kong Clipper,* a Pan Am Sikorsky S-42, was moored to a harbor dock. Dive bombers targeted the flying boat, turning it into a charred carcass in a matter of minutes.

Captain Fred Rolf and his crew were evacuated later by a CNAC plane that took them to Calcutta; theirs was just one of many rescue flights out of Hong Kong for Pan Am's Chinese subsidiary. Forced to fly mostly at night and often under enemy fire, CNAC carried nearly 400 officials and civilians, including 100 children, to safety before Hong Kong fell.

The *Philippine Clipper*, one of Pan Am's big Martin M-130 seaplanes, almost suffered the same fate as the *Hong Kong Clipper*. On the morning of December 7, it had departed Wake Island heading for Guam. When news of the Pearl Harbor attack reached Wake, Captain John Hamilton was told to dump 3000 pounds of gasoline and return to Wake. The Marines manning the island's defenses, short of scouting aircraft, asked Hamilton to make a patrol flight—in effect, the Pan Am crew was about to join the United States Marine Corps on a very unofficial basis. Before they could take off, however, Japanese bombers swept over the island and machine gun bullets riddled the defenseless flying boat while it was being refueled.

Although nine of Pan Am's sixty-six station employees were killed in the attack, the Martin's damage miraculously was confined to numerous but nonfatal bullet holes (the crew counted ninety-seven); ninety minutes after the raiding planes left, Hamilton took off—without making any repairs—and flew almost 2500 miles to Hawaii, with a single stop at Midway.

Another drama involving Pan Am's seaplane fleet also unfolded after the Pearl Harbor attack. This time it involved a Boeing 314, the *Pacific Clipper*, commanded by Captain Bob Ford. The outbreak of war caught the giant flying boat in New Zealand, where Ford received War Department orders to get home by any route that would avoid enemy interception, no matter how long it took. Normally Ford would have flown east across the Pacific to California, where the *Pacific Clipper* was based. Inasmuch as the Army officially now owned all of Pan Am's Boeings—as had been arranged under Stallter's mobilization plan—Ford followed orders.

After covering the seaplane with a hasty camouflage paint scheme, he took off from Aukland and flew west to Australia, then to India, Arabia, Central Africa, and South America, and finally headed north to New York. En route, the flight almost ended in disaster over Surabaya in the Dutch East Indies, when British fighters mistook the Boeing for a Japanese flying boat and were about to open fire when one pilot saw part of an American flag under the camouflage.

The next difficulty occurred just before they landed at Ceylon, when the number three engine failed. There were two Pan Am flight engineers in the crew, Swede Rothe and Jocko Parish, and in those days most flight engineers also were fully qualified airframe and engine mechanics. Rothe and Parish found that ten of the sixteen studs holding a cylinder in place had ruptured; they had enough spare studs, but they needed a special tool to attach them.

Parish paid a visit to a British warship he had spotted in the harbor, borrowed some cold rolled steel along with the ship's lathe, and hand-fashioned a makeshift tool which he used to repair the cylinder. This little incident was a forerunner of things to come; while ATC and NATS pilots did perform almost daily miracles, so did those less glamorous flight engineers and mechanics who made a science out of improvision.

The *Pacific Clipper* finally landed at Pan Am's Marine Terminal, adjacent to La Guardia Airport, completing a trip that mileagewise—31,500—had taken the big flying boat around the world, a distance which theoretically made the *Pacific Clipper* the first seaplane to circumnavigate the globe. One account, in fact, logged the mileage at 34,500. However far the Boeing flew, the honor was somewhat diluted because to complete a true world flight back to its California base, the seaplane would have had to have crossed the continental United States.

When the *Pacific Clipper* landed at New York, the tired crew learned that their doughty flying boat was no longer in the Army. While they were en route, the Army had transferred all but three of the Boeings to the Navy. The Army retained as C-98s the *Capetown, Anzac,* and *California* clippers and assigned them to ATC. The *Pacific, Honolulu, Yankee, Atlantic, Dixie,* and *American* clippers donned the sea-gray colors of NATS. All were to survive the war except one, the *Yankee Clipper,* whose fate will be described in a later chapter.

What the *Pacific Clipper* had accomplished theoretically was achieved officially later by another B-314, the *Anzac Clipper,* commanded by Pan Am Captain Bill Masland and operating as an ATC aircraft: a legitimate around-the-world flight. But while the feat was legitimate, it also was mostly accidental. Masland flew from New York to the Casablanca summit conference, where he was supposed to pick up President Roosevelt, Prime Minister Churchill, and Premier Stalin, and take them to Australia for a secret meeting with Chinese leader Chiang Kai-shek. Allied intelligence had reason to believe the Japanese had found out about the meeting, so the trip was canceled. Masland went ahead with the flight anyway, albeit with a less distinguished passenger list: he flew General Albert Wedemeyer and his staff to Australia. Next, instead of reversing course and heading back the way he had come, he continued westward over the Pacific to San Francisco, and then nonstop across the United States from San Francisco to New York, completing a global flight that covered nearly 37,000 miles.

Pan Am's seaplanes, the B-314s in particular, were often used for flying VIP passengers, but the Boeings completed plenty of tough cargo missions before PAA acquired land planes like the C-46 and C-54. Just before Christmas of 1941, three of the 314s flew from New York to Calcutta, carrying ammunition and spare aircraft parts for some forty fighters of the Flying Tigers grounded in Burma. Other B-314s were assigned to a regular military cargo shuttle service between Natal and Fisherman's Lake on the west coast of Africa. ATC C-47s and C-53s operating as part of Pan Am's Latin American division would fly emergency cargo from Miami to Natal, and the flying boats would take it across the South Atlantic. Virtually every flight was labeled RUSH—among the items the Boeings hauled across the ocean were spare parts for crippled tanks, ammunition, and 12,000 pounds of dust filters for aircraft operating in desert conditions. The B-314 crews had to be as durable as their airplanes; one PAA captain made twelve transatlantic crossings in thirteen days.

Unlike the land transport planes the Army and Navy acquired from the airlines that had been stripped of all civilian vestiges, clippers used to fly VIP passengers were allowed to retain at least a reasonable semblance of their luxurious interiors, for it was hard to imagine a president, a prime minister, or a four-star admiral or general sitting on a metal bench seat, squeezed in by cargo, all the way across an ocean.

And the Boeing flying boats *were* luxurious, for the B-314 literally was the grandfather of the mighty Boeing 747 that was born three decades later. Like the 747 of the future, it was a double-deck aircraft of incredible spaciousness, with an especially large flight deck that could have been a ship's bridge. The cockpit, twenty-one feet long and nine feet wide, had more than adequate room for the 314's six-man flight crew: three pilots (one served as a relief pilot on long flights), navigator, radio operator, and flight engineer—the latter the first on a U.S. commercial transport. The B-314's six-man contingent had far more working space than there was for a five- or even four-man crew on one of ATC's C-54s or C-87s.

There were two to four cabin attendants usually assigned to a prewar Boeing transatlantic flight, and they worked in an environment of roomy airborne splendor; at the then-hefty round-trip transatlantic fare of $675, passengers expected such luxury and service. The B-314 could seat eighty passengers by day and accommodate forty in sleeping compartments at night, although Pan Am later changed this configuration to seventy-four day and fifty night for all trips of up to 1500 miles. On transatlantic flights, however, passenger capacity was cut to only thirty-five, and transpacific flights never carried more than thirty. In addition to seating and sleeping accommodations for passengers, the 314's lower deck also included a dining salon, cocktail lounge, separate lavatory/dressing room facilities for men and women, and what had been a bridal suite in peacetime became a private stateroom for the likes of such VIPs as FDR and Churchill. The upper deck aft of the cockpit contained rest quarters for the crew and a large baggage area. It was no wonder the B-314 carried what was then a record price tag: $514,000 per airplane, and that figure didn't include the spares every airline ordered when they bought a new airplane.

The lower-level passenger deck featured thick carpeting, deep-upholstered davenport couches in individual Pullman-type compartments instead of seat rows, soft indirect lighting, and sound-proofing—the latter a relatively new gimmick first introduced on airliners in 1932. The lower deck main lounge became the dining room when meals were served—three servings at staggered hours because the four-table dining salon seated only twelve persons—and at night the couches were converted into beds.

If the forty-one-ton B-314 was slow (even under ideal conditions it was lucky to cruise at more than 180 miles an hour), its range was unprecedented for a transport of that time—nearly 4000 miles with a thirty-passenger payload. It would have been hard to find a wartime passenger, whether military or civilian official, who would have traded the flying boat's roominess and comfort for getting someplace a few hours sooner. The Boeings seemed to offer an incongruous, nostalgic touch of peacetime graciousness in the middle of a brutal war, and they appealed to every world leader who ever flew on one.

Winston Churchill, in fact, fell in love with the B-314 the first time he traveled on one. Following a meeting with FDR in Washington a few weeks after Pearl Harbor, Churchill planned to fly on the *Berwick,* one of the three B-314s BOAC operated during the war, from Baltimore Harbor to Bermuda, where he was supposed to board the battleship *Duke of York* for the trip back to England. By the time they reached Bermuda, however, the PM had become enamored with the giant aircraft, and insisted on going the rest of the way by air. He was to write later how much he was impressed by the peacetime bridal suite that served as his sleeping quarters, by the thirty to forty feet he had to walk to get from the suite to the dining room, and—after he was allowed to handle the controls briefly—by how easy the big ship was to fly.

Such testimonials, however, couldn't save the B-314s or their sister flying boats from postwar extinction as viable commercial aircraft. They were not only slow, but unprofitable; they were fuel guzzlers because of their great weight, to achieve the virtues of range it was necessary to reduce payload, and assigning a ten-man crew to an airplane carrying as few as thirty passengers made no economic sense. It also was expensive for a single carrier to maintain a seaplane base, whereas airport costs were borne by several airlines. Significantly, when the Army and Navy returned their B-314s to Pan Am ownership before war's end, the airline had already decided to sell them.

The last flight of any Pan Am flying boat was made by the *American Clipper* from Honolulu to San Francisco on April 8, 1946. A few 314s saw brief postwar service with charter airlines, but all eleven that survived the war were eventually wrecked in accidents or wound up on the scrap heap, an ignominious fate for one of aviation's greatest airplanes. Pan Am itself had ended the war flying mostly land planes, and its vast ATC/NATS operations had carried its crews to virtually every theater of combat.

Basically, PAA geared most of its wartime operations to the airline's three main divisions: Atlantic, Pacific, and Latin America. It flew the North Atlantic for NATS and the South Atlantic for ATC, combining the latter with its Latin America division, while its Pacific military flights were largely in behalf of NATS, in whose organization the airline played an indirect though important role: a Pan Am captain serving in the Navy helped establish its transport arm. Pan Am's long experience in flying the vast reaches of the Pacific, building bases, and pioneering the routes themselves, made it a natural partner for a navy fighting for survival from Hawaii to Australia. Navy Secretary Frank Knox created the Naval Air Transport Service only five days after Pearl Harbor, acting on the recommendation of former Pan Am Captain Dutch Schildhauer; the first NATS squadron, using four R-4Ds (the Navy's designation for the DC-3/C-47), was formed three months later.

Most of the major bases served by this and subsequent squadrons had been established by Pan Am years before: familiar names like Aukland, Canton Island, Wake, Midway, New Caledonia, Suva, and Noumea; unfamiliar Pacific outposts such as Funafuti, Espiritu Santo, Efati, Wallis, Samarai, Kaneohe, Tangatabu, Upolu, Penrhyn, Nasilai River, Nandi, and Milne Bay—even some of these bore a PAA stamp.

But the Navy also had a huge stake in the defense of Alaska, and it was a military cargo/personnel contract with NATS that Juan Trippe signed in September of 1942. The Navy wanted additional logistical support for United and Northwest's airlifts to the northern territory, and PAA began operating ten flights a week from Seattle to Fairbanks via Juneau, five weekly flights to Nome, and one a week to Bethel. Within months, Pan Am had expanded its Alaskan operations to Kodiak, Dutch Harbor, and Adak.

Providing an Alaskan airlift for the Navy represented another natural partnership, for Pan Am already was serving Alaska and had spent considerable sums on badly needed navigation aids, new radio facilities, and airport construction. One of the airline's less-appreciated and sometimes historically ignored achievements was its know-how in creating or at least improving crucial airfields in areas that could only be called primitive. Pan Am's construction personnel were as skilled at such projects as its airmen were in the skies, and the support they received from Juan Trippe and the rest of Pan Am's top management was admirable, to say the least.

Witness, for example, PAA's massive airport development program in Africa. British author P. St. John Turner, in researching Pan Am for his *Pictorial History of Pan American World Airways*, was particularly impressed by the airline's consumate professionalism, which he thought far surpassed similar British efforts in building airfield facilities at remote sites, and this included the living conditions provided the workers.

Pan Am's contruction crews equipped in whole or in part a total of fourteen stations across Africa, consisting of hangars, laboratories, barracks, and power houses. Workshops were air-conditioned, 14 metal cold-storage buildings kept food protected, and the sleeping quarters contained more than 4000 comfortable spring mattress beds. Sufficient rest was essential, for the usual 48-hour-work-week maximum was generally ignored.

The threat of malaria was always present and Pan Am tried hard to reduce exposure risk. Daily quinine tablets were mandatory, while workers constantly drained stagnant water and screened every ditch within range of a construction site; actually, delays in mail deliveries affected morale more than the heat and mosquito raids. The final bottom line was impressive: the trans-African airlift Pan Am eventually turned over to the Air Transport Command already was a superbly organized operation in virtually every respect.

(PAA even did something to correct the slow mail deliveries about which employees complained. One of the war's lesser-known yet most widely used and praised achievements was the development of a system for microfilming mail to save weight, the result of a joint research effort by Eastman Kodak, Pan Am, and BOAC. Its technical name was Airgraph, but it quickly acquired the more popular label of V-mail, the "V" appropriately standing for Victory.)

While the giant flying boats of Pan Am lumbered across the world's oceans on special missions, the airline's growing fleet of C-47s, C-54s, and C-46s began joining the ATC/NATS airlifts of the other carriers. PAA's planes flying under a NATS contract crossed the North Atlantic 3800 times during the war, and its NATS aircraft made more than 3000 transpacific flights. When these are added to the airline's ATC operations across the South Atlantic between Natal and Africa, Pan Am's wartime ocean crossings totaled some 15,000—and all this occurred routinely less than twenty years after Lindbergh's New York–Paris flight made the Lone Eagle a national hero.

Pan Am crews also flew the Hump for ATC; while not in such numerical numbers as other carriers, the airline was heavily involved in airlift operations affecting the CBI theater. Aircraft and crews from the PAA-Africa division joined with the ATC's CBI Ferry Command to evacuate more than 4000 wounded British and Indian troops from Burma ahead of advancing Japanese troops. The Pan Am crews and their C-47s were based at Dinjan in northeast India, flying ammunition and weapons to units trying to hold back the enemy, and taking off again with at least sixty evacuees packed into every airplane—one plane carried seventy-one. The C-47s stunk with the odor of gangrene, vomit, and unwashed bodies. The pilots' wildest nightmares couldn't match the conditions under which they carried out these missions. They flew, unarmed and unescorted, from 4 A.M. to 7 or 8 P.M., often through blinding monsoons, enemy fire, and usually at night through and over mountainous terrain.

Pan Am also established the "Cannonball" route for ATC from Miami direct to Karachi, India—an 11,500-mile flight using C-54s exclusively, and these were airplanes benefitting from a PAA experiment. Every airline flying the oceans for ATC had its technical people working on ways to stretch range. Pan Am's idea was to strip every ounce of camouflage paint off a C-54 and replace it with a thin, high-gloss finish. Much to their surprise, this added about five miles an hour to the average cruising speed of 200 mph, and also enabled loadmasters to up each transatlantic payload by about 1200 pounds.

Pan Am's airlift to and across Africa is credited with helping the British defeat Rommel and preserve the Suez Canal as a vital transportation supply link. It established an AWTI school that trained 1800 navigators for both ATC and NATS. And its airmen contributed their rightful share of individual exploits—to cite one typical incident, there was Captain William Moss, who pulled off a miraculous rescue in the middle of the storm-tossed Pacific.

Moss and the rest of his PAA/NATS crew were refueling at a remote Pacific base when the Navy was advised that a troop transport, the *Cape San Juan*, had been torpedoed and sunk, and that there were about fifty survivors. Moss took off and started looking for them in a Consolidated PB2Y, a four-engine seaplane patrol bomber converted into a transport. He flew 300 miles from the base before the swimming, oil-coated men, waving weakly, were spotted.

Moss managed to make a safe landing in the rough sea and took forty-eight survivors aboard. Then came the challenge of taking off in the heavy swells. He just made it after bouncing fifty feet in the air on the top of one huge swell. The Navy awarded him a commendation, and after the war he not only flew jets for Pan Am but became a flight operations director for the airline—one of the most interesting pilots who ever wore the four stripes of an airline captain. It was Bill Moss who in the mid 1960s did the first and most comprehensive study of world jetliner accidents that had ever been conducted. One of its most important conclusions was a subtle tribute to the airmen of ATC and NATS: Moss found that sixty-three percent of all jet accidents occurred during the landing phase, *with eighty percent of these taking place in areas of the world where only seventeen percent of the landings were being made.*

That italicized (by the author) phrase could have described, and probably understated, the conditions under which these wartime air transport crews operated so many times: frequent poor visibility, primitive airports ringed by mountains, often a lack of accurate charts—or sometimes no charts at all, sporadic availability of navigation aids, and exposure to every kind of foul weather from desert sandstorms that could reach 25,000 feet to arctic blizzards, from ocean storms to jungle monsoons with rain so heavy that flying through one was like being underwater in a submarine.

It was impossible for either ATC or NATS to maintain a perfect or even an above-average safety record; there had to be numerous accidents, although many were unexplained disappearances and may very well have been due to enemy action. The Luftwaffe is known to have shot down at least one of the ATC's C-54s, and there probably were more such fatal encounters. But overall, airlift operations were remarkably safe in spite of all the handicaps and life-or-death decisions that had to be made, in the amount of time it takes to blink an eye.

There may have been some PAA pilots who began the war needing a refresher course on instrument flying, but by the time the war ended they were as good as their brother airmen on Eastern, or any other airline.

Including, it must be added, those flying for the one carrier Juan Trippe would have been happy to see operating a single ATC cargo route between Philadelphia and Pittsburgh: TWA.

Transcontinental & Western Air

On December 24, 1942, TWA president Jack Frye signed one of the most important documents in the airline's history.

Officially, it was the War Department's contract number DAW 535 ac-1062. Its legalistic language was similar to several other airline military contracts for overseas operations, in that it directed TWA "to hire and train all personnel, procure necessary facilities, materials and supplies, and to secure necessary certificates of convenience and necessity, licenses, and permits essential to providing air service on a worldwide basis for the United States Army."

On the same day Frye signed the document, which designated TWA as Contract Carrier No. 16, he established TWA's Intercontinental Division (ICD). Under wartime pressures and amid the uncertainties of a global conflict yet to be fought and won, he had laid the foundations for his airline's future as an international carrier that would become Pan Am's bitterest competitor. Nor was it any wonder that Trippe feared TWA most of all; if Jack Frye had the airline's majority stockholder looking over his shoulder all the time, he also had his checkbook at his disposal all the time, for said majority stockholder was Howard Hughes.

As Frye had promised Hap Arnold a year before, the five Stratoliners were the first to leave TWA's fleet, and if the airline's mechanics shed tears as they prepped them for delivery to the Army, they could have been forgiven. The interiors were gutted, and all five aircraft converted into combination cargo/passenger airplanes. Out came the vaunted pressurization systems that made the Boeing 307 so unique. Four auxiliary fuel tanks were installed between the cockpit and cabin. The proud red stripes on the tail and fuselage were removed and replaced by olive drab; the only insignia was that of the Air Transport Command plus the names they had carried in civilian service: each was named after an American Indian tribe: *Comanche, Cherokee, Zuni, Apache,* and *Navajo.* This had been Frye's idea; he had great respect for Native Americans (and he was reputed to have Indian blood).

Frye ordered the DC-3s remaining in the decimated fleet to undergo a slight cosmetic alteration; the italicized lettering that proclaimed TWA as THE TRANSCONTINENTAL LINE above the cabin windows was changed to VICTORY IS IN THE AIR—BUY BONDS.

The new ICD organization was set up hastily in makeshift quarters—a small room on the second floor of the terminal building at Washington National Airport, which had opened only six months before Pearl Harbor. Otis Bryan had been named to head ICD, an assignment which came as a complete surprise to Otis. He had been overseeing the training program at Eagle's Nest and decided to go home to Kansas City for Christmas. When he landed, at 6 A.M., he was greeted by a secretary from Frye's office.

"Mr. Frye wants to see you," she informed him.

"I'm tired and pretty grubby," Bryan said. "Let me go home and get cleaned up first."

"I'm sorry, Captain Bryan, but he wants to see you right now."

Bryan sighed resignedly, wondering what was so important, and went to Frye's office, where Jack broke the news that he had signed over the Stratoliners to the Air Corps. Then he dropped the bomb.

"They want someone to set up a group to operate them between Washington and Cairo, and they want it done in a hurry. We don't have much time, Otis. Rommel's kicking the hell out of the British in Egypt and Montgomery's running short of proximity fuses for his artillery shells. That'll be our first load, and we're already stripping the 307s and putting in extra fuel tanks."

"Okay with me," Bryan said, expecting Frye to assign him to the first flight. "Who's going to run this outfit?"

"You are."

The five "Indian tribes" were ready before Bryan's new ICD was. It took him two months to get everything organized, including transferring crews from domestic schedules, although part of the delay was due to the Civil Aeronautics Board's inevitable procrastination in granting TWA authority to operate a Washington-Cairo route; not even a war could interfere with a bureaucratic process. The Stratoliner *Navajo* was selected for the first flight and, typically, Otis assigned himself to command it. Before the takeoff, witnessed by all five CAB members, someone asked Bryan if this would be the first time he had ever been out of the United States.

"Second time," Bryan said blandly. "I spent a week in Mexicali once."

With Milo Campbell, a colorful ex-cowboy as his copilot, Bryan flew the Stratoliner to Cairo via West Palm Beach, Puerto Rico, Belem and Natal in Brazil, then across the South Atlantic to Monrovia, Liberia, Accra and Kano in Nigeria, and Khartoum. He insisted on making this a survey as well as a cargo mission. While he didn't waste much time getting to Cairo, the return trip was spent conferring with Army personnel all along the way, gaining information on operational problems so he could establish future procedures and standards. That was why the round-trip took seventeen days, the crew receiving a "well done" from Hap Arnold upon *Navajo*'s return—ending the first of nearly 10,000 wartime Atlantic crossings by TWA alone, compiling more than 15.6 million logged miles.

ICD's personnel during the war was to reach a maximum of 1753—more than TWA's total employment in 1939—with 634 in Flight Operations and 783 in Maintenance. The ICD fleet mushroomed accordingly; the five Stratoliners, which served right through V-E Day, were joined by a dozen C-87s, and later by eighteen C-54s and C-54As. Forty-five TWA flight crew members were killed in nine crashes while on ATC missions.

One of Bryan's first tasks was to hire radio operators and navigators, professions that were not necessary in airline domestic operations. Until he acquired graduates of the AWTI schools, most of the early navigators came off ships. Flight engineers largely were drawn from the ranks of mechanics, and one had to be good to win promotion from a maintenance hangar to a cockpit; the first class for mechanics hoping to qualify as Stratoliner flight engineers started out with thirty hopefuls and graduated only five.

The war also brought the airline's first male flight attendants since the days when TWA was Transcontinental Air Transport (TAT) and flew Ford trimotors. They were hired as pursers for ICD trips that carried passengers, because the War Department adamantly refused to let the airline use any of its hostesses.

"We've got guys in places like Africa and Greenland who haven't seen a woman in two years," an Army official explained to Frye.

The most available source for men with flight attendant experience was Eastern, the only major domestic carrier that had refused to hire women; this had been Rickenbacker's unyielding policy, Captain Eddie claiming that stewardesses were a waste of money because after an airline spent a lot of money training one, she flew only about six months before leaving to get married. Rickenbacker gave Frye his grudging approval to hire some of his stewards because he knew many of them were going to be drafted anyway.

So ICD's first pursers were half a dozen former Eastern stewards extremely happy to be recruited; ICD was an honorable way to avoid getting drafted into the Army, and the pay was a lot better than the $85 a month and dollar-a-day meal allowance Eastern was paying. ICD purser salaries started at $200 a month, which was not only satisfactory but downright seductive. The transitional training was virtually nonexistent; one former Eastern steward remembered that the new hirees simply took their old Eastern manuals and copied them word for word, substituting "TWA" for "Eastern" whenever necessary.

The need for more pursers increased as ICD's operations expanded. One month after the inaugural Cairo flight, Arnold asked TWA to start flying the North Atlantic, and Bryan assigned three of the Stratoliners to this route—from the east coast to England and beyond, via Gander and Prestwick, Scotland. By the fall of 1942, TWA was operating not only C-87s over the Atlantic but brand-new C-54s and C-54As. The big Douglas transports were welcome additions, especially the latter which were built specifically for ATC/NATS operations. The first C-54s to go into ICD service were basic DC-4s, originally ordered by United and American, and converted into cargo aircraft. The C-54A had a beefed-up metal floor and a large door, ideal for loading cargo, on the port side of the aft fuselage. Extra fuel tanks behind the cockpit held 2500 gallons, and maximum gross takeoff weight was 70,000 pounds— 5000 more than the standard C-54.

Ed Betts, a senior TWA captain who after retirement became the airline's unofficial historian, provided one of the best descriptions of the C-54's interior as it appeared to its wartime occupants:

"The crew and cockpit area had its own 'john,' a small compartment for storing the ever-present box lunches and coffee jugs, and crew rest bunks. The cargo or passenger area did not have sound-proofing; metal benches ran the length of the cabin walls. At regular intervals a major depression was made in the benches for passenger [bucket] seats. Nobody ever figured out who the model might have been for the size of the depression, since it didn't fit the average size fanny and was *very* uncomfortable. The wide aisle generally resembled a sloppy dormitory with sacks of mail or cargo tied in the center along with suitcases, duffel bags, blanket rolls, and other paraphernalia arranged to make a comfortable spot to take a nap."

The C-54 was about fifty miles an hour faster than the Stratoliner, roomier, and pilots loved the added advantage of its tricycle landing gear. The 307's single gear created problems on the heavily loaded ICD flights, for the Stratoliner was nose-heavy to begin with and the problem was even worse in its military configuration, due to the four extra fuel tanks in the forward cabin. On any heavily loaded 307 flight, no one in the cabin could sit down during takeoffs because all passengers and nonflying crew members had to stand as close to the cockpit as possible; this was the only way to get the tail wheel off the ground during the takeoff roll. Former ICD purser Russ Robbins recalled that the cabin occupants couldn't start returning to their seats for an hour after takeoff.

"They'd return in order of rank," Robbins added. "If there was a general on board, he'd be the first to sit down. After about two hours, everybody finally got a seat. But if you had to go to the john, which was in the rear section, somebody else had to go forward to balance the trim. That Stratoliner was really something. You never took off like in a normal airplane. You just bounced and bounced until it bounced high enough to raise the gear."

But these were skin blemishes on the Stratoliner's overall reputation for durability, reliability, and safety. The B-307 may have been a son of a bitch to get off the ground, but once in the air it was quite an airplane. To its takeoff difficulties should be added the story of one Stratoliner that made seventeen round-trips over the South Atlantic in three weeks, the eastbound flights carrying fuses for antitank shells needed by British General Montgomery's forces at El Alamein.

ATC had spread the word on Pan Am's speed-enhancing experiment with unpainted C-54s, and TWA removed the olive drab from all such aircraft. That the practice added a modest five mph to the cruising speed must have galled Jack Frye. Every time he looked at a C-54 he could only think of what might have been if war hadn't interfered. TWA had ordered DC-4s but as early as 1938, even before the first Stratoliner was delivered, he and Hughes had been working secretly with Lockheed on the design of the Constellation, a four-engine, 300-mph fully pressurized airliner that would have done to the DC-4 what the DC-2 did to the Boeing 247: render it obsolete overnight. The triple-tailed Lockheed transport, actually faster than the early models of the swift Japanese Zero fighter and still considered one of the most beautiful airliners ever built, was almost ready for TWA's transcontinental service when the Japanese hit Pearl Harbor; every Constellation that would move down a Burbank assembly line was immediately earmarked for the Army, which designated them as C-69s.

But trust Howard Hughes to upstage even the United States Army in the middle of a world war. This was an airliner considered so important to Lockheed's own future that the manufacturer had borrowed Boeing's Eddie Allen, regarded as the finest and most experienced test pilot on four-engine aircraft in the world, to make the first flight. After the initial test flights, Hughes talked Lockheed into loaning him the airplane and on April 17, 1944, he and Jack Frye took off from Burbank and flew nonstop to Washington, D.C., setting a new transcontinental record of six hours and fifty-eight minutes. The ICD division had provided him with a flight engineer, navigator, and radio operator, while he shared the piloting duties with Frye. Reportedly they had an angry argument before takeoff over who would fly the first leg, and Hughes seems to have won; Frye didn't take over the controls until they were over eastern Kansas, approximately halfway.

The Air Corps didn't object to the flight—they thought it was good publicity for its new transport—but not until the big airliner landed at Washington National Airport did the military brass learn that Hughes had ordered the Connie painted in TWA colors. There were double red stripes on the three tails, TWA in large letters on both sides of the rear fuselage and the wings, and the old prewar slogan THE TRANSCONTINENTAL LINE gleamed above the cabin windows just as in peacetime. Air Corps officials were furious when they saw the Constellation land at National—a flying billboard for an airline that didn't even own the plane.

True, the paint used wasn't real paint, but easily washable watercolors. But the Army was peeved anyway. There is reason to believe Hughes did it not only to boost TWA but also as a thumb-nosing gesture in the direction of Hap Arnold. He disliked the general intensely, considering him more of a politician than a soldier, and the ill-feeling was mutual—the pair had more than one shouting match during the occasions when their paths crossed. Howard's incorrigibility even went beyond the paint scheme episode; he was supposed to turn the Connie over to the Army immediately after the flight, but somehow he managed to keep it for a few more days while he took various government officials on demonstration rides.

Frye had assigned nine hostesses to serve snacks on the demonstration flights but Hughes, who was in a foul mood (reportedly because actress Ava Gardner had turned down his invitation to go on the record flight), refused to have any women on the plane—including hostesses. Many of them, in fact, resented the Army's ban on female flight attendants aboard ICD aircraft, and there were many times when the hard-working pursers would have welcomed their help.

Pursers were not only responsible for serving meals on the long Atlantic flights but for buying the food in the first place. Russ Robbins found this out just before his first ICD flight—the Stratoliner was brand-new to him and a TWA commissary manager was showing him the aircraft's galley with its cooking utensils, pots and pans, and three hot plates.

"Great, but where's the food?" Russ asked.

"There isn't any on board. You're the guy responsible for buying it."

There wasn't time to go grocery shopping, so Robbins talked a soft-hearted Army mess sergeant out of enough meat and bread for sandwiches that fed his passengers until they reached Gander nine hours later. At Gander he scrounged additional supplies that sufficed for the more-than-fifteen-hour flight to Prestwick—a fully loaded 307 often averaged only 130 mph.

"We pursers would spend most of our layovers buying food for our next flight," Robbins related. "Some of it was hard to get—you needed ration coupons for sugar, for example, and TWA didn't have any coupons to give us. We'd go from store to store bargaining and begging, picking up whatever we could. Inevitably, we had to rely on the black market. One thing in plentiful supply was canned fruit cocktails which you could buy in large cans. Occasionally we'd acquire a black market turkey, chicken, or ham. I'd take it home and my landlady would let me cook the night before a flight. I used a file cabinet to pack the food and I'd take the cabinet out to the airport the next day."

If the pursers had it rough at times, ICD's mechanics had equal reason to wonder if even the infantry might have been easier. There were constant debates over the relative hardships to be suffered at the African vs. Brazilian bases, the ICD facility at Natal usually drawing the most votes. John Cooper, a TWA welder, was en route to Africa on a C-87, but when they landed at Natal to refuel for the South Atlantic crossing, the base supervisor had heard there was a skilled welder aboard and pulled him off the plane.

"We need you here," he told Cooper.

Cooper had heard some horror stories about life in Natal, sheer boredom rating high on the list of complaints. "I'd rather go to Africa," he pleaded in vain. Sorrowfully, he watched the C-87 take off, leaving behind the luckiest welder in ICD—the same C-87 disappeared later that day, with no trace of its fate. And Cooper, who some time after the war became TWA's vice president of maintenance, always remembered the Natal assignment more for mechanics' exploits than the base's living conditions.

"Actually, it was tolerable if you could get used to eating not much more than Spam," Cooper said. "Natal itself was gorgeous, with a great beach. The flights would leave about 9 P.M., heading for Ascension Island (in the Azores). We had about a dozen mechanics there plus a few passenger agents and clerks. The first thing we learned was how to steal stuff off airplanes, and we learned how to improvise. For example, a C-54 came through one day and it needed exhaust ball joints for a sick engine. Hell, I don't think there was a ball joint replacement within a radius of two thousand miles. So another mechanic and I worked all night scrounging through piles of spare parts. We finally found some old joints which we pruned down to fit an R-2000 engine.

"There were always some wrecked airplanes around. If a plane came in with some faulty part you usually could cannibalize one out of a wreck. But even cannibalizing had its limits, so we'd resort to stealing stuff from aircraft parked there overnight by military transients. A pilot would leave his airplane and go off to get some sleep. He'd come back the next morning and find it had a wheel missing. The stealing got so bad that ATC crews started leaving a guard by their airplane all night long."

Union rules didn't apply to the ICD stations like Natal, the mechanics working from ten to twelve hours a day. The shifts varied; a man might be on duty only four or five hours on one shift and then work unrelieved stretches of twenty-four hours. For entertainment, the Natal base had a makeshift movie theater, and the town of Natal wasn't too far away. Its main attractions were the Staff House, the hotel where the ICD flight crews stayed, and the Wonder Bar, which all TWA, Pan Am, and Eastern ATC alumini remember with mixed feelings.

It was a combined watering hole and occasional brothel, periodically raided by the local police or U.S. Marine MPs who constituted the base security force. Downstairs were a bar and dance floor, and upstairs were a few bedrooms reached by "the longest staircase in South America," to quote one Natal veteran. The back of the building had a second-floor balcony from where the Pan Am flying boats could be seen taking off or landing on a nearby river.

The ICD mechanics were as colorful and resourceful as the flight crews. There was Red McKenny, who reached his assigned ICD base in Africa after spending thirty-seven days on what apparently was the slowest freighter in the Merchant Marine. Red was confronted one day with a balky engine that wouldn't start. The trouble was diagnosed as a failed condensor, and the next ICD plane carrying spare parts wasn't due for another week. So Red built a makeshift condensor out of an empty sardine can. This was rated an even better job of improvision than the one performed by a TWA flight engineer whose Stratoliner was rendered hors de combat by an inoperative starter. The crew faced being temporarily marooned at the remote military base where they were grounded, until the flight engineer noticed a captured German bomber on the premises. An hour later the Stratoliner was taking off, thanks to a starter the flight engineer had filched from the enemy aircraft and hastily retooled to fit a B-307.

The Stratoliners were frequently blowing cylinders, a habit at which the Natal ground crews took personal offense—any grounded ICD airplane was an unacceptable sight. One of the base supervisors, Jack Robinson, was convinced that the cylinder headaches could be traced to sloppy engine overhauls by the ICD maintenance base in Washington. He hitched a ride on a northbound ICD flight so he could personally supervise a major overhaul on the four engines of a Stratoliner scheduled to head back to Natal as soon as the overhaul was finished. A test hop was perfect, and Robinson decided to go back to Natal on the same airplane, confident he had set a perfect example for engine overhauls.

They got as far as Richmond, Virginia, only 100 miles from Washington, when a cylinder blew.

Perhaps the most famous and officially honored ICD mechanic was a chunky, cigar-smoking maintenance supervisor named Roy Davis. He started with ICD early in 1942 as a mechanic in Washington and was asked if he'd serve overseas "for a couple of weeks." He spent the rest of the war supervising aircraft repairs at seven wartime overseas bases—Goose Bay in Labrador, Stations BW-1 and BW-8 on Greenland, Stevenville and Gander in Newfoundland, Casablanca, and the Azores. One base commander, writing to General Charles Jeter, who headed ATC's North Atlantic Division, praised Davis in language that would have earned a military man some kind of medal:

"Regardless of the time, day or night, (he) was always available and willing to aid in any maintenance work, not only on his own carrier's aircraft but on any aircraft that might be experiencing difficulty . . . Furthermore, Mr. Davis has been instrumental in the training of inexperienced [Air Corps] mechanics at this station to the degree that their proficiency on C-54 type aircraft is unexcelled.''

Davis received commendations from Jeter and another ATC general, A.W. Kissner, but he was to value them no higher than the postwar honor he received from the Air Line Pilots Association. He was one of the first four men awarded honorary lifetime memberships in ALPA. The others were Lindbergh, Doolittle, and Rickenbacker, Davis being the sole nonpilot. He also turned out to be the most famous mechanic in airline history. After the war, he seemed to be making a career out of freeing airplanes that had become mired in deep mud or snow—the first one was a TWA Connie that had landed in Paris in a heavy fog and skidded off the runway into thick muddy clay.

After watching futile efforts to pull it loose, Davis chomped down on his ever-present cigar and growled, ''I'm gonna fly the damned thing out.''

Which he did, by gunning the engines until they howled in protest. Reassigned to domestic stations, he repeated the feat at Chicago's O'Hare, driving a 707 and two Convair 880s out of snowbanks. An author doing research for an aviation novel heard about Davis, interviewed him, and that was how Arthur Hailey's fictitious ''Joe Patroni'' entered literary and film history as the TWA mechanic in *Airport.*

After Otis Bryan's brilliant organization of ICD earned him promotion to vice president of War Projects, Cliff Mutchler—director of cabin service—headed the division before being transferred back to domestic operations. His successor was Hal Blackburn, a slim, veteran captain with a dapper mustache whose appearance tended to confirm an industry suspicion: that due to the Howard Hughes influence, most TWA pilots looked like Greek gods who had obviously been recruited from Central Casting.

Blackburn was indeed a handsome man, but he also was one of the toughest, most rule-abiding, and demanding bosses any airline possessed. As ICD's chief, he won the respect of all TWA's pilots, including those free souls who considered him a company-minded martinet. Like Bryan, Blackie never asked an airman to do anything he wouldn't do himself. He had flown many ICD missions personally and continued to fly them even after he took over the division. On one ICD flight, he was trying to duck under German radar and came down so low that the ocean waves were slapping against the airplane's belly and salt spray covered the windshield.

At one point it came to Jack Frye's attention that Blackburn had authorized TWA planes to fly over the German V-bomb experimental center at Peenemünde on the Baltic coast. He summoned Blackburn and demanded an explanation.

"We've been taking pictures of the installation," Blackie confessed.

"Jesus, Blackie, it would be very serious if we had a TWA pilot shot down or captured."

"We won't do it anymore," Blackburn promised.

"You'd damned well better not. By the way, did you get any pictures?"

"Yes, sir," Blackburn said proudly.

Frye grinned. "Keep it to yourself."

On another occasion, Blackburn was told TWA had to ferry a C-87 to Miami for delivery to Pan Am. He couldn't find an available crew, so he ferried the big airplane himself—solo.

"If Bryan had found out about it, he would have fired me retroactively," Blackburn said later. "But hell, we did some crazy things in wartime."

But Hal Blackburn could be unforgiving of pilot transgressions. Captain Al Sherwood was commanding a C-54 on a North Atlantic ICD passenger flight and all four engines quit when the carburetors iced up. He came down to a lower altitude and got them restarted. The passengers not only applauded, but several wrote Blackburn letters praising Sherwood's skill in saving them from probable death. Blackburn called Sherwood to his office.

"You dumb son of a bitch!" he scolded. "If you had shot alcohol into those carburetors, they wouldn't have iced up—and now you're a goddamned hero!"

Blackie tried hard not to play favorites among the ICD airmen, but he had a few captains he particularly liked—such as Larry Chippiano and Milo Campbell. No one could figure this out, because Campbell and Chippiano were as far apart in personality as the North and South poles are geographically. Larry's ICD crews could have passed a Saturday morning inspection at West Point.

Yet although he insisted on a spit-and-polish operation, from shined shoes to spotless aircraft interiors, copilots, flight engineers, navigators and radio operators would tell Blackburn, "That Captain Chippiano's real tough, but can I fly with him again?"

Campbell dressed like the cowboy he was before learning to fly, and he walked like one, with a pronounced bowlegged Western waddle. A typical Milo Campbell ICD crew resembled four kitchen sinks filled with unwashed dishes. But every man who flew with him would ask Blackburn the same question: "Can I fly with him again?"

(Chippiano died during the war of a heart attack on his fortieth birthday, a few hours after taking Orville Wright for a ride in a Constellation. Milo survived the war but was killed in a crash while riding as a passenger on a survey flight in Ethiopia.)

A host of VIP names appeared on ICD manifests: FDR, France's Charles de Gaulle, presidential advisor Harry Hopkins, Generals Marshall, Bradley, Eisenhower, Arnold, Stilwell, and Patton, Admirals King and Leahy, Jimmy Doolittle, the Chiang Kai-sheks, King Peter II of Yugoslavia, Queen Wilhelmina of the Netherlands, Secretary of War Stimson, and Ambassador Joseph Davies on his famous "Mission to Moscow."

Patton was on one of the many ICD flights conducted in such secrecy that even the captain wasn't briefed on its full itinerary until after takeoff. Operating under secret orders, the C-54 flew a load of military brass—with briefcases chained to their wrists—from England to Casablanca, where the next day Captain Joe Carr and his crew were restricted to the cockpit area while a large column of Army vehicles delivered a new batch of passengers. After takeoff, Carr was informed they were to proceed nonstop to Prestwick.

It was a long flight, but no one in the cockpit still knew who was on board until the middle of the night, when there was a rap on the cockpit door. A high-pitched voice asked permission to come in—it was Patton, who explained he owned and flew a small Cessna and would like to see the C-54's far more complicated instrument panel.

"Especially your Artificial Horizon. All I got on my Cessna is the standard needle and ball. Besides," he added with a smile, "I'm getting goddamned bored sitting back there."

Carr let Patton sit in the copilot's seat and explained the workings of the Artificial Horizon and other instruments unfamiliar to a private pilot. He also let the fiery general handle the controls for a while. As Patton finally got up to leave, he asked the crew not to disclose his presence on the flight or that of his staff. Later they learned Patton was being transferred from North Africa to England, where he was to begin training tank units for the Normandy invasion. And after the war, they also learned that as soon as Patton boarded their ICD flight, the Army had an actor, a look-alike double, parading around Tunis posing as the general.

ICD also got involved, quite innocently and indirectly, in the media and political flap that erupted when FDR's son Elliot, a highly respected Air Corps colonel with an exemplary war record, used an ICD plane to ship a dog named Blaze from England to his wife in the States. Somehow, Blaze was assigned a Priority 1, which was reserved for members of the president's immediate family (see Chapter Nine) and the dog apparently bumped a returning serviceman off the plane. For Republican congressmen and the anti-administration press, the incident was manna from heaven. In the middle of all the furor, the Pentagon issued an order prohibiting dogs from being carried on any ATC aircraft, whether airline or military operated.

Then came the Battle of the Bulge, and the Army discovered that it was extremely difficult to evacuate casualties from the snow-covered battle zone. So orders were issued to ship a dozen dog teams with sleds and drivers from station BW-1 in Greenland, and an ATC C-54A flown by a military crew landed there to pick them up. But the aircraft also was carrying important cargo that couldn't be off-loaded, and there was room for only eleven of the dog teams. At that point, an ICD C-54 heading for Prestwick landed at BW-1 with space for the twelfth team. And that's when the fun began.

Dogs, sled, and driver boarded the TWA plane, whose captain had strict orders not to tell Prestwick what and who he was carrying—for some reason, the Army didn't want the Germans to know about the dog teams. When a ground radio operator in Greenland sent Prestwick a message anyway, it was garbled in the transmission; relayed to the ATC base at Prestwick, it read: "Expect woof-woof and attendants on Mess House Dog."

The message, in return, was handed to the base commander who did some translating of his own. He apparently interpreted "Mess House" as meaning "White House," he figured "woof-woof" and "dog" must refer to Fala, President Roosevelt's pet

Scottie, and he therefore deduced that FDR himself must be on the ICD plane.

The C-54 landed at Prestwick to be greeted by a hastily convened honor guard, immaculate in white gloves and helmets. A special loading ramp normally used for boarding or deplaning ambulatory patients had been rolled out to accommodate the polio-crippled President. It was debatable who was more surprised: the TWA crew at the reception, or the base commander, when the aircraft disembarked a full team of barking Alaskan huskies, a large sled, and a bewildered driver.

If occasional humor is a part of war, however, so is tragedy. Of the forty-five TWA flight crew members who died flying for ATC, six of those deaths were the result of the worst kind of fatal mistake: friendly fire. On March 25, 1944, a TWA C-54A flying between the Azores and Casablanca flew over a convoy escorted by two U.S. "jeep" carriers. Navy fighters intercepted the ICD plane, came close enough to identify it as an ATC aircraft, and flew away. But a few minutes later, British fighters jumped the unarmed transport and shot it down. One of the RAF pilots later claimed credit for destroying a German Focke-Wulf 200 patrol bomber.

The gallant Stratoliners plodded across the Atlantic on ATC missions almost until the end of the war. TWA's five B-307s alone logged more than 21,000 transatlantic flying hours, while achieving a perfect safety record. Overall, TWA ranked fourth in total ATC operational hours, behind American, United, and Pan Am; the airline's total profit from all wartime contracts was only $181,900. But ICD contributed more to the Atlantic airlift than planes and people; it was one of three wartime partners who developed and proved the practicality of "pressure pattern" flying: taking advantage of prevailing winds and the most favorable weather for minimum flight time, instead of just choosing the shortest distance over an extended course.

TWA assigned a specially equipped C-54A to the project, dispatching it across the North Atlantic day after day with an Army and TWA meteorologist aboard, charting wind and weather patterns by using a new radio altimeter which made it possible to determine significant changes in barometric pressure systems. By following these patterns, the "weather planes" could transmit current weather and wind data to Gander, where it would be relayed to all affected flights. Because the weather research flights were not only long but conducted over some of the most desolate terrain in the world, and more frequently during the winter months, each aircraft carried arctic survival equipment: parachutes, heavy clothing and boots, sleeping bags, emergency rations, and rifles. ATC itself credited this research for its ability to fly the North Atlantic the year round, rather than being forced to shift operations to the more circuitous routing over the South Atlantic to Africa.

The pressure pattern flying in standard use today is basically what ICD and its two partners developed during the war. One of the weather research partners was the Air Transport Command. The other was the airline C.R. Smith had left for ATC duty.

American Airlines

"Of all the big U.S. domestic carriers, American Airlines's [wartime] role was the most varied."

That quote, by eminent aviation historian R.E.G. Davies, in his *Airlines of the United States Since 1914,* is an accurate appraisal of how the symbolic Eagle of AA went to war.

Its pilots and ground crews served ATC and the Navy over the North and South Atlantic, the CBI theater, and the dreaded Hump, the Pacific, Alaska, and the continental United States. Its aircraft flew every type of mission from cargo and personnel flights to weather research, from medical evacuations to route surveys and range-stretching experiments. It put floats on C-47s. And it was one of the carriers that declined the usual cost-plus-fixed-fee contracts— American netted $16.5 million during the war, but not one cent of that profit came from its ATC operations; all its war contracts were performed at cost.

American and Northeast were the principal contributors to the establishment of the North Atlantic airlift, AA being the second carrier to launch survey flights over the Great Circle route adopted by ATC. On a chilly day in February 1942, *Flagship Cleveland* waddled to a stop at La Guardia, discharged the last civilian passengers this particular DC-3 would carry for a long time, and then was taxied to Hangar 5, where it went through the denuding process for transformation into an Army transport. For the next few weeks, mechanics swarmed over the airplane, installing such unfamiliar equipment as extra fuel tanks, a radio room, a plywood table for a navigator, survival gear including snowshoes and two rifles, parachutes, life rafts, fishing lines, and medical kits.

Not for almost two months was the job finished. On April 24, the former *Flagship Cleveland* took off for Presque Isle, Maine, one of the old Ferrying Command's first bases. Aboard was a handpicked seven-man crew that included a pair of million-mile captains—H.G. "Robby" Robinson and Frank Bledsoe—and the airline's chief meteorologist, C.E. "Doc" Buell. Frank Ware, chief of maintenance at La Guardia, had assigned to this important flight a man he considered to be the best mechanic around—namely Frank Ware. It was said of Ware that he was one of the few men in aviation who could start a balky engine without invoking the name of the diety, either in prayer or in vain. Commanding the expedition was Dan Beard, American's chief engineering pilot and one of its top technical experts.

The mission, ordered by C.R. himself as one of his last acts before joining ATC, was to supplement the earlier Northeast Airlines survey flight to determine the practicality of a regular North Atlantic airlift. The navigator assigned to the AA survey, C.H. McIntosh, wanted to use a highly touted new $500 drift indicator designed for the Army, but permission was refused. So he and young Dixon Speas, a genuine Mr. Fixit assigned to the airline's engineering department, built an improvised indicator out of a ruled celluloid disk they mounted in the floor near the navigator's table; McIntosh gleefully claimed it worked better than the Army's $500 model.

Within weeks of the survey flight's confirmation of Northeast's cautious optimism about flying the North Atlantic, the first of thousands of ATC flights were spanning the Great Circle route. By mid 1945, American alone had made some 7000 North Atlantic crossings, and at the peak of ATC operations its C-54s were averaging almost 500 flights a month.

Before the airlift could reach such proportions in four-engine airplanes, whose speed and range literally shrank the North Atlantic, American first had to figure out how to stretch a DC-3's range for transatlantic military operations. Allowable gross weight was a key factor; maximum DC-3 gross weight in normal airline service was slightly over 25,000 pounds—too low for a military cargo flight. So Dan Beard ran a series of flight tests at La Guardia to determine how much additional weight the airplane could safely carry, gradually increasing the gross in increments of 500 pounds until he got up to 30,000 pounds. At that point, he set the new maximum at 29,500 pounds, "to give the boys a little margin," as he put it, although in actual service many of the converted DC-3s were flown routinely at more than 31,000 pounds.

Then Beard handed Dixon Speas another assignment: how can the pilots stretch a DC-3's (or C-47's) range when they're taking off in an airplane that's almost two and a half tons heavier than normal? Speas developed a series of charts and graphs that established new "cruise control" power settings and fuel mixtures for every phase of every North Atlantic DC-3 flight, taking into account such factors such as winds, payload, altitudes, etc. Initially, his goal was to attain maximum miles per gallon. Later he modified these procedures to "maximum ton miles per hour," which meant the airplane would consume more fuel, but would get to its destination faster. The operating procedures he created for American were adopted by the Airline War Training Institute for general use.

While writing the book on range-stretching, Speas started pestering Beard to let him go out on one of the ATC survey flights so he could judge firsthand whether he was on the right track with all these new procedures.

"Absolutely not!" Beard ruled. "You go out and get yourself killed and there won't be anyone around who can finish all those charts and graphs."

Operating on the principle that the squeaking wheel gets the most grease, Speas kept nagging, pleading, and arguing until Beard finally relented, but with a stern warning:

"All right! All right! But don't go beyond Greenland. Do you understand, Dix? Do not go beyond Greenland!"

So Speas boarded a converted DC-3 for Greenland, via Presque Isle, Botwood in Newfoundland, and Goose Bay, arriving at BW-8 (BW for Bluie West, the code name for the U.S. military base on Greenland's west coast) to be greeted by the base commander, who turned out to be Colonel Bernt Balchen, the famed Norwegian arctic explorer and pilot; he had flown against the Germans while in the Norwegian Air Force, and had joined the U.S. Army after the Nazis occupied Norway.

From BW-8, Speas flew to BW-1, another air base that had been established in southern Greenland, and here he encountered none other than Ernie Gann, the American Airlines captain who was now flying ATC contract flights and had just landed at BW-1. Gann grabbed Speas as soon as he spotted him.

"Dix, I think one of my engines needs an overhaul. Can you take a look at it?"

Speas had Army mechanics remove the cowling on the suspect engine, found no telltale trace of oil leaks, and reported his findings to Gann.

"Ernie, I figure that engine's about thirty-five hours overdue for a tear-down, but I don't think it'll give you any trouble. Where do you go from here?"

"Reykjavík, Iceland," Gann said. Then he added, with a wry grin that was more of a challenge, "Come on—go with us."

Speas knew exactly what Gann was saying without saying it: If Speas thought that engine was okay, prove it by coming along.

Ignoring Beard's stern admonition, Speas did go along, and discovered that flying the North Atlantic included some risks that couldn't be avoided by opening an operations manual and studying some graph; before they landed at Reykjavík, American almost lost a highly respected young technical expert and a captain who was destined to become a famous author.

Gann let Dixon occupy the left seat and fly the Greenland-Iceland leg, Speas having acquired some cockpit experience as part of his job. As they approached the British base at Reykjavík, Dixon requested landing clearance. All he got was silence.

"They're not answering, Ernie," he worried. "They've gone off the air."

Gann took over the controls and tried to raise the Reykjavík tower himself. Still no response. They couldn't land without clearance, and when Gann decided to head for their alternate—Stornoway in northernmost Scotland—he was advised that the field there was under air attack and closed. Nor was there any chance of returning to Greenland—there wasn't enough fuel.

Gann decided to violate regulations, and headed for the runway. At that point, what seemed to be the beams from every searchlight in Iceland impaled the DC-3. Frantically, copilot Cotton Johnson flashed the coded identification "signal of the day" on an Aldis lamp and kept repeating it until Gann landed. As the DC-3 rolled to a stop, it was met by a British army staff car whose driver yelled, "The commanding officer of this airfield wishes to see the captain of this aircraft immediately!"

Ernie returned a few minutes later with the explanation for their reception. Someone in Greenland dispatch had forgotten to notify Reykjavík that the flight was en route. This in itself wouldn't have been so serious, except that the British thought their plane might be a captured KLM DC-3 trying to pull off a sneak bombing raid.

"Captain Gann," the commander remarked, "every gun on the base was focused on you. If you had so much as backfired, we would have shot you down. By the way, I don't know whether you noticed that cruiser at the mouth of the harbor, but last week it shot down two friendly aircraft."

Speas, at least, had the satisfaction of seeing that his procedures really did work and he modified them later to apply to larger aircraft, like the C-87 and C-54. But no set of figures could guarantee complete safety; between those early first survey flights and the aircraft armada of the later war years, lay many tales of adversity and adventure. And one of the most dramatic involved an American C-87 commanded by Captain Owen "Chuck" O'Connor, westbound early in 1943—before the North Atlantic route had been fully developed—from England with the usual ATC Liberator crew of five—two pilots, navigator, radio operator, and flight engineer/ mechanic. As far as O'Connor was concerned, his cargo was more precious than a load of gold bullion: he had on board seventeen battle-weary soldiers returning to the U.S., seven of them for medical treatment and rest.

Almost the entire flight was spent battling stiff head winds and ice, the latter so severe that O'Connor was forced to descend from 18,000 feet to warmer air at only 3000. But at the lower altitude, the C-87 was gulping fuel voraciously, and as they neared the Canadian coast, O'Connor knew they were running into trouble. At 3000 feet, they were in an overcast and the navigator had only two brief glimpses of the stars—not enough time in which to take bearings. Their can of worms opened wider when the freak weather conditions began producing false radio navigation signals; O'Connor was homing in on a station west of the one he thought he was contacting.

By this time they had reached landfall, but all four engines were running on not much more than fumes. He sent one final radio message before deciding he had to gamble on a forced landing:

"Low on gas. I've got to land the ship. Landing on uncharted lake."

At dusk, taking advantage of what daylight was left, he put the

C-87 down with incredible smoothness on an ice-covered lake some-where in the wilds of northern Quebec. The date was February 4. The good news was that no one got a scratch and the airplane was unharmed. Fortunately for their morale, they didn't know the bad news: they were going to be marooned on that frozen lake for the next thirty-two days.

What happened was a grim application of Murphy's Law—every-thing that could go wrong, did. The day after they landed, O'Con-nor and his navigator took solar sights to establish their position, without realizing that the bitter cold had damaged their octant. The position they radioed to the ATC at Presque Isle was miles off. They got a break, however, when their signal was picked up by two search planes whose pilots instinctively ignored the erroneous position report and homed in on the C-87's battery-operated trans-mitter, using their unerring radio direction finders. The ordeal might have ended right then and there, but before the search planes could reach the downed aircraft, O'Connor's battery failed. Low on fuel, the searchers had to turn back.

A third search plane actually stumbled on the lake a few hours later, and dropped supplies. Again, their troubles should have been over—except for a blizzard that swept into the area and grounded all rescue efforts for the next three days. When the search was renewed, the C-87 was covered with snow and almost impossible to spot from the air. Not until February 10 did the air probes sight the marooned party. A C-47 piloted by Ernie Gann and Breezy Wynne dropped fresh supplies and radioed the position to the rest of the searching aircraft. O'Connor and his half-frozen charges figured they had it made. After Gann's sighting report, other planes arrived and began circling the lake.

One of them was a Northeast C-47 commanded by Fred Lord, who decided to land and fly the whole party out. He figured if a C-87 could get down on that lake, he should have it even easier with the smaller C-47. What Lord hadn't taken into account, how-ever, was the deceptive amount of snow that the blizzard had dropped. He did land safely, but he came to an abrupt stop after rolling only a couple of hundred feet.

"I'm stuck," he radioed helplessly. Now "Lac O'Connor," as it was dubbed later, had two stranded airplanes and three more marooned men.

The following day, another blizzard struck, dumping another

six inches of snow. Lord figured out a way to fashion a makeshift snowplow out of assorted parts from the two planes and they staked out a runway outline. Eight men pulled the improvised plow trying to clear away enough snow for a takeoff attempt, but even working in shifts they made little headway. The men were terribly weakened by temperatures that at one point dropped to seventy degrees below zero.

Each morning, O'Connor held sick call and treated mushrooming cases of frostbite as best he could. The captain in his airline days was known as a rather easygoing, friendly man who seldom pulled rank on young copilots even though he was one of American's most seasoned veterans, with more than 20,000 logged flying hours. Now he seemed to be drawing on inner resources and strengths he himself didn't know he possessed; he went out of his way to sound optimistic and keep morale up.

All that saved them was the fact that at least ATC knew where they were, although all the frustrated rescue pilots could do was continue dropping survival supplies and equipment: sleeping bags, tents, stoves, warm clothing, axes, shovels, boots, and even blow torches. The sleeping bags were lifesavers; it was so cold each man used two.

O'Connor appropriated the C-87's cabin as a storage place for the food planes kept dropping: ham, beef, bread, beans, and flour for hotcakes. It was a vast improvement over their fare for the first few days, when a typical meal consisted of one can of soup in a pot of boiling water, to which had been added the defeathered carcasses of small birds. One soup pot contained an owl one of the men had shot. Nourishment and better protection from the freezing weather did the trick. On February 26, enough men had gained sufficient strength to clear what passed as a runway. On that day, a ski-equipped C-47 managed to land and take off again with the seven wounded soldiers. But weather continued to harass the rescue attempts and it was not until March 6 that the last of the men were taken off the frozen lake—O'Connor was among them.

Miraculously, there were no serious medical consequences; O'Connor, whose courage and discipline had played such a large role in their survival, had only one complaint: he was suffering from sunburn. A few weeks later, as the weather turned warmer, Ernie Gann's copilot—Breezy Wynne—returned to the lake with a crew, filled up the C-87's tanks, and flew it back to La Guardia for an overhaul. When the airplane was returned to its ATC transatlantic schedules, it carried a new name beneath the cockpit windows:

LAC O'CONNOR.

There was a further sequel to the ordeal of Captain O'Connor and his men. Ernie Gann turned this true story into a novel, *Island in the Sky*, and it also was made into a film starring John Wayne.

Gann was one of those rare men who seemed to excel in anything he tried. An accomplished musician, a talented artist, and a skilled, sensitive writer, he also was an excellent pilot—a kind of latter-day Antoine de Saint-Exupery. He flew many missions for ATC and was typical of those senior airline pilots who could be extremely pragmatic about facing the dangers of the North Atlantic.

When American began acquiring C-54s for its North Atlantic ATC schedules, Dixon Speas worked forty-eight consecutive hours without sleep, preparing manuals on emergency procedures for the new plane. The morning after he finished, he encountered Gann, who was standing in front of his locker in La Guardia operations. They knew each other well long before their Reykjavík experience, and only recently Speas had been Ernie's instructor in C-54 ground school.

With pride of authorship, Dixon handed Gann the new manual. "What's this all about?" Gann asked.

"Dammit, Ernie, it tells you what to do in an emergency."

Gann smiled. "You gave us all that stuff in ground school, Dix."

"Sure, but this is all written down."

Gann thumbed through the pages, pausing to examine some of Dixon's complicated graphs and charts. "And what's all this stuff?"

"Well, those tell you what to do if you lose an engine—how far you can go, fuel management, power settings on the remaining three, and so on."

Gann smiled again. "Do you suppose we could go up to flight control, and you give me the power settings for four segments of about three hours each, assuming everything's working right?"

"Sure."

"Fine. Now we can put this manual where it won't do any harm." He opened his locker, shoved in the manual, and closed the door. Then he put his arm around Speas. "You know, Dix, that damned thing could hurt somebody. If I get into an emergency, I'm not going to have time to look something up in a book. I've got to remember what you've already told me or I'm lost."

Ernie also was an inventor of sorts. He eventually transferred from the North Atlantic airlift to the South Atlantic airlift operated out of Natal, and on one trip was complaining to a fellow pilot about the smoke bombs they carried, used for checking wind drift over water.

"They don't work half the time," Gann groused. "The government's charging American two hundred bucks for every bomb and I'll bet I could make a better one and a hell of a lot cheaper."

A few weeks later, he had built a prototype that looked so promising, he wrote the War Department that he could produce a $20 bomb that would work ninety percent of the time. Much to his surprise, the Army sent him a contract and told him to go ahead, but Gann was too busy flying and never did anything about it.

Ernie was only one of the colorful American pilots who flew for the Air Transport Command. At the top of the Interesting Characters' list was a diminutive veteran captain named Si Bittner, easily the airline's most notorious practical joker, and perhaps the most fiendish in the entire industry. He pulled them on fellow pilots, stewardesses, and even passengers, and the latter included a woman sitting in a forward window seat on one of Bittner's prewar DC-3 flights.

She heard something banging on her window and, startled, looked up to see a chicken bone tied to a long string. Quite naturally, she screamed, and the stewardess sprinted to the cockpit to report this unique menace to air safety. There she found Captain Bittner, still unwinding a long piece of string through his open side window, and wondering out loud if he had enough string to reach row seven.

Not even war could suppress his sense of humor. He got off a C-54 at Prestwick and started pulling a long pole out of a cargo hatch. A mystified mechanic asked him what the pole was for.

"Well," Bittner explained, "I've heard there are British women who wouldn't touch an ATC pilot with a ten-foot pole, so I brought along an eleven-foot pole."

It was another AA North Atlantic captain who formed the Honorary Order of the F.B.I.—which stood for Frozen Bastards of Iceland. The informal organization boasted members from every crew exposed to the route's wintery blasts, including one C-87 pilot who radioed Prestwick his aircraft was experiencing strange vibrations. He sent the flight engineer back to look for the source, which turned out to be passengers stamping their feet to keep warm. The F.B.I.'s reputation for Spartan endurance was slightly tarnished when some members complained that when they arrived at La Guardia, New York City was colder than Iceland.

If things were tough for the North Atlantic air crews, the ground crews deserved equal respect and even more sympathy. Winters at the North Atlantic ATC bases could be brutal, yet the mechanics who manned them were all volunteers; the quartet of American's maintenance supervisors who opened many of the airline's ATC stations collectively were to compile eight years of foreign service, cross the ocean thirty times, and work in thirteen different countries.

Goose Bay, Labrador, was known as Station 685; the closest railhead was at Moncton, 550 miles away. The station was opened the day after Pearl Harbor, with a single dirt landing strip; during the summer it was possible to bring supplies in by boat, but in the winter everything had to be flown in. There were no hangars and the mechanics worked in the open, often in temperatures forty degrees below zero.

Station 765 was at Stephensville, Newfoundland, which became the hub of North Atlantic operations. The seventeen men American stationed there achieved an on-time dispatch record that compared favorably with the airline's domestic operations. The station's general foreman, R.M. Smith, who had been one of the first six men sent to Presque Isle, was told he'd be coming home in about six weeks; he stayed overseas for four years.

Meeks Field in Iceland was Station 720—heaven in the summer, when there were twenty-four hours of daylight, and a dark, frozen hell in the winter. Not even the low living costs (25 cents for a steak or chicken dinner, and 15 cents for a haircut) could compensate for the working conditions. To quote one of the sufferers, lead mechanic George Stoneking:

"Did you ever see horizontal rain and snow? Did you ever have to dig your way out of a Nissen hut—a fancy name for a dark alley with doors at both ends? The wind starts blowing at forty-five miles an hour, with gusts often reaching 120. You start walking up the road against that wind, rain or snow blowing in your face, and before you've gone a hundred feet you feel as though Joe Louis has given you a ten-round beating."

In addition to the previously mentioned ATC/TWA/AA pressure pattern research, American assigned two crews who flew a C-54 on alternate North Atlantic crossings all winter, each round-trip taking about three days. Aboard every flight was an Army meteorologist making and recording weather observations. His data was transmitted to Army stations every hour on the hour from the eastbound flight, and every hour on the half hour from the westbound flight. All this weather information was passed on to the USAF bomber squadrons based in England, and used in planning their raids over the European continent.

(The Navy also took advantage of the airline's reputation for weather expertise. It signed, on a three-month trial basis, a costs-only contract under which the Navy's ferrying command was given complete access to American's transcontinental communications and weather advisory systems. The Navy used the service to ferry new fighters and bombers from east coast factories to the west coast, and this proved so successful that the contract was renewed and stayed in effect until the end of the war.)

Far from the frozen north, at Tezpur, India, was an American Airlines ATC operation known by its code name: Project 7-A. It began in July of 1943, when General Arnold asked American to divert ten C-87s and 150 pilots and mechanics from its South Atlantic ATC schedules and fly them to Tezpur. Captain Ted Lewis, who had just been transferred from Burbank to Natal, suddenly found himself in charge of organizing another emergency airlift to one more place American had never served before. Arnold's directive mentioned that the men probably would have to camp out in tents, but that spare engines weren't needed because there were plenty of them available in India.

Lewis took that last bit of assurance with a grain of salt the size of a basketball; he put brand-new engines in all ten airplanes and begged, borrowed, or stole every C-87 spare part he could locate in both Brazil and Africa. Many of the pilots, however, were drawn from the North Atlantic crews. Nobody knew much about the mission except what Arnold's terse orders had spelled out briefly: they were to take enough supplies and equipment to operate the ten-plane fleet for ninety days, and that the mission involved flying the infamous Hump over that part of the Himalayas which formed a towering barrier between India, Burma, and China.

Project 7-A was activated July 18 with a phone call from Arnold. On August 1, only fourteen days later, Captain Toby Hunt landed the first C-87 at Tezpur, with a contingent of twenty-five men. The next day, Hunt took the same plane over the Hump; three months later, American's crews had set a cargo record for the CBI theater, and they did it with fewer planes that the Air Corps was using for the same Hump operations.

Yet Bill Evans, one of the AA pilots assigned to Tezpur, had both sympathy and respect for the far less experienced military airmen. "I have to give them a lot of credit," he reminisced after the war. "Those guys came right out of advanced training and most of them had never flown the C-46s and C-47s they threw at them. They were terribly inexperienced at first. We had ADF [Automatic Direction Finder] stations all along the route, and if one of the kids got lost, he'd ask you to recite poetry or start counting, so he could get a fix.

"One Air Corps pilot bailed out over what the maps said was unexplored territory. He found his way to a mission, and the priest was a guy who had lived a half block away from him in Chicago— they had grown up together.

"When we got there, the Army pilots were getting the Air Medal for fifteen trips over the Hump, and the Distinguished Flying Cross for thirty flights. They never flew it at night. We were making three round-trips a day, and when we started flying the Hump at night, that ended the medals."

(It should be said, however, that the young Army pilots *earned* those medals. At the start of the Hump missions, they were flying unarmed C-47s, an airplane whose airline DC-3 version seldom cruised above 8000 feet, into terrain studded with 15,000-foot or even higher mountain peaks usually hidden behind innocent-looking clouds. One of the first C-47 Hump pilots, incidentally, became a United States senator and a candidate for president of the United States. He was a first lieutenant named Barry Goldwater.)

As might be expected, the ubiquitous Captain Bittner turned up at Project 7-A, but generally behaved himself—there wasn't that much to laugh at. The Tezpur base had no indoor plumbing, and the toilet facilities consisted of a six-hole "Chic Sale" privy which the British Army had built and sold to American for $10,000. Captain

Bittner's zeal also may have been curbed by the presence of the wild animals that abounded in the area; Tezpur, in fact, had been the locale where "Bring-'em-Back-Alive" Frank Buck did much of his hunting and filming. No one ventured very far from camp.

The C-87s Lewis had mustered may have had new engines, but those engines were among the very few parts on the airplane that could be classed as new. All ten, plus two more that arrived later, were former B-24 bombers that had been damaged in accidents and converted into cargo aircraft. The pilots found that one of them wouldn't climb higher than 12,000 feet, a decided handicap when flying the Hump. The mechanics discovered that it had been built with a negative stagger in the tail section.

There were no scales for weighing cargo loads; weights were guessed at by how far the landing gear struts depressed. Bill Evans came out to his plane one day and gaped—the struts were so flat they were almost touching the ground. It turned out that a rookie loadmaster had put railroad ties through the cabin and then placed the rest of the cargo on top of the ties. How a C-87 was loaded was important to a pilot's health. The nose wheel wasn't steerable, and the pilots steered by applying a combination of brakes and throttles. Improper loading resulted in a tail-heavy airplane that Superman couldn't have budged.

It was bad enough having to fly airplanes that no sane pilot would have tolerated in an airline operation, but to cross the Hump in one of these battered, marginally airworthy C-87s was the epitome of bravery. The veteran American pilots went out of their way to act as mentors to the increasing number of young Army airmen arriving at Tezpur as Project 7-A's ninety-day assignment progressed. The airline pilots often used their days off to fly with the rookie military crews, imparting all the knowledge they had acquired themselves flying the Hump.

Sometimes knowledge didn't help even the sagest veteran. American lost six crewmen during Project 7-A, among them the man who had flown the first trip. Toby Hunt had gone over the Hump sixty-four times and had just completed his sixty-fifth crossing, but when he reached China, the weather was too bad to land. Hunt turned around and was heading back to India, still carrying a heavy load of small-arms ammunition, when an engine failed and another began to lose power. It was impossible to maintain altitude and Hunt ordered his four crew members to bail out through the cockpit escape hatch. All four did, and eventually reached safety, but Hunt stayed with the plane—whether by choice, or because he was a huge man who may not have been able to squeeze through the hatch, no one ever knew.

He evidently tried to crash-land into the cushioning of a rice paddy, but the airplane couldn't make it over a hill on the edge of the paddy. The Chinese found the C-87's wreckage and carried Hunt's body out of the mountains in a hand-hewn coffin so heavy that when Lewis and other pilots arrived to claim it, it took ten men to lift it. They flew the coffin back to Tezpur, where Hunt was buried in the shadow of a small Buddhist temple, next to the remains of the five other crew members killed in a previous C-87 crash.

It was part skill and part luck that these were the only fatal accidents during Project 7-A, because flying the Hump was rated the most dangerous noncombat assignment of the war, even riskier than the North Atlantic. The delivery point was at Yunnanyi, China, apparently the home port for every thief in the Orient. The ATC crews were losing so much stuff out of airplanes that they started drawing lots to see who would stand armed guard at night on layovers. Then some of them started spurning the layovers; the Yunnanyi field had no runway lights, but the first night departure out of Yunnanyi was made anyway by a captain who had just drawn all-night guard duty.

"The hell with it," he told his crew. "We're going back to Tezpur." They took off with an Army jeep stationed at the end of the runway—they just headed for its lights.

By the time Project 7-A's allotted three months were up, American had flown the Hump more than 1000 times, carrying some 5 million pounds of cargo, from bombs and aviation fuel to medical supplies and spare parts for tanks. Passengers were infrequent, but one was a Singer Sewing Machine Company salesman who somehow had wangled permission to make regular trips into China. And there was one Hump flight that angered every man associated with Project 7-A. The incident occurred on a C-87 that was heading for China and ran into a thunderstorm. The turbulence jarred open a box marked SIGNAL CORPS EQUIPMENT. A crew member looked inside to check on damage and discovered the box was filled with lipstick, nylon hose, and other feminine items, all consigned to Madame Chiang Kai-shek.

When the Army took over the Hump mission completely, an Air Corps engineering officer inspected American's C-87s and condemned all ten as unairworthy.

"We were supposed to deadhead home in style," Bill Evans remembered, "but when they condemned the airplanes, we had to fly them back ourselves."

The crews got them as far as Charleston, South Carolina, where they phoned New York and asked what they were supposed to do with ten beat-up C-87s.

"We don't care what you do with the goddamned planes—just don't bring 'em to La Guardia," was the answer.

But there was no other place to go, so they were flown to La Guardia anyway, and parked on some grass, where eventually the Army sold them for scrap. But while the airplanes were quickly forgotten, the six men who didn't return from Tezpur were not. Those who served in Project 7-A took what remained out of their mess fund and used it to buy a memorial plaque that hangs today on a wall at American's Flight Training Center in Dallas.

While Project 7-A was an exciting yet brief wartime episode, American's South Atlantic base at Natal was as big an operation as the North Atlantic airlift, and during the winter, when North Atlantic schedules often had to be reduced, even bigger. The number of smaller stations blossomed into a huge global network; employees who once thought it an adventure when they traveled 500 miles in the States found themselves working in far-off places they had trouble spelling.

Such as Marrakech, in French Morocco; American had made the first survey flight establishing a direct route from Newfoundland to Morocco, although mechanics assigned to Marrakech must have equated it to a sentence in purgatory; temperatures soared to 130 degrees, so blistering hot that tools couldn't be left on the ground. Picking up a wrench in that heat could burn the skin off a man's hands. The mechanics learned to put their tools in a pail of water.

By 1944, American had become the second largest international carrier in the world, its ATC operations topped only by Pan Am. Like so many other carriers, however, its involvement didn't stop with ATC and NATS flights.

One of American's engineers invented a hoist for changing a 600-pound airplane tire, a device that went into service at virtually every air base. It used to take six men twenty-four hours to change a pair of tires; two men using the new hoist could do it in one hour. Then there was the airline's experimental shop at La Guardia, known as "Department X." There, in Hangar 5, engineers, mechanics, and draftsmen worked with General Electric technicians on a top secret project: modifying an XB-23 twin-engine bomber into a flying test bed for high-altitude flying. The end result was a pressurized cabin that eventually went into late models of the B-29 bomber. One of Department X's more prosaic achievements was conducted at the request of the Navy—figuring out a way to put pontoons on a DC-3.

American, too, operated a large modification center at La Guardia, that started out converting B-24s into C-87s, then ironing the bugs out of C-46s. Thirty of the fat-bellied airplanes came into the center straight from the Curtiss factory. They left the center having undergone more than 180 engineering changes; American's engineers had recommended about 180 additional modifications, but the Army rejected them because there wasn't enough time.

The center's other major assignment was the conversion of C-54s into flying ambulances, some of them subsequently flown by American's ATC crews. But this is an appropriate time to emphasize the mercy side of the wartime airlift, for all the airlines directly serving the war zones operated medical evacuation aircraft—usually C-54s and C-54As. Ironically, in the early days of the war some medical authorities advised against such transportation, in the belief that flying would be harmful to the more seriously wounded, who had to travel in litters. The opposite proved to be the case; there is no way of knowing how many lives were saved by air evacuation, but the most conservative estimate runs in the thousands. According to a War Department report issued near the end of the war, only one patient died aboard a med evac flight, and he was so seriously wounded that survival would probably have been impossible in any event.

Unlike the Navy's white-painted hospital ships, marked with prominent red crosses, ATC and NATS operated unmarked, unarmed aircraft for the medical flights. A homeward-bound ship carrying wounded from a war theater like the CBI would take up to three months to reach a U.S. port; a C-54 delivered its patients within a week. To assure en route care, every med evac plane carried at least one Army or Navy flight nurse, and many of them were former airline stewardesses and hostesses. The transition from cabin attendent to a lieutenant in the Army or Navy Medical Corps was easy, for in the prewar years most airlines required flight attendants to be registered nurses.

The usual practice was for regular troop carrier planes to airlift wounded from as close to the battlefields as possible (helicopters didn't come into use until the Korean War), and fly them to an air base for transfer to the big litter-equipped aircraft. Sometimes, however, the latter flew wounded right out of combat areas.

The ATC's first long-range ambulance flight carried five litter patients from Karachi, India, to Walter Reed Hospital in Washington, D.C.; from then on the evac flights took on the frequency and efficiency of an airline within an airline. ATC evacuated 12,000 wounded by air in 1942. By the end of 1944, it was operating 2000 short- and long-range ambulance flights a day and had flown more than 123,000 wounded and sick back to hospitals in the United States—a total that does not include those carried out of battlefield areas by troop carrier planes. As good as the field medical stations were, they lacked the full facilities and staffs of stateside hospitals.

Ernie Gann was one of the many airline pilots who flew a number of medical flights, C-54s whose three tiers of litters were often jammed with wounded so fresh from combat that the airplanes stank with the odor of excretion, emergency medicines, and sweat that seemed to generate the smell of fear mixed with shock. The most effective opiate against pain was the knowledge that the aircraft was heading home.

Gann and his fellow airmen sensed the latter; if they went back into the cabin to converse with the troops, as Ernie himself tried to do on every air-evac flight, the pilots were struck by the unrelenting similarity of the questions tossed at them. No complaints. No self-pity. No crying out for sympathy. Just questions. What's their present position? How fast is the plane going? And—always—the last and most important question: when would they arrive home?

Older airline pilots like Gann had their hearts and souls touched by more than just the wounded. They also saw the ravaging effects of combat on young bombers and fighter pilots flying back to the U.S. on leave or for stateside reassignment. These young men were no longer the baby-faced, cocky, unbloodied youngsters the transport crews remembered flying over to their squadron bases only a few months before. No trace was left of their jaunty confidence and feisty swagger. They seemed to have aged virtually overnight, their expressions somber as if any semblance of celebration at their own survival would demean the memories of comrades who could never go home.

This, of course, happened in World War II. But airline pilots flying military airlift missions in the Korean and Vietnam wars were to find themselves feeling the same sympathy, however futile it often seemed to be, toward those afflicted with the emotional residue of war.

★ ★ 6 ★ ★
War Wings—Part III

United Air Lines

United's Pat Patterson and American's C.R. Smith were the airline industry's version of the Odd Couple.

These two powerful airline tycoons were totally unlike in many respects, not the least of which was physical appearance. Smith was tall and heavyset, Patterson short and a bit pudgy. As chieftains of the nation's two largest domestic carriers, they were unrelenting rivals who clashed on more than one occasion, including a knockdown, drag-'em-out donnybrook over one of American's prewar advertising campaigns that described the airline's southern transcontinental route as "the Low-Level Airway Through Southern Sunshine to California," and "The Southern Sunshine Route."

Those slogans were to Patterson what "Marching Through Georgia" was to a resident of Atlanta; he felt, with considerable justification, that "low-level" and "southern sunshine" were phrases indirectly but unmistakably implying that United's northern transcontinental route, admittedly exposed to more bad weather in the winter months, was therefore more hazardous. Angry words were exchanged, followed by United's counterattack: an ad campaign of its own denying the safety implications and pointing out that, in fact, American's planes systemwide flew over more mountainous terrain than United's.

Both campaigns violated an unofficial industry rule which *Fortune* magazine, in a commentary on the advertising war, described as the airlines' First Commandment: "Thou Shalt Not Do Anything to Reflect Directly or Indirectly on Air Safety."

"Essentially," *Fortune* noted, "the industry is a collection of independent states that are joined by common interests as well as common hazards. The greatest of these hazards is the ordinary man's fear of air travel."

C.R. had approved the ads, but meant them as promising passengers fewer delays because of more favorable winter weather, and not as a reflection on United's safety. So he invited Patterson to a quiet dinner, where the hatchet was buried. The truth was that these two titans really liked and respected each another even though the tough, taciturn Smith and the paternalistic Patterson were miles apart in their executive styles and personalities. The big Texan had the instincts of a riverboat gambler, and he undoubtedly was an industry pacesetter in many passenger service innovations. Patterson, who got his start in the banking industry, was typically conservative and cautious. He didn't take part in Smith's persistent needling of Eddie Rickenbacker at ATA meetings, but he openly enjoyed the sharp digs and would even allow himself an occasional discreet chuckle, as he did the time Rickenbacker challenged C.R. to toss a coin "to see who's the biggest son of a bitch in the industry."

"Eddie," Smith said gently, "no mere flip of the coin could possibly rob you of that distinction."

At one postwar ATA meeting, however, the usually genial Patterson lost his temper when the captain went into one of his typical tirades against his fellow executives. Rickenbacker was accusing them of spending too much money on food service. In-flight food service, on which United prided itself, was a subject close to Patterson's heart. He had great sympathy for the captain, who still showed the physical effects of injuries suffered in a prewar Eastern DC-3 crash and a wartime episode in which he was marooned on a raft in the Pacific for twenty-two days (see Chapter Seven). But this latest attack against the industry was too much, even for Patterson.

"Some of us wish you were back on the raft!" Patterson snapped.

"Guys like you make me wish I was!" Rickenbacker retorted.

Despite his innate paternalism, Patterson had a lode of steel under his benign personality. He once prevented a pilots' strike by threatening to resign as president if his airmen walked out; that was something else he shared with C.R.—both men were trusted and even adored by the people of their respective airlines. And each man was convinced there were instances when the best interests of the industry deserved a higher priority than any competition between two airlines. This, even ahead of the reputation for personal integrity they also shared, was the single most important thing they had in common. They fought like wildcats for their respective companies, but they knew when it was time to close ranks for the good of commercial aviation as a whole.

On February 9, 1937, a UAL DC-3 making a routine night approach to the San Francisco airport (Mills Field in those days) in perfect weather suddenly went into a dive and crashed into the bay, killing all eight passengers, the stewardess, and both pilots. The wreckage was pulled out of the water the next day and examined, but nothing was found to explain that forty-five degree dive, and investigators were ready to tag the United captain with pilot error.

Five weeks after the accident, an American DC-3 was rolling down a runway at Newark and about to take off when the captain found the controls had jammed. He managed to abort the takeoff, came to a stop, and tugged again at the control yoke, trying to determine why it wouldn't budge. Looking down, he discovered that the copilot's radio microphone had fallen off its hook and become wedged in a small, V-shaped well at the base of the yoke. He pried the mike loose, the controls moved normally, and he took off. The near mishap was reported to his chief pilot, and a few hours later Smith was on the phone to Patterson recounting the Newark incident.

"Pat, we think this is what might have caused your San Francisco accident," he told the UAL president.

The crash probers took another look at the wreckage and found the copilot's radio mike still wedged into the well. Douglas promptly advised all DC-3 operators to install a rubber boot over the well, no similar problem ever reoccurred, and the Smith-Patterson friendship was solidified.

When war came, they found they had something else in common: Each was determined that his airline was not going to profit from its military activities. Patterson, in fact, tried to go a patriotic step further than anyone else by establishing a nonprofit company, which he incorporated as "The United Air Lines Victory Corporation" Ten shares of capital stock were issued at $100 a share, all owned by UAL. Its sole purpose was to handle all military contracts on a nonprofit basis, and keep them completely separate from the airline's commercial operations.

The altruistic gesture went in one government ear and out the other. Washington decreed that the Army and Navy couldn't do business with a company subsidiary created deliberately to avoid making any profit, because this wasn't fair to those carriers signing cost-plus-fixed-fee contracts. So United had to dissolve the Victory Corporation although, following American's and TWA's leads, its fixed fees were set so low it was almost impossible to make much, if any, profit. In place of the Victory Corporation, which lasted less than three months, Patterson established another separate unit to handle all war business: the Military Transport Service.

The airline's first major commitment to the war effort began one month after Pearl Harbor, when a pair of brand-new B-17 bombers ferried in from the Boeing factory in Seattle arrived at United's big overhaul base in Cheyenne, Wyoming. The modification orders indicated that they were obviously being prepped for some kind of special mission; UAL's mechanics were told to cram extra fuel tanks into every available space, remove all guns and bomb bay racks, and install new racks that would hold photographic equipment. Seven weeks later, in mid February, the two Flying Fortresses left Cheyenne and headed for Alaska, leaving behind a lot of curious workers wondering what their mission could be.

They found out much, much later, when the wraps of secrecy finally could be removed. These were the B-17s that flew photo reconnaissance flights over Tokyo preceding Jimmy Doolittle's bombing raid against the Japanese capital the following April. Preparing them for these long-range missions marked the start of what was to be the nation's largest airplane modification center, and one many later airline centers would be modeled after. Cheyenne may have been Indian country to someone like a native New Yorker, but during the war this small western city—once just a refueling and pick-up stop on United's early transcontinental air mail route— became a bustling hatchery for thousands of modified warplanes. By the time the war ended, 5680 bombers, most of them B-17s, had gone through the center's two huge new hangars.

Cheyenne provided another classic example of the ability of these airline maintenance shops to handle their double wartime role: they could not only turn themselves virtually overnight into aircraft manufacturing facilities, but they also created, again almost overnight, highly skilled production workers out of civilian greenhorns. United hired every available man and woman in the Cheyenne area, then roamed through the entire Rocky Mountain states for additional help. Base employment boomed to more than 1600, about half of them commuting to Cheyenne from Greeley and Fort Collins, fifty miles away, via a bus service United established. And the government eased Cheyenne's housing shortage somewhat by bringing in 300 trailers.

The recruits included cowboys, gas station attendants, housewives, and clerks; many of them had never set eyes on a lathe, drill press, or rivet gun before, but at the peak of the center's operations they were turning out eleven finished airplanes a day, and in a single year manufactured some 4 million parts. As each modified aircraft was rolled out of the hangar, a United test pilot would check it out and then turn it over to an Army ferry pilot. A visiting United official one day counted a total of ninety-nine B-17s either undergoing modification work in the hangars or parked on the field awaiting test or ferry flights.

Just as busy but in a different kind of activity was another United facility in Oakland, California: the Boeing School of Aeronautics, its name dating back to the airline's early years, when United was known as Boeing Air Transport, as a member of the United Aircraft & Transport Corporation conglomerate. The Boeing Airplane Company no longer had any connection with the school, which had been training new United copilots and mechanics for more than a decade. Hap Arnold enlisted the resources of this "university of the air" two years before the school became part of Sam Solomon's Airlines War Training Institute. Arnold knew that if war came, the Air Corps was going to need aviation mechanics in large numbers, so in 1940 he asked the Boeing school and similar institutions to launch a mass training program.

The Oakland school began the project by starting a new mechanics' class every ten days; by the end of 1942, it had graduated more than 2000, and at its peak the school had over 100 instructors assigned to three daily shifts of classes. When AWTI was organized, the United school expanded into additional training areas: navigators, radio operators, and special technicians for both the Army and Navy. The school never resumed its original role of training copilots for the airline, but United established three military copilot schools at Tracy, California, Reno, and Denver.

Historically, United for years had operated extensively in the western and northwestern states; it came as only a mild surprise when the airline's first major airlift contract involved Alaska—an assignment that followed an emergency telephone call from ATA president Edgar Gorrell to Pat Patterson early in 1942.

"Pat, how soon could United start a scheduled military cargo and personnel service to Alaska?" Gorrell asked.

"From where in the U.S. to where in Alaska, Ed? What kind of a route are you talking about?"

Gorrell explained that the Army needed an airlift as soon as possible from Dayton, Ohio, to Fairbanks, Anchorage, and Nome via Calgary and White Horse in the Yukon Territory. Patterson realized this would be entirely new territory for United's pilots, but he accepted the "Operation Alaska" assignment without hesitation. Three days later, a United DC-3 carrying the airline's best meteorologist and several experienced communications technicians took off from Salt Lake City and headed north for a survey flight over the unfamiliar proposed route.

There were no real surprises; like all the other airlines that would be operating in Alaska, United's survey team learned that pilots would have to fly through 7000-foot mountain passes, dodge peaks like Mt. McKinley that towered 20,000 feet and higher, work with maps that called for considerable guesswork, and use widely scattered, rather primitive airfields that from a decently high altitude looked like truncated country roads in the middle of a forest.

According to Frank Taylor's official history of United (*High Horizons*), the three veteran pilots and several communications specialists on the survey flight found Alaska's radio navigational aids better than expected—a more optimistic appraisal than the ones made by Western and Northwest's crews. Based on the survey's findings and recommendations, United inaugurated the Dayton-Nome airlift May 15, 1942—which happened to be only three weeks before the Japanese invaded the Aleutians. That was the point at which the Army and Navy mounted an emergency airlift that involved United and ten other carriers in rushing men, equipment, and supplies to the threatened northern territory. Taylor succinctly described the swift adjustment these airline pilots had to make, from what they thought would be fairly routine cargo flights to hair-raising missions that on some occasions could be as studded with as much danger as actual combat.

"Crews soon found out that they were flying not only a supply line, but were answering emergency calls from all over the vast Alaskan territory," Taylor wrote. "They flew anything—troops, generals, guns, ammunition, high-octane gas, tools, clothing, medicine . . ."

The experience of United Captain Bob Dawson and his brush with a Japanese carrier was related in an earlier chapter. Add to this nail-biter the story of UAL Captain Jimmy Johnson, who on Memorial Day of 1942 was assigned the job of flying an Army officer, two technical sergeants, and a load of ammunition from Anchorage to Cold Bay in the Aleutians. He delivered personnel and cargo to Cold Bay after a routine flight, returned to Anchorage, and was immediately dispatched to another Aleutian base, this one at Unmak, with 5000 pounds of airplane bombs. That was when Jimmy Johnson learned that flying for Operation Alaska wasn't always routine.

When he reached Unmak, he had to land in a sixty-mph crosswind on a short metal landing strip. The cargo had just been unloaded when a strong gust of wind tipped the C-47 over on its nose, slightly damaging both propellers. Just as Johnson and a ground crew were almost finished repairing the props, Japanese planes swept over the field, guns blazing. Pilots and ground crews dove for the nearest ditch. Thanks to poor visibility and marksmanship, the attackers didn't hit anything, and after they flew away, Johnson and his crew climbed out of the ditch, back into their plane, and returned to Anchorage—thoroughly convinced that wartime Alaska was a long way from those peacetime trips Johnson used to make between Chicago and New York.

Captain Hugh Worthington would have murmured "amen" to that conclusion. He was in Anchorage on a layover when the Navy notified United that it had a crippled destroyer laid up at Adak, in dire need of a new crankshaft. The crankshaft replacement that had been delivered to Anchorage weighed 3500 pounds and was twenty feet long, almost enough to fill the entire length of a C-47 cabin. Worthington took off with his heavy load and an equally heavy load on his mind: the weather forecast called for the deepest low pressure center ever recorded for the Aleutians, and it was parked just west of Adak.

He laid over at Unmak for the night, hoping for a more optimistic weather report before leaving the next morning. Adak radio told him to expect a 600-foot ceiling with two miles visibility—that was the good news. The bad news was a forecast of sixty-five-mph surface winds cutting across the only runway, which meant Worthington would have to sideslip into that stiff crosswind at a thirty-five-degree angle in order to land. Tough, he thought, but not impossible. By the time he reached Adak, however, visibility had dropped to only three-fourths of a mile, while the crosswind had increased to ninety mph and was now blowing at a forty-five-degree angle to the runway.

Worthington knew the low-pressure front had swept in faster than expected. But he also knew something that wasn't being taught to young military transport pilots at the time, little survival tricks based on knowledge of weather behavior that UAL pilots had been accumulating since the old air mail days. Many storm fronts, like hurricanes, have relatively calm centers; Worthington timed his final approach and landing to sneak in during that brief lull in wind violence. He timed it so perfectly, in fact, that while ground crews were unloading the crankshaft, the surface wind suddenly accelerated to a shrieking crescendo and they had to tie the airplane to heavy tractors so it wouldn't be blown over. Throughout the war, even as the planes of ATC and NATS were flown increasingly by all-military crews, many were pilots who had been trained the airline way—either in formal classes or riding in cockpits absorbing valuable practical lessons from their older, more experienced airline brethren.

United's flight crews, like those with Western, Northwest, and Pan Am, learned the tough lessons of Alaskan flying in a hurry. UAL operated its C-47s with a three-man crew, adding a radio operator to the captain and copilot. A radio man was a valuable asset to have aboard on these ATC missions to the far north, particularly on flights to the Aleutians. Wartime UAL radio operator Ralph Lewis, in an entertaining autobiography (*Dead Reckoning*) that related his ATC experiences in both Alaska and the Pacific theater, explained the reasons as only a veteran crew member of those days could.

"Weather signals were transmitted in Morse code in groups of five-digit numbers," Lewis wrote, "and were coded differently each day to prevent weather data from being deciphered by the Japanese. In Aleutian flying it was necessary to monitor weather reports continuously for fifteen or twenty landing facilities at a time, then decode the reports into usable information immediately. It was a demanding routine.''

So demanding, he added, that he usually was too busy to worry about the miserable weather that was par for the course. Landings were made in visibility of less than a quarter of a mile and under ceilings as low as 300 feet. The C-47/DC-3, with reasonably effective deicing boots on the leading edges of the stabilizers, fin, and wings, was far superior to the DC-2 in its ability to combat icing. But thermal deicing hadn't been developed yet, and even the boots couldn't always dislodge a heavy ice buildup. Alaskan winters also could produce one type of ice that defied the rubber boots: rime ice, so porous that only heat could melt it. If a plane iced up despite the boots, pilots learned to land at the nearest field and hope it had a warm hangar so the wings could be defrosted. Lewis remembered occasions on which he and the two pilots had to wipe every inch of the wings, stabilizers, and rudder dry with rags before they could take off again.

The undramatic but vital logistical history of World War II was written in the items that appeared on military cargo manifests, and United's were typical. One Dayton-Nome flight carried nearly 4000 pounds of fleece-lined flying suits for shivering Army pilots in Alaska. UAL C-47s hauled a daily 800-pound shipment of sensitive equipment from the Sperry Gyroscope Company in New York to Boeing in Seattle. Although Operation Alaska was an Army/ATC contract operation, United drew varied missions for the Navy as well, Worthington's crankshaft "special delivery" being one instance. One UAL crew, flying in weather that had grounded regular west coast flights, took off from San Francisco and delivered 800 pounds of serum to San Diego in time to make a Navy ship that was leaving for the Pacific war theater. The airline repeated this "don't miss that ship" deadline when it flew two tons of gunsights from Akron to Oakland in time to catch a Navy transport ship, then loaded 7800 pounds of bearings on three C-47s and flew them from Akron to Puget Sound, in Seattle, where a battleship was undergoing emergency repairs.

United's participation in the Alaskan airlift was supposed to end early in August 1942, when it turned Operation Alaska's Dayton-Nome supply route over to Northwest Airlines. The pullout was intended to release UAL crews for ATC missions in the Pacific, but only five months after the last United crew had left Alaska, the airline was called back again for another emergency: the retaking of the Aleutian islands held by Japanese occupation forces.

This latest emergency supply line ran from Seattle to the Aleutians via Vancouver Island, Ketchikan, Juneau, Yakutat, Cordova, and Anchorage. United surveyed one of the two airways chosen for the airlift, an Alaskan coastal route mostly over open sea; the other was an inland route that was safer but took two hours longer to fly. After one month of flying both, the pilots reported overwhelming preference for the shorter coastal route, with one proviso: if they could have more accurate, up-to-date weather forecasts for the Seattle-Alaska flights, they could make the trip with only two stops—the first at Juneau or White Horse, and the second at Anchorage—ninety percent of the time.

United promptly assigned Howard Hoffman, chief of its meteorology department, to the task of setting up a joint airline/ATC weather bureau called the Alaska Air Transport Meteorological Office, or AATMO. As soon as it went into operation, the supply flights doubled in frequency until the Japanese unexpectedly abandoned Kiska, the largest Aleutian island they had occupied, without a fight. And UAL, having completed more than 2 million miles of Alaskan operations with no serious accidents, shifted its resources to the airline's chief wartime mission: Operations Pacific.

This enormous responsibility, handed to an airline with no transocean flying experience, came from ATC chief Harold George in mid 1942, a time when American forces in the South Pacific were just beginning to recover from their initial setbacks and humiliating defeats that had carried the tide of Japanese conquest almost to the shores of Australia. The agreed-upon strategy for the Pacific counteroffensive, Hal George knew, involved taking back important occupied islands one by one, and considering the vast distances a Pacific campaign involved, that meant an aerial supply line.

George ignored UAL's lack of overseas experience; he wanted United's participation partially because except for the Alaskan contract and the airline's domestic military cargo flights, United had no other major operational commitments. UAL wouldn't be pioneering the route he wanted it to serve; Pan Am and Consairways already had flown it. But American, Eastern, and TWA were heavily involved in the Atlantic, Pan Am had plenty on its own plate, and George had liked United's performance in Alaska. It also is very possible that C.R. Smith recommended United for the Pacific; although there is no evidence that he had anything to do with UAL's selection, George did seek his advice on any matter pertaining to the airlines. C.R., it should be remembered, had the utmost admiration for Pat Patterson's company, which he considered second only to his own in every aspect of air carrier operations—including training, passenger service, a tradition of technical excellence, and a reputation for superb maintenance.

So United was given one of the toughest assignments of the war, and its difficulties were well outlined by historian Frank Taylor:

"The task outlined by General George was flying an oceanic airline with one end in San Francisco and the other constantly changing. President Patterson accepted the job and agreed to start within forty days flying an 8269-mile overseas route entirely new to United's pilots, who were to operate strange equipment few of them had ever seen. The pilots got an idea of the scope of the hurry-up new run when they saw a schedule of the route, as long almost as all of the airways flown by the company on the mainland. It read: 'San Francisco to Hickham Field, Honolulu, 2446 miles; Hickham to Canton Island, 1908 miles; Canton to Nandi, Fiji Islands, 1250 miles; Nandi to New Caledonia, 865 miles; New Caledonia to Amberly Field, near Brisbane, Australia, 1800 miles.' Alternating points in the Pacific were Palmyra Island and Christmas Island."

The mind-boggling distances to be flown didn't concern the pilots as much as the C-87s assigned to Operations Pacific; these were greeted with a marked lack of enthusiasm, for most of the pilots were hoping to fly new C-54s—after all, United's own engineers had helped Douglas develop the Skymaster. But this was in the earlier days of C-54 production and as soon as the big transports left the Santa Monica assembly line, ATC and NATS grabbed virtually every airplane. For that matter, there weren't many C-87s around for allocation to United; at first the airline couldn't even scrounge one up for crew training purposes until less than a month before "Ops-Pacific" actually began. The result was a lot of on-the-job training aboard this unfamilar airplane; the crews had to learn even as they started flying the Pacific, armed mostly with what they had been taught hastily at the Boeing School of Aeronautics—and this was ground school, not flight training.

United's pilots, most of them veterans of the Alaskan airlift, bid for the Pacific route on the basis of seniority and, as expected, twenty-five very senior captains, the same number of copilots, and other flight crew members constituted the cadre initially assigned to Ops-Pacific, a total later tripled to seventy-five individual crews who were put through the Oakland school with as much speed as decently practical. The same five-man crew—captain, copilot, flight engineer, navigator, and radio operator—stayed together over the almost four years United flew the Pacific for ATC. Pilots assigned to Ops-Pacific studied or took refresher courses in celestial navigation, navigation by dead reckoning, radio codes, meteorology, and survival procedures. The school also put rookie navigators through a ninety-day course, considered the minimum time needed to teach overwater navigation to the likes of ex–ticket agents, accountants, and draft-eligible college students who preferred the possibility of an ocean ditching to being drafted.

Ralph Lewis was one of the first radio operators hired; he applied after reading in a newspaper that United had signed a contract to fly the Pacific for the Air Transport Command, but didn't know he'd be flying to the frozen north before he got a chance to cross the balmy Pacific. He never forgot the proud day he was sent to an Air Corps clothing depot and was issued the ATC wardrobe authorized for civilian crew members: a complete officer's uniform, a fleece-lined leather flight jacket, khaki trench coat and jumpsuit, military headgear (visor cap and soft overseas cap), ATC insignia, and a B-4 bag—the latter always gave crews the impression that they could stuff anything into a B-4 except a DC-3 landing gear.

The first C-87 was delivered into less-than-eager hands early in September 1942, and all twenty-five cockpit crews were checked out in it. On September 23, five more C-87s arrived at Mills Field in San Francisco, and on the same day Captain Jack O'Brien, who became United's superintendent of Pacific flight operations, took off for Australia. It didn't take long for O'Brien to discover that C-87 training had omitted certain vital information concerning the airplane's less desirable qualities. Taylor's account of the incident speaks volumes:

"Three hours out, the crew undertook to pump fuel from the emergency tanks to the main tanks. The gauges showed NO PRESSURE, indicating no fuel. O'Brien decided to turn back while the turning was good. Before he reached the San Francisco airport, the gauges started working again. At the airport a check revealed plenty of fuel in the tanks. Somebody had neglected to warn O'Brien that on the C-87s the gauges worked sometimes, and sometimes they didn't. The captain took off again, and this time, as on subsequent trips, nobody worried about gauges. Then ten days later the plane was back from Australia after flying over 16,000 miles.''

United's pilots flew C-87s for almost a year before the Army finally allotted Ops-Pacific its first C-54s, an average of two flights a day leaving Mills Field and heading toward Hawaii after stopping first at Hamilton Field to pick up military cargo and personnel. Navigation across the Pacific was accomplished either by celestial sightings at night—satisfactory if there was no cloud cover—or dead reckoning by day using data from an octant, almanac, star tables, and forecast winds. There were a few radio beacons in the South Pacific, but they didn't begin to cover enough airspace. Lewis, who later became a navigator himself, discovered that this was the busiest job on the airplane and nerve-racking as well, what with so many postage-stamp islands that had to be located with absolute precision. There was no other field close enough to Canton Island, for example, to use as an alternate; miss the island's seven-mile length and three-mile width after at least ten exhausting hours in an uncomfortable C-87, and there was nothing but empty ocean ahead. ATC aircraft operating over the Atlantic were able to use, with increasing frequency as more equipment became available, the radio-wave navigational aid known as loran—the acronym for Long Range Navigation—developed by the U.S. during the war. Loran would not be installed on ATC's Pacific transports, however, until late 1944.

ATC radio operators like Lewis had little time to relax on a long flight, either. Voice communications were extremely unreliable in the Pacific because of the distances involved, and the operators usually kept in contact with ground stations via the old-fashioned dots and dashes of Morse code. The most reassuring leg to fly was the 2400-mile stretch between San Francisco and Honolulu; three U.S. Coast Guard air/sea rescue cutters, equipped with homing devices and powerful radio transmitters, were stationed along the route just in case an ATC airplane had to ditch. And, naturally, Honolulu was the favorite place for layovers.

The flight crews stayed at the old but still rather plush Moana Hotel, a six-story wooden building not as fancy as the Royal Hawaiian, where the submarine crews enjoyed their R and Rs, but a lot nicer than some of the other layover sites. Brisbane started out as the terminus of the Pacific airlift, but by early 1944 UAL's flights were terminating at Townsville, about 600 miles to the north of Brisbane, on the Queensland coast.

The UAL ground crews assigned to Townsville had it a lot worse than the men on the incoming flights. When the mechanics first got to Townsville, they had to sleep in tiny unlit tents erected in the middle of a muddy field. There was an Australian army barracks and mess hall available, but the Australian commander decreed that no civilians could sleep in the same building as the Aussie soldiers, nor were they allowed to sit at the dining room tables, so the mechanics had to eat standing up. Seely Hall, named Ops-Pacific manager, arrived in Townsville with superintendent of maintenance Bill Hoare, and both went ballistic when they saw the ground crews' living conditions.

Hall pulled more strings than a master puppeteer and finally arranged for the mechanics to live in three small wooden barracks, while five large tents were erected to serve as workshops and shelter for tools and parts. Every night one mechanic pulled guard duty to keep thieves away. Hall managed to billet the flight crews in Townsville's only hotel; by no stretch of the imagination was it the Moana, 5821 miles away, but even Townsville seemed like hotel heaven when the ATC crews started landing in the middle of such battle zones as New Guinea, Guadalcanal, and Kwajalein. There they shared the same crude sleeping and eating facilities as the troops, and many were the hungry, tired UAL crew members, including lordly captains, who didn't turn up their noses at ordinary field rations and a tent with an Army cot.

Nadzab Field in New Guinea's Markham Valley became Ops-Pacific's new terminus just when Townsville conditions had improved, and from Taylor's description of life at Nadzab one may gather that even Townsville was life at the Moana by comparison. "The field had three landing strips," Taylor wrote, "with no lighting facilities. The area was strewn with the wrecks of Japanese and American planes downed in battles preceding the paratroop landing which captured the valley from the Japanese. Here, living quarters were three miles up the hillside, where the temperature was cooler but where the rains turned the road into gumbo. Freshets poured down through the tents during the rains. Where meat and vegetables had been plentiful in Australia, they were nonexistent in New Guinea. The crews learned to eat C rations and like them. Between rains, the bright equatorial sun beat down, hot and blinding. Crews, working in shorts, turned as brown as natives."

Seely Hall visited Nadzab and saw the mechanics washing clothes in a stream. He asked them what they needed most and the unanimous reply was "a washing machine." So Hall, on his next trip back to San Francisco, acquired a hand-powered washer and brought it to New Guinea, along with two fir trees, in time to celebrate Christmas with the decorated trees and clean clothes. As of that Christmas Day, 1943, at long last even New Guinea was beginning to look civilized.

On December 26, ATC ordered the entire UAL contingent to Guam.

C-54s began replacing the C-87s in mid July of 1943, much to the relief of the flight crews who no longer had to watch helplessly if one of the lighter, faster LB-30 Liberators operated by Consairways, which was flying the same route, passed them in the air; the Liberator pilots were sure to remind them of it if they happened to cross paths later on layovers. There were also three fatal crashes out of a total of United's some 7000 Pacific flights, and all three involved C-87s, with eight crew fatalities.

The first occurred February 7, 1943, when a C-87 approaching Canton Island landed short of the runway and hit the water. Only two of the sixteen passengers, all Army officers, survived, and there was only one surviving crew member, copilot Hoot Moninger, who told investigators that when they were turning from base leg into final approach, the flaps on one wing deployed asymmetrically— the equivalent of the brakes on one side of a car locking during a turn.

On August 2, 1943, a UAL/ATC C-87 crashed a few seconds after taking off from Aukland, New Zealand, around 1 A.M. on a rainy night. This one was blamed on a combination of fatigue (the crew had flown 123 hours in the past twenty-six days) and a caged (inoperative) gyro that gave the pilots a false horizon when they went into a sharp turn after getting airborne. Aboard were the most unusual passengers Ops-Pacific carried: twenty-four Japanese prisoners of war, along with their wives and children, who were being flown to New Guinea, where they would be exchanged for American POWs. Only about half the passengers and two of the five crew members survived the crash; the direct cause was failure to check whether the directional gyro had been activated before the takeoff, yet technically the pilots hadn't done anything illegal. The mandatory pretakeoff "challenge and response" checklist that became normal airline cockpit procedure after the war did not exist in 1943.

Far luckier was the crew of a heavily loaded C-87 that was taking off from Townsville bound for Port Moresby and stalled twenty feet from the ground. It pancaked down on its belly and skidded more than 2000 feet before it plunged into a soft marsh. All five crew members walked away.

Canton Island was the scene of the third fatal C-87 accident on May 3, 1944, when a nose wheel tire blew on takeoff; two crew members, the flight engineer and the navigator, died in the crash, which destroyed one of the last C-87s United operated during the war. Meanwhile the airline's ATC C-54s were compiling a brilliant record of their own, on more than one occasion hauling cargo that was beyond the capability of the smaller C-87. Jack O'Brien flew one such flight, a load of replacement stabilizers for damaged B-17 bombers of the Fifth Air Force, based at Port Moresby.

UAL still was waiting for its first C-54 to be delivered when General George Kenney, commander of the Fifth Air Force, asked for the emergency shipment. The stabilizers were too long and cumbersome to load into a C-87, so ATC diverted a C-54 from its Atlantic airlift and O'Brien, with famed test and racing pilot Benny Howard as his first officer, flew the transport from San Francisco to Brisbane, covering 9000 miles in thirty-five hours, with only two refueling stops: Honolulu and Canton Island.

The C-54 already had proved itself over the Atlantic; this was a stunning demonstration of its ability to handle the far greater reaches of the Pacific. Another C-54 flew an even longer mission than O'Brien's, an airplane commanded by W.E. "Dusty" Rhoades, who had started the war as a copilot and was upgraded to captain shortly after Ops-Pacific was launched. Dusty and his crew were in San Francisco awaiting assignment for his next routine ATC Pacific flight when he got some exceptionally nonroutine orders: he was to fly a C-54 nonstop from San Francisco to Washington, where he would receive further orders of a secret nature. He didn't know he was about to undertake one of the longest missions of the war.

In Washington, Rhoades boarded fourteen State Department officials plus a load of priority mail and classified cargo. He flew south to Brazil via Miami and Puerto Rico, then across the South Atlantic to Morocco and Algiers. At the latter city, he picked up Major General Richard Sutherland, General Douglas MacArthur's chief of staff, and the C-54 finally landed in Cairo in time to deliver the civilians and Sutherland to the summit meeting being held by FDR, Churchill, and Chiang Kai-shek.

There was more to come for Dusty Rhoades, including his wartime future. After the conference ended, he headed the C-54 east, this time with more mail and cargo, and with Sutherland and other staff officers as passengers. Sutherland, however, was a notch above the average passenger; he was a pilot himself, and Dusty let him take over the controls occasionally. Rhoades unloaded mail and cargo in India, then flew Sutherland back to Australia before crossing the Pacific and home to San Francisco via New Caledonia, the Fifi Islands, Canton Island, and Honolulu. He had flown a total of 150 hours, logged 31,380 miles, and had impressed Sutherland so much that the general recommended him to MacArthur as his personal pilot.

So Dusty Rhoades, who at the time of Pearl Harbor was only a lowly UAL copilot, became the commander of the special transport assigned to MacArthur, a C-54 known as the *Bataan;* MacArthur chose the name himself, as might be expected from a man who couldn't even say the word "Bataan" without choking up from his painful memories of the Philippines defeat, the Bataan Death March, and the last stand at Corregidor. Dusty took a leave of absence from the airline to don the uniform of an ATC major— and later a colonel—and he was the one who flew MacArthur and the *Bataan* to Tokyo for the surrender ceremony and the start of the occupation. Twelve other ATC transports piloted by United crews were in the victorious air armada that swept over the Japanese capital on V-J Day, but most eyes were on the C-54 carrying MacArthur.

ATC and NATS military crews were expected to assume the bulk of Ops-Pacific operations when the war ended, but so many Air Force and Navy transport pilots holding high discharge points left the service that MacArthur complained to Washington about inadequate mail and cargo service to the occupation forces in Japan. ATC asked United to launch "Ops-Tokyo," a new transpacific airlift involving three daily flights from San Francisco to Tokyo. The operation, which for a brief time included eight daily San Francisco–Honolulu round-trips, tied up seventy-five crews who otherwise could have been used to fly UAL's reviving domestic schedules. But saying no to an obvious military need, even if the war was over, was not William A. Patterson's style.

UAL's extensive Pacific experience did much to shape the airline's future, for it affected Patterson's own visions of that future. Unlike TWA and American, Patterson had no interest whatsoever in the postwar transatlantic market. He was, in fact, the lone airline president to support Juan Trippe's unsuccessful postwar attempt to establish a single U.S. overseas flag carrier; in 1944, Patterson predicted that it would take as few as a dozen and not more than twenty-three planes to carry all the transatlantic air traffic for the next ten years, one of the few inaccurate predictions he made in his entire career.

Shortly after the war ended, United subcontracted and subsequently turned over all of its ATC responsibilities in the Pacific to Trans-Ocean Airlines and Pacific Overseas Airlines, two postwar charter carriers organized by ATC and NATS veterans. The only Ops-Pacific leg that UAL continued to operate commercially was San Francisco–Honolulu, the route the airline eventually expanded into a full-scale transpacific service. Patterson found some irony in his refusal to enter the transatlantic brawl. There was one other major airline chief who, despite his own carrier's extensive wartime overseas operations, felt the same way as Patterson, and carefully limited its postwar expansion activities to the Americas.

That was Edward Vernon Rickenbacker.

Eastern Air Lines

Like many of its sister airlines, Eastern found itself operating more airplanes during the war than it had given up to the Army at its start.

On September 1, 1942, Eastern established a Military Transport Division (MTD), inaugurating its wartime missions modestly. It assigned six converted DC-3s to domestic cargo flights, but MTD quickly expanded its operations, starting with a military cargo route between Miami and Natal. Over the next three and a half years, MTD flew more than 45 million pounds of war cargo and 130,000 passengers while compiling one of the best safety records of any

ATC carrier—not one scheduled flight was ever canceled, and only one airplane was lost. In peacetime, Eastern was known as a "bad weather" airline, and MTD lived up to that reputation.

The queen of the MTD fleet was the C-46, Eastern adding fifteen of them to the Miami-Natal route by February of 1943. Between MTD's formation and the introduction of the C-46, however, were five months of extensive modifications—some 300 factory changes recommended by the airline's technicians in Miami before EAL considered them acceptable.

MTD headquarters were in Miami, and its operations really got into full gear in mid April of 1943, beginning with a survey flight that took a number of senior captains over the route that would be the airline's prime ATC responsibility: a 6500-mile hop from Miami to Accra, Africa, via San Juan, Trinidad, Georgetown (in British Guiana), Belem and Natal (Brazil), and Ascension Island. The Trinidad-Georgetown-Belem-Natal legs were flown over uninhabited jungles, while the other legs involved ocean flying.

Eastern lacked previous ocean-flying experience, and only pilots with at least 10,000 hours of logged flying time were assigned to MTD. The restriction made sense, for the logistics and handicaps were enormous. The Trinidad airstrip, for example, was surrounded by jungle and located at the base of a mountain range whose peaks were usually shrouded in clouds. There was no such thing as a missed approach at Trinidad; a pilot had to be right the first time.

Maintenance was a problem, particularly at the start, when there were few if any facilities along the route—these were stations that hadn't been involved in the prewar Pan Am airport construction program. In MTD's early days, a mechanic went along on every flight, but this became impractical as the Army began beefing up "the Great Chocolate Fleet" with new C-46s, and Eastern found that its airplanes outnumbered the available mechanics.

A temporary solution was to station two mechanics at Borinquen Field, Puerto Rico. One would work on two planes each morning, board the second aircraft, and then fly with it down to Trinidad, where he would service the same two airplanes for their return trip the next day. He would come back to Puerto Rico on the second aircraft, service the two ships all over again, and then get some sleep while the other mechanic would repeat the identical grueling schedule.

This arrangement lasted only until Eastern received enough C-

46s to extend its military transport flights beyond Trinidad. MTD then had to station mechanics at every stop, and it took a war for any man to work under the horrendous conditions they put up with. The airfields at Georgetown, Belem, and Natal were airports only in the sense that they had runways. Atkinson Field in George-town was a good example. Located halfway between Miami and Natal—it was 2000 miles from either point—its only runway was nothing more than a narrow clearing hacked out of the jungle. For a time, Eastern's sole and very lonely employee at Atkinson was a mechanic who lived in a mud hut with a roof made of dung and palm leaves. Not until later in the war was a crude barracks built for the additional men assigned there.

The pilots had to avoid flying over French Guiana, which had come under German control after France collapsed. They usually stayed five miles offshore, but more than one MTD plane flew home with bullet holes in the fuselage because it had wandered too far inshore.

Eastern's base at Belem was Van de Cans Field, located twelve miles from the Amazon delta town. The Brazilian facilities there, like the field at Georgetown, had been carved out of solid jungle and some of the trees surrounding the airport towered as high as 200 feet—it was another so-called "airport" where no pilot dared try a missed approach, especially in a heavily loaded C-46. Over-nighting pilots stayed at Belem's misnamed Grande Hotel, and occasionally so did the mechanics. The maintenance crews worked on an average of four airplanes a day, often finishing up at midnight a shift that had begun early in the morning. At that hour a mechanic usually was too tired to make the twelve-mile trip into Belem over a road that was more of a wide path, so he would curl up on top of some cargo inside a plane and grab what sleep he could. For such mechanics, a typical breakfast consisted of emergency rations he got out of the aircraft, and not even the stiffest martinet of a captain ever begrudged this appropriation of supplies.

Conditions were slightly better at Natal, where there also was a Grande Hotel even more inappropriately named, and a good fifteen miles from Natal's Parnamirim Field. At least the weather was some-what drier and cooler than at either Belem or Georgetown, but Natal's biggest problem was the field. It was built on fine sand; a stiff ocean breeze could whip up the first cousin to a Sahara sandstorm. About the best one could say about the Grande was that in case of rain, it had a roof. The beds were straw mattresses plunked down on wood planks, but the sleeping quarters were palatial compared to the hotel's food service. The meals ranged from poor to unbearable, a culinary shortcoming magnified by the waiters who spoke no English. A reporter named Bill Wooten, assigned to cover MTD activities, later provided a firsthand account of the language barrier problem:

"If a guy from Eastern wanted an egg, he almost had to lay one himself. He'd flap his arms and cackle until the waiter got the message. Until the boys got to pick up a little Portuguese, they had to work out some ingenious sign language to get served."

When the Army finally got permission for ATC aircraft to bypass French Guiana entirely, Eastern began operating a different course that took MTD flights over the Brazilian interior. It was a more direct route that saved time, but the entire thousand-mile stretch was over almost solid jungle, as wild and dense as any in the world. There were few dependable radio aids, and the outdated, inaccurate maps were even worse than those in Alaska, which were Rand-McNally masterpieces by comparison. Many of the high mountains in the area weren't even displayed on pilot maps; those that were shown turned out to have higher or lower elevations than indicated, and also were as much as fifty miles away from their designated locations. Added to this thousand-mile unmarked obstacle course, and frequently blotting out most landmarks, was the intertropical front, a barrier of turbulent cumulus clouds often towering into the stratosphere and extending to within 500 feet of sea level. The MTD crews usually adhered to one rule: cruise at around 9000 feet—no higher and no lower.

The Army took over the bases at Belem and Natal late in 1942, and MTD ground personnel began operating in a quasi-military environment. Employees were required to wear uniforms and were subject to Army regulations, including trial by court-martial for violations of the Articles of War. There was even a system of rank that followed that of ATC flight crews—top administrative officers wore the three shoulder bars of an airplane commander, chief mechanics and station managers two bars, and mechanics and assistant station managers one.

The Commando's reputation as a brawny weight lifter collided frequently with its reputation as a temperamental pilot-killer. Its hydraulic system was so unreliable that at one point Eastern grounded every C-46 for two weeks until its engineers could correct the problems. The C-46's fire-extinguishing system, as one mechanic put it, "couldn't have put out a match in a high wind." Its electric propeller-feathering system had a habit of feathering inadvertently at embarrassing moments—such as on takeoff. The feathering headaches, however, eventually disappeared when the temperamental Curtiss electric propellers were replaced with new Hamilton-Standard props. With all its faults, some of them never eliminated entirely, the C-46 had great range as well as tremendous load capacity for a two-engine transport. And some pilots, like Captain Warren Metzger of Alaska Airlines, who flew them on Navy contract missions, considered the Commando one of the best transports ever built.

"Once they got rid of those electric props," Metzger declared, "it was a very fine airplane. If you flew a C-46 at its proper maximum weight, it would handle its load on one engine better than a DC-3. But during the war they constantly operated them about five thousand pounds over maximum. Sure, if you're carrying fifty thousand pounds on a C-46 and you lose an engine, you'd better start grabbing a rosary."

Late in 1943, Eastern extended its aerial pipeline from Natal across the South Atlantic to Accra via Ascension Island and the airline was willing to operate the Commando across 1500 miles of water between Natal and Ascension; in view of the airplane's inadequate engine-out performance, this had to have been almost as risky as flying one over the Hump. That MTD's C-46s crossed the South Atlantic without serious incident was a tribute to the mechanics who nursed them on the ground, to the pilots who nursed them in the air, and to the airplane itself.

Ascension Island was the refueling stop for the African flights, and landing a C-46 there was like trying to park a Greyhound bus in a suburban driveway. Hills lapped each side of the runway, which also happened to be humped; the middle was fifteen feet higher than it was on the approach end, and forty-five feet higher than at the other end. The result was that pilots landed uphill until they reached the top of the hump and then rolled downhill the rest of the way. The crews had to get used to the illusion that they were running out of runway until they could see the downgrade.

Flights always left Natal at night in order to land at Ascension Island in daylight, because Ascension had no runway lights. There were no night takeoffs from Ascension, either, for besides the hazard of an unlighted runway, there was the problem of terns—a species of bird roosting by the landing strip, with the unpleasant habit of conducting takeoffs of their own as soon as darkness fell. There were thousands of them, and they had already wrecked one airplane before Eastern started operating there.

EAL stationed only one employee at Ascension, a mechanic who lived with Army personnel. He got along fine with his military companions, and they all welcomed the sight of an incoming MTD airplane, usually carrying mail, fresh reading material, and sometimes special food treats. Like virtually every ATC unit, MTD was close-knit, a proud wartime fraternity that quickly built up its own traditions and esprit de corps. The living and working conditions may have been abominable, yet griping was at a minimum; boredom was the worst enemy.

Accra was a place as miserably uncomfortable as any on the MTD system. It was malaria-infested, and its population was heavily weighted with giant mosquitoes so voracious that MPs checked cots every night to make sure the men were sleeping under nets. If anyone was found in bed without a mosquito net, it was a court-martial offense. The airfield was in bush country inhabited by primitive natives, and while they were harmless and even friendly, nobody felt much like straying away from the base. Maintenance work was performed in the open, either under scorching heat or in teeming rain. Nights were cooler, but darkness also brought the bombing raids by hordes of mosquitoes; the insects would wait until perspiration washed away repellants, and then attack.

For anyone assigned to MTD, laughs were few, the work hard, and the hours long—a fifteen- or sixteen-hour day was the norm for a mechanic, not the exception. The flight crews didn't pull duty to that extent, but they had their own brand of fatigue and tension. No pilot who ever flew the Natal-Ascension Island leg can ever forget the difficulty of finding a dot in the middle of the ocean, with no other land within 700 miles and the closest alternate landing strip at least 1000 miles away. Navigation was celestial and by dead reckoning plus, on more than one occasion, the power of prayer. A mistake of a couple of degrees meant a flight would miss Ascension entirely and make ditching inevitable, but even this kind of strain was no worse than over the rest of the route, where a forced landing gave the crew a choice between the ocean and the jungle.

The chief compensation was the knowledge that MTD's missions were helping to win the war, and the undeniable fact that flying a transport plane, even with all the risks, was infinitely better than getting shot at on a regular basis. Plus, the discovery so many provincially smug young Americans made when exposed to life in something other than a prosperous democracy. They learned there is a human urge for dignity and pride, no matter how primitive or uneducated a person may be. Pan Am's people were probably the first to absorb this lesson, and eventually all the ATC/NATS crews had similar experiences—namely, giving such people dignity by giving them jobs.

The MTD station managers, whose chief duty was to serve as liaison men between the airline and the Army, hired South American natives for about 30 cents a day. To many of them, the pay was secondary to the satisfaction of working around airplanes, something that gave them a sense of responsibility and importance they had never known before, and quite possibly would never know again. One station manager hired a tall, dark-skinned native who seemed lackadaisical and indifferent until the manager gave him a title: *Jefe de los Lavatorios*. From then on, he literally strutted through his daily chores, menial though they were. Translated, his title was Supervisor of Lavatories—which meant his job was to clean out the airplane "honey buckets," or toilets.

At Borinquen Field, a young Puerto Rican was assigned the task of waking up the flight crews overnighting at the barracks. Many, worn out by hours of tough flying, would have slept through a major earthquake and waking up some sleepy and very grouchy senior captain was only slightly less dangerous than challenging a mother grizzly bear with cubs. The youngster would shine a flashlight in pilot faces and shake the men until they opened their eyes. But this proved unsatisfactory, because a few weary pilots would go right back to sleep after the boy left, and then blame him for delaying their flights.

A few such unjustified scoldings forced him to take drastic action, demonstrating that while he may not have been educated, he was smarter than some of the pilots. He drew up a list of the airmen he was to wake each morning and took it with him when he made his before-dawn rounds. The minute a pilot stirred into semiconsciousness, the boy would deliver the one English sentence he had carefully memorized: "Sign de paper!" The flashlight stayed on until the bleary-eyed man had signed next to his name, and if he went back to sleep his human alarm clock was in the clear.

The MTD C-46s carried everything that could be squeezed into a Commando's dirigible-shaped cabin, including—on one occasion—a disassembled Army observation plane. As with all the airlines flying for ATC, practically anything could show up on a cargo manifest. Eastern's MTD flights carried cryptograph machines, spare parts, ammunition, artillery, mail, soap, and millions of dollars in payrolls. The same variety applied to the passenger manifests; one MTD flight carried railroad engineers bound for Iran, and another had "sappers" aboard—men trained to detect and destroy land mines.

The return flights didn't come back empty. They hauled mica and quartz crystals from Brazil to the U.S. when a shortage of these critical materials threatened to halt production of radar and radio tubes. They flew tons of crude rubber, tons of captured German weaponry to be tested and evaluated by American ordnance experts, and ferry pilots returning to the U.S. to pick up more planes.

The latter often performed their ferrying missions over Eastern's MTD route, but their safety record was alarming. They were young and inexperienced, with very little instrument training—the AWTI schools weren't in full swing yet—and for a time scores of them were victims of violent and totally unexpected tropical storms they were ill-equipped to handle. Army officials discussed the high accident rate with MTD personnel, and the result was the use of Eastern planes as "weather ships." Many southbound MTD flights began carrying Army weather observers, radioing firsthand en route weather information back to ferry bases. If there was no Army meteorologist aboard, Eastern's own radio operators provided weather data to any military aircraft operating in their area; if a ferry pilot needed a forecast update, he could contact the nearest Eastern flight.

Only two weeks after the program went into effect, the ferry accident rate dropped dramatically, and stayed low for the duration of ferry operations over the route. Eastern's own AWTI school helped improve the safety record, too; the airline opened a training facility in Atlanta for military pilots, flight engineers, and mechanics that turned out 1200 graduates, and later EAL provided on-the-job training in heavy cargo aircraft to almost 800 Army pilots.

And while the Great Chocolate Fleet roamed unfamiliar skies over jungles and oceans, the man who ran Eastern with an iron fist joined two other airline presidents in writing their own chapters in the saga of World War II.

★ ★ 7 ★ ★
The General, the Colonel, and the Man in the Raft

Hundreds of airline officials entered the armed forces in World War II, many of them joining the Air Transport Command or Naval Air Transport Service, where their abilities were best utilized.

Robert J. Smith, a Braniff Airways vice president, went into the Air Service Command as a lieutenant colonel and supervised all ASC cargo contracts. There was C.H. "Dutch" Schildhauer, a veteran Pan American pilot who had pioneered many of the airline's Pacific and Atlantic routes; he had been a Navy airman before joining Pan Am, and as a wartime Navy captain he was largely responsible for organizing NATS. Similar examples would fill an entire chapter, and mention must also be made of the ex–airline pilots who flew "the high and the mighty" for ATC and NATS: generals, admirals, prime ministers, and presidents.

A former American Airlines captain, Edward Coates, was operations chief of the ATC's "Brass Hatters" squadron whose crews transported high-ranking military and civilian officials all over the world. TWA's Otis Bryan helped ATC develop many of its overseas routes and, as will be related in a later chapter, was President Roosevelt's favorite airman. American's Hank Myers also commanded presidential transports, as well as serving as ATC chief Hal George's aide. It was Commander W.H. "Slim" Larned, a United captain in peacetime, who flew Navy Secretary Frank Knox on a grueling 17,000-mile inspection trip; he also was chief staff officer for NATS's Atlantic operations.

That kind of list, too, could go on for page after page. But the airline people most subject to critical scrutiny, by the very nature of their enormous prewar executive authority, were the two air carrier presidents who donned uniforms: American's C.R. Smith and Continental's Bob Six. They both worked for Hal George's Air Transport Command, but that was all they had in common during the war, their military careers going in different directions. C.R. "flew a desk," while Six served as an active transport pilot.

The General

If C.R. Smith "flew a desk," so to speak, he flew it like no one else in the U.S. Army Air Corps. As American's president, C.R. was known for his fervent hatred of bureaucratic red tape, long-winded memos, and the use of even one sheet of carbon copy paper in practically any kind of correspondence. About the only item he brought from American to his ATC job was his manual typewriter. On this he continued to write the same pithy notes to subordinates that were his modis operandi at American, addressed directly and solely to the person who was supposed to carry out his orders; carbon copies of a C.R. Smith directive were as rare as five-engined airplanes.

This couldn't last, of course, the military being fueled as much by paper as by high-octane gas. Eventually, C.R. was apprised of the Pentagon's unofficial Eleventh Commandment—*Thou Shalt Make Carbon Copies of Damned Near Everything*—and he was forced to reform. He acquired a fancy typewriter with a perforated paper roll that produced six copies, usually typed professionally by a Pentagon clerk, although Smith claimed later that he never intended to apply his no-copy, I'll-write-my-own-memos habit to *all* his official correspondence.

"I knew from long experience that the outfit [ATC] would not function well unless the top hands knew what the others were doing," he explained virtuously. Maybe so, but one of his closest wartime associates swore that before the arrival of that Gatling gun version of a typewriter, and his accepting secretarial help, C.R. once sent an important order to Casablanca, brusque and self-typed as was his airline style, with no copies.

"The Pentagon found out about it and raised hell with C.R.,

who ignored all the protests," the associate related. "But it was after this that he got the typewriter with the perforated rolls."

Any top airline executive going into ATC or NATS was immediately suspect of favoring his old company, and Smith was no exception. C.R. made sure such criticism could never apply to him; he deliberately avoided as many contacts with American as possible, and during the entire war devoted 100 percent of his loyalty and time to ATC. He tried to keep himself posted on what the airline was doing, but even when he heard things that bothered him, he made no effort to interfere. He adhered to this hands-off policy even when American, during the war, applied for permission to acquire American Export Airlines and its postwar international routes, thus creating what was to become American Overseas Airlines. C.R. had reservations about certain aspects of the merger, but said nothing. Not until several years after the war did he order AOL's routes and aircraft sold to Pan Am.

Despite his position as George's deputy, C.R. did relatively little traveling during the war. He did manage to visit the CBI theater once, and some of his ex-pilots then flying for ATC gave him a royal welcome. At a festive party in his honor, former AA Captain Cotton Johnson took a machete and chopped off Smith's tie. Many years later, C.R. was on a flight from Dallas to New York, and Cotton, who was flying the trip, asked Smith if he remembered him.

"I don't remember your name," C.R. growled, "but I remember that goddamned machete."

How much he missed the airline during the war no one really knew; C.R.'s large streak of sentimentality was always carefully guarded and it was even more invisible during wartime, buried under his strict hands-off policy. Yet some of his old airline friends suspected that figuratively speaking, his uniform never really fit him. Bill Dunn, a former American public relations director who was attached to General MacArthur's staff, was in Washington on leave and stopped in to visit his old boss. When they went out to lunch, Dunn noticed that Smith looked miserable when he had to return a salute—and there were plenty of them, because C.R. had just been made a brigadier general.

Dunn voiced some comment about all the saluting and Smith frowned.

"This general stuff isn't for me," he said unhappily. "In business, if you're smarter than the other guy you'll get ahead. In the military, if you're smarter than some other general, you'd better watch your step or you'll wind up in some place like Samoa."

Dunn quickly found out, however, that his being an old friend and former airline colleague cut no mustard with his ex-boss. He was scheduled to return to the Pacific theater by ship and decided it would be better to fly. He phoned Smith.

"Any chance of getting me on an ATC flight, C.R.?"

"No!" was the curt reply.

End of conversation. And Dunn realized what others already had discovered in any wartime contacts with Smith: To C.R., the Air Transport Command, not American, was his airline for the duration, and there was no point in anyone even remotely connected with the airline asking the slightest favor.

Unlike a few self-important airline executives who took off their uniforms after the war, but still insisted on being called by their former military rank, C.R. became a civilian again in a hurry. It was once more "C.R." or "Mr. C.R." More important, to most people he hadn't changed one bit. There were a few who thought he seemed a little more arbitrary, even dictatorial, but this might have been due to the contrast with the easygoing Ned Kemp, or the personable Ralph Damon, who was the airline's executive vice president and was really running American at war's end.

Smith spent the first few days after his discharge—with the rank of a three-star major general—getting briefed on the airline's current problems. The terse notes began pouring from his typewriter again, and it was almost as if he had never been away. He professed to be damned glad he was out of the Army, but many years later a close friend asked the old lion what had been the most interesting period of his life.

"The war," C.R. replied without hesitation.

The Colonel

Bob Six didn't reach the exalted status of a general—he entered the Army Air Corps as a mere captain, and was discharged not quite two years later wearing the silver oak leaves of a lieutenant colonel.

But in those two years, Continental's volatile founder proved to be as colorful an ATC pilot as he was an airline president. He enlisted in August of 1942, and left his airline in the hands of Terrell C. Drinkwater, Continental's executive vice president and general manager. The night before Six took the military oath, he met with Ted Haueter, his vice president of operations, whom he trusted more than anyone else in the world.

"Ted, keep me informed," was all Six said—and Haueter understood. Drinkwater was capable and experienced, but also intensely ambitious. Those four words Six had uttered to Haueter were to save his airline for him.

So Bob Six went off to war and was immediately assigned to the Air Transport Command. He was a licensed pilot, but he had to earn a multiengine rating at the Thunderbird School in Phoenix. His first ATC outfit was the Sixth Ferry Command based at Hamilton Field, California, and his first ATC flight was ferrying a B-24 bomber to Australia, where he was greeted by a change in orders: proceed to New Caledonia and take over a small ferry command post there.

Six felt like an exile on the island, and was overjoyed when he was ordered back to Hamilton. He flew copilot on the return trip, with Roy Pickering—later to become American's chief pilot in San Francisco—in the left seat. They were so happy to be going home that they carelessly packed away their aircraft identification codes. En route to the West Coast, they flew over a Navy convoy which demanded their coded identification.

Six groaned. "Hell, they're in our bags in the rear of the plane. I'll go get 'em."

Pickering looked down at the convoy, which was beginning to zigzag, while every antiaircraft gun on the escorting warships was swiveling in their direction.

"By the time you get those codes, we'll have been shot down," he told Six. "Let's get the hell out of here."

Pickering ducked safely into a cloud bank just as the guns opened up.

Six arrived at Hamilton to find he had a new commanding officer: General Karl Truesdale Jr., a veteran Air Corps pilot who wasn't exactly thrilled about his newly reporting subordinate.

"I figured when the Air Force assigned Six to me, they were just trying to stash an airline executive in a cushy job," Truesdale confessed. "Maybe the Air Force felt that way, but Six sure as hell didn't. He pitched right in and worked his tail off. He was one fine officer."

That he was, but he also was a maverick who could be a thorn in the side of any commanding officer. At Hamilton, Six was reunited with two old friends from Continental who also had joined the Army: former vice president Clarence West and John Bender of sales, both of whom had been with United before Six recruited them for Continental. West was sworn in as a major, which galled Six, who hated to be outranked by any former airline subordinate. Yet a few months later, when Six was promoted to major, he always stood on West's left in dutiful accordance with military protocol requiring the senior officer to be on the right.

Bender was only a lieutenant, but as far as Six was concerned, he was the most valuable shavetail in the entire United States Army. He was the outfit's "official bandit," capable of begging, borrowing, or even stealing anything the Sixth Ferry Command needed, from whiskey to a two-and-a-half-ton truck. There seems to be one in every military unit, and Bender was tops at a profession demanding the most devious skills, brazen ingenuity, and total lack of conscience.

He was willing to go anywhere and do anything his former boss suggested, although on more than one occasion he regretted being so pliant. One day, Six was ordered to pick up some spare airplane parts at a Sacramento depot, using whatever aircraft was available. He spotted a two-place, single-engine trainer all fueled up and commandeered it.

"Come on along with me," he suggested to Bender, who hesitated. He knew Six had flown mostly B-24s and B-17s on ferry trips.

"You checked out in that plane?" he asked doubtfully.

"Hell, no," Six said confidently. "But if I can fly a B-24 I can fly that little thing."

They took off in the trainer and immediately ran into a problem. Six couldn't find the lever that retracted the landing gear and Bender, who was a ground officer, was no help whatsoever. Six shoved and pushed at various unfamiliar switches, levers, and buttons, but the wheels still refused to come up, and finally, swallowing his pilot's pride, he radioed the Hamilton tower.

"How the hell do you get the gear up on this bucket?" he inquired.

"What kind of an aircraft are you flying?" the tower wanted to know.

"Damned if I know," Six admitted.

"Suggest you do a flyby so we can identify your airplane."

Six buzzed the tower as requested. "Okay, now where's that goddamned lever?" he repeated.

"There isn't any," the tower controller sighed. "You're in an aircraft with a fixed landing gear."

Like all ATC units, the Sixth Ferry Command was more of an airline than a military outfit. About ninety percent of its flight crews were ex–airline pilots whose main job was ferrying airplanes and airlifting personnel and materials to combat zones. Six was in charge of operations, including all flight scheduling and crew assignments, and when Truesdale was transferred to the much larger Morrison AFB in Florida, he insisted on taking Continental's "Three Musketeers"—Six, West, and Bender—with him.

Truesdale was happy about the Morrison transfer for a reason that had nothing to do with its being a bigger ATC base. He agreed with a War Department assessment that Hamilton, semiringed by mountains and with its longest runway only 6000 feet, was too small. So his final assignment at Hamilton was to select a site for a new air base, and he gave this job to Six.

Six, accompanied by an engineering officer, inspected various sites throughout California and the Pacific Northwest, finally agreeing that one particular location was superior and reporting their recommendation to Truesdale. The site they picked became Travis Air Force Base, fifty miles from San Francisco, and now rated as one of the finest in the world.

The Morrison tour of duty involved far more difficult duties than at Hamilton. Morrison, located near West Palm Beach, was the jumping-off base for ferry flights to Africa, via Brazil. Truesdale was handed a can of worms the day he reported. The Morrison ferry planes were flying a route that took them down the east coast of Brazil to the seaport city of Natal from where, after refueling, they took off across the South Atlantic toward North Africa.

The route looked simple, logical, and reasonably safe on paper, but it had a fatal drawback. Severe storm fronts built up almost daily, and numerous planes never reached Natal; Tom Harmon, the All-American halfback from Michigan, was the pilot of one aircraft that went down in a storm and he reached safety only after a harrowing trek through jungle country that would have intimidated Tarzan. Truesdale discussed the problem with Six.

"We need an inland route that circumvents those weather fronts," he said. "Take a B-17 down there and see if an inland route's possible."

Six, in command of a five-man survey flight that included a weather expert, flew to Natal on a route taking them over 17,000-foot mountains that weren't on any aeronautical charts. There were no storms, but severe mountain turbulence was prevalent and at lower elevations the terrain was so desolate that survival after a forced landing would have been almost impossible. Six returned to Morrison and reported his findings to Truesdale.

"An inland route won't work," he advised. "For one thing, it's too tough for some of the kids flying down there—hell, a lot of 'em have only a couple of hundred hours and that mountain country would scare a condor. I'll bet we'd lose more planes and pilots than what the coastal route's costing us right now."

"We're losing too many of them along the coast," the general reminded him. "You got any ideas?"

"Yep. We found out those fronts don't start building up until mid morning. If we dispatch the ferry flights from dawn until about 10 A.M., then shut down operations until late afternoon, we'll miss just about all the bad weather."

Truesdale quickly adopted the plan and the accident rate dropped sharply, as it had with other ferry pilots aided by Eastern's weather planes. But while Six's new seven-day scheduling system was a boon to the young ferry pilots, those in charge of dispatching the flights encountered severe ground turbulence. The twice-a-day departures, one dispatch operation starting at dawn and the other close to sunset, made for a very long workday. It was particularly tough on Sundays, for Saturday nights at Morrison were reserved for relaxation and the early Sunday morning dispatching duties were performed through bleary, often bloodshot eyes.

"We gotta do something about it," Six informed his two Continental cohorts after a few torturous weeks of the Sunday-morning-must-follow-Saturday-night ordeal.

"Yeah," Bender agreed. "But what? You were the one who came up with this damned schedule."

"I'll think of something," Six promised.

He did, and it was sheer genius. He rented rooms for himself,

West, and Bender in a West Palm Beach hotel under assumed names. After the early Sunday morning flights had left Morrison, the trio would sneak off to the hotel for a few hours of badly needed sack time. Truesdale, during his entire tenure at Morrison, never was able to locate his Sunday truants, and it was not until after the war that Six confessed to him where his operations officer, administrative officer, and official bandit, had been hiding every Sunday.

On one of his flights to Natal, Six ran into a Pan Am ATC pilot who was so impressed by the privilege of having a few drinks with the president of Continental that he insisted on presenting him with a gift. It was a jaguar cub that Six named Whiskey, which he crated up and brought back to Morrison. Whiskey wasn't much bigger than an ordinary cat and Six at first tried to turn the cub into a house pet; he built a small cage for him where Whiskey slept at night, outside his quarters, and took him to the office every morning, allowing him to romp around freely.

Few shared Six's affection for the baby jaguar, especially as he began growing at an alarming rate. Once Whiskey wandered into the ventilating ducts and was lost for six hours while half the base turned into a search party. Visitors to Six's office, never expecting to see a live uncaged jaguar, started getting nervous, and Truesdale suggested that maybe Whiskey was becoming a liability.

"He wouldn't hurt a fly," Six assured the general. "You never saw such a gentle little fella."

Truesdale finally ordered Bender to "do something about that damned beast," and Bender's solution was not only drastic but painfully effective. Somehow, he managed to surreptitiously attach a piece of raw liver to the seat of his superior's pants without Six realizing it. Whiskey reacted as any red-blooded young jaguar would—he charged and sunk his fangs into both the liver and several inches of Robert Forman Six's posterior. Whiskey was banished permanently to his cage, and eventually was donated to the West Palm Beach zoo.

No one knew what Six was liable to bring back from any flight. He showed up one day with a South American anteater, but never got a chance to turn it into a house pet—Truesdale took one look at it and ordered Six to make another donation to the zoo. After one B-24 ferry mission, Six arrived back at Morrison with a kangaroo he had somehow acquired. Bender managed to sneak the strictly contraband animal into Bachelor Officers Quarters, where he kept it hidden from Truesdale for weeks.

The official bandit always suspected that Bob Six had excellent communications with the Almighty. He and Six were passengers aboard a B-25 on a flight from Morrison to Dallas. They ran into bad weather but passed up a chance to refuel at Houston and then found Dallas completely socked in. The fuel warning lights began to blink indicating only ten minutes of fuel remaining, and even the wing tips disappeared in a thick fog. Bender got out of his bucket seat and started to strap on a parachute.

"Where the hell do you think you're going?" Six demanded.

"I'm bailing out before we crash," Bender croaked.

"We aren't gonna crash," Six assured him. "I'll go up to the cockpit and see how things are."

Bender followed him. Just as Six stuck his head into the cockpit, the fog suddenly dissipated and there was a runway dead ahead.

"See?" Six chided. "I told you not to worry."

"It was just like the parting of the Red Sea," Bender reported to Truesdale later. "I know how close we were to buying it, because we ran out of fuel while we were taxiing to the gate."

Six was probably the only major in the armed forces with a personal aide, which helped compensate for Clarence West being promoted to lieutenant colonel while Six was still a major. Truesdale never officially assigned Bender to his operations chief, nor did he have to; Bender, now a captain, attached himself and did as much foraging for his old boss as for the base commander. Came the day when Six, with Bender present, asked Truesdale if he could have a jeep assigned to him on a permanent basis.

"I'm sorry, Bob," the general apologized, "but we're really short of ground vehicles, especially jeeps."

Bender disappeared for a few hours, telling Six he had an errand to run. He came back not only with a jeep he had filched from an army unit, but also a sergeant who somehow had found himself assigned to Major Six as his personal driver. Bender never did explain to either Six or Truesdale how he achieved the double theft of a jeep and a driver without getting court-martialed.

Despite Bender being color-blind, he did win his wings while at Morrison, although having Six as head of the pilot rating board at the time may have had something to do with his qualifying. Bender's limited flight duties included a regular mail run in a twin-engine

Cessna between Morrison and Homestead AFB. When he wasn't flying the mail, Bender occasionally accompanied Six to Cuba for fresh meat, and Nassau in the Bahamas for scotch, both items in short supply at Morrison.

Continental's Three Musketeers were inseparable during off-duty hours, but Six never confided in either of them his growing concern over what was happening back at the airline's headquarters in Denver. True to his word, Ted Haueter had been keeping him informed—and what Six was hearing was Terry Drinkwater's open desire to turn Six's temporary military duty leave into permanent banishment from Continental. Six got the first disturbing hint when he flew to Wichita on Army business and had dinner with Haueter and a few other old friends from Continental. Because airline business was discussed, Six told Ted to put the $263 dinner tab on his expense account. Haueter did, only to have Drinkwater personally reject it. Then Haueter learned that the executive committee, of which he was a member, had been holding meetings without telling him they had been scheduled.

Fed up, he resigned and applied to the Navy for active status under his old reserve commission. The Navy wanted to assign him to a bomber squadron in Alaska, but said he needed permission from his board of directors to leave the airline. It was then that Haueter found out Six had given the directors a flat order not to let Ted leave under any circumstances. He gave up and continued to correspond with Six, who by then was having serious health problems.

He was proud of a promotion to lieutenant colonel, but he was overweight, suffered from high blood pressure, and one morning he awoke to find his legs paralyzed from a pinpoint cerebral hemorrhage. Although he recovered the use of his legs quickly, he was obviously a sick man. Three times he went before a disability board, which refused to let him return to flying duties. If Six couldn't fly, he wanted out, but the board also refused to give him a disability discharge.

It was at this Catch-22 point that Haueter got a call from Hap Arnold, who was worried over a threatened strike at Continental's modification center. Production had fallen off sharply even before the strike threat.

"That mess in Denver has to be straightened out or else," Arnold warned, and Haueter knew the "or else" meant cancellation of a contract that was keeping the airline afloat.

"I don't have the authority to do it," Haueter said bluntly. "If you want a guy to clean up this mess, get Bob Six back here."

Ted knew Six already had someone in Denver fully capable of fixing the center's problems. He was an ex–Air Corps colonel named Harry Short, whom Six had met at Morrison and liked well enough to make him the unofficial fourth Musketeer. When Short received a medical discharge, Six pulled some strings and got him assigned to the modification center as general manager, a post for which he was eminently qualified; Short had once been in charge of a modification facility in Britain with 8000 employees under his supervision.

The problem was that Short lacked the clout to fight Drinkwater, and Haueter knew this when he urged Arnold to get Six back on the scene. Arnold responded by giving Six a thirty-day leave, sending him to Denver with a crack team of Air Force efficiency experts. He scrupulously avoided any interference with Drinkwater, but took over the modification center. Before his month's leave elapsed, he and Short had successfully negotiated a new labor contract. Six returned to Morrison with production levels back to a satisfactory level, but his military days were nearing an end.

He had no desire to be a desk jockey and Truesdale sympathized with him, finally suggesting that Six talk to Oliver Gasch, the base judge advocate.

"I'll be honest with you," Six told Gasch. "If I stay in the Air Force, I could lose my airline. But if I can get back to Continental, I think I can do more for the war effort at the modification center than sitting around here on my ass sharpening pencils."

Gasch nodded understandingly, and then showed him an Army regulation which in effect declared that if a serviceman could prove he'd be more effective as a civilian, he could get an honorable discharge. "If you honestly feel your situation fits that regulation," Gasch added, "I'll draw up the papers myself."

Those papers were still being processed when Haueter phoned Six to warn that the simmering corporate feud was about to explode. Drinkwater had called a special board meeting at the Biltmore Hotel in Los Angeles; the purpose was to demand Six's resignation from Continental on the grounds of health problems so serious that when he was discharged from the Army, he would no longer be capable of running the airline effectively. The directors would be asked to name Drinkwater as his successor.

Duly alerted, Six obtained an emergency leave and showed up at the Biltmore, much to Drinkwater's surprise. His very presence wrecked the attempted coup as he assured the directors his health was fine. A few weeks later his discharge from the Air Force came through. Drinkwater, his influence at Continental virtually destroyed, left to become a vice president at American and later was named president of Western.

To his dying day, Robert Forman Six was extremely proud of the two years he spent in the Air Transport Command. He didn't talk about his war experiences much, especially to fellow airline executives. He ran into one of the latter in Kansas City once and agreed to have a few drinks with him. For reasons Six himself could not explain, he did not tell him that their paths had almost crossed during the war and under dramatic circumstances—when Six was commanding one of the search planes looking for a B-17 that had ditched in the Pacific.

The hawk-nosed airline mogul sitting across from Bob Six in that Kansas City hotel bar, drinking martinis as if they were plain water, had been a passenger on that same B-17.

The Man in the Raft

Edward Vernon Rickenbacker of Eastern Air Lines was an avowed isolationist, and an indefatigable foe of President Roosevelt, whom he hated with unrelenting passion. Politically and philosophically speaking, Captain Eddie was judged to be several miles to the right of Calvin Coolidge; as Bob Six once remarked, "Compared to Eddie, a John Bircher was a liberal."

But he also was a sincere patriot who loved his country; like so many Americans who opposed involvement in another European war, once we were in it he was willing to do anything for the war effort. If he had preached isolationism, he also had preached preparedness in the absolute belief that no one would dare attack a powerfully armed United States.

Rickenbacker was only fifty years old when the U.S. entered the war, and there is some reason to believe he secretly wished he could have put on a uniform again—after all, he had been America's leading fighter ace in World War I, with twenty-five confirmed air victories. But he had given up his reserve colonel's commission in 1934, as a symbolic protest against FDR's seizure of the airlines' air mail routes—Rickenbacker had publicly called the deaths of twelve Army pilots trying to fly the mail, "legalized murder." And he was too proud to ask any favors from a president he openly despised.

If Captain Eddie was tempted to seek active military service, he kept it well hidden. In fact, when Bill Knudsen of General Motors became a three-star lieutenant general and was placed in charge of war production, Rickenbacker told him that by accepting the commission, "your usefulness to the country will be cut in half." Yet Rickenbacker himself leaped with eagerness at any wartime job or mission Washington suggested, as long as the suggestion didn't come from the White House.

(Rickenbacker apparently never appreciated or even grasped the fact that FDR actually never tried to keep him out of the war, as the President attempted to do with the nation's other leading isolationist: Charles Lindbergh.)

His initial conduit to war assignments was Hap Arnold, who was fond of the old pursuit pilot and admired his blunt honesty, if not his isolationist sentiments. In March of 1942, Arnold asked Captain Eddie to go on a nationwide tour of Air Corps training bases where morale was reported low. Rickenbacker happily accepted the invitation and went on the tour, accompanied by General Frank "Monk" Hunter, who had flown with the captain in the 94th Pursuit Squadron. They made an interesting pair; both were recovering from air accidents. Rickenbacker still walked with a limp from the injuries he had received in that 1940 crash near Atlanta, and would for the rest of his life. Hunter, who had suffered a serious back injury, took a masseur along to help keep him upright. But the two crippled men finished the tour successfully, Rickenbacker establishing surprising rapport with rookie pilots. Arnold was impressed to the point of mentioning this to Secretary of War Henry Stimson, who asked Rickenbacker to go on another mission: to England as a "nonmilitary observer" of Army bomber and fighter commands, evaluating the morale situation at bases in Britain.

The request first was made in writing and repeated in a subsequent face-to-face meeting Rickenbacker had with both Arnold and Stimson. They offered him a commission as a brigadier general,

American's C.R. Smith as deputy commander of the Air Transport Command. He was proud of the uniform but hated the saluting ritual. (*Photo courtesy of American Airlines—C.R. Smith Museum*)

The unsung hero of global airlift was Col. Edgar S. Gorrell, first president of the Air Transport Association of America. He led the nation's airlines in peace and war, from January 1, 1936 to March 5, 1945. (*Photo courtesy of Air Transport Association*)

The only known photograph of C.R. Smith (*left, standing*) and President Roosevelt together, believed to have been taken at an unnamed air base in the U.S. early in the war. (*Photo courtesy of American Airlines—C.R. Smith Museum*)

William A. "Pat" Patter
of United. There was alw
a twinkle in the eye of
paternalistic airline ch
ranked along with De
C.E. Woolman as one of
industry's truly beloved
ecutives. This photo sh
a younger Patterson, as
looked during the
*(Photo courtesy of Ur
Airlines)*

A rare group shot of four
endary commercial avia
icons, taken at a 1968 W
Club dinner in their he
Left to right: Wings
president R. Dixon Sp
W.A. Patterson, C.R. Sn
Eddie Rickenbacker
Juan Trippe. *(Photo cou
of Wings Club of New York)*

Pan Am's dynamic leader was
Juan Trippe. (*Photo courtesy of*
Airways International Magazine)

Captain Edward Vernon Rickenbacker of Eastern Air Lines.
(*Photo courtesy of* Airways International Magazine)

Robert Forman Six, Continental
Airlines's founder and president.
(*Photo courtesy of* Airways Interna-
tional Magazine)

The 747's grandfather. Cut
away drawing displayin
the spacious interior of pr
war Pan Am Boeing 314 fl
ing boat. Note the forwa
staircase leading from tl
lower lounge to the uppe
level flight deck, a featu
duplicated some 30 yea
later on the 747. (Pho
courtesy of The Boeing Compa.
Archives)

One of Pan Am's 314s i
wartime service with tl
Naval Air Transport Servic
(Photo courtesy of The Boein
Company Archives)

A Boeing 307 Stratoline
the world's first pressurize
airliner, in Air Transpo
Command garb. *(Photo cou*
tesy of The Boeing Compar
Archives)

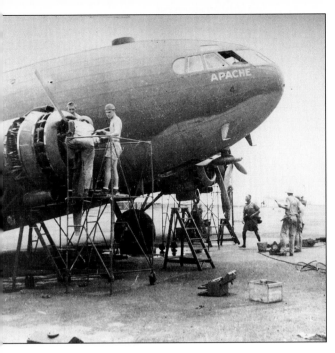

Servicing the ex-TWA Stratoliner *Apache* at Natal, Brazil, jumping-off spot for wartime South Atlantic airlift flights. (*Photo courtesy of The Boeing Company Archives*)

The famous—or infamous—step in the center of the Boeing 247's cabin. It hid the plane's main wing spar. (*Photo courtesy of The Boeing Company Archives*)

A C-47 taking off from a unidentified air base. Th odds are that the Goone Bird was carrying more tha its supposed allowable max mum load. (*Photo courtes of McDonnell Douglas*)

This shot of a C-47 shows the navigation dome on the top of the fuselage just behind the cockpit. The dome was one of the few features that distinguished the military transport from its civilian DC-3 sisters. (*Photo courtesy of McDonnell Douglas*)

Paratroopers boarding fleet of C-47s somewhere England. Notice the sm artillery piece being loac on the aircraft in the lo left corner—the "Goor bird" could carry alm anything. (*Photo courtes McDonnell Douglas*)

e DC-4E, prototype of the
med DC-4/C-54 transport
ries. The triple-tail proved
be a mistake and Douglas
ed a single tail on the pro-
iction model—the largest
nd transport plane of
WII and mainstay of the
erlin Airlift. (*Photo cour-
sy of McDonnell Douglas*)

The wartime C-54 assembly
line in Douglas's Santa Monica plant. (*Photo courtesy of
McDonnell Douglas*)

WWII workhorse. A perfectly-
estored C-46 Commando,
ow part of the Pima Air &
pace Museum's 200-plus
ircraft collection in Tucson,
rizona. One of the 3,200
-46s built during the war,
his particular airplane flew
he dreaded Hump in the
hina-Burma-India (CBI)
heater. (*Photo courtesy of
ima Air & Space Museum*)

Another military transpo[rt]
workhorse: the Consolidat[ed]
C-87, passenger/cargo versi[on]
of the B-24 heavy bomb[er.]
Despite several "bugs," it w[as]
a major airlift contributor [in]
WWII. (*Photo courtesy of Lo*[ck]
heed-Martin Tactical Aircr[aft]
Systems)

A C-53 bearing both Northeast and ATC insignia being
readied for a North Atlantic
route survey flight. The C-53
was the long-range version
of the C-47. (*Photo courtesy
of Delta Air Transport Heritage
Museum*)

Trailblazer: Northeast Ca[p-]
tain Milton H. Anders[on]
who commanded the fi[rst]
North Atlantic route surv[ey]
mission for the Air Tran[s-]
port Command. Crews w[ore]
arctic gear on the dangero[us]
survey flights. (*Photo co*[ur-]
tesy of Delta Air Transport H[er]
itage Museum)

7 bombers in United's
e Cheyenne, Wyoming
lification center. (*Photo
tesy of United Airlines*)

Ready for war. An aerial
shot of B-17s awaiting ferry
crews at United's Cheyenne,
Wyoming modification cen-
ter. (*Photo courtesy of United
Airlines*)

WII's airline-military part-
rship is graphically illus-
ated in this photo of a
nverted DC-3 being loaded
th priority cargo by UAL
d army personnel. (*Photo
urtesy of United Airlines*)

Like all airlines during WWII, Delta relied heavily on women to staff its airplane modification center. This quartet of "Rosie the Riveters" is working on a Douglas A-20 light bomber at Delta's Atlanta facility, rated one of the nation's best. (*Photo courtesy of Delta Air Transport Heritage Museum*)

Flight nurses caring for just a sample few of the thousands of wounded servicemen who were flown home for medical treatment. This picture was taken aboard a litter-equipped C-54, circa 1944. (*Photo courtesy of United Airlines*)

Whoops! The maroo crew of a Northeast/A C-47 mired in the snow Canada's "Lac O'Conn They landed in an effor rescue the crew and p sengers of Captain Ch O'Connor's C-87 that forced down on the fro lake. (*Photo courtesy Delta Air Transport Heri Museum*)

otain Eddie Rickenbacker
ter) after his wartime res-
—54 pounds lighter than
ore the Pacific ditching
l hardly able to walk
uided. Helping him is
onel Robert L. Griffin (*left*)
l a member of the rescue
ne's crew. (*Photo courtesy
P / Wide World Photos*)

sion Manpower 1943.
rican honored partici-
ts of the CBI theater's
ect 7-A at this 1944 dinner
Jew York. Note the num-
of ATC uniforms scattered
ughout the assemblage.
*to courtesy of American
nes—C.R. Smith Museum*)

sion Manpower 1991.
s American Trans-Air
bo jet crew—two pilots, a
ht engineer and nine
ht attendants—was typi-
of airline troop charters
he Gulf War. (*Photo cour-
of American Trans-Air*)

Even in a far-away war, a line reservists serving w the armed forces liked remember their old carrie This Vietnam med evac he copter sports an Aloha A lines insignia. (*Photo courte of Aloha Airlines*)

The Huff-Deland crop-dusting biplane was the ancestor of Delta's future fleet and forerunner of a technique adopted during WWII, when specially-equipped C-47s sprayed insect-infested jungles throughout the Pacific. (*Photo courtesy of Delta Air Transport Heritage Museum*)

An All-American Aviati (today's US Airways) Stins about to pick up mail at small-town airport in t 1930s; the hook that grabl the mail bag from a su pended wire is faintly visi between the landing g wheels. This primitive s tem led to the developmen towed troop-carrying glide (*Photo courtesy of US Airways*

uess Where II, a specially-built C-87 intended as the rst presidential aircraft, though the Secret Service refused to let President Roosevelt fly in it. *(Photo courtesy of Lockheed-Martin Tactical Aircraft Systems)*

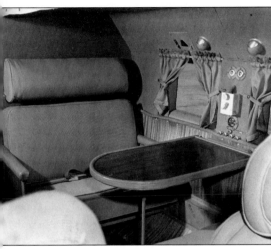

A vivid look at part of *Guess Where II*'s luxurious interior. *(Photo courtesy of Lockheed-Martin Tactical Aircraft Systems)*

Consolidated workers installing seats on a conventional C-87 being equipped as a military passenger transport—a VIP transport if the leather upholstering is any indication. *(Photo courtesy of Lockheed-Martin Tactical Aircraft Systems)*

The bulkhead map and presidential seal are featured in this rare shot of the *Sacred Cow*'s interior. (*Photo courtesy of McDonnell Douglas*)

The *Sacred Cow*'s rear lounge; the Clipper ship painting was largely for the benefit of President Roosevelt, who loved everything about the sea and ships. (*Photo courtesy of McDonnell Douglas*)

Exterior shot of the only elevator ever installed on an airplane, to facilitate enplaning and deplaning by polio-afflicted FDR. The small ramp accommodated his wheelchair. (*Photo courtesy of McDonnell Douglas*)

The plushly-furnished Lockheed C-121A Constellation used by General Eisenhower when he commanded NATO forces after the war. The same airplane participated in the Berlin Airlift. *(Photo courtesy of the Pima Air and Space Museum)*

One of Alaska Airlines's C-130s during the carrier's postwar U.S. Navy scientific mission to the North Slope. The barren Alaskan landscape is graphic evidence of the stark environment. *(Photo courtesy of Ron Suttell, Alaska Airlines)*

A Lockheed C-130, one
aviation's greatest milit:
transport planes, in unus
civilian livery. Alaska A
lines's "Golden Nugget" l
on the tail was a postv
trademark. (*Photo cour*
of Ron Suttell, Alaska Airlin

A far cry from the transport
planes of WWII is this Federal Express 747, assigned
to the massive Desert
Shield/Desert Storm airlift.
(*Photo courtesy of Federal
Express*)

Military airlift capability of
the 1990s. A contingent of
U.S. troops preparing to
board an American Trans-
Air Lockheed L-1011 bound
for the Persian Gulf war
zone. (*Photo courtesy of
American Trans-Air*)

which was politely declined. Surprised, they upped the ante to major general, and got the same answer.

"You pay me the same as you did when I toured the domestic bases," he told them. "A dollar a year, and I'll pay my own expenses."

"You might be more effective as a high-ranking officer," Arnold pointed out. "Some people might clam up to a civilian, even someone as well known as you."

"No, sir!" the captain declared. "When I get back, I want to be able to pound the table, point to the facts, and get some action."

He was in England for several weeks, meeting with a number of British officials, including Prime Minister Winston Churchill, but he spent most of his time observing, studying, and interviewing crews at U.S. air bases. His most comprehensive report concerned the B-17 bomber, on which he submitted more than twenty criticisms and seventeen recommendations for improvements. The latter included better oxygen masks, installation of armor plate under the cockpit and navigator station (in 1918, he had improvised his own "armor plate" by placing a metal stove lid under the seat of his Spad), and more electrical power to gun turrets, to keep them from freezing at high altitudes.

His written reports to Arnold and Stimson were made public after the war, but what he told them verbally was kept confidential; he may have been more critical than he or Stimson ever wanted anyone to know—remember, this was in 1942, when there was still a lot to learn about the early deficiencies of U.S. combat aircraft, and when the airline modification centers were really just getting up steam. Rickenbacker did bring back with him one set of plans for the North African invasion, the other four copies going by special courier on three ATC airplanes and a U.S. Navy cruiser.

Rickenbacker was prouder of this courier role than anything else he did during the war. It was no wonder that only six days after he returned from England, Rickenbacker was off on another inspection tour, this time to the Pacific, but also carrying in his head a carefully memorized, confidential message from Stimson to General Douglas MacArthur. Rickenbacker never revealed what he had to memorize; he would only describe it as a matter "of such sensitivity that it could not be put on paper."

He did deliver it, in person, but almost two months behind schedule . . .

* * *

Rickenbacker left San Francisco October 17, 1942, on a Pan Am Clipper that flew him to Hawaii. His traveling companion was Colonel Hans Adamson, an Army public relations officer who had accompanied him on both the U.S. and British tours. After a brief rest stop, and visits to Air Corps bases in the area, they boarded a B-17 for the long flight to MacArthur's headquarters at Port Moresby, New Guinea.

There apparently was a clash of personalities the minute Rickenbacker met the aircraft commander: Captain Bill Cherry, a tall Texan who had been an American Airlines copilot before the war. Cherry sported a goatee and wore cowboy boots, and both the facial adornment and the unconventional footwear seemed to offend Rickenbacker; he was to comment later that Cherry's appearance was "a little surprising," and anyone who knew Captain Eddie might well have interpreted that remark as a snide criticism disguised as an innocent observation.

The rest of the B-17 crew was somewhat more military: First Lieutenant Jim Whittaker, who Rickenbacker thought looked a little too old to be only the copilot; First Lieutenant John De Angelis, the navigator; Sergeant Jim Reynolds, the radio operator; and Private John Bartek, the mechanic—a freckled, red-haired youngster who was only three months out of an Air Corps mechanics school. In addition to Captain Eddie and Colonel Adamson, there was a third passenger: Sergeant Alex Kaczmarczyk, a young Air Corps crew chief who had been hospitalized in Honolulu with appendicitis and jaundice, and was returning to his unit in Australia.

The B-17 ground-looped after blowing a tire on takeoff, and the party had to transfer to another B-17. This time their departure was uneventful, and the bomber grumbled peacefully toward the first refueling stop: tiny Canton Island, 1900 miles southwest of Hawaii. The estimated flying time was ten hours, and for what actually transpired in that airplane and what went wrong, the main historical sources have been the two accounts written later by Rickenbacker himself: in his autobiography *Rickenbacker,* and in his earlier book, *Seven Came Through,* which he always insisted was a completely factual account of the ill-fated flight.

They were scheduled to land on Canton at 9:30 A.M., and an hour before their ETA, Cherry began a gradual descent. For the next two hours, they squinted in vain for the first sight of the island, that Pacific flyspeck only seven miles long and three miles wide. All they saw was empty ocean. At 10:15, the now-worried Rickenbacker asked Cherry how much fuel they had left.

"A little more than four hours' worth," Cherry said.

Rickenbacker suspected they had already missed Canton. He wanted to know how much of a tailwind they had been encountering, and Cherry told him the weather briefing he had received before leaving Honolulu had estimated it at about ten knots. But Rickenbacker was to say later that he had a gut feeling the tailwind was much stronger than Cherry's ten-knot figure, and that after he was rescued, his hunch was confirmed by the navigator of another plane that had left Hawaii only an hour before their own takeoff. The navigator, Rickenbacker wrote, told him he had been given the same forecast of a ten-knot tailwind, but after shooting the stars had indicated a tailwind of more than thirty knots, he revised his calculations, and they had brought him straight to Canton.

Captain Eddie informed Cherry they must have overshot the island and suggested they get cross-bearings to establish their exact position. But when radioman Reynolds asked Canton for a bearing, he was told the necessary equipment—which had been delivered weeks before—hadn't been uncrated yet.

There was a radio station on Palmyra Island, midway between Honolulu and Canton, and Reynolds contacted it with a request for a continuous radio signal that might give the B-17 a bearing. Meanwhile young navigator De Angelis took a sun shot with his octant and gave Cherry a new heading which the pilot followed for the next half hour.

It was a wasted thirty minutes, because at that point De Angelis, understandably flustered, gave Cherry a different heading. Cherry asked why. De Angelis voiced his suspicion that the octant, which he had transfered from the first B-17, might have been damaged in the ground-loop. Rickenbacker said later that the entire flight could have been predicated on the deadly combination of an erroneous tailwind forecast and a damaged octant, throwing them hundreds of miles off course.

The radio station at Palmyra suggested that they climb to 5000 feet and circle while the station took a bearing. This was done, and Palmyra gave them another heading, which Cherry followed. There was still nothing but open water ahead of them. Getting desperate, Cherry even followed Rickenbacker's suggestion that he ask Canton to fire antiaircraft shells timed to explode at 7000 feet, so the B-17 might spot them. Canton advised a few minutes later that the guns were being fired and that search planes had taken off, but no one on the bomber saw anything.

Cherry decided to try another idea: to "box the compass," which involved flying west for an hour, then north, east, and finally south, hoping to stumble on the island. The trouble was that by now they didn't have enough fuel to complete all four legs. When the gauges showed they had only an hour's fuel left, Cherry told Reynolds to send a "Mayday" and at the same time he ordered his crew and passengers to start lightening the B-17 in preparation for a ditching. They began throwing everything out of the airplane that wasn't bolted to the airframe.

Rickenbacker, limping on the cane he had been using since the Atlanta crash, went back to the tail to help; among the items he tossed out were an expensive Burberry coat he had purchased in England, the suitcase Eastern employees had given him the previous Christmas, and his briefcase. Before he dumped the suitcase, he took out a carton of cigarettes, put three packs in his pocket, and divided the rest of the carton among the others. Adamson suggested that they should drink all the water they had on board before ditching, but Rickenbacker vetoed this—"we may need it more later," he warned.

The only items that weren't thrown out were two mattresses they needed to help cushion the shock of the ditching impact, and various emergency supplies: water, thermos jugs filled with coffee, and food rations. Most of them removed their shoes and some even took off their trousers, but Captain Eddie stayed fully clothed and that included the special high-topped shoes he was required to wear after the Atlanta accident.

Everyone donned Mae West life jackets and waited for Cherry to ditch, one of the most difficult and riskiest procedures any pilot can face. There was a heavy swell below, and this made the ditching even tougher. The carefully taught technique was to descend parallel to the swell and land in the trough, using the swell to reduce speed and lessen impact; hitting water at high speed is akin to colliding with concrete.

With all passengers and crew braced, Cherry timed the ditching perfectly and with admirable precision. The impact shock, nevertheless, was violent. Adamson hurt his neck and back, and Reynolds smashed his face against the radio panel. The already crippled president of Eastern was just shaken up, however. Bartek managed to get three rafts released and the B-17, filling rapidly with water, was quickly abandoned. Cherry, copilot Whittaker, and Reynolds climbed into one raft. Rickenbacker, Adamson, and Bartek occupied the second, and De Angelis and Sergeant Alex as everyone called him—he had told Captain Eddie not to bother trying to pronounce Kaczmarczyk—were in the third.

A sudden wind gust blew the rafts away from the sinking plane, and it was at this point that the eight survivors realized that help had better arrive soon; all rations, including the precious water and coffee, had somehow been left aboard. There was a hasty debate over whether someone should go back to the plane and try to salvage the rations, but all agreed the B-17 might sink at any minute. Obstinately, it stayed afloat for another six minutes, enough time for them to have retrieved at least the water and coffee, and they watched the bomber sink with the sickening knowledge that they had probably made a terrible mistake.

The rafts themselves were half full of water, and Rickenbacker began bailing out the one he was in with the old felt hat he always carried; no one, not even his wife, had ever been able to talk him into buying a new one. He did throw his cane over the side, explaining that "the Lord never taught me to walk on water with it."

Thus began one of the most dramatic, harrowing, and in some respects controversial sagas of survival in sea and air history. They were marooned in those rafts for twenty-two days of suffering, near starvation, and—in one tragic case—death. (By contrast, the 316 survivors of the cruiser *Indianapolis* were rescued after five days in their own shipwrecked hell.)

Young Sergeant Alex died on the thirteenth day of the ordeal; he had begun the flight still in a weakened condition from the surgery and jaundice, he had swallowed seawater getting into the raft after the ditching, and his constitution was just not strong enough to sustain him. At one point Captain Eddie himself held him in his arms, trying to warm the boy's shivering, emaciated body. After he died, Cherry removed his wallet and dog tags so they could eventually be sent to his family, and they rolled his body over the side into the sea.

Most of the survivors' accounts, including Rickenbacker's own recollections, acknowledge it was he who took command, almost from the first moments after Cherry's brilliant ditching, to the day the seven remaining survivors were rescued. *Time* magazine described him as "the flotilla's Captain Bligh," an apt reference to the British commander's amazing forty-two-day, 3700-mile voyage in an open boat after the famous 1789 *Bounty* mutiny. Still dressed in his business suit, Rickenbacker cajoled, comforted, taunted, scolded, and led them in prayer, although Adamson, a full colonel, was the ranking officer and Cherry had been the aircraft commander.

"The seven men bobbing with me in these crowded rafts made up a typical cross section of young American manhood," Rickenbacker was to write later. "They had their strengths, and they had their weaknesses. Somebody was going to have to hold them together, and that somebody would have to be me."

The only food saved from the B-17 were four oranges that Cherry had stuffed into his leather flight jacket. Rickenbacker had taken a Hershey bar off the plane, and Sergeant Alex had half a dozen chocolate bars, but the saltwater had made all the candy inedible and also ruined the cigarettes. They took an inventory of the equipment stored on each raft: folding aluminum paddles so light and flimsy that wielding them in any kind of rough sea was virtually impossible, a patching kit, two hand pumps for bailing and maintaining raft air pressure, two collapsible bailing buckets, two sheath knives, a compass, and a pair of pliers. But no water, and no food.

They went without water for eight consecutive days; on the ninth day it rained, and they managed to catch the precious drops in whatever was handy—bailing buckets, Captain Eddie's ancient hat, canvas, clothing, and even handkerchiefs. The life-saving rain perversely almost cost lives; it came in the form of a vicious squall that tipped over Cherry's raft. Weakened as they were, it was a miracle that the two pilots and Reynolds mustered enough strength to get the raft righted and haul themselves back in.

Until they encountered the squall, their only liquid and food came from the four oranges, which Rickenbacker doled out in pitifully small portions. Not until the fifth day was the third orange divided among the eight men, and the last one was consumed the next day, because Captain Eddie figured it was the only way to keep Sergeant Alex alive. They were all haunted by culinary memories of things they had once taken so much for granted. Reynolds kept talking about soda pop. Cherry swore that if he ever got back, he was going to gorge himself on chocolate ice cream. Rickenbacker, for reasons he could never explain, began thinking of chocolate malted milk—something he hadn't tasted for twenty-five years.

Tempers flared under tension. Merely jostling a raftmate who was stinging from sunburn was enough to ignite cursing. Rickenbacker, as the self-appointed leader, became a natural target for a kind of sullen hatred. Yet after they were rescued, most of them said it was his strong willpower that had kept them alive. One man tried to commit suicide to make more room in the crowded raft. He suddenly dove into the water, and Rickenbacker yanked him back in, cursing him for cowardice. When Captain Eddie heard anyone praying for death, he lashed out with invectives and insults. Long before they were rescued, some of them were swearing they'd stay alive just to "get even with the old son of a bitch." And at least one man apparently never stopped hating him: Bill Cherry.

The man who commanded the ill-fated flight returned to American Airlines after the war and became a respected senior captain, retiring at the mandatory age of sixty. Through the years, he adamantly refused to be interviewed about the raft ordeal, talk about Rickenbacker in any way whatsoever, or, according to pilots who flew with him, even discuss the events of those twenty-two terrible days.

"You couldn't even mention the name Rickenbacker to him," one of his fellow airline captains and closest friends once told a writer. "I think Bill Cherry will go to his grave carrying inside of him his own version of what happened in that plane and on those rafts. If you brought up the subject, he'd just walk away. Someone who knows him pretty well had a theory that Rickenbacker may have been the one who got them lost over the Pacific, by getting panicky when they first had trouble finding Canton, and issuing the wrong orders. But that was scuttlebutt, and I never heard Bill himself say anything like that."

Even if Cherry or any of the others on the rafts were justified in resenting or even hating Captain Eddie, their feelings and emotions had to have been affected by the ordeal. Certainly the evidence points to his powerful leadership, his indomitable will, and to a courage that had to spring from his faith in God. The Rickenbackers and the Pattons of this world could inspire hatred, but they also could inspire men to do things of which they had never dreamed themselves capable.

The most widely publicized incident that occurred during this ultimate test of human endurance and resolve involved a seagull. It was day eight and Rickenbacker was dozing when the gull landed on his hat. Instinctively he grabbed the bird, wrung its neck, defeathered it, and calmly carved up the carcass, dividing the raw, stringy, fishy-tasting flesh into equal shares. They saved only the intestines, which they used for fishing bait.

The seagull nourishment brought only temporary relief. The rainwater was finished the night before Sergeant Alex died, and they went another forty-eight hours suffering horribly from thirst. A fish caught on the ninth day was the last for a long time; they lost the lines and hooks trying for more, and they found they couldn't even eat the one they had caught. It was a small shark, and even hunger pangs weren't enough to overcome the foul, rancid taste of shark meat. All they could do was chew tiny pieces and then spit them out, gagging.

Sharks were constant and unwelcome companions, coming up under the rafts and jolting them hard enough to raise them out of the water. Another enemy was the ocean saltwater, corroding all their watches (except, inexplicably, the one Whittaker was wearing), compass needles, and even the Army .45 automatics that Cherry, Whittaker, and Adamson carried. They had tried to shoot seagulls with them, but the swift corrosion froze the guns' mechanisms and the frustrated officers finally threw the useless weapons overboard.

Other than the unfortunate Sergeant Alex, Adamson was the worst off physically. The injuries he had suffered in the ditching were extremely painful, and they were aggravated by saltwater sores and blistering sunburn over almost his entire body. The miracle man was the oldest one in the rafts, the fifty-year-old president of Eastern. His already battered frame grew thinner and thinner until he began to resemble a living skeleton, and his prominent nose took on the shape of a big meat hook. Yet while his body shriveled and weakened, his personality seemed to become even stronger and more domineering. By the fifteenth day, they were all cursing at each other, but at Rickenbacker more than anyone else. The rafts were tied together, and it was easy to hear what was being said.

"You're the meanest, most cantankerous son of a bitch who

ever lived," one man swore at him. Captain Eddie heard another man tell a companion, "I swear I'll live so I can have the pleasure of burying that old bastard at sea."

The only moments of calmness, of comradeship, even lucidity, came at night, when they prayed together. Before darkness fell, they took turns reading out of a Bible Bartek had brought off the plane. Yet even the prayers led to bitterness, most of it directed against Rickenbacker. As the days and nights passed and hopes for rescue faded, some of the men questioned the existence of a God they felt had ignored their prayers and deserted them. Such sentiments were heresy to the devout Captain Eddie, who not only voiced angry denials, but scolded them for their weakness and lack of faith.

They all dreamed fitfully, of rich foods, home, loved ones, and the days when the worst pain to be suffered was that of a mild toothache. Then the dreams became nightmares, for they always awoke to the realities of slow death in three rubber coffins. Rickenbacker's raft held three men in a space less than seven feet long and not quite three feet wide, and one of the other rafts was even smaller.

On the seventeenth day, overcast with the sea running rough, Cherry heard the sound of an airplane engine. Then they saw the aircraft, a single-engine scouting seaplane, and began shouting. They might as well have been calling to the wind; the seaplane was too far away to spot the seven tiny figures yelling and waving, and soon disappeared.

The letdown was demoralizing, but at least it had been the first sign of human life they had seen for two and a half weeks. Maybe, just maybe, it was an indication that search planes still were looking for them, and if so, a ship had to be close by—perhaps even land. Their hopes soared the next afternoon when they saw two more aircraft in the distance, but these, too, flew away without spotting them. They experienced more frustration on the nineteenth day, when four airplanes appeared, with the same results, and they realized that even though the rafts were painted a bright yellow, a plane had to be virtually on top of them to see anything. It was at this point that Cherry and Rickenbacker had their most serious confrontation.

Cherry wanted to take the smallest raft, which now held only De Angelis since Sergeant Alex's death, and try to make land by himself. The navigator, he suggested, could take his place in the raft with Whittaker and radio operator Reynolds. Cherry argued that there was no use in staying together. He thought if they separated, search planes might have a better chance of spotting at least one of them, and that if he could find land it was likely he'd also find rescuers. De Angelis objected, and Rickenbacker sided with him.

"You're crazy," Captain Eddie told Cherry. "You don't even know what direction to take. Those planes we saw came from the north, south, east, and west. And if they couldn't see three rafts bunched together, how in the hell are they going to spot just one?"

"I still think our only hope is to scatter," Cherry insisted. "It'll give us two chances to be seen instead of only one. But I won't go unless you agree it's right."

"It's wrong," Rickenbacker snapped, "but I don't see any use in prolonging the argument."

"Then I'm going," Cherry said firmly.

De Angelis climbed into the raft holding Whittaker and Reynolds, the latter so weak he could hardly talk. Cherry got into the smallest raft alone, and drifted away. As he disappeared from sight, Rickenbacker heard De Angelis and Whittaker muttering that maybe Cherry had the right idea about splitting up. Captain Eddie, whose temper was attached to a short fuse anyway, blew up. Angry words flew back and forth until sheer fatigue ended the argument— even Rickenbacker lacked the strength to keep it up. When De Angelis and Whittaker announced that they were taking off on their own, too, Captain Eddie told them to go ahead.

He watched gloomily as the second raft drifted from view. Now he was alone with Adamson and Bartek, both more dead than alive, and for the first time he began to doubt their chances of being saved. They had some drinkable water, laboriously saved from the occasional rain squalls they encountered, and before the rafts separated, the survivors had managed to scoop up with their hands small, sardinelike fish they found swimming close to the surface. But Rickenbacker had only to look at his two remaining companions to know they were growing weaker by the minute. When he doled out the morning ration of water, the equivalent of what a one-ounce whiskey jigger would hold, both Bartek and Adamson were too almost too feeble to raise their heads and drink.

He had just about given up all hope on the afternoon of the twenty-second day when two more planes showed up, flying only a couple of hundred yards away, yet still not seeing them. By this time, Rickenbacker was the only one with the strength left to wave and he had to do this while sitting down. There went their last chance, he thought.

The miracle happened thirty minutes later. Two aircraft roared out of the sun and headed straight for the bobbing raft, flying so low that Rickenbacker saw one pilot waving and swore he could even see him smiling. The planes flew off, but just before sunset other aircraft appeared, including a seaplane that landed and picked them up; they were only forty miles from Funafuti in the Tuvalu Islands chain, called the Ellise Islands at the time, where the Navy had a base. The pilot, Navy Lieutenant William F. Eadie, told Rickenbacker that Cherry's raft had been spotted the previous afternoon by a Navy plane on routine patrol; Cherry's subsequent rescue had sent every available search aircraft into the air.

The rafts had drifted some 500 miles southwest of Canton Island to the Tuvalu group. While Cherry was being rescued, the raft with Whittaker, De Angelis, and Reynolds had reached a beach on one of the chain's uninhabited islands. They were seen by natives on an adjacent island, where an English missionary had a small radio transmitter. He notified the Navy and the three survivors were picked up as soon as a plane could be dispatched.

The excruciating ordeal had ended. Captain Eddie, who had weighed 180 pounds at the start of the Pacific trip, was down to 126 pounds when he was rescued; when they were undressing him at the small base hospital, his clothes fell apart. He had a dirty brown beard with hair almost two inches long, and he had grown a drooping mandarin mustache—he took one look into a mirror and immediately demanded a shave. He admitted later he wished he'd had a picture taken of the beard, but the impulse to get rid of it fast was almost as if he were ridding himself of the nightmare.

Officially, they had been missing for twenty-two days, although Rickenbacker thought they had been picked up on the twenty-first day, Wednesday, November 11. The discrepancy was explained later: the rafts had drifted across the international date line, thus losing a day, so that the final rescue was made on Thursday, November 12. He also may have been wrong—although he never admitted it—on an even more important point: his opposition to Cherry's wanting the rafts to split up. No one will ever know if any survivors would have been rescued in time if the three rafts had stayed together, as Captain Eddie had urged, but the odds seemed to be against it. It was unlikely that the raft with Rickenbacker, Adamson, and Bartek would have been found if the other two rafts hadn't been sighted.

With incredible resilience, Rickenbacker recovered almost as quickly as the much younger Cherry, Whittaker, and De Angelis. Bartek and Reynolds took a little longer and Adamson, who developed pneumonia, was in critical condition for some time before medical treatment pulled him through the crisis. But instead of returning to the U.S., as the Navy doctors recommended, Captain Eddie insisted on resuming and completing his Pacific mission: delivering Secretary of War Stimson's oral message to MacArthur and inspecting air bases. His session with the general was especially cordial, as was to be expected with two men who held strongly conservative political views.

But when Rickenbacker did get home, he laid on Stimson's desk far more than a report on his meeting with MacArthur and the base tour. He wanted something done about survival equipment and survival methods, and he wanted it done in a hurry. He learned that Bill Cherry already had been assigned to work with the designers of new survival gear, but Captain Eddie was anxious to provide his own recommendations, which he delivered to Stimson in person, verbally, and frequently spiced with expletives that told the Secretary of War exactly what Edward Vernon Rickenbacker thought of current survival equipment.

He informed Stimson that rafts had to be bigger—much longer and wider—while each should be equipped with some kind of durable sheet that could perform three functions: serving as a sail, providing protection from the sun, and acting as a rain catcher. Remembering all too vividly the precious water and food rations that had gone down with the B-17, he said every raft should contain adquate emergency supplies such as liquids, concentrated food, vitamins, sedatives, a first-aid kit, rubber patches and waterproof glue, flares, Very pistols for signaling, a large jackknife, fishing tackle with appropriate bait, and some kind of chemical water distiller that could make seawater drinkable. His final recommendation: enclose all this emergency equipment in watertight containers.

It was at Rickenbacker's instigation that a group of scientists developed a practical water distilling apparatus that became standard equipment on ships and aircraft. And a team of technicians from ATC, NATS, Pan Am, American, and TWA soon developed vastly improved self-inflating life rafts, fully equipped with the survival gear Rickenbacker suggested, including two different types of water distilling devices, that are still in use today.

Despite what he had just gone through, Captain Eddie willingly took on more assignments from Stimson. He spent three months after his return from the Pacific touring U.S. war plants. In the spring of 1943, Stimson sent him to Russia with inspection stops along the way in North Africa, Iran, India, and China. He flew 55,000 miles on ATC aircraft, talked to an estimated 300,000 American airmen, and brought back from the Soviet Union a voluminous report on Russian use of American military equipment.

Before he left on this final wartime assignment, however, Stimson had arranged for him to speak at the Pentagon to an audience of Air Force and Navy officers on his raft experiences, an invitation that Captain Eddie accepted with alacrity. He unloaded his salty, uncensored views on current survival equipment—or the lack thereof—and one of the officers present, a young Air Force colonel and ex–airline pilot flying for ATC, was impressed not only with Rickenbacker's remarks, but the force with which they were delivered.

"It was the first time I had ever seen Rickenbacker," he recalled. "Frankly, I had been one of the guys who had to implement an Air Force order to strip everything possible off our life rafts so we could save weight. The theory was that if you went down in the ocean, your chances of ever being found were too slim anyway. But when Rickenbacker came back from his ordeal, he showed up at that Pentagon meeting and read us the riot act—every fourth word had four letters. Actually, we already had started putting survival gear back on the rafts, including chewing gum, but I have to admit we felt like little schoolkids getting reamed out by a teacher."

The name of that young colonel was Floyd Hall. Twenty years later, he would take over a demoralized, almost bankrupt Eastern Air Lines while Rickenbacker stood helplessly on the sidelines, his own reputation in shreds, his name anathema among disillusioned employees, directors, and stockholders.

And what he had done for his country during the war was forgotten amid the corporate carnage for which he bore a large share of the blame. He had been betrayed by his own stubbornness, with sad irony the same stubbornness that had kept him alive on that raft.

☆ ☆ 8 ☆ ☆
The Flying White Houses and the Feuding Flyboys

When it came to travel, Franklin Delano Roosevelt loved ships and trains, and in that order. Airplanes ran third—a very, *very* distant third, although he became the first president to fly while in office.

Until a global war and summit conferences thousands of miles away made air travel an obvious necessity, he not only accepted but secretly welcomed the Secret Service's edict that flying was too dangerous for the president of the United States. It wasn't that he was afraid to fly; he simply preferred the leisurely pace of a sea voyage (especially on a U.S. warship) or riding the rails in his private car, named the *Ferdinand Magellan,* which was built for him early in the war by the Association of American Railroads. This was a monster, with bullet-proof windows three inches thick that could stop a .50-caliber bullet fired at point-blank range, and a heavily armored underframe that made it impossible to tip the car over even if a bomb went off underneath. The truth was, however, that Roosevelt also avoided flying because his confinement to a wheelchair made boarding the airplanes of that day rather difficult.

His cousin and predecessor, Theodore Roosevelt, was the first former president to fly, and typically for the ex–Rough Rider this wasn't just as a passenger. In 1910, about a year and a half after he left office, TR went up in a flimsy Wright pusher biplane and the pilot, pioneer aviator Arch Hoxsey, let him handle the controls briefly. Very briefy, because Hoxsey was more nervous than Teddy, who insisted on standing up and waving with both arms to onlookers below.

Almost two and a half decades later, FDR—then the governor of New York—decided to fly from Albany to the 1932 Democratic National Convention in Chicago, where he was scheduled to accept the party's presidential nomination. It would be, incidentally, the first acceptance speech by a presidential candidate in the history of nominating conventions.

FDR's many biographers have made no secret of the fact that the polio-crippled candidate flew to Chicago, aboard an American Airlines Ford trimotor, as a symbolic gesture intended to demonstrate he was healthy enough to run for the nation's highest office. That an airline flight seemed to provide such proof was a stark commentary on the public's attitude toward air travel in 1932.

The flight left Albany at 8:30 A.M., with refueling stops at Buffalo and Cleveland, ran into strong head winds plus considerable summer turbulence, and didn't land in Chicago until 4:30 P.M.—two and a half hours late. Some unflattering news photographs of Roosevelt deplaning from the Tin Goose generated reports that the New York governor had been airsick most of the trip. This was untrue; it was the nominee's 15-year-old son John who used several "barf bags" during the flight. His father professed to have enjoyed every minute of the experience and pronounced it "delightful," although it was to be ten years before FDR boarded another airliner. And this time it was under the wraps of wartime security.

In the dawn hours of January 11, 1943, at Pan Am's Miami marine base, Captain Howard Cone and his crew awaited the arrival of the nine passengers scheduled to board the *Dixie Clipper,* a camouflaged Boeing 314. Cone, a naval reserve lieutenant, was wearing his Navy uniform—appropriate for the commander of a flying boat that was now a U.S. Navy airplane flying officially for NATS. Cone already knew he was carrying VIPS; the passenger list included such names as presidential advisor Harry Hopkins, presidential physican Admiral Ross McIntyre, and Admiral William Leahy, top White House naval advisor. It didn't take the IQ of Einstein to figure out the identity of the name that headed the passenger manifest, a "Mr. Jones," who arrived beside the *Dixie Clipper* in a Navy launch, and had to be helped aboard the seaplane.

Thus did Franklin Roosevelt, en route to the Casablanca conference, become the first U.S. president to travel abroad by air, the first to visit a war theater since Abraham Lincoln, and the first chief executive to visit Africa. Ironically, it was the Secret Service that insisted he make the trip to Casablanca by air, because the German submarine campaign in the Atlantic was at its height, and the agents feared a submarine attack more than any by the Luftwaffe, or the perceived hazards of air travel. The *Dixie Clipper* was accompanied by another B-314, the *Atlantic Clipper,* that carried a contingent of lesser war planners, assorted officials, and Secret Service agents; it also served as a backup plane in case the seaplane carrying FDR should have any mechanical problems. Both Cone and the commander of the other flying boat, Dick Vinal, were among Pan Am's most senior captains, boasting the airline's highest pilot rank: Master of Ocean Flying. And Cone himself set a precedent: the first airplane to carry a U.S. president, although it was operating under military orders, was commanded by a former airline captain, and this would be the case until well after the war ended, Cone being succeeded as a presidential pilot by two other ex–airline captains.

The two big seaplanes flew first from Miami to Trinidad, for an overnight stop, then to Belem and across the South Atlantic to the African port of Bathurst, not far from Dakar; the trip from Florida to Bathurst covered 5860 miles, but Casablanca was still 1500 miles away. At Bathurst, the presidential party boarded a pair of TWA C-54s flying for ATC, FDR's aircraft being in charge of none other than Captain Otis Bryan, who right then and there seems to have become Roosevelt's favorite pilot.

Not that he had any reason to complain about Cone or any of his crew. His preference for ships notwithstanding, the president obviously had enjoyed himself on the long seaplane flight, despite the necessary confinement—which he was used to anyway, being a permanent wheelchair prisoner. The President, dressed in baggy slacks, an open-collar shirt, and a loose, V-neck sweater, played solitaire, read, studied maps, ate well, and enjoyed dry martinis.

Actually, he had a much more difficult time boarding and deplaning from the C-54, whose main loading door, on the port side of the aft fuselage, was so high off the ground in this tricycle-gear airplane that large and bulky stepless ramps had to be built to accommodate his wheelchair. And in the middle of what was supposed to be the strictest security measures of the war, the ramps were a dead giveaway to FDR's presence. Security as well as convenience and concern over submarine warfare was to be a major motivating factor in the Secret Service's desire for a special presidential airplane.

Folllowing the Casablanca war strategy conference with Churchill, FDR flew back to Bathurst on Bryan's C-54, where he reboarded the *Dixie Clipper* for the long trip back to Miami, this time by way of Natal and Trinidad. The 17,000-mile round-trip journey between Florida and Casablanca—highlighted by the celebration of FDR's 65th birthday en route—had consumed three days of actual travel time in each direction, to which were added three stopovers and two changes of planes. Some fifty years later, the Boeing 747-400 that is today's Air Force One could have flown nonstop from Washington to Casablanca in seven hours.

It was the length of that marathon Casablanca trip, most of it in a comfortable but slow flying boat, that convinced the Secret Service, not to mention the Air Corps and ATC chief Hal George, that the president of the United States needed and deserved to have a well-equipped land transport aircraft assigned to the White House. George not only had a specific airplane in mind, but the command pilot as well. His name was Henry Tift Myers, who had won his Air Corps wings at Kelly Field, Texas, in 1931, before joining American Airlines.

Myers, a soft-spoken Georgian whose maternal grandfather had founded the town of Tift, Georgia, was one of the many airline pilots holding reserve commissions when war broke out and then called to military service. Hank went to Washington and was wandering around ATC headquarters trying to find out what his assignment was supposed to be, when he was told C.R. Smith wanted to see him.

"You're going to be an aide to General George," C.R. announced. "I've recommended you."

"The hell I am," Myers protested. "I want to fly, not sit around behind some goddamned desk."

"You'll get plenty of work," Smith assured him, and took him in to meet George.

"I understand you're going to be my aide," the ATC chief said.

Myers may have been soft-spoken but he also was decidedly outspoken. "Look, General, with due respect, all you need is a fourth for bridge and I don't play bridge. So get yourself another aide."

George chuckled. "You like to fly, don't you?"

"Sure, but . . ."

"So we have bases all over the world and I need someone to take me there. And C.R. tells me you're a hell of a pilot."

From then on it was Colonel Henry T. "Hank" Myers. For the next seven years he flew not only General George, but two presidents, two first ladies, many other generals, admirals, senators, congressmen, cabinet officers, and assorted statesmen to virtually every country on earth. He was to remark later, "There were about sixty of them, and I think I missed only three."

The aircraft George picked as a presidential airplane was a specially equipped C-87, and he had FDR's physical handicap in mind when he chose it over the C-54. Even with a tricycle landing gear, the big Consolidated bomber-turned-transport had a fuselage whose cabin floor was very low to the ground, and FDR's wheelchair would need only a small, very inconspicuous ramp for enplaning and deplaning. Furthermore, the C-87 was several miles per hour faster than the C-54 (it had set several ATC speed records), and while it didn't have the cargo-carrying muscle of the Douglas plane, when fitted out as a VIP transport it wouldn't be carrying heavy loads.

After the Air Corps signed a contract with Consolidated-Vultee for converting three regular C-87s into VIP transports, fuselage number 159 was pulled off the regular assembly line in Fort Worth, along with two other C-87s under construction, and moved to a remote area of the factory where they were completed under tight security. All three airplanes were subsequently assigned to the ATC's "Brass Hats Squadron," and Aircraft 159 became Hank Myers's personal pride and joy. It was Hank who dreamed up its name: *Guess Where II,* which he had painted in flowing script above the main cabin door. He picked it in the belief that most of its flights would involve important passengers traveling on secret missions, although he always assumed its chief duty would be to fly the president of the United States.

The career of *Guess Where II* began in a blaze of glory when, on one of its earliest missions, it flew 3500 miles nonstop from Ceylon to Australia, without military escort and unarmed, although much of the trip was made over Japanese-controlled waters and bases on Sumatra and Java. The flight was part of a round-the-world fact-finding mission with five senators and a load of high-ranking military officers aboard. Myers, with a hand-picked crew that included copilot and close friend Elmer "Smitty" Smith, continued to fly his beloved C-87 anywhere in the world George or anyone else decided he should go. Eleanor Roosevelt was a passenger several times, and eventually there came the day when *Guess Where II* was handed the assignment Myers had been waiting for: flying FDR overseas to another summit meeting, this one in November of 1943 at Teheran and Cairo, involving the Allies' Big Three—Roosevelt, Churchill, and Stalin. The travel arrangements called for FDR to cross the Atlantic to Oran on the new battleship *Iowa*, and then board *Guess Where II* for the rest of the trip.

The sea voyage was not without an embarrassing incident. En route, an escorting destroyer accidentally fired a torpedo that just missed the *Iowa*, which also happened to be carrying Navy Chief of Staff Ernest King, the shortest-tempered, meanest-dispositioned admiral in the U.S. Navy. An unnamed Navy officer commented later:

"It was bad enough that Roosevelt was on the battleship, but if that destroyer captain knew Ernie King was also aboard, he would have tied himself to an anchor and jumped overboard."

Thanks to the Secret Service and the various idiosyncrasies of the C-87, however, Hank Myers was destined to become the most disappointed colonel in the U.S. Army Air Corps. Only a few days before Myers and his crew were scheduled to leave for Oran, the White House advised General George that the president and his party would use an ATC C-54, operated by TWA, and commanded by Otis Bryan. *Guess Where II* would be used only as a backup plane. And this being the Army, Myers could do nothing but fume in private while his resentment for Bryan and TWA festered into a real feud.

Hank honestly thought that Jack Frye had "sneaked in the back door" of the White House and exerted political influence for the benefit of his airline. Actually, Myers was wrong; neither Frye nor anyone else at TWA knew anything about the switch of airplanes and crews until the White House itself passed the word. The decision was made by the Secret Service, which had become alarmed over persistent reports of C-87 problems. In-flight fires were just one of the bugs plaguing the transport; equally disturbing were cases of severe tail buffeting and other oscillation incidents, one of them so bad that the crew couldn't maintain control and had to bail out.

ATC investigators and Consolidated engineers traced the vibration troubles to a simple cause: toggle switches controlling the props and another set of switches controlling the engine cowl flaps were not only next to each other, but very similar in appearance. Pilots were accidentally hitting the cowl switches when they meant to be using the prop toggles, and opening cowl flaps in flight and at cruising speed generated severe buffeting, especially in the tail section. The solution in the form of relocating the flap toggles, however, came too late to save *Guess Where II* from a demotion that, much to Myers's sorrow, was to be permanent; the Secret Service didn't object to the president's wife flying on the C-87, so long as the president himself avoided the blacklisted airplane.

Guess Where II and its crew were assigned to the first lady when FDR sent his wife on tour of American bases in the Caribbean and South America in March of 1944. They were gone a month on the 13,000-mile mission, in the course of which she not only wore out the flight crew but the military officers accompanying her—not with excessive demands, for she traveled unusually light and hated any fuss or special treatment, but with her sheer energy. Myers always thought the Secret Service code name for Mrs. Roosevelt was the most appropriate of them all: "Rover."

When they returned to Washington, Eleanor presented the crew with three dozen exquisite orchids she had picked up in South America. Later, she gave each member a beautiful inscribed salad bowl commemorating the trip.

The pleasure of flying Mrs. Roosevelt, adored by every man who ever served as her pilot, still didn't soften Hank Myers's resentment over the Teheran mission being taken away from him and given to Otis Bryan, now a major in ATC. The TWA veteran remembered Roosevelt as being an amiable, uncomplaining passenger the first time he flew with him—"very much interested in the territory over which we flew, and always asking questions. But he didn't ask for special privileges. We had removed several seats so he'd have a bed, but I can't recall his using it very much, if at all. He said he'd rather sit up and stay awake because the others in the plane didn't have the same privilege. Another thing that impressed me was how good-natured and chipper he was when he boarded. It was about 7 A.M. and he had been flying steadily for almost three days since leaving the United States, but you'd never know it.

"I admired him greatly. He had a strong personality and the

ability to put you at ease right away. I was awed at first, but we had some wonderful conversations."

When Bryan picked up the presidential party after the *Iowa* delivered him to Oran, FDR had to be enplaned via a makeshift ramp. It was a sight that always jolted Bryan, because it brought home so starkly the extent of Roosevelt's incapacitation.

"I knew we had been ordered to build ramps," Bryan said, "but I only thought of them as a convenience. I was aware of FDR's polio, but until I actually saw him being wheeled into the airplane, I didn't dream it had left him like that."

He was to be reminded of that physical helplessness again after the meetings in Teheran and Cairo had ended. Before they left Cairo, the president confided to Bryan that he wanted to visit Malta and Sicily on the return flight, although neither were on the itinerary.

"The Secret Service will tell me no," FDR admitted, "but I'm also going to tell them I not only want to stop at those two places, but also visit troops in Naples, a real combat area. They'll be so worried about my flying into Naples, they won't say a thing about Malta and Sicily. Is that okay with you, Otis?"

Bryan agreed not to make waves, although later he almost regretted it. Approaching Malta, he discovered that a hydraulic pump had failed, making it impossible to lower the wing flaps for a normal landing. He sent the navigator back to inform the president that they would have to land much faster than usual, which presented an element of danger.

"Well, just tell Otis to do the best he can," Roosevelt said calmly. Then he added with a chuckle, "Sounds like we'll have a good time."

Secret Service agents grabbed every pillow in sight and placed them around FDR as cushioning protection against impact. But Bryan, landing at well over 100 mph, touched down so gently that the tire blowouts he feared never happened. Later he was asked how it felt to make such a landing, knowing that one mistake might kill the outstanding leader of the free world.

Bryan shook his head. "That didn't cross my mind," he insisted. "What really worried me was getting caught by German fighters just as we landed."

He wasn't being modest or even kidding. He had real reason to fear such an attack on an unarmed transport carrying the president. He strongly suspected that the Malta visit, supposedly top secret, was no secret to the enemy. While in Cairo, Roosevelt had asked him to fly to Ankara, where he was to pick up the Turkish president and bring him back to Cairo. Bryan landed at Ankara and was having coffee with the U.S. base commander when the voice of German propagandist Lord Haw-Haw came over the radio.

"Major Bryan, Roosevelt's pilot, has just landed in Turkey," Lord Haw-Haw announced, much to Bryan's dismay.

"How the hell did he know that?" he demanded.

The base commander sighed. "They've probably got spies right in the Ankara control tower that the Turks operate. One of them evidently called Berlin the minute you landed."

The Air Corps had wanted to provide Bryan with an escort of P-38 fighters into Turkey, but Otis declined, even though he respected those twin-engine, long-range Lockheed Lightnings with the twin tail booms, so feared by the Germans that they were known as "those fork-tailed devils." Bryan wasn't too sanguine about the effectiveness of escorts, because they weren't much use at the moment a transport was most vulnerable: when it was landing.

The Teheran/Cairo meetings marked the last time a U.S. president was to fly overseas, or virtually anywhere else, in anything except a transport designed specifically as a Flying White House. *Guess Where II* was supposed to fill that role until it was victimized, in some ways unfairly, by the C-87's suspect reputation. Some Pentagon officials thought the new C-69 Constellation would be ideal, but in mid 1943, when the Air Corps decided it needed a new presidential airplane, the Connie still was an unproven design in the middle of an unfinished flight test program. The most immediately available choice was the C-54, and in October of 1943, Douglas removed fuselage 78 from the Santa Monica assembly line and parked it in a corner of the factory so secluded that many workers didn't even know it was there. One indication that there might be something different about this airplane—designated as Project 51—was the unusual number of Douglas and Air Corps inspectors in constant presence.

To the untrained eye, the aircraft's external shape was identical to those of the seventy-seven C-54s that had preceded it. The factory serial number was 7451, but the contract the Air Corps had signed with Douglas specified the design and construction of a C-54 the likes of which had never been seen before. The Douglas engineers who first saw the blueprints had a pretty good idea of what this airplane was going to be used for, and the identity of its number one passenger. They called for the installation of a battery-powered elevator in the aft fuselage that eliminated the need for the telltale wheelchair ramps.

The engineers, aware that the Secret Service had ordered the elevator for security reasons, figured out a way to hide its presence other than when it was in use. They installed it behind the main passenger cabin, where it was concealed so well that Air Force officers used to bet civilian passengers they couldn't find the elevator during their flight. And Gil Mason, who designed aircraft interiors for Douglas, went far beyond this new means of enplaning and deplaning to assure that Franklin Roosevelt was going to enjoy traveling on this airplane. J.E. terHorst and Colonel Ralph Albertazzie, in their definitive and fascinating history of presidential aircraft, *The Flying White House,* said the designer's solution for FDR's boredom was an ingenious one.

Mason knew the president hated to be confined for long periods, even on a ship; on an airplane his impatience and discomfort were even greater. During Roosevelt's first two overseas air trips, he had managed with considerable difficulty to pay visits to the flight decks where he thoroughly enjoyed himself observing crew activities. Mason set out not only to make such visits easier, but to give the president some degree of greater mobility within the C-54.

His first contribution was to design a collapsible lightweight wheelchair fashioned out of chromium steel and leather. It easily could be rolled into the special elevator at ground level and hoisted into the aft cabin corridor from where it could be wheeled anyplace in the airplane. To facilitate entrance to the cockpit level itself, Mason installed removable steel rails over which the wheelchair could roll; once inside, the wheelchair was locked securely into a position just behind and between the two pilots. From all accounts, FDR loved the entire arrangement.

The interior of *Guess Where II* was no slum area, but it paled in comparison to what Mason and his associates put into the new plane. The presidential suite, an area of about eight by twelve feet that sat seven people, included a conference table in the middle of the compartment and an upholstered swivel chair for the president that was attached to the floor. A sofa, convertible into a bed, was at one end of the suite, and a telephone connected the compartment to the airplane's three other staterooms and the cockpit. Four big maps on rollers were placed on one of the cabin walls, and next to the maps were enlarged duplicates of major flight instruments including speed, altitude, and time. The furnishings were laid out in such a way that Roosevelt could move his wheelchair around with ease.

One exclusive feature worried the Secret Service, with its passion for absolutely security. Douglas installed a large, bullet-proof picture window by FDR's swivel chair, and while Roosevelt loved it, the window immediately proclaimed to all onlookers that this was no ordinary C-54 Skymaster, and announced FDR's presence just as surely as stepless ramps. The Secret Service objected so vociferously that a compromise was reached: Douglas fashioned an aluminum template that could be fitted over the picture window from the inside of the aircraft. In the center of the template was a hole the exact size of a C-54's typical round window. The agents assigned to the flight would decide the most appropriate time to attach the disguising template, usually just before landing, so that anyone looking at the airplane's exterior would think it was just another ATC Skymaster.

Aircraft 7451 had a few important technical differences, too. The landing gear doors were beefed up to protect the wheels, and the plane's ailerons were larger than those on conventional Skymasters. It took Douglas almost eight months to complete Project 51; Hank Myers flew the new transport from Santa Monica to Washington National Airport, where it became part of the Air Transport Command's 503rd Wing, the ATC unit assigned to VIP air transportation.

The Air Corps let it be known, albeit unofficially, that it would like Aircraft 42-107451 (the assigned serial number carried on the tail) to be called "The Flying White House." The Air Corps should have known better; this was like naming a child Percival, and then wondering why he was called Butch for the rest of his life. The airplane quickly became known as "The Sacred Cow," which supposedly was the idea of the irreverent White House press corps. This is what every World War II historian has accepted as gospel— with a single exception. John Toland, one of the war's finest chroniclers and an indefatigable researcher, credited presidential advisor Bernard Baruch with naming the plane; according to Toland, the White House reporters heard what Baruch was calling the airplane and quickly adopted it themselves. Roosevelt himself thought the press was responsible.

"So the reporters are calling it 'The Sacred Cow,' eh?" he laughed. "Suits me."

Much against the Army's wishes, "Sacred Cow" stuck like instant glue. Yet the *Cow*'s first official mission wasn't a presidential flight; Myers flew Secretary of War Henry Stimson and a group of senior military officials to Naples via Casablanca on July 1, 1944, about a month after the Normandy invasion. Seventeen days later, Myers took the same passengers from London to Washington nonstop, covering 3800 miles in the record time of seventeen hours and fifty minutes. He may have still missed *Guess Where II* for sentimental reasons, but he was rapidly falling in love with the new airplane.

The next VIP to enjoy the *Cow*'s palatial comforts was someone used to demanding such amenities: Roosevelt ordered Myers to pick up Madame Chiang Kai-shek in Rio de Janeiro and bring her back to Washington without delay. He made the round-trip of more than 5000 miles in less than twenty-four hours, the first time in aviation history that any airplane had flown that many miles in a single day.

Mission number three, late in 1944, took Myers and the *Sacred Cow* on a 25,000-mile trip, carrying three high-ranking generals and admirals to both the European and Pacific war theaters; it was a fact-finding tour ordered by Roosevelt and aimed at future reorganization of the Army and Navy. And in February of 1945, the *Sacred Cow* finally boarded not only the President, but an ATC major assigned to the flight as Myers's copilot—an airman Hank didn't particulary like, from an airline he cordially hated.

This was the flight to the summit meeting at Yalta on Russia's Baltic coast; it would be Franklin Roosevelt's first trip on the luxurious transport that had been hand-tailored to cope with his infirmity. Tragically, it also would be his last trip on the *Cow*. He apparently wasn't aware of the cockpit friction he himself had fomented by going over General George's head and insisting that Otis Bryan serve as Hank Myers's copilot.

The new U.S. cruiser *Quincy* carried FDR and his party as far as Malta, where the *Cow* was waiting, a fake serial number on the tail replacing "AF 42-107451" for security reasons. The president was boarding an airplane commanded by a colonel who was not merely unhappy, but boiling mad. Myers was surprised to learn that Bryan was to be his copilot and second-in-command, and that while this crew arrangement ostensibly had come from FDR's staff, Hank had every reason to believe the orders reflected Roosevelt's personal wishes that Bryan be assigned to the Yalta mission.

Myers not only didn't think much of Bryan, his opinion of TWA was even lower; he seemed to rank that airline somewhere in the general vicinity of the German Luftwaffe. So Hank proceeded to exercise his authority as aircraft commander and placed his regular copilot, Elmer Smith, in the right seat. This probably was his prerogative in a technical sense, but FDR was the commander in chief of the armed forces and Myers's defiance of the president's wishes might have been interpreted as insubordination.

Apparently, Roosevelt wasn't even aware of any cockpit friction. He genuinely liked Hank Myers, but enjoyed a special rapport with Bryan, who from all reports did little if any flying during the entire trip. "He might as well have been a passenger," copilot Smith remarked later. Otis always denied there was any rancor between Myers and himself, and this was probably true on Bryan's part. And there was one thing on which both men agreed: Roosevelt's deteriorated physical appearance.

In the two years since Bryan had seen him, the TWA pilot thought the president had aged at least fifteen. Myers was shocked, too. FDR may not have even been aware of what trouble he had caused by insisting on Bryan's presence, because neither pilot would have wanted to mention anything so minor to a man not only on the way to one of the most important international conferences in history, but also a man who was obviously seriously ill and, in fact, dying.

After the war, Bryan recounted a poignant incident that occurred on the return flight from Yalta. FDR asked Otis to come to his stateroom, and the pilot thought he seemed bored, lonesome, or maybe even depressed.

"I guess he just wanted someone to talk to," Bryan related. "He talked about Stalin and his mistrust of Churchill and vice versa. He said too much of his time had been taken up dealing with that situation."

There was no mention, of course, about the "other situation"— the one in the cockpit.

Myers landed the *Sacred Cow* and its distinguished passenger, "Sawbuck"—FDR's Secret Service code name—on the morning of February 3 at Saki, a Russian airfield about sixty miles from Yalta. It was Colonel Myers's second landing at Saki; a week before, he had made made a dry run from Malta to the airfield, arriving in a thick overcast, ahead of time—so early that he decided to make a straight-in approach, so fast that he was on the ground before Russian antiaircraft guns could be trained on the plane.

From Saki, Myers flew a dry run to Cairo, because this was where Roosevelt was planning to visit after the Yalta conference ended. This time the *Cow* experienced her first mechanical malfunction, when an engine connecting rod broke. The crew commandeered a healthy engine from another C-54 and flew back to Malta in time to meet the *Quincy* on schedule.

Hank Myers's judgment and calmness were never tested as thoroughly as on the real flight from Malta to Saki. P-51 Mustang fighters were escorting the *Cow* (Myers, unlike Bryan, welcomed such protection) when a Soviet plane suddenly crossed into the transport's flight path in what for one heart-stopping moment seemed to be a collision course. The Mustang flight leader ordered an attack, but Myers radioed an instant countercommand and dropped the C-54 a thousand feet, out of the way. The unknown Russian pilot continued on his way, apparently unaware that he had almost changed the course of history.

Myers and his crew got a taste of Soviet paranoia, even toward Russia's allies, when they were assigned to a building normally used for resort guests. He shared quarters with copilot Smith and navigator Ted Boselli, and it didn't take them long to discover their room had been clumsily bugged. They found the poorly concealed microphone about five minutes after entering, left the bug where it was, and reportedly spent much of the night loudly relating stories of imaginary secret weapons and juicy gossip about various celebrities they claimed to know personally.

Naturally, there was considerable curiosity on the part of the Russians toward the *Sacred Cow*. They had seen C-54s before, but nothing like this one, and one of the most interested visitors was the head of the Soviet naval air forces, Admiral Yermachenkov, who made not just one, but several visits. Myers, following orders to "be cooperative," kept showing him brand-new equipment. Albertazzie and terHorst, relating the incident in *The Flying White House,* noted that on each visit Yermachenkov was accompanied by impassive agents of NKVD, the Soviet secret police. So the frustrated

Russian airman was forced to display total indifference toward everything he saw.

Myers showed him an altimeter, emphasizing that it was new and secret. Yermachenkov nodded indifferently, an obvious "we already have it" gesture. Hank pointed out the plane's loran navigational equipment, so new that some ATC officers didn't even know it existed. Yermachenkov almost yawned and remarked that he already knew all about this navigation device. It finally dawned on the hospitable Americans that this high-ranking Russian air officer didn't dare display interest in front of the NKVD, for it would have been an admission of Soviet technological inferiority. Myers got proof of this when he slipped Yermachenkov some current American magazines from the airplane's stock of reading material. The magazines were returned within a few hours by a poker-faced messenger who said they weren't needed.

The *Sacred Cow's* next trip ended in sadness; it carried Bernard Baruch on a diplomatic mission to London, but shortly after Myers landed word came that FDR had died in Warm Springs, Georgia. The badly shaken Baruch, a close friend of Roosevelt for many years, asked Hank to fly him back to Washington immediately; three weeks later, Myers took President Truman to Missouri to visit his mother—a one-day round-trip that was to be repeated often, because Truman loved flying and preferred it to any other mode of travel.

Truman used the *Cow* on every possible occasion: to San Francisco for the adoption of the United Nations charter; from Brussels to Potsdam, Germany, where the feisty successor to the aristocratic Roosevelt met "Uncle Joe" Stalin for the first time and, unlike FDR, decided that Stalin was nothing but a ruthless tyrant bent on world conquest. Myers had picked up the president in Belgium because Truman had been talked into crossing the Atlantic in a more leisurely way, aboard the cruiser *Augusta*, that gave him time to confer with top advisors before the Potsdam conference.

Harry Truman was an impatient man to begin with, and from all accounts he hated the sea voyage. Before returning home, he asked Myers about the possibility of flying him all the way back to Washington. The colonel said if they left Berlin at 5 P.M., he'd have him landing at National Airport by nine the next morning; Truman told him to go ahead and make the arrangements. Once again his advisors argued against it, insisting he needed the rest that a sea voyage would provide. They were about to lose their case until Bess Truman intervened—thanks to a telephone call arranged by the White House staff—and the President returned home on the cruiser.

But he continued to fly on the *Cow* every chance he could, and so did members of his administration. Myers flew Secretary of State Byrnes and General Marshall to Europe in a trip that marked the start of the famed Marshall Plan for rebuilding the war-shattered continent, and the flight included New York to Paris nonstop— the first such crossing since Lindbergh's 1927 feat.

Originally, the *Sacred Cow*'s official call sign for Air Traffic Control identification purposes was "Army 7451"—the last four digits of the airplane's registered tail numbers. After the National Security Act of 1947 unified the armed forces and established an independent Air Force (Truman signed the Act into law aboard the *Sacred Cow*), the *Cow*'s call sign was changed to "Air Force 7451." This, in turn, was superceded by the prefix "Special Flight" followed by "7451" or more commonly by the phonetic initials "Sam Fox." Later the prefix was shortened to "Sam."

The call sign Air Force One (Navy One, or Marine One, if the President is using an aircraft operated by the Navy or Marines) was first used by President Eisenhower's Lockheed Constellation, *The Columbine I,* although it wasn't adopted officially until the first presidential jet, a Boeing 707, was delivered in 1961.

Four piston-engine transports—a Douglas DC-6 and a trio of Constellations—followed the *Sacred Cow* into postwar White House service, but Myers flew only the DC-6 as the presidential command pilot, and Truman was his last presidential passenger. If FDR had been close to Otis Bryan, Truman's relationship with Hank Myers was even closer. Myers would do anything for him, and that included doing practically anything with an airplane.

The president once talked his favorite pilot into buzzing the White House in broad daylight, because he expected Bess and daughter Margaret to be on the roof of the executive mansion watching jet fighters put on an air show over the nation's capital. Truman, accompanied by two Secret Service agents, sneaked out of the White House, drove to Bolling Field, where Myers was waiting with the *Cow,* and a few minutes later the Flying White House roared over the real White House at an altitude of only 500 feet.

Truman was sitting by the picture window laughing and waving at the small group of startled people on the roof.

He didn't see his wife and daughter there, however, so Myers made a second pass. By this time, Bess and Margaret had joined the roof spectators, jumping up and down and waving as the C-54 thundered by again at about 450 feet. Myers could have been in an ocean of hot water, but he escaped censure or a possible fine because he was following the president's orders. Harry Truman took the heat—a savage lambasting in the press for what was called a foolish stunt, although anyone who knew Hank Myers might question whether anything he did with an airplane could be regarded as either foolish or a stunt. Hap Arnold once called him "the Paderewski of our profession."

Not until long after Harry Truman left office was it revealed that he had involved his pilot in another presidential caper. Truman's bitterest political enemy was Senator Robert Taft, a conservative Republican from Ohio. Myers knew that Truman's opinion of Taft couldn't be printed on asbestos three inches thick, but he didn't realize the extent of the president's contempt until Truman began making frequent flights to Independence, Missouri, to visit his aging mother. He gave Myers standing orders that he be notified as soon as the *Cow* passed over the Ohio state line, a presidential command that mystified the pilot until he discovered what Harry was doing with the information.

As soon as Myers told him they were over Ohio, Truman would go to the nearest lavatory in the airplane and relieve himself by what a child would refer to as "tinkling." Then over the cockpit intercom would come the familiar Missouri twang: "Hank, activate the disposal system."

The gesture was purely symbolic, of course, because whatever liquid departed the disposal system evaporated long before it hit the ground. But that a dignified colonel in the U.S. Air Force willingly joined in such horseplay underlined the unusual rapport between these two men, both with small-town backgrounds and possessing the same simple likes, dislikes, and basic philosophies. Albertazzie and terHorst, in their history of presidential airplanes, stressed that Truman, perhaps more than any other chief executive, really loved to fly, and regarded the *Sacred Cow* almost as a refuge, a sanctuary from the pressures of office and the occasional odors of Washington politics.

The *Cow*'s glory days had to end eventually; after all, it was an airplane whose basic design dated back to early 1938. When the war ended and there was no longer any reason to keep the plane's movements secret, the Air Force seriously considered sprucing up its military exterior with some kind of special insignia. The Walt Disney studios submitted a design that showed the face of a smiling cow wearing a halo over one horn, and a striped Uncle Sam top hat over the other. The public also mailed in an avalanche of various suggestions, one of them winning the admiration of Myers and his crew. It depicted a cow, covered with medals and a bright halo, flying over a globe.

But the *Sacred Cow* never got to wear any special insignia because the White House—presumably its staff—decided that a presidential airplane needed dignity more than some comic drawing. Myers's suggested compromise, however, did win approval. The flags of every country the *Cow* had visited were painted on the left side of the C-54's nose; there were forty-four of them, with seven more added before the *Cow* was retired as a presidential airplane in July of 1947 and became just another VIP transport, albeit still a very well-furnished one.

The *Cow* had started running out of time in 1946, when the Air Force decided to replace it with a modern pressurized airliner of postwar design. The two candidates were the latest model of the Lockheed Constellation, which happened to be the queen of TWA's fleet, and the Douglas DC-6 which American and United had ordered in large numbers. Hank Myers reportedly lobbied behind the scenes in favor of the Douglas entry, while Jack Frye was doing likewise in behalf of the Connie; it would be an obvious honor for any airline to be operating the same transport as the president of the United States. When Douglas won the competition, American willingly gave up a coveted early delivery position so that fuselage number 29, which was supposed to go to the airline, could be diverted from the regular assembly line and transformed into the new presidential airplane.

There is reason to believe that Myers had Harry Truman's ear when it came to the final decision, although that decision was supposedly made by the Air Force alone. And it definitely was Myers who gave Truman a name for the new Flying White House, one the President loved: *Independence*.

Hank continued to fly the *Sacred Cow* until the *Independence* was delivered and put into service in 1947. The new DC-6 was not only pressurized, but even more luxurious than the old C-54. Yet while it won Myers's respect in the one year he flew it, the plane never earned the affection he felt toward the gallant *Cow*. After the war, he was flying back to the U.S. from Paris with a load of returning soldiers when the *Cow* slammed into a series of violent updrafts. One of them shot the plane from 8000 feet to more than 14,000 in seconds, followed by a sudden downdraft that sent it plunging toward the ocean, out of control. Myers tried everything to halt the dive; he was to say later he kept thinking that if the *Sacred Cow*—the proud presidential aircraft—crashed into the Atlantic, it would be a devastating and lasting blow to all aviation.

They were still out of control at 1000 feet, gripped by the killer downdraft, when a lightning bolt hit the C-54 with the impact of an antiaircraft shell. An explosive flash of white and blue fire momentarily stunned and blinded Myers, so that he couldn't even see the instrument panel. Instinctively, he pulled back on the yoke; instinctively and miraculously, the *Cow* responded as if the bolt had somehow freed her from the downdraft's clutches. Her nose came up and the altimeter readings started to climb. Myers, fearing there must have been structural damage, diverted to Iceland, where mechanics found that the lightning strike had put more than twenty-five tiny scorched holes into the fuselage. Yet that was the only damage, and Myers continued the flight to Washington.

That dive had produced the worst five minutes in the three years Hank Myers spent as the *Sacred Cow*'s commander. He flew the *Independence* until January of 1948, when he decided to resign from the Air Force and return to American Airlines. He had the satisfaction of being succeeded by another former American pilot, Lieutenant Colonel Francis "Frenchie" Williams, and he admitted he was glad to get back to the more regular, structured life of an airline captain; what Myers didn't miss about being the presidential pilot were the days and months the job kept him away from his wife and young son.

Truman tried to talk him into staying in the Air Force a little longer, not as an aircraft commander but as his military aide—not only a very handsome compliment but an assignment that would have earned Myers a promotion to brigadier general. Hank declined; he had spent six years in uniform and that was enough.

The other wartime presidential pilot, Otis Bryan, also resumed his former airline career, rejoining TWA after the war but not staying very long. Bryan worshipped Jack Frye, and after Howard Hughes fired Frye early in 1947, Bryan clashed repeatedly with Jack's successor and finally quit—although both Hughes and even Frye urged him to stay. Otis became the U.S. representative for a large Philippines conglomerate.

In 1955, the Air Force transferred Aircraft 42-107451 to Headquarters Command at Bolling Field, just outside Washington. Its status as a VIP transport was gone; now it was used, rather sparingly and even more prosaically, for what was termed "administrative military flights." Technological progress resulted in a "nose job"; the Air Force extended the *Cow*'s nose section to accept a weather avoidance radar unit, which gave the airplane the snout of a winged Pinocchio who had just told a lie.

The last flight of the *Sacred Cow*, which took place October 17, 1961, was also the shortest in its seventeen-year career; an Air Force general ferried it from Bolling to Andrews Air Force Base, a distance of roughly ten air miles. To those must be added the 1.5 million miles the Air Transport Command's own logs showed for the *Sacred Cow*, although only 43,000 miles involved presidential flights. When this magnificent veteran touched down on an Andrews AFB runway, those were the final seconds of the 12,135 hours and twenty-five minutes she had spent in the air.

Forty-eight days after the flight to Andrews, on December 4, 1961, the *Sacred Cow* was decommissioned in a brief but moving ceremony and officially turned over to the Smithsonian Institution to become part of its historic aircraft collection, joining such renowned birds as the original *Wright Flyer*, Lindbergh's *Spirit of St. Louis*, and Wiley Post's world-circling *Winnie Mae*. The Smithsonian's ancient buildings were far too small for an airplane the size of a C-54—one of them barely held the Wright and Lindbergh planes—so the *Cow*'s wings were removed and the airplane was trucked to the museum's aircraft storage facilities in Maryland. There it sat unnoticed and ignored for twenty-two years, gathering dust and generally deteriorating into a mere facsimile of its former magnificent self.

When the Smithsonian's new National Air & Space Museum opened in 1976, there still wasn't room to squeeze in the first Flying White House and even if there had been, the airplane was in no condition to be put on display. So in 1983, the *Cow* was shipped by truck to Dayton, Ohio, home of the huge U.S. Air Force Museum. The restoration process began in August of 1985, with an army of dedicated and skilled volunteers contributing almost 35,000 hours of work over the next ten years. When they finished, one of the most famous airplanes in history had been reborn in all its former pristine glory and put on display along with two other presidential survivors of the piston age: the *Independence* and the last of the Connies that served President Eisenhower, *Columbine III*.

Two wartime airplanes that certainly earned a place of honor by the *Sacred Cow*'s side ended instead on the scrap heap. After the war, the *Dixie Clipper* was cannibalized for spare parts needed for six other Boeing flying boats operated by a charter and cargo airline. *Guess Where II* had a short-lived postwar career, serving a number of ATC bases briefly until the War Department decided to declare the airplane war surplus. Its final flight was to a warbird graveyard at Walnut Ridge, Arkansas. An Air Force officer saw the C-87, parked in the middle of hundreds upon hundreds of battered combat aircraft, just before the wreckers got their hands on it. He said it looked brand-new, which made its end even more poignant.

Hap Arnold had wanted at least one model of every airplane used in World War II preserved and protected so future generations could view them at museums, understanding and appreciating the role each played in history's greatest conflict.

Unfortunately, no one bothered to save what was supposed to be the first Flying White House.

★ ★ 9 ★ ★
Bumps in the Night

The emotional thunderbolt of the Pearl Harbor attack brought war home to a nation's civilian population only partially prepared for what commitment to global conflict meant in terms of personal sacrifice at worst, and inconvenience at best.

Inconvenience sums up how the war affected civilian air travel although, relatively speaking, it didn't even affect that many people. In 1940, the last full year of normal, unrestricted peacetime airline operations, slightly in excess of 1 million people traveled by air. Many of them, however, were "repeaters"—businessmen who flew frequently, so that the 1 million figure actually represented the number of tickets sold, not a head count of each separate individual who flew. It was estimated that in 1940 less than ten percent of America's adult population had ever been on a scheduled airline flight, and taking the "repeater" factor into account, a more realistic figure would have been five to seven percent.

Even before Pearl Harbor, there were some military authorities who believed that if war came, *all* civilian air travel should be banned for the duration. Edgar Gorrell sold the War Department on a far more practical and fairer plan: the establishment of a priority system that controlled the boardings of every airline flight. Gorrell, on January 20, 1942, advised all Air Transport Association members that they were to honor the Military Director of Civil Aviation's directive to that effect, a directive which spelled out a specific passenger pecking order.

"Complying with orders from the (MDCA)," Gorrell's letter began, "these instructions will be kept available to each person who is assigned the responsibility of representing the industry in each city, to check the validity of each request for priority with existing orders from the MDCA."

In abbreviated form, these were the priority categories:

Priority 1 - *Any person properly identifying himself as a member of the President's family or as a member of the President's immediate staff in the White House.*

Priority 2 - *Army, Navy, or Marine Corps airplane pilots of their respective Ferrying Commands traveling under orders, upon presentation of such identifying orders.* (This category was extended to include civilian ferry pilots.)

Priority 3 - *Military personnel (War, Navy, and Marine Corps, including Allied military personnel) who present travel orders directing travel by air.*

Priority 4 - *Army and Navy equipment, ammunition, supplies, and materials essential to the war effort ordered for air movement by the War Department.* (This applied to priority cargo whose weight might necessitate blocking out passenger seats.)

Priority 5 - *Personnel of government departments and agencies and personnel whose activities are essential to the war effort (other than military personnel), traveling on specific orders for priority travel by air which certifies such travel is necessary to the successful prosecution of the war effort.* (Later in the war, when the crunch for space eased somewhat, civilians making essential trips were placed in this category, which gradually became part of Priority 3.)

Gorrell also accomplished something that his members regarded as a minor miracle: he convinced the Army to let an experienced airline man administer the priority system. The choice was United's traffic manager, Ray Ireland, the only catch being that he had to join the Army first; he was sworn in as a colonel and ran the program throughout the war, playing no favorites and doing his best to assure full compliance.

The would-be air traveler who didn't qualify for any priority category went to the end of every standby line; it made no difference that he or she might hold a confirmed reservation, because in effect there was no such thing as a confirmed reservation. Civilians got used to receiving a dreaded phone call the night before their flight, or even a few hours before departure, when the tired voice of an airline agent would intone the litany of bad news:

"Sir, we're sorry to inform you that the government has requisitioned the space you hold for priority use . . ."

It was not surprising that Joe Citizen found space not only difficult to obtain but most of the time virtually impossible. For at least the first two years of the war, ferry pilots alone were occupying up to ninety percent of all available airline space.

Even a passenger holding a priority ticket could be bumped by someone with a still higher priority, and this happened all the time. The only assurance anyone had was that once the flight took off, he or she was safe until the next stop, which wasn't of much help on the longer multistop trips. The average transcontinental DC-3 flight between New York or Washington and the west coast, at a one-way fare of about $170, involved at least two stops en route, and sometimes as many as six, each landing a potential bumping ordeal generated by priority passengers boarding at airports all over the country.

There were extremely few cases where airline agents violated the priority boarding regulations, a remarkable record of compliance considering the frequent temptations they faced. Passengers holding no or low priorities would try everything in the book to get on a flight—from sob stories that would have flooded an 8000-foot runway, to astronomical bribe offers. Airlines serving Washington, D.C.—and these included American, United, Eastern, and TWA— were most frequently exposed, because the nation's capital was heavily populated by citizens with large egos; these were the days of dollar-a-year industrialists doing their best for the war effort, but sometimes chaffing under wartime restrictions and shortages.

Yet rare was the instance where an appeal either to sympathy or avarice worked. As a matter of fact, it dawned on the public, including even the most influential and powerful travelers, that the five priority categories were right up there with the Ten Commandments—and undoubtedly enjoyed more compliance. Eddie Rickenbacker, flying on his own airline with a Priority 5, found this out the hard way when an enlisted man holding a Priority 3 bumped him off an Eastern plane just before takeoff.

An equally prominent VIP who suffered the same fate was Eleanor Roosevelt, who consistently refused to ask for the Priority 1 rating to which she was entitled as a member of the president's immediate family. The first lady was flying from Washington to New York and holding the Priority 5 she invariably requested. At the last minute, an Army pilot, and only a second lieutenant at that, showed up clutching a Priority 2. Everyone else on the plane had a Priority 2 or 3 except Mrs. Roosevelt, so American's station manager, Jack Mullins, had to ask her to give up her seat.

He hated to do it, very much aware that Eleanor Roosevelt was not only the wife of the president and deserving of the highest travel priority, but also happened to be a close personal friend of C.R. Smith, who openly adored her. A man of few words, especially when it came to admitting he admired anybody, C.R. unabashedly called Mrs. Roosevelt "one of the most unusual women I ever met, in intelligence and energy—always interested in doing for someone else instead of someone doing for her."

Mullins tried to apologize when he told her she was being bumped from the flight, but Mrs. Roosevelt merely smiled. "My goodness, young man, of course I'll get off. There's no question those pilots should go ahead of me."

Mullins, a tough boss who would have tossed his own mother off an American flight if she lacked a priority, almost sighed with relief. After the war, that incident was the one he remembered best.

"We took all sorts of people off our airplanes," he reminisced. "Usually the bigger and more important a person was, the more understanding and easier to handle he was. It invariably was the little guy who just thought he was important who gave us the most trouble."

(American's Admirals Clubs, the airline's VIP lounges, at one time had an official "men only" membership policy. C.R. waived it for Mrs. Roosevelt to the extent of sending her what amounted to a permanent guest pass. She responded with this friendly thank-you note: "I realize that it is not essentially a women's club! I do not think that I shall very often avail myself of the Club privileges, but it is nice to know that I can do so if I wish.")

Not all the priority-displaced passengers were as understanding and cooperative as the first lady, although the system ran smoother than the airlines actually expected. Eastbound flights were a little easier to get on, with less bumping; westbound flights, however, were usually booked solid with Priority 2 ferry pilots who had just returned from flying planes to Europe and were heading for the west coast to pick up more aircraft. Any nonpriority civilian who had managed to board a westbound transcontinental flight was virtually certain to lose his seat somewhere along the way. A Los Angeles newspaper sent a reporter to cover an important story in New York. The eastbound trip, normally a fifteen hour flight, took forty-four hours, which wasn't bad in wartime. When the assignment was finished and he flew back to Los Angeles, he was en route for nine days.

The chances of getting bumped increased sharply unless a passenger held at least a Priority 3, which didn't always help, because a lot of Priority 3s were bumped by 2s. Trains were just as jammed, of course, and gas rationing held down interstate automobile travel, which put additional strains on air travel. In retrospect, the airlines did an incredible job; in 1943 alone, they carried 1.5 million more passengers than in 1939, using less than half the number of planes. In 1944, the passenger count totaled more than 4.6 million. Utilization was one explanation; virtually every carrier was operating every available aircraft up to fifteen hours a day. Even flights leaving at such ungodly hours as 3 A.M. were usually packed, because inconvenient departure times offered about the only chance a nonpriority passenger had of getting on a flight, especially if he or she had been bumped off a previous one. Vacation air travel naturally became nonexistent, and also in sharp decline were airline advertising and promotion budgets; why spend money advertising when every seat on every airplane was practically guaranteed to be filled? Wartime load factors—the percentage of available seats occupied by paying passengers—averaged ninety percent, compared to the sixty percent of the immediate prewar years.

The airlines stopped selling tickets through travel agents and also suspended discounts to holders of the Universal Air Travel Card, the industry's first use of paying by credit. Another category affected was the percentage of women flying, dropping from twenty-five percent in 1940 to no higher than fifteen percent during the war. Conversely, the number of women employed by the airline industry boomed as more and more men went into the armed forces. Even crusty, chauvinistic Eddie Rickenbacker had to abandon his long-standing, inviolate rule against hiring female flight attendants.

Not many had to be hired at first, because Eastern's fleet late in 1943 was down to only twenty DC-3s. The company's employee newspaper hailed their advent with far more enthusiasm than the captain demonstrated. Commenting on the effects of fleet reduction, the paper noted that "many details of the passenger service were reduced correspondingly in quantity," and then added:

"One very pleasant and outstanding exception to this reduction is the addition of Flight Stewardess Service, supplementing our Flight Stewards aloft."

It is tempting to wonder what Captain Eddie thought when he read that statement; even during the war he accepted stewardesses only as a necessary evil. Invariably, he addressed every one he encountered as "girlie," and he did so as long as he ran the airline. He took a perverse delight in trying to catch them in some rules violation, and one of his tricks was to charge past the flight attendant standing by the boarding stairs to see if she'd ask to see his pass. He probably tried this at least fifty times and never nailed anybody.

His reluctance to put any woman in a position of responsibility extended beyond airplane cabins. Eastern once had a very efficient sales representative named Alice Eckhoff, whose sales territory was the tough New York garment district. Before and even during the war she was carried on the payroll as "A. Eckhoff" so Rickenbacker wouldn't find out she was a woman. But the war circumvented such prejudices, and not only Eastern but also a lot of other airlines found themselves short of male talent and finally assigned women to tasks supposedly beyond female capability. Typical was the story of a young lady named Margaret "Maggie" Robinson, who joined Eastern's reservations staff in St. Louis during the war, and her own account could be that of hundreds of such women working for any airline at any one of its smaller stations:

"We had a small office on the second floor of the Lambert Field terminal. Our reservations table was borrowed from the coffee shop downstairs and covered wth a green oilcoth. We recorded all reservations on three-by-five cards and filed them in a cigar box, arranged by days of the month, alphabetically and current.

"Eastern was very strict about our wearing correct uniforms. I remember we had to have blue shoes and sometimes we had to borrow ration coupons from friends in order to buy a pair. And we figuratively had to wear many hats—even if you were assigned to reservations, you were also expected to work the ticket counter prior to a flight departure.

"Forty-five minutes before a flight left, you rushed from reservations down to the counter and began to check in passengers. I always wondered how we could ever take care of a full planeload—twenty-one passengers! Actually, there was almost as much to do checking in twenty-one as (there was later) in checking in two hundred. There'd be a long manifest on which you had to record each passenger's weight, destination, and baggage (the limit was forty pounds)—how many pieces, their weight, and the check numbers. And, of course, what kind of priority he was traveling on. You started talking to passengers the minute the first one came up to the counter and you could never stop talking because if you did, you were dead. We used to keep one eye on the clock, seeing how close we were to flight time. After everyone was checked in, you'd lock up the counter, put on a uniform hat, and run outside to help load last-minute baggage—after you made the flight announcement.

"When the last bag was loaded and everyone on board, you'd salute the captain and run back to reservations, where you'd start teletyping information to downline stations—who's making connecting flights, who's going straight through, and so forth. I worked from four A.M. to noon, six days a week. There were no such benefits as shift differential pay, overtime pay, or holiday pay. On your day off, you'd usually come out to the airport to see how things were going and invariably you'd wind up helping out. All this for a starting salary of a hundred and twenty-five dollars a month. But the airlines were like that, not just in the war years but before and for a while after the war.

"The training program for reservations consisted of reading Eastern's traffic manual. There was only one desk in reservations, so I'd have to study in the terminal lobby. Once you read through the manual, you were considered trained. We did have a training school in New York, and I wanted to go there badly, but once I read the traffic manual, they figured I had enough of an airline education."

Rickenbacker's dreaded station inspections were diminished during the war, but he still tried to make as many as possible and he hit St. Louis four weeks after Maggie had started working there. The station manager warned her, "Don't say anything to him unless you know what the hell you're talking about."

Captain Eddie arrived and as usual began chatting with whatever employees happened to be on duty. For some reason, the topic of conversation centered around the difficulties of landing at certain airports, and Rickenbacker cited one that presented a particular problem because "the beam sways"—meaning the electronic range signal was erratic.

Maggie Robinson didn't know a radio range signal from a spark plug, but she was positive she knew everything there was to know about beams—after all, Lambert had one that revolved on the top of the control tower. She spoke up before anyone could stop her.

"I know just what you mean, Captain," she chirped. "I come to work every morning at four o'clock and I see the beam on the control tower, going around and around and around . . ."

There was dead silence. The station manager mentally crossed himself. Rickenbacker gave her a long, hard, disbelieving look— and then started to laugh. From that day on, Maggie Robinson— her sex notwithstanding—became one of his favorites.

His reaction to another wartime gaffe was never recorded, and it is possible no one dared tell him. A brand-new and very nervous young lady assigned to the Eastern ticket counter at Washington National Airport had to make her first departure announcement. She was scared stiff, cleared her throat three times, and then delivered her message:

"Ladies and gentlemen, Eastern announces the departure of Flight 420, service to New York. Passengers will please show your tickets to the plane as you board the stewardess."

All of the carriers had to drop their prewar requirement that flight attendants had to be registered nurses, and this prerequisite was to be abolished permanently after the war. The presence of an attractive cabin attendant helped compensate for the uncertainties of wartime air travel, and, assuming one held a high boarding priority, flying still remained a reasonably pleasant experience. The in-flight food service wasn't that bad, either, although the airlines substituted cardboard trays for the usual metal ones and thereby saved about 100 pounds per airplane. Dinner on a United DC-3 reflected the airline's reputation for culinary excellence—UAL was the first U.S. carrier to operate its own flight kitchens, manned by top-rated chefs. Carl Solberg, in his fine history of commercial aviation (Conquest of the Skies) cited this menu for a typical hot meal served aboard a wartime Mainliner: bouillon soup, filet of beef, fresh green beans, hot potatoes, salad, rolls, lemon meringue pie, mints, and coffee; on Fridays passengers had a choice of fish or beef.

Those lucky enough to find space on one of the few Pan Am/ NATS Boeing 314s operating scheduled transatlantic passenger service during the war had it even better, although eastbound flights took at least twenty-six hours and averaged about four hours longer westbound, because of the invariably strong headwinds. Certainly it was a more enjoyable and relaxing way to cross the Atlantic than aboard an unheated ATC C-54 or C-87, where passengers on some midwinter flights put on gloves as soon as they boarded and didn't dare remove them after takeoff for fear of frostbite.

Despite the sharp increase in night flying and virtual round-the-clock operations, the airlines compiled an above-average safety record during the war. There were several fatal accidents, however, and two of them produced some of the biggest and blackest headlines of the war, because each airplane had a celebrity passenger aboard.

On February 22, 1943, Pan Am's *Yankee Clipper*, the same Boeing 314 that had pioneered commercial transatlantic flying, was on final approach to land on the Tagus River, where Pan Am maintained a seaplane base as the New York–Lisbon terminus. Officially, the flying boat was a NATS airplane although it was being flown by a Pan Am crew headed by one of the airline's most senior captains, Rod Sullivan, an ex–chief petty officer who had learned to fly in the Navy.

It was dusk, with darkness coming on fast, and as the big Boeing banked just prior to touching down, the left wing hit the water. The plane did a half cartwheel and broke up under the violent impact. It sank in ten minutes; of the thirty-nine passengers aboard, only fifteen survived, and one of them was famed Broadway singer Jane Froman, who was traveling with a USO group. Paralyzed below the waist from crash injuries, she would have perished in the freezing river if it were not for a kind of storybook hero from the crew: fourth officer John Burns, who held her up until a rescue boat arrived. They were married later, although their truer-than-fiction romance eventually ended in divorce.

The crash of the *Yankee Clipper,* the only B-314 to be lost in an accident during the war (neither of the two Martin M-130s survived), ended the career of an airplane that had logged over half a million air miles that included 240 Atlantic crossings. The official verdict was pilot error, and the evidence did seem to point to Captain Sullivan's misjudging his altitude when he banked. Yet he had a reputation for liking to make flat, fast landings, and other Pan Am pilots thought the fatal one at Lisbon was more of a "lazy pilot's approach."

He survived the crash, but his career didn't; he was forced to resign, although many of his fellow Pan Am airmen wondered if he deserved such severe punishment. Some figured Sullivan may have been a victim of the so-called "black hole" phenomenon, a tendency for a pilot to become visually disoriented while making an approach over water at night, and thinking he is higher than he actually is. But if that's what happened, it still wouldn't have been enough to erase the pilot error stigma. Sullivan's only vindication, an empty one at that, came in the 1952 film *With a Song in My Heart,* starring Susan Hayward, who played Froman. The imaginative scriptwriter had the Boeing hitting a submerged log in the Tagus River.

The other, even more spectacular fatal accident occurred January 16, 1942—a tragedy that began at 4 A.M., when a glamorous passenger boarded TWA Flight 3 at the Indianapolis airport. She was not only one of Hollywood's most beautiful and genuinely popular stars, but she was married to the most famous leading man in film history.

Her name was Carole Lombard, the wife of Clark Gable.

A native of Indiana, she had been in Indianapolis winding up a war bond tour. The Treasury Department told her it would be happy if she sold $500,000 worth in the Indiana capital, the last scheduled stop on the tour; she hung up about $2 million in sales in one day, with 3000 people lined up to buy bonds at her first public appearance in the lobby of the State House. Later that night, wearing a black evening gown (everything she wore on the tour was in black, which she considered appropriate for wartime), she wowed an overflow audience at the Cadle Tabernacle, impressing everyone with her enthusiasm and sincerity. If anyone showed the slightest sales resistance, she would turn on that dazzling thousand-watt smile and crack, "If my husband was here, you'd buy, I'd betcha!"

No more well liked film star ever lived. Bawdy with the vocabulary of a dock worker, one of the most renowned practical jokers in

Hollywood, and a woman of great natural beauty, she was worshiped by everyone from lowly grips to studio executives. Director Garson Kanin called her "the only star I have ever known who did not want a dressing room on the set. What little makeup she used, she would put on herself."

She called Gable "Pappy," he called her "Ma," and theirs was a love affair untainted by the fragility and destructive egos that mark so many film marriages.

The original tour itinerary called for her to return to Los Angeles from Indianapolis by train, accompanied by MGM press agent Otto Winkler and Carole's mother, Mrs. Bessie Peters. But the actress was tired, she missed Gable, and the train trip would have taken three days, so she insisted on flying. Neither Winkler nor Mrs. Peters were happy over that decision. They both disliked airplanes, and Mrs. Peters had an additional reason for preferring the train. She was a great believer in numerology and astrology, and fearfully pointed out that they would be leaving on the sixteenth day of the month; the number sixteen, according to numerologists, was a warning of an impending accident or death.

The pragmatic Carole scoffed at such fears, logically pointing that if the numerologists were right, all flights taking off on the sixteenth day of any month were in dire peril. But she agreed to a compromise. She was willing to let a coin toss determine their mode of travel: train if it came up heads, plane if it came up tails. Winkler flipped a nickel and it came up tails, so he went to work trying to get space on any westbound flight out of Indianapolis. The only available seats were on TWA Flight 3, and that added fresh ammunition to Mrs. Peters's numerology worries. She warned there were too many threes connected with this trip, starting with the flight number. They would be on a DC-3. They were a party of three. Carole was thirty-three years old. The astrological portents were ominous, too; Mrs. Peters's astrologer had advised her to stay off airplanes during all of 1942. Carole just laughed and shortly before 4 A.M., the trio boarded the DC-3, whose upper fuselage appropriately carried in flowing red script the same message Lombard had been preaching to enraptured audiences: VICTORY IS IN THE AIR—BUY BONDS.

Flight 3 originated in New York, and there had been a crew change in St. Louis, where the captain who took over was forty-one-year-old Wayne Williams, a veteran from the air mail days who was considered one of TWA's best instrument pilots. He had been hired in 1931, in fact, to teach instrument flying to Ford trimotor crews. At the time he boarded Flight 3, he had accumulated some 12,000 hours of logged flying time. The logbook of his twenty-five-year-old, far less experienced copilot, M.A. Gillette, showed slightly over 1300 hours.

There was a brief flap after they landed in Albuquerque. Because of a heavy load of mail and priority cargo, two of the twenty-one seats were blocked off, which left only nineteen passengers who could be accommodated, and there were a number of Army pilots, all graduates of Eagle Nest, who had been ordered to report to their ferrying command base in Los Angeles. TWA found space on the plane for fifteen of them, plus another serviceman with travel orders, and an agent asked the Lombard party to give up their seats. Carole normally would have complied without the slightest fuss; if there was ever a star totally devoid of all prima donna attributes, it was Carole Lombard. But she was exhausted, anxious to get home to Gable, and she didn't know how long they might be stranded in Albuquerque.

So she "pulled rank." She argued that her bond tour was, in effect, a government mission, and therefore her party deserved as much priority as the Army pilots. This wasn't true; she was traveling on a Priority 5 and the pilots held Priority 2s, but being Carole Lombard, she won the debate without any protests from the three airmen who would have taken their seats. They were the luckiest pilots in the U.S. Army; they had no way of knowing, nor did Lombard, that she had saved their lives.

Ordinarily, Flight 3 would have flown nonstop from Albuquerque to Burbank, which was then the principal airport serving the Los Angeles area. But Williams was told to expect strong head winds, and with the heavy load he was carrying, he decided to make refueling stops at Winslow, Arizona, and Las Vegas. He took off at 4:40 P.M., approximately three hours behind schedule, with only 350 gallons of fuel. A few minutes out of Albuquerque, he changed his mind, and received permission to bypass Winslow. By the time he landed in Las Vegas, it was past 6:30, and already dark. He refueled and took off again an hour later—thus setting the stage for a mystery that to this day still fascinates TWA pilots who knew Captain Wayne Williams.

* * *

Clark Gable was preparing a royal homecoming for his wife, her mother, and Winkler—a surprise dinner party to which he had invited his two brothers-in-law and Winkler's wife. The dining room had been decorated with red, white, and blue balloons and paper streamers, and upstairs in the master bedroom he had planted another surprise for his "Ma" who loved playing her own practical jokes. Just before leaving on the tour, she had put a blond woman mannequin in their bed, and told him, "it's to keep you company while I'm gone." He was going to get even with her; she was going to find a far more realistic dummy in that bed—a replica of an aroused naked man.

He pulled the blanket over the dummy's head and, chuckling in anticipation of her reaction when she pulled off the bed covers, went downstairs to await a call from an MGM publicity man who was meeting her flight. The phone finally rang, but it wasn't the publicist; it was Eddie Mannix, second-in-command to MGM mogul Louis B. Mayer himself, and one of Gable's closest friends.

"Eddie, can I call you back?" Gable asked. "I'm waiting for Larry Barbier to call me from the airport when Carole's plane gets in."

Mannix swallowed hard and broke the news. "Clark, Larry just phoned me from the airport. Carole's plane went down a few minutes after it left Las Vegas."

"How bad is it?" Gable wanted to know.

"Nobody knows yet, but we'd better get over to Vegas right away. The studio's chartering a plane and someone will stop by in a few minutes to drive you to the airport."

It took three days before rescue workers crawling up a mountain covered with ice and snow could reach the pulverized wreckage, not that there was anyone alive to rescue. Mannix refused to let Gable climb the mountain to look for his wife's body, and it was just as well. The studio executive did accompany one of the search teams and found out Carole had been sitting in the forward section of the cabin, which had been compressed into a mass of crushed, charred aluminum only ten feet long; most of the bodies, including hers, were burned beyond recognition and could only be identified from dental records.

When Mannix returned from the grisly trek, Gable kept asking, "Why Ma, Eddie? Why did Ma have to go? . . . Why?"

But there was an equally important "why" that had to be answered.

Why did an airliner commanded by an experienced captain fly into the side of a mountain on a clear, cold night with perfect visibility? And that "why" never did get a conclusive answer.

Westbound flights out of Vegas followed an airway whose compass heading was 205 degrees, taking them safely to the south of Potosi Mountain, an 8500-foot peak northwest of the Las Vegas airport. Yet witnesses who saw Flight 3 take off told investigators it headed in a *northwesterly* direction. It was an exceptionally clear night with good visibility.

Williams had filed a flight plan that established 8000 feet as his cruising altitude. This was not only 500 feet below the summit of Potosi Mountain, but the flight plan further specified a departure heading of 218 degrees, *almost directly toward the mountain*. Also puzzling was the fact that the flight plan itself violated TWA's operating procedures, which required such plans to be made out by the copilot but personally signed by the captain as assurance that he had seen it and agreed with it. Flight 3's carried only Gillette's name in printed letters; Williams never signed it, a mysterious omission suggesting that he probably never even looked at it.

Most of the airway beacons in the Las Vegas area had been blacked out because of the war, but there was one still operating on January 16: Beacon 24, also known as the Arden beacon, located about two and a half miles to the right of the center line of the Las Vegas radio range leg that marked the airway. Flights heading southwest out of Vegas passed to the left of Beacon 24. But when the Civil Aeronautics Board was investigating Flight 3's fate, it learned that the last time Williams had flown the Las Vegas–Burbank leg, about three weeks earlier, Beacon 24 was inoperative. It seemed logical to suspect that Williams, seeing the lighted beacon, mistook it for one situated directly on course and, assuming he was on course, flew to the right of it without realizing he was looking instead at Beacon 24.

The CAB, in its final report on the accident, conceded the possibility that this might have happened. But it also pointed out that in addition to the lighted beacon, the lights of the town of Arden and those of automobiles on U.S. Highway 91, plus the lights of the town of Goodsprings farther on, were plainly visible from the air and "afforded reliable reference points."

"Moreover," the CAB continued, "under contact conditions such as existed on the night of the accident, if the cockpit lights are kept dimmed, it is possible to see the outline of the mountains, especially when they are snow-covered as they were on January 16."

Of course, there was considerable Monday morning quarterbacking in that damning conclusion, for it assumed that (1) the pilots found the time to look down on the lights of automobiles and towns instead of concentrating on their instruments, and (2) that the cockpit lights were dimmed.

But the report added:

"Furthermore, it appears . . . that the available radio range facilities were operating properly at the time of the accident. Had the captain and first officer been listening to the Las Vegas radio range, a moderate 'A' signal would have been heard, which would have definitely indicated the plane was off course . . . It seems obvious that the pilots were not using the radio range for navigational purposes."

Flight 3 impacted Potosi Mountain at a point 730 feet below the crest. All twenty-two aboard were killed instantly, and the CAB's subsequent verdict was pilot error: ". . . failure of the captain after departure from Las Vegas to follow the proper course by making use of the navigational aids available to him."

Wayne Williams's fellow airmen didn't question that verdict, but they also believed it left unanswered a question that begged for an answer:

Why?

Why did an airline captain of his reputation and experience violate so basic a rule as mandatory signing of flight plans—and this was a grossly erroneous flight plan that chose a departure gateway to doom?

Why did Williams, who had flown in and out of Las Vegas scores of times, steer the DC-3 on a compass heading he must have known led straight into the peak of an 8500-foot mountain?

Why did a captain, especially skilled in instrument flying, blithely ignore all the navigational aids available to him, including a simple radio signal that would have warned him he was off course?

The majority of TWA pilots who knew Wayne Williams well could draw only one conclusion, however speculative:

He wasn't in the cockpit when Flight 3 crunched into the rocky hide of that mountain.

Frank Busch, not only a veteran TWA captain himself but one who rose high in the airline's management ranks, had a theory that drew a lot of support.

"On the Lombard plane were pilots Wayne and I had trained at Eagle Nest," Busch explained. "What I and others think happened was that Wayne went back to the cabin to bull with them about me and some of the other guys we all knew. He left the copilot flying the plane and the kid flew right into the mountain. The way we found Wayne's body, it didn't look as if he had been in the cockpit when they hit. He was the kind of guy who gave his copilots a lot of responsibility. They put me in with him and every time we'd approach a thunderstorm, he'd leave the cockpit and I'd have to wrestle through the damned stuff. I finally got up the nerve to ask him why and he says, 'because those things scare me to death.' "

Gordon Parkinson, who spent forty years in various TWA operations posts, also knew Williams, and after the crash asked a number of pilots what they thought might have happened. "The scuttlebutt was that he was back in the cabin talking to Carole Lombard," Parkinson reported. "They couldn't prove this, but it was widely believed, because that's exactly what he might have done."

Otis Bryan was among those who agreed that Williams must have left the cockpit almost immediately after takeoff.

"He was a good friend of mine," Bryan related, "but he was a show-off. I don't mean that in a derogatory sense—he was a hell of a good pilot, but I can just see what happened. He had a copilot who was strange to him, and that plane was no sooner off the ground than Wayne was back there talking to Lombard."

If Williams did leave the cockpit while Flight 3 was still climbing, that would answer one "why," but not another: why didn't he sign the flight plan or not even look at it and therefore immediately spot Gillette's deadly departure heading? This was just as responsible for sending twenty-two people to their deaths as any failure to utilize available navigation aids—or look out the cockpit window for visual indications that they were off course?

The hostess on Flight 3 was Alice Frances Getz, Kansas City—based. TWA asked the chief hostess at the base, Ida Staggers, to notify Alice's parents, and Ida related the sad experience later:

"She came from a farm in northern Illinois, and there was no telephone. Personnel finally got me a number to call, that of a neighbor who had to drive a wagon over to the Getz farm, wake up Alice's father, and drive him back to the phone. By this time, it was about two or three in the morning, and I still don't know why I didn't wait until later that morning. I don't even remember how he took the news, I was so stunned myself."

So was everyone else, including the entire airline and film industries.

Ernst Lubitsch, who had directed Lombard's last and perhaps her finest comedy, *To Be or Not To Be*, felt it necessary to cut one line of dialogue before the picture could be released. The excised line, spoken to costar Jack Benny, was: "What can happen in a plane?"

Howard Hughes reportedly sent Gable a personal condolence note and the grief-stricken actor received this telegram from the White House:

"Mrs. Roosevelt and I are deeply distressed. Carole was our friend, our guest in happier days. She brought great joy to all who knew her and to millions who knew her only as a great artist. She gave unselfishly of her time and talent to serve her government in peace and in war. She is and always will be a star, one we shall never forget nor cease to be grateful to. Deepest sympathy."

FDR later was to award Lombard a posthumous medal, with a citation that called her "the first woman to be killed in action in the defense of her country in its war against the Axis powers," a sentiment that Lombard herself would have dismissed, in her own salty language, as "pure BS." And Gable turned down the Army's offer of a military funeral; he coped with his own grief by enlisting in the Air Corps less than eight months after the crash. He was to come out of the war a major with the Distinguished Flying Cross and Air Medal. To the surprise of many, including a large chunk of the legal profession, he never attempted to sue TWA for negligence, and according to one of his most objective biographers, Warren Harris, he even talked Otto Winkler's widow out of filing a lawsuit by promising to build her a house and provide her with a $100,000 annuity, which he paid for himself.

One prominent and respected radio news commentator had the temerity—or what a few might call the courage—to question all the attention being given to Carole Lombard's death, treating it as a national calamity and forgetting that twenty-one other Americans also died on Potosi Mountain. This lone dissenter was the caustic Elmer Davis.

"If you judge from the newspaper headlines of the past few days," Davis said in that memorable dry, nasal twang of his, "this is still a country where the death of a movie actress is more important than the death of fifteen Army fliers in the same accident. Fortunately, there is plenty of evidence that, in this instance, the newspaper headlines misrepresent the feeling of the public. Certainly an immense number of Americans have come to realize by now with the sort of times we live in that the death of an artist, however distinguished and popular, is of less importance to the future of the nation than the loss of fifteen of the highly trained men on whom we must depend for victory."

The most angry rebuttal to this journalistic heresy came from Walter Winchell. "I expect we can train fifteen more pilots, dreadful as their loss was," Winchell observed sarcastically. "I expect we can find other ways to sell more than $2 million in defense bonds in one day. But you could dredge Hollywood from end to end and not find another girl who could get out there and sell that many that fast solo."

There undoubtedly were many Americans who agreed with Winchell. It seemed futile to rate the importance of big bond sales by a beautiful and beloved film star vs. the future potential of fifteen young Army airmen; it was the classic case of trying to compare oranges with apples. But Elmer Davis probably could have found supporters among airmen themselves; thanks to Lombard's prominence, the crash of a single civilian DC-3 on a lonely Nevada mountain really did produce bigger headlines, heavier newspaper coverage, and more radio news air time than all the ATC and NATS fatal accidents combined. This may have been natural, easily understood, and even forgiven in the context of Lombard's death being a tremendous human interest story. Yet she would have been the first one to remind all those mourning her, "Hey, how about shedding a few tears for some very important people on that plane—those fifteen pilots who would have preferred living long enough to fly for their country."

All pilots would have welcomed that kind of epitaph for their fifteen dead comrades, aware of the importance of trained pilots. The flight crews themselves understood, far better than anyone else, how much the airplane had revolutionized warfare, even on the high seas, where the aircraft carrier had replaced the battleship as the true capital ship; carriers, not dreadnoughts, became the powerful axis around which every task force was built. No ground offensive could succeed without tactical air support. True, contrary to the overblown prewar predictions of air power enthusiasts, the strategic bombing campaign against enemy production centers didn't win the war all by itself, but the war couldn't have been won without it. And among those recognizing sooner than most people how far and how fast aviation had progressed during the war were the airline pilots flying for ATC and NATS.

They saw progress in terms of the equipment they were flying, transports like the reliable C-54 and the fifteen pressurized Constellations that had joined the ATC by V-J Day as C-69s, plushly equipped command transports seating forty-three passengers in comparative luxury. They saw it in the development of better navigational aids like loran, in such technological innovations as radar, jet engines, and the first actual use of two war-developed bad weather landing aids: instrument landing systems (ILS) and GCA, or Ground Controlled Approach. They saw a subtle glimpse of their industry's future: the thousands upon thousands of young Americans exposed to travel by air for the first time in their lives, and who would be the passengers of postwar America. These airmen, who had turned the Atlantic into a pond and the even vaster Pacific into a lake, knew better than anyone else that the airplane had finally become a true instrument of *international* travel and commerce.

At the same time, they recognized what the unforgiving crucible of war had also exposed: aviation's inadequacies, the achievements still needed, the advances yet to be made. Some of the airline pilots who flew for ATC and NATS were among those who after the war made the Air Line Pilots Association a professional organization as well as a labor union, fighting for legitimate safety reforms; in some cases, airline pilots were directly responsible for important innovations, such as centerline runway lighting and strobe anticollision lights, to cite just two examples.

ALPA was only ten years old at the start of the war. Officially born in 1931, against the determined opposition of virtually all top airline management, its very existence was kept secret for fear of company retaliation until an ALPA membership card was found in the wallet of a pilot killed in a crash. Even farsighted industry leaders like C.R. Smith, Pat Patterson, and Jack Frye were lukewarm at best or flatly opposed to unionizing pilots, although they were proud of the many personal friends they had among their airmen. And if there were a few who didn't object to ALPA itself, almost to a man they detested the union's founder and leader.

ALPA's first president was an ex–airline pilot named Dave Behncke, who had flown the mail for Northwest and passenger planes for Boeing Air Transport when it was part of United. Professor George Hopkins, in his official history of ALPA (*Flying the Line*), described him as "a man who had all the prerequisites for a successful labor leader—suspiciousness, lack of sentimentalism, and a good deal of personal drive."

The description was most accurate. Behncke was irritating, abrasive, stubborn, extremely difficult to deal with, and every airline executive who had to negotiate a contract with him dreaded it as he would a summons to appear before the Spanish Inquisition. The ALPA chief had some disconcerting habits, too, such as always having a dictionary with him, even during contract sessions. If anyone used a word he didn't understand, he would look it up while the conversation was still going on. Many of his own pilots disliked him, but the bottom line was his loyalty toward his members and his tireless efforts in on their behalf; he was interested in results, not popularity polls. He founded ALPA in an era when airline management as a whole regarded pilots as the equivalent of overpaid bus drivers. Behncke gave the airmen their first voice, their first sense of dignity and importance, and their first taste of bargaining clout.

After Pearl Harbor, Behncke reluctantly had to give up the eighty-five-hours per month limit on flying he had so laboriously negotiated with both the government and the industry before the war, and agree to a new 100-hour limit. But he kept collecting horror stories of members flying double or beyond that limit on ATC and NATS missions; some Pan Am and United pilots flying the Pacific, for example, often were in a cockpit twenty out of twenty-four hours. Dave Behncke swore things would be different after the war, for the union itself was growing in strength. In 1940, ALPA had only 1400 members; by V-J Day it represented more than 5700 (and today numbers some 45,000).

It was ATC's and NATS's increasing use of four-engine airplanes that provided Behncke with what would be a major and controversial postwar issue. He reasoned, quite correctly, that such multiengine transports would form the bulk of the industry's fleet after the war and that pilots flying larger, faster, and more sophisticated equipment deserved higher pay. This made sense even to the airline chiefs he would be dealing with, but his professed arguments in favor of increased pay were incredibly illogical.

Behncke based his demands on the curious supposition that because an airplane flew faster and covered more miles, it would encounter more hazards. In effect, he was demanding "hazard pay" for flying airplanes that in most respects were safer than any two-engine airliner, even the DC-3. After the war, targeting TWA first because it was the first to start operating Constellations, he ended up with a pilots' strike that cost Jack Frye his job and almost wrecked the airline.

The "hazard pay" issue was one of several that would plague postwar industry-ALPA relations, including a bitter dispute over whether the third cockpit crew member should be just a flight engineer or trained as a third pilot. This one would take several years to resolve, one of the stumbling blocks being Behncke's refusal to accept flight engineers as members, thus forcing them to form their own small but very militant union. And the cockpit comradeships of the ATC years disintegrated in the heat of this intralabor feud. The wartime navigators, who had no strong union to fight their battles, gradually were phased out after the war, replaced by electronic navigation aids.

The turbulent management-labor battles that plagued the airline industry after the war are not part of this story, but the seeds of future strife were planted before the war ended—by the swift pace of technological progress that featured the transport airplane itself. ALPA was to fight a lot of wars over safety issues and problems the war had exposed; the airlines, in turn, felt that too often those safety issues didn't really involve safety at all, but were thinly disguised economic demands. This was one of the industry's biggest complaints about Dave Behncke, who seems to have invented the technique with his "hazard pay" strategy that came right out of ATC's shift to larger airplanes.

Months before the guns were stilled and World War II ended in total victory, the airlines had begun adjusting to more normal

operations with the repossession of most of the twin-engine transports they had given up at the start of hostilities. By November of
1944, even prior to the Battle of the Bulge, ATC had returned 101
DC-3s, twelve DC-2s, three Lodestars, twenty-six Electras, and twenty-
five B-247s; all eight Stratoliners were returned shortly before V-E
Day.

Few of them went back into airline service immediately, for most
showed the effects of their military careers—the DC-3s, DC-2s, and
Stratoliners in particular. Some DC-3s had to be completely rebuilt.
It had taken major carriers like American and United four days to
convert a civilian DC-3 into a military cargo configuration; the
reconversion process took twenty-one days. Virtually every airplane
needed new flooring, in some cases new outer skin, and either new
or completely overhauled engines.

Each aircraft had to be weighed carefully to determine the exact
center of gravity, without which no airplane can be flown safely.
The problem was that the standard fleet weights used in peacetime
were useless, because frequent wartime repairs to ATC aircraft
usually changed their balances. American had budgeted some $2.75
million for its entire reconversion program and spent almost that
much on just the first few airplanes the Army returned.

The DST sleeper planes were a thing of the past; no one
reinstalled their berths. In fact, with the demand for space still high
on domestic flights, some carriers used the reconversion process to
increase the capacity of their returned DC-3s from twenty-one seats
to twenty-eight, simply by narrowing the aisle space, decreasing
legroom, and adding a row of seats that provided two-and-two
seating instead of the old two-and-one.

Four carriers—American, United, TWA, and Northwest—took
part in the industry's last major domestic wartime mission: the
massive redeployment of thousands of troops from the east to the
west coast after Germany began to collapse. ATC allotted eighty C-
47s to the airlift, a spartan operation; the troops loaded and
unloaded their own baggage and ate box lunches.

The airlines fortunately were able to stay clear of a nasty political
imbroglio involving the 1944 presidential election. By that time,
industry participation in the military airlift had dwindled considerably, but both ATC and NATS got caught in the crossfire. President
Roosevelt, running for an unprecedented fourth term against
Republican Thomas Dewey of New York, had wanted to give the

11 million soldiers, sailors, marines, and airmen stationed overseas a chance to vote in the election. But in a measure introduced in Congress by his Democratic lieutenants, FDR insisted on two provisions: no serviceman should have to pay the poll tax required by southern states, and the mail ballot itself should be a one-sheet affair limited solely to candidates for federal offices.

Southern congressman went ballistic over the poll tax proviso, and Republicans said it was criminal not to allow servicemen to vote for local and state candidates. The debate raged for days, Ohio's Senator Bob Taft leading the fight for all-inclusive voting. According to David Brinkley, who covered the Senate for United Press during the war, Taft really feared that Roosevelt's plan "was to march the troops to the polls under orders to vote for the only name they knew—his own; to line them up as WPA workers had been lined up at the polls in past elections."

"Republicans and Southerners together could not defeat the bill outright," Brinkley wrote in his brilliant *Washington Goes to War*, "but they could, they hoped, defeat it indirectly by insisting that state and local ballots be sent to the camps and battlefields along with the federal ballot. That, as everyone knew, was impossible."

Impossible to everyone but Taft, it seemed. Democratic Senator Scott Lucas of Illinois told the Senate that he had checked with the Air Transport Command and Naval Air Transport Service, and was informed that ATC and NATS combined couldn't possibly carry ballots from forty-eight states with more than 3000 counties and thousands of towns and cities. In a presidential election year, Lucas remarked, Illinois alone had 102 counties, each with a different ticket.

Taft scoffed at such statistics. He argued that if ATC could carry 10,000 tons of cargo over the Hump every day, why should it have so much trouble flying ballots weighing a mere 250 tons overseas?

No one ever knew where he got that 250-ton figure. ATC itself estimated that 11 million ballots listing every candidate for every state, county, and local office, plus 11 million federal ballots carried in a separate envelope, would weigh not 250 but *160,000* tons.

The bill Congress finally passed and sent to the White House was so riddled with confusing and restrictive amendents that Roosevelt refused to sign it. He didn't want to veto it, either, so he let it become law without his signature, and the result was that very few servicemen overseas voted at all. FDR, of course, won the election anyway.

It was, in a political sense, the last hurrah for the man who had made the airplane an integral component of the presidency.

★ ☆ 10 ☆ ★
Postwar Postscripts

By the end of the war, the Air Transport Command and the Naval Air Transport Service were operating the equivalent of the biggest airline in aviation history. Between December 7, 1941 and V-J Day, ATC and NATS airmen had flown the equivalent of more than 28,000 times around the world at the equator. In cold numbers, the airlines' contribution was small: a total of slightly over 200 airplanes, 1200 pilots, and 3000 mechanics and technical specialists. Those numbers, however, in effect were out of context; that tiny cadre of planes, pilots, and ground crews not only launched the airlift, but mapped its routes and helped prepare the military to fly the 3000 aircraft that eventually constituted the ATC/NATS air armada.

The nation's top military aviation leaders knew the real score: that results, not numbers or statistics, were a better yardstick for judging what the U.S. airline industry accomplished in World War II.

"The contribution to the military of our competitive civil carriers in equipment, trained personnel, operating methods, and knowledge have been of first importance in this war," Hap Arnold said after victory had been won. "We have learned and must not forget that air transport is an essential of air power, in fact of all national power."

"Unqualified praise is due the airlines of America," declared Vice Admiral A.W. Fitch, Deputy Chief of Naval Operations for Air, "for the magnificent way they stepped into the breach at the time of our greatest need. When we were attacked at Pearl Harbor, our cargo and transport force was inadequate to meet the sudden transportation demands for vital supplies, munitions, and men. The airlines closed the gap by putting their skilled manpower, ground facilities, and flying equipment at the disposal of the Armed Forces. Equally important was their administrative know-how, which they also generously contributed. The airlines blazed new routes to war-strategic points, assisted in specialized flight and ground service training, and flew high-priority passengers and cargo on dependable schedules."

From the man who ran ATC itself, Hal George, came this kudo for the civilian carriers: "If it had not been for their whole-hearted cooperation, it would have been nearly impossible for us to carry on the job the way it has been done."

But Edgar Gorrell, whose member airlines had helped create and man this colossal, unprecedented air transport fleet, never lived to see the final outcome of the war in which his own foresight, determination, and sound judgment had played such an important role. Without his unique abilities, not the least of which was the courage to confront the president of the United States, the airlines in all likelihood would have been nationalized, trapped in a clumsy, unwieldy wartime bureaucracy not of their own making, just as the railroads were in the first World War.

Gorrell not only saved them from that fate, but gave the industry the cohesiveness, determination, and unity that made its achievements possible.

The Little Colonel's own military background contributed mightily to the industry's surprisingly excellent relations with every branch of the armed services; Gorrell understood generals and admirals, just as he understood the diverse collection of rugged individualists, mavericks, paternalistic leaders, and ego-driven moguls who were his nominal bosses at the Air Transport Association. He earned the enmity of more than one; even far-sighted Pat Patterson of United tangled angrily with Gorrell during the war when the ATA president announced his intentions of investigating alleged excessive premiums being charged by two big airline insurers. Patterson informed Gorrell that ATA's directors had never authorized such an investigation and threatened to pull United out of ATA if Gorrell didn't back off.

The colonel did back away, realizing that he couldn't buck anyone with Patterson's clout and reputation and still keep his job. In the long run, Edgar Gorrell knew when to push and prod, when to compromise or temporize, when to hang tough, and when to use diplomacy or fall into a dignified retreat. He would not hesitate to occasionally sit on the industry's freewheelers, nor was he afraid to argue the airlines' case before military powerhouses like Hal George or Hap Arnold. The ATA president walked one of the war's thinnest, most precarious tightropes, while simultaneously juggling a score of balls, a masterful balancing act. That he could consistently give the highest priority to the war effort, yet with equal consistency protect the airline industry's legitimate interests, represented an amazing combination of patriotism and statesmanship.

He had moved ATA from Chicago to Washington just prior to the outbreak of war, and he brought his workaholic habits with him. During the war years, he seemed to regard even twelve or fourteen-hour days as insufficient to accomplish everything he wanted done. He never came to work later than 7 A.M., and often stayed at his desk until well into the night. Eventually, the grind took its inevitable toll; he developed a heart condition and typically ignored all advice to slow down.

On February 22, 1945, he married for the second time, but his new bride, Mrs. Mary Frances O'Dowd Weidman, was to become a widow in less than two weeks. On March 5, Gorrell suffered a fatal heart attack. At his request, his body was cremated and an Air Force plane scattered the ashes over the place where the Little Colonel had once been known as the Little Corporal: the United States Military Academy at West Point.

Germany would surrender in less than two months and Japan in another five, yet amid all the accolades for the war's great military leaders and statesmen, somehow the name of Edgar Staley Gorrell slipped only too quietly into the history books.

The airlines, like their pilots and ground crews who had been part of ATC and NATS, had a lot of readjusting ahead of them in the transition to peace. In operational and technical areas, they were fairly well prepared for the new peacetime challenges. Millions of miles of transocean flying on military missions to faraway lands had provided them with an enormously skilled pilot force, superbly equipped to handle an international air travel market that previously only Pan Am had served—and of a potential size that had never existed before. By 1957, only twelve years after V-J Day, as many passengers were flying across the Atlantic as were crossing by ship. And when the jet age dawned a year later, the giant ocean liners that had ruled the North Atlantic became virtual dinosaurs, doomed to extinction as major carriers of traffic between Europe and the United States. Less than five years later, in 1962, transatlantic ocean liner passengers numbered fewer than 500,000 while 2 million flew across.

There was a similar revolution in domestic travel, as the airplane gradually began to replace the Pullman as the dominant transporter of long-range, first class interstate passengers. As Carl Solberg pointed out in his *Conquest of the Skies:*

"As late as 1945, [the airlines'] 397 airliners still carried only one-eighth of the traffic that went by Pullman. But in the years after Pearl Harbor, 1.5 million Americans had learned to fly, another million had flown the oceans and continents as military passengers [including airlifted wounded, the actual figure was closer to three million—author's note], and uncounted millions at home, kept from the air by priority restrictions, had witnessed the spectacular advance of aviation around the globe."

The domestic air travel revolution suffered severe birth pains; the immediate postwar years brought chaos to the airlines, most of them saddled with war-bloated payrolls and facing huge debts in the rush to order such new airliners as the Constellation, Douglas DC-6, and the later Martin 202, Convair 240, and Boeing's four-engine Stratocruiser, with its famous little belly cocktail lounge, still remembered fondly by every passenger who ever flew in a Stratocruiser.

Technically known as the B-377, the Stratocruiser gave one of its operators—Pan Am—a chance to relive the glory days of its Boeing flying boats, although the comparatively small lounge (its curved divan could seat fourteen adults, but only in a tight squeeze) actually was a far cry from the spacious accommodations of a B-314. Nevertheless, Pan Am tried hard to convince customers they'd be flying in unprecedented luxury. In addition to the lounge, the airline's advertisements promised (at a small surcharge) "magnificent seven-course dinners, champagne and liqueurs, music, bed-length sleeperettes, five extra cabin attendants, and—for the ladies—Lanvin's *Arpege* perfume and orchids."

Such ostentatious service, however, was generally confined to the long transocean flights; domestic travel was something else. The industry had an Achilles' heel in the form of airports that weren't capable of handling the immediate postwar avalanche of air travelers. What the public got were jammed terminals, too many delayed or canceled flights, and an overall sour taste of air transportation that was more like purgatory than the utopia so many had expected. Too many airplanes cruising at more than 300 miles an hour were being guided by radar originally designed to handle twenty-five-knot warships. Nor did several fatal crashes and the mandatory grounding of both the Constellation and DC-6 for correction of serious design errors (the Connie's electrical system and the DC-6's fuel transfer arrangement) help public confidence. And the Stratocruiser itself, although it was a passenger's delight, suffered so many engine shutdowns that it became known as "the best three-engine airplane flying the oceans."

Yet all this was part of the transition from war to peace, a gut-wrenching readjustment period no less traumatic for the airline industry than it was for the millions of soldiers, sailors, and airmen who came home to an America that had changed in so many ways. When public disappointment and disillusion set in, the carriers had to resell air travel and reestablish public confidence, a task that couldn't be accomplished overnight. Until they reequipped their fleets with the vaunted, fully pressurized, 300-mph new postwar airliners (and eradicated all their bugs), the airlines relied on the airplanes that had won the war of the airlift: primarily the C-54, now wearing civilian clothes as the DC-4, and even the venerable DC-3, whose C-47 version literally glutted the used airliner market—there were some 8000 war surplus Gooney Birds available at bargain basement prices.

While the larger airlines were signing contracts for DC-6s and Connies, they were also interested in an intriguing postwar equipment question: what new short-range transport was going to replace the DC-3? There were still smaller cities to serve, shorter routes to fly, and the concept of regional or local service airlines was just over the horizon—if anyone needed a modern replacement for the aging DC-3, it supposedly would be these new subsidized carriers, created to bring scheduled air service to the nation's smaller communities. They would be the "airlines of Main Street," and initially were called "feeder" airlines, whose chief purpose would be to fly people from small towns to larger cities, where they could connect with flights to destinations served by the major carriers.

There were several pretenders to the DC-3 throne, including a prewar Douglas design that produced one of the most forgotten transports in aviation history: the DC-5. Yes, there really *was* a DC-5! It was a high-wing, two-engine airplane that retained many of the DC-3's systems, so many that a few cynics claimed—inaccurately—that the DC-5 was just a DC-3 with the wings on the top of the fuselage instead of underneath. Douglas built only twelve of them before the war, four going to the Netherlands, one to William Boeing as his private airplane, and the remaining seven to the U.S. Navy and Marines as personnel transports. Because it was a 1939 airplane (it actually flew before the DC-4E and was thus out of numerical sequence), and also because Donald Douglas wasn't very enamored of high-wing airplanes, the company never even considered the DC-5 in its postwar plans. Nor did it attempt a new short-range transport project, but turned instead to a far less expensive program: modernizing the DC-3.

Douglas called it the "Super DC-3," and for what amounted to a mere face-lift, it was an admirable effort, involving bigger wings, more powerful engines, and a slightly larger fuselage carrying thirty-one passengers. It was the first of several transports that were to give Douglas the reputation of building "rubber" airplanes—existing designs that could be stretched into larger, improved versions at a minimum of development costs. The Super Three was a good try, but futile; its base price was $140,000, and one with the kind of attractive interior the average airline would want carried a $200,000 price tag. There was no way this souped-up Gooney Bird could compete against war surplus C-47s selling for so much less. A C-47 in mint condition went for only $25,000, and a truly beat-up airplane could be bought for under $10,000.

(If war surplus C-47s were going for a song, ex–combat aircraft could be bought for only a whistle. In the late 1950s, *Twilight Zone* producer Buck Houghton needed a B-25 Mitchell medium bomber for an episode called "King Nine Will Not Return." The wartime price of a new B-25 was $345,000; Houghton bought one from the Air Force for $2500.)

Lockheed designed and built two prototypes of a high-wing, twin-engine postwar airliner specifically aimed at the feeder market. Called the Saturn, it was a sixteen-passenger transport and while

Lockheed priced it attractively at only $85,000, it not only had to compete against much cheaper war surplus planes, but against the scores of well-maintained DC-3s that the big trunk airlines were phasing out. By and large, these formed the nucleus of the feeder airline fleets, and the supposed market for a DC-3 successor turned out to be just a continued demand for used DC-3s.

Boeing's postwar entry in the short-range transport field was the Model 417, another high-wing twin but one that never even reached the prototype stage; Boeing terminated the B-417 project as economically unfeasible because it was too far behind the forthcoming Martin 202 and Convair 240; if there never really was a DC-3 piston-engine successor, in fact, the 240 came the closest.

While waiting for full-scale production of brand-new transports, the major carriers spent the immediate postwar years overhauling and refurbishing their regular DC-3s and the C-54s they acquired from the Army and Navy. Pennsylvania Central was the first to put converted C-54s into regular passenger service, and the airline hit the jackpot with one of the airplanes ATC turned over to the airlines: it acquired, much to its surprise, the same C-54 that flew President Roosevelt to Casablanca in 1943. For as long as PCA/ Capital operated the former Skymaster in commercial service, the aircraft carried this commemorative plaque prominently displayed in what was now a standard DC-4 cabin:

IN THE PLANE
PRESIDENT FRANKLIN D. ROOSEVELT
AND MEMBERS OF HIS STAFF FLEW TO
THE HISTORIC CASABLANCA CONFERENCE IN
FRENCH MOROCCO JANUARY 1943.
AT THIS CONFERENCE UNITED NATIONS LEADERS
PLANNED THE OFFENSIVE DESTINED TO
BRING ABOUT UNCONDITIONAL SURRENDER
OF THE AXIS POWERS.

Because of the plaque, this particular DC-4 was undoubtedly subject to the slowest boarding process on PCA or any airline; passengers would stop to read it in awe before finding their seats. It made no difference that the plaque's reference to the "United Nations" might have been questioned by historical purists—in a technical sense, the UN wasn't officially formed until June 26, 1944.

At any rate, this and other four-engine Douglas transports, unpressurized though they were, ruled the civil airways as they had the skies of the global airlift—a long way from the "Grand Hotel with wings" prewar promise, but nevertheless an uncomplaining, thoroughly reliable airplane possessing very few faults. Admittedly, it was expensive and laborious to convert them from military cargo configuration to civil use; United, for example, bought surplus C-54s for a modest $90,000 per airplane but had to spend another $200,000 for the ninety-day conversation process—longer than Douglas had taken to build a new C-54.

The C-54's one unpleasant wartime habit—leaking fuel tanks—had been eliminated by an American Airlines maintenance trouble-shooter named Abe Hoyt. On the C-54, and the DC-3/C-47 as well, the wings themselves, thanks to their cellular construction, served as integral gas tanks. But when the C-54's larger wings twisted in flight, they occasionally sprang fuel leaks around the rivets if the twisting force hit a certain area. Hoyt solved the problem by applying a very thin first layer of sealer over the cracks, and then adding any number of additional layers as needed; once word of the process spread among ATC and NATS ground crews, there were no more reports of leaking fuel.

Scores of similar undramatic little tricks were carried over from the war into peacetime airline operations. One example: the weight- and space-saving methods of packaging cargo, developed jointly by the airlines, ATC, and NATS. They designed shipping crates fashioned from specially processed cardboard and fiberboard instead of the far heavier, bulkier ones made out of wood and/or metal, a substitution that increased the payload on one NATS cargo seaplane by as much as 6000 pounds. A typical shipment of spare airplane engines packed in wooden or metal crates would have weighed more than 26,000 pounds and taken up all the cargo space available in five or six C-47s. The new packaging reduced the weight to less than 9000 pounds, and the crates could fit into a single plane.

The C-54 was the only four-engine wartime transport that success-fully transitioned its way into extensive postwar airline passenger service. The eight Boeing Stratoliners that had pioneered pressur-ized commercial flights did see some service after the war. The five TWA operated for ATC were all returned to the airline during April 1945, and after overhaul went back to flying domestic schedules minus their pressurization systems. One airplane, the *Comanche,* completed a special final military mission, but under TWA colors and not as an ATC aircraft: it carried thirty-one Seabees and six sailors home from the Aleutians at no charge.

The airline's "Strats" were operated on various domestic routes, for less than four years, including a few transcontinental flights (the one-way fare was $149.95, exactly as it was in 1937, and the same held true for the New York–Chicago fare of $44.95). In 1949, all five were sold to the French-owned Aigle Azur airline for a total of $525,000, including spares; TWA had paid $268,000 apiece for each of the six it had originally ordered in 1937.

Pan Am continued to operate its three Stratoliners as ATC aircraft, flying Latin America routes, until 1946, and then sold the planes to a Florida aviation school, the first of a succession of different owners. The ninth Stratoliner, which Howard Hughes had appropriated as his personal airplane, spent the entire war parked in a hangar at Glendale, California.

In 1946, he remodeled the interior, at a cost of $250,000, into a "Flying Penthouse" that boasted a master bedroom, living room, galley, bar, and two bathrooms. Two years later, he sold the plushly furnished airplane to Texas multimillionaire Glenn McCarthy, who seldom used it. In 1962, a hurricane seriously damaged the Stratoliner, and after it was repaired a Florida yachtsman bought it, removed the wings and tail section, and mounted the entire cabin, including the cockpit, on a boat hull, thus creating one of the most unique houseboats afloat. As recently as 1994, it was seen moored in one of the river tributaries in the Fort Lauderdale area.

The workhorse C-87 had one brief, albeit unsuccessful shot at a civilian career. Late in the war, Consolidated-Vultee designed a B-24/C-87 civilian derivative, officially called Model 39 and dubbed the "Liberator Express." It was a four-engine, high-wing airplane that utilized the B-24's wings—the best feature of both the bomber and transport version because of their low drag at all speeds—the same landing gear, and the same engines: four Pratt & Whitney Twin Wasp radials. The fuselage was totally new, circular with a "hemispherical" cockpit section that closely resembled the front end of Boeing's B-29 bomber.

Only a single prototype of the Model 39 was built and sold to American Airlines, which operated it briefly after the war as an experimental air freighter. Consolidated designed it primarily as a cargo plane, but it could also be configured to carry forty-eight passengers. Other than American's one-aircraft order, however, Model 39 failed to attract any airline interest; the well-seasoned DC-4's performance matched or exceeded it in almost every respect, and the Liberator Express was far slower than either the DC-6 or the Constellation.

Just two carriers, Eastern and National, evidenced serious interest in another wartime workhorse, the C-46, although in Eastern's case it would be more accurate to limit that interest solely to the airline's president. Eastern actually placed an order for twenty CW-20s, the civil version of the Commando, late in 1944 for postwar delivery, while National ordered six. The EAL contract was strictly Eddie Rickenbacker's decision, and he made it in the face of determined opposition from Charlie Froesch, the airline's highly respected chief engineer, who had represented Eastern in the five-airline group involved in the DC-4 project.

Froesch warned Rickenbacker that the big Curtiss transport, despite the fine job it had done for MTD, was not what the airline needed for the postwar period.

"I'd like to know why, Charlie," the captain grumbled.

"Because it was never really designed for airline operations. I've seen their shop facilities in Buffalo, and they're not too hot. Second, the airplane's too damned slow. Third, their engineers don't have the transport design experience we get at Lockheed and Douglas. And let's face it—every postwar transport airplane will have a tricycle landing gear except the CW-20. It'll be a comedown."

"Well, Curtiss assures me it'll do a great job for us," Rickenbacker muttered unhappily. "I'll have to think it over."

Froesch knew the real reason Rickenbacker had gone for the Curtiss sales pitch—he was close friends with the Curtiss-Wright president, Guy Vaughn, and the captain was nothing if not loyal to his friends. On paper, at least, the CW-20 looked promising, except for that outmoded landing gear; its big cabin was to be configured for at least thirty-eight passengers, and the factory mock-up included one feature that would be welcomed by today's flight attendants: a divanlike stewardess seat with a folding desk for in-flight paperwork.

Curtiss itself took the captain off the hook. First, it informed Eastern it was moving its engineering department from Buffalo to St. Louis, a transfer that would delay CW-20 deliveries. Then the company decided to move its manufacturing facilities to Columbus, Ohio, necessitating more delays, and that was all the excuse Rickenbacker needed to cancel the contract—this and the similarly aborted contract with National were the closest Curtiss-Wright came to postwar CW-20 sales. Nor did the CW-28—an improved version with a tricycle landing gear—win any orders. But war-surplus C-46s were widely used as freighters and, in several cases, as passenger planes by the so-called "nonskeds."

The latter were a postwar phenomenom that was both good news and bad news. Officially, they were called by various names: large irregular carriers, charter airlines, supplemental airlines, and nonscheduled airlines more commonly shortened to "nonskeds." Unofficially, the established airline industry referred to them as illegal trespassers, unfair competitors, fly-by-night pretenders, and shoestring upstarts. The trespassers, unfair competitors, and shoestring upstarts, in turn, considered themselves pioneers who for the first time in history were offering low-cost air transportation to the public. As with most controversies, there was a certain amount of truth to both perceptions, as R.E.G. Davies, the dean of aviation historians, objectively observed:

"A legion of ex-pilots, among others, founded their own companies . . . Most were doomed to failure from the start. Good military pilots, fighter or bomber, do not necessarily adopt themselves to civilian conditions. The early nonscheduled airline promoters could not always reconcile their spirit of enterprise with the many regulations for navigation, safety, and maintenance. Many were unable to cope with the administrative necessities, and the nonskeds, as they quickly became known, acquired an unfortunate reputation for unreliability and even sharp practice. Those whose true pioneer spirit was combined with a dedication to providing good public service were damned by association with the unscrupulous."

According to Civil Aeronautics Board records, no fewer than 2730 companies that called themselves "airlines" were founded almost as soon as the war ended in 1945, and they acquired more than 5000 aircraft. Many confined themselves strictly to air cargo, a few occasionally taking on charter business.

The problem the scheduled airlines had with the nonskeds, however, went far beyond the horde of marginal operators whose financial standing matched the dubious status of their war-weary airplanes—usually beat-up C-47s or equally decrepit C-46s. An airline whose captains often had to use their own gasoline credit cards to pay for aviation fuel, because the airline itself had no credit, posed no real competitive threat. And if a pilot using his personal oil company credit card to fill up the tanks of a big transport plane sounds unbelievable, we offer this absolutely true postwar story:

In December 1946, a group of West Point cadets wanting to fly home on their short Christmas leave had pooled enough money to charter a plane—"enough money" meaning all they could afford was an ex-ATC C-47 operated by one of the shoestring nonskeds, Coastal Cargo Airlines, which was willing to fly twenty-nine cadets from Teterboro Airport, New Jersey, to San Francisco by way of Atlanta, Dallas, Phoenix, and Los Angeles, for $55 per man, or $110 round-trip.

They landed in Atlanta about 2 A.M. to refuel, but the fixed base operator who was supposed to provide the gas refused to let the captain charge it to his company; Coastal Cargo, it seems, had the credit standing of a bankrupt bookie.

"Then take my Esso [today's Exxon] card," the captain pleaded.

"For eight hundred gallons of gas? You think I'm nuts?"

The crestfallen captain reported the dilemma to the two cadets who had organized the charter.

"I'm sorry, guys," he apologized, "but I'm afraid we're stuck here."

The two entrepreneurs took up a collection among twenty-seven fellow passengers, but this strategy didn't raise enough cash to fill the tank of a Model A Ford. In desperation, one of the organizers decided he'd try to get someone in authority at Standard Oil of New Jersey to authorize acceptance of the captain's Esso card. By now it was past 3 A.M., but somehow the brash cadet managed to filter through several layers of management by phoning the oil company's emergency night number, and finally got through to— and we repeat, this is a true story—none other than the president of Standard Oil of New Jersey.

The cadet identified himself and launched into his tale of woe.

"Sir, I'm sorry to bother you at this time of night, but I'm in charge of a load of West Point cadets flying home for Christmas. We're stuck in Atlanta because the fixed base operator here won't let the pilot charge the gas to his airline."

"What the hell do you expect me to do about it?" the sleepy president demanded.

"Well, sir, the pilot wants to use his Esso card, but they won't honor it."

"Who did you say this is?"

The cadet repeated his name, which meant absolutely nothing to the president of Standard Oil of New Jersey but who, it turned out, had a heart larger than the stranded C-47.

"Lemme talk to that fixed base guy," he sighed.

They took off a few minutes later, all tanks filled with gas charged to the captain's Esso card.

Incidentally, the name of the resourceful cadet who got the president of Standard Oil out of bed at 3 o'clock in the morning was Frank Borman, the same Frank Borman who as an astronaut would command the Apollo 8 moon mission, and later become president of Eastern Air Lines.

Companies like Coastal Cargo were too undercapitalized to survive, and their mortality rate was about 100 percent. But there were several larger, adequately financed nonskeds who flew decent, well-maintained equipment—and that spelled competition to the scheduled carriers, because the new arrivals began operating what amounted to regularly scheduled flights over the prime long-haul routes of the certificated airlines, including lucrative transcontinental trips.

They got away with the route invasion at first by classifying their flights as charters, even though a typical "charter" trip might have only five passengers traveling as a group and the other fifty-five passengers flying as individuals. And their fares—such as $99 from New York to Los Angeles—attracted passengers who otherwise would have flown on a scheduled airline, and for $99 they were willing to put up with such drawbacks as the occasional practice of deliberately delaying a departure until enough passengers showed up to fill every seat.

Eventually, the CAB ruled that a large irregular carrier could operate a maximum of only eight to twelve flights per month between any two points. The nonskeds got around this by organizing multicarrier alliances; each member adhered to the monthly limitation, but eight to twelve flights a month by several airlines came close to matching the flight frequencies of the scheduled airlines—and over their most profitable routes.

The established carriers fought back by resorting to the "if you can't beat 'em, join 'em" strategy. In 1948, Capital Airlines (formerly Pennsylvania Central) introduced night coach service between New York and Chicago, packing sixty seats into a few DC-4s and charging four cents a mile instead of the usual six cents. They were appropriately called "Nighthawk" flights, and were an instant success soon copied, with some initial reluctance, by American and TWA, who began offering coach fares on some transcontinental flights using DC-4s refitted to carry at least sixty passengers.

Conservative United was the last transcontinental holdout but finally fell in line, although UAL's initial opposition had ignored its own history. United had actually pioneered the concept of discounted fares as early as 1940, when it operated the first air coach service between Los Angeles and San Francisco, via intermediate stops, at a one-way fare of $13.50. United assigned ten-passenger Boeing 247s to the experimental service, winning CAB approval only after it justified the lower fares by pointing out it was using obsolete, fully amortized aircraft. The experiment ended prematurely when the Army took over a large chunk of the airline's fleet, but it was a portent of things to come—as was TWA's postwar introduction of the first "two-class" service.

In 1949, Howard Hughes's airline modified some of its older Connies to carry a dozen coach passengers in the forward section of the cabin, this being the noisiest and least desirable area in which to sit, because it was closest to the propellers. Never before had any airliner carried two classes of passengers paying different fares, but it marked a natural evolutionary step from all-coach service; it was also a brilliant piece of marketing strategy that set the pattern for fare structuring in the jet age to come.

The war between the scheduled airlines and the nonskeds gradually diminished to a few minor skirmishes and eventual peace, as the latter were assigned the new and far more respectable status of "supplementals" under CAB regulations that in effect gave them unlimited authority to carry cargo and legitimate charter passengers. For all their faults and frequent winking at the rules, the nonskeds made significant contributions to commercial aviation. They widened the air travel market by offering lower fares, they did much to develop air cargo, they conceived the idea of group travel, and the better-run ones became part of the postwar Civil Reserve Air Fleet (see Epilogue); such supplementals as American

Trans Air, for instance, were to contribute heavily to the massive Gulf War airlift. The larger so-called irregulars, in fact, carried twenty-five percent of the passengers and fifty-seven percent of cargo tonnage during the 1948–49 Berlin Airlift, and half the total cargo tonnage flown to the Korean war theater.

Several well-capitalized all-cargo airlines were also launched after the war, the largest and most successful being colorful Bob Prescott's Flying Tiger Line, named after the American volunteer fighter group for which he had flown in China. Prescott was wise enough not to rely entirely on freight revenue; he diversified into other areas, including military charters, but he wanted no part of the nonsked war and, in fact, applied for and was granted membership in the ATA.

Another successful airfreight venture was Seaboard World Airlines, founded by World War II veterans whose numbers included a large contingent of former Air Transport Command airmen. Seaboard flew cargo across the North Atlantic for a number of years until it was merged into Flying Tiger in 1980.

The likes of ex–military pilot Bob Prescott, with his business acumen and flair, were few in number, for there were only a handful of survivors among the nearly 3000 hopefuls who in 1945 had started out, mostly on the power of prayer, with only one or two heavily mortgaged airplanes flying freight and whatever occasional passengers they could scrounge up. They also found themselves competing with the established scheduled airlines, which not only operated all-cargo air freighters (albeit not very successfully) but packed freight into the bellies of their passenger planes.

Eventually, it took an ex–Marine Corps pilot from the Vietnam war named Fred Smith to unearth a golden nugget: an untapped market niche that concentrated on overnight delivery of small packages and priority business and banking correspondence. Thus was born Federal Express, whose radical concept first appeared in a college term paper Smith wrote in 1965, while still an undergraduate at Yale. It wasn't until 1972 that he was able to launch the company whose very name is synonymous with the concept of guaranteed next-day delivery.

Smith's term paper proposed funneling freight, mostly small packages, into a central distribution point and then redispatching them to their destinations. He pointed out that most air freight shippers were missing potential customers by sending cargo almost exclusively over major airline passenger routes between the largest cities. His professor was less impressed than the investors Smith would corral six years later; the term paper received a lukewarm grade of C. The "Federal" in the company's name was derived from one of its first contracts: the Federal Reserve system needed a reliable overnight check-clearing service. Incredibly, for several years the Civil Aeronautics Board blocked Federal Express's expansion by refusing to let it operate large jets; when that ban finally was lifted in the late 1970s, FedEx also became part of the airline industry's military airlift reserve, assigning forty aircraft to the program, including nineteen 747s acquired when it merged with Flying Tiger, and sixteen DC-10s (see Epilogue); FedEx flew more Gulf War missions than any other airline.

While new carriers like Flying Tiger, Slick, and later, Federal Express, Emery, and UPS, became established cogs in postwar commercial aviation, failures far outnumbered successes. Among the casualties, however, was the superbly run air organization that ran second only to the Air Transport Command in the scope and efficiency of its wartime operations: the Naval Air Transport Service.

NATS was less than seven years old when the stroke of a presidential pen signed its death warrant.

It had been created December 12, 1941, by Navy Secretary Frank Knox, who agreed with a number of his admirals that the Navy should operate its own air transport system. The Navy, while gladly accepting the same kind of airline assistance the Army was receiving, wanted to run its own show. Knox's insistence drew criticism from those who believed Navy pride mixed with traditional interservice rivalry had run roughshod over sheer common sense. Why duplicate the Air Transport Command's efforts? Why establish two separate organizations with essentially the same missions, the same objectives, and in many cases even using the same types of airplanes?

The Navy's answer was that the missions and flying equipment were not always the same, the proof being that NATS had to operate a lot of seaplanes as well as land-based aircraft, and that its airlift needs were somewhat different because virtually every admiral in the fleet gave the Pacific war a higher priority than the European theater; the Pearl Harbor disaster was a large and irritating burr under a lot of Navy saddles. Such arguments might be considered somewhat specious, because jealousy on the part of the Navy may well have been the primary motivating factor in establishing a separate air transport system. Yet neither Hap Arnold nor Hal George had enough muscle to go over Knox's head. They knew the next head they'd face was that of Franklin Roosevelt, who tried to be impartial, but was so pro-Navy he even referred to it as "my Navy," in a tone of decided pride; it was never "my Army" or "my Air Force."

So the Navy got its own airline, its first transport squadron based at Norfolk, Virginia, with four R4Ds assigned to Atlantic operations, being too short-ranged for Pacific missions, along with Pan Am and American Export Airlines transports operating under NATS contracts. Within the next few months, the entire Atlantic divisions of both Pan Am and AEA became part of NATS.

Additional squadrons were formed at Alameda, California, to cover the Pacific, and at Kansas City to link the Navy's domestic bases with its proliferating Pacific bastions. NATS began operating Douglas Skymasters—R5-Ds—in the spring of 1943. These were the Navy's first four-engine land planes and, like their C-54 Army counterparts, served as the queens of the NATS fleet. The Navy configured some R5-Ds to carry fifty airborne troops, equipped others as hospital planes with twenty-four litters, and beefed up a few to carry light tanks, howitzers, or scout cars.

The R5-D, however, was not the Navy's biggest airplane. NATS also operated the Martin Mars, a monster of a flying boat that weighed 148,000 pounds, 64,000 pounds more than Boeing's 314. In November of 1943, a Mars carrying a 50,000-pound payload flew nonstop from Patuxant Naval Base outside of Washington, D.C., to Natal, Brazil, covering the 4250 miles in twenty-nine hours. The other seaplanes in the NATS fleet included the Martin PBM-3 Mariner, and the four-engine Consolidated PB2Y-3 patrol bomber which the Navy converted into a transport.

NATS continued to expand throughout the war. New squadrons were established at San Diego, Seattle, Honolulu, Oakland, and Patuxent. A Naval Air Ferry Command was created late in 1943, with three new squadrons based in Columbus, Ohio, New York, and San Pedro, California. A few months before Germany surrendered, NATS was elevated to the status of a Fleet Command of more than a dozen transport squadrons totaling 26,000 officers and men and a fleet of 429 airplanes, more than a third of them R5-Ds.

At the height of the war, NATS was carrying upwards of 22,000 priority passengers a month on flights averaging 1200 miles, along with 8 million pounds of cargo and mail. ATC, of course, with a much larger fleet and correspondingly greater manpower, compiled even more impressive figures, yet the Navy proved it, too, could operate a global airlift.

But the glory days of "the Navy's airline" ended with the passage and signing of the National Security Act of 1947, unifying the Armed Services under a newly created Joint Chiefs of Staff. NATS officially went out of existence in June of 1948 when, in accordance with unification's requirements, all Air Force and Navy long-range military airlift operations and responsibilities were merged into a new organization: the Military Air Transport Service, bearing the acronym MATS—which, according to some of its less reverent pilots, stood for More Aggravation Than Service.

Almost simultaneously with its creation, however, came a new challenge to U.S. airlift capability—one that in many respects was tougher than anything the nation had faced in World War II. It involved supplying such essentials of life as food, fuel, and medicine to a city of well over 2 million people *entirely by air for almost an entire year.*

History knows it as the Berlin Airlift.

The crisis began in June of 1948, instigated by Soviet Premier Stalin, the paranoid dictator of Communist Russia—the man FDR had so instinctively liked that he coined the benign nickname, "Uncle Joe," but the same man Harry Truman had instinctively distrusted, considering him about as benign as a rattlesnake. The seeds of this first and, until the Cuban missile crisis of 1962, most menacing of all Cold War confrontations, were sown when postwar occupational control over defeated Germany was divided among the victorious powers: the U.S., Russia, Britain, and France. The three Western allies occupied West Germany, including the western half of Berlin; the Soviet Union East Germany and East Berlin.

It was a division that invited trouble, thanks to Stalin's suspicions about the western democracies, the U.S. in particular. He perceived these nations as posing a constant threat not merely to the Soviet Union, but to the cause of communism itself. All his fears and hatred came to a boil in 1948. Stalin saw Western Europe recovering almost miraculously from the war, a comeback fueled largely by American aid and one that was also affecting the western area of conquered Germany. Stalin's convoluted reasoning interpreted any aid to Western Germany as encouraging renewed German aggression against the Soviets.

He was determined to establish communist domination over most of Europe, particularly the east, so that Russia's borders would be lined only by nations not just sympathetic to communism, but ruled by communist governments. This was the infamous iron curtain, that descriptive phrase so adroitly coined by Churchill, and the curtain had already fallen over Poland, Hungary, and East Germany. In February 1948, Soviet troops seized Czechoslovakia, one of Europe's most democratic countries. The one remaining hole in the curtain was West Germany and its nerve center: the three western sectors of Berlin occupied by American, British, and French troops and collectively constituting the city of West Berlin, a city obviously recovering from the war a lot faster than its eastern counterpart.

On June 16, 1948, Soviet representatives walked out of the four-power council jointly governing Germany's occupation, a performance of staged petulance first preceded and then followed by a succession of deliberate provocations. Rail traffic between West Germany and Berlin was stopped for two days without warning and without explanation. A highway bridge in perfect condition would suddenly be closed for two days, ostensibly for so-called "repairs." The Russians for months flooded West Germany with their own worthless paper currency, hoping to force economic chaos by inducing inflation. The Soviets would call important conferences and then abruptly walk out of the meetings in feigned anger over some imaginary affront.

Then came the most threatening, potentially combustible provocation Stalin's mind could conceive. He was apparently only too willing to ignite a military showdown, knowing that Soviet occupation forces dwarfed those of the western allies, for Russia had never really demobilized after the war; in 1948 its army was the largest in the world by a huge margin. As of June 24, 1948, the U.S. occupation force in Germany consisted of only two divisions. That was the day Stalin forced the issue, deliberately trying to take over all of Germany by striking at the helpless civilian population of its western capital.

He established a rigid, brutally ruthless blockade of West Berlin, completely severing access to every highway, railroad, and waterway that carried food, coal, and medical supplies into a metropolis whose population at the time was greater than that of Los Angeles, Cleveland, Detroit, or Philadelphia. He assumed that President Truman had only two choices—retaliate with force, or knuckle under—and he was gambling, correctly, that the heavily demobilized U.S. didn't want to fight another war over besieged West Berlin. Unfortunately for good old "Uncle Joe," however, he left one avenue of entry open.

Three avenues, actually. Three air corridors, a northern, southern, and central, each twenty miles wide, leading into West Berlin's two airports: Tempelhof Field in the American sector, and Gatow in the British. Three large loopholes in Stalin's master plan to drop the iron curtain over all of Germany.

They weren't very large loopholes at first, more like tiny cracks, and at the start of the Berlin Airlift, Stalin had every reason to ridicule it as a tangible menace to his blueprint of conquest-by-starvation. The figures supported his contempt for "Operation Vittles," the name the U.S. Air Force gave the airlift: Berlin needed a minimum of about 1500 tons of food and medical supplies daily for no one knew how long. It meant taking off or landing an airplane loaded with ten tons of supplies every three and a half minutes twenty-four hours a day, seven days a week, and an airlift of such gargantuan proportions had never been attempted before; the Normandy invasion had required far greater tonnage, but most of it was delivered by sea, not by air.

Furthermore, the 1500-ton minimum requirement applied to the warm weather months; if the siege was still in effect by winter, the daily requirement would have to include heavy coal shipments and would increase to 4000 tons—which would necessitate airlift planes taking off or landing within every two or three minutes around the clock. And all the Air Force had available to launch the Berlin Airlift were fewer than 100 C-47s.

Operation Vittles, however, possessed a few underrated weapons—underrated by the Russians, certainly—in the form of leadership, flight and navigation equipment, and the support of the airline industry, none of which Stalin had taken into account. His overconfidence ignored the proud traditions of military transport pilots and airlift logistical experience, so much of it originally airline-taught and airline-developed—quite literally, the best-trained airlift cadre in the world. Nor had Stalin ever grasped the importance of radar's development into a bad-weather landing aid of monumental proportions.

He had also failed to realize the brains behind the Berlin Airlift, not to mention the powerful personalities guiding those brains. The USAF in Europe was headed by cigar-smoking General Curtis LeMay, of whom a subordinate once said: "When the son of a bitch walks into a room full of junior officers, you can hear their spines crack." The man LeMay put in charge of Vittles, when it became apparent this was going to be a long haul of undetermined duration, was General William Tunner, architect of the Hump airlift. The overall commander of U.S. occupation forces in Europe was General Lucius Clay, no renowned combat leader, but the Army's most consummate diplomat and an exceptionally skilled administrator. It was Clay who contacted Washington as soon as the blockade began, and recommended an airlift as the only alternative to military action.

LeMay and Tunner knew C-47s were simply too small for the job ahead; it would be like trying to supply eight combat divisions with half a dozen jeeps. In June and July, the C-47s were able to fly in less than 1200 tons a day, Vittles was looking like a lost cause, and Clay flew to Washington, where he pleaded for bigger airplanes. He got them: virtually every C-54 in the new Military Air Transport Command's fleet. Skymasters began winging their way toward Germany from MATS bases around the world. From Panama. From Hawaii. From Alaska. From scores of domestic bases. The Navy contributed two squadrons of R5-Ds, at the time just about its entire postwar four-engine transport strength. As soon as each Skymaster completed its transatlantic crossing, it would land at Rhein-Main, the big USAF base near Frankfurt, load tons of cargo, and head for Berlin on what would be the first of many such missions.

(Rhein-Main was a mother lode of aviation history; it was adjacent to the former site of the Zeppelin Company's home base, and it was from here that the dirigible *Hindenburg* had taken off a decade before on its final, ill-fated trip to Lakehurst, New Jersey.)

To handle many of the assignments and missions normally flown by MATS C-54s, the Pentagon called on the same source as in World War II: the airlines, this time both scheduled and nonscheduled, who took over regular, nonemergency cargo assignments normally flown by C-54s by operating hundreds of military contract flights. Several scheduled carriers flew military personnel and cargo shipments within the U.S., while Seaboard & Western, Pan Am, TWA, American Overseas, Alaska Airlines, and Trans-Ocean began the first of some 600 transatlantic crossings loaded with supplies for Berlin—106 of them by Seaboard & Western alone. Slick Airways operated a vital supply link from Texas to Westover Air Force Base in Maine, that fed the overseas flights.

No airline cargo planes were allowed to fly into West Berlin itself, because it was considered too dangerous. They usually landed at Rhein-Main and unloaded their cargoes for transfer into MATS C-54s. The more the Russians tightened the siege screws, the more Operation Vittles stepped up its own tempo as the C-54 armada swelled to some 300 airplanes, and the Royal Air Force built its own Berlin Airlift fleet up to more than 100 transports. The RAF role was vital; into what the British first called "Operation Knicker" and later "Operation Plainfare" was thrown virtually every transport airplane the RAF had, including twin-engine Dakotas (C-47s) and four-engine converted Lancaster bombers. The RAF even used Short Sunderland flying boats in the airlift, seaplanes almost as large as Boeing's 314. The Sunderlands would land on Havel Lake within the perimeters of West Berlin and unload their cargoes.

At the height of the airlift, the two allies were operating 700 flights a day into Berlin, but this was a figure achieved only after Clay accepted a French offer to open a third field at Tegel in the French sector to relieve the congestion at Tempelhof and Gatow. Clay was irked by initial construction delays—he had set a December 1948 deadline for the new field and Paris officials insisted it couldn't be finished until the following March. Yet it was finished in time to meet Clay's timetable, and this was partially due to the no-nonsense commander of the French occupation zone, General Jean Ganeval, who seems to have been a kind of French George Patton.

He discovered that a tall Russian radio tower, located on the fringe of the Soviet zone, had been erected in the middle of what was to be the new runway's approach path, posing a definite hazard to incoming flights. Ganeval politely asked the Russians to remove the tower. The Russians refused, not nearly as politely. So one night Ganeval sent a demolition team into the area and blew it up.

The third field, opening just at the start of the cold winter months, was all the Berlin Airlift needed. Also crucial was the construction of a third runway at Tempelhof. Those same months brought the worst flying weather—days and nights of virtually no visibility and ceilings so low that in airline operations, landings under these conditions would have been illegal. But the thunder of Pratt & Whitney and Rolls-Royce Merlin engines bouncing off the rooftops of besieged Berlin never ceased. The Germans looked at leaden skies and wondered how these young Americans and Britishers could possibly land their precious cargoes when people on the ground could hardly see across the street.

The answer, of course, was that wartime technological achievement called Ground Controlled Approach (GCA), developed as part of radar (Radio Detection and Ranging) research. Most of the experimental work was done by an American physicist named Luis Alvarez, who first conceived the idea of using new precision radar to guide planes down safely even under extremely limited ceiling and visibility conditions.

The system he created sent two radio beams toward incoming aircraft—the first to pinpoint the target and the second to establish a safe glide path beam for the pilot to follow. The GCA operator, usually parked in a truck next to the runway, would lock onto the approaching airplane with one beam, and then monitor his path down the glide scope beam on a radar screen, while transmitting any necessary corrections via voice radio. The USAF identified its eastbound airlift planes as "Big Easy," followed by the aircraft's tail numbers; westbound flights out of Berlin were "Big Willy."

So the airwaves around Tempelhof, Gatow, and Tegel were constantly crackling with GCA litany . . . "Big Easy Fiver-Fiver-Twenty-Two, you are slightly to the right of glide slope . . . turn left two degrees . . . you are back on glide slope but a little high . . . bring your nose down a bit . . . you are correcting nicely . . . very good . . . you are now lined up and cleared to land."

The MATS pilots loved GCA, which wasn't true of the airline pilots who tried it. They didn't really trust GCA, even though most military airmen considered it extremely accurate, and it still is hard to find an airline pilot who isn't leery of any system that puts complete control of an airplane into the hands of someone on the ground during a bad weather landing, the most critical and potentially dangerous phase of any flight.

"Let the motorman do the approach and landing," argued American's Sam Saint, the respected pilot/scientist who invented centerline lighting for runways.

Over strenuous objections from airline pilots, there were several postwar attempts to require GCA at major civilian airports in the U.S., and GCA equipment actually was installed at some of them, although sparsely used, if at all. The airlines went along with their pilots' preference for Instrument Landing Systems (ILS) instead.

With ILS, the airman also lines up his airplane with two radio beams emanating from a ground station, but there is no voice guidance. The beams appear on the cockpit instrument panel as tiny arrows which the pilot aligns until they are centered perfectly, telling him he is on the right final glide path.

The truth was that GCA was far more precise than the earlier ILS equipment, and some claim it is still superior even to more modern ILS hardware. The best of both worlds was the double system installed at Andrews Air Force Base just outside Washington, where ILS was used to monitor GCA approaches, but this was never adopted on a widespread scale either by the military or the airlines.

Regardless of the GCA vs. ILS debate, there is no doubt GCA was largely responsible for Operation Vittles's mind-boggling success during the critical winter months of 1948–1949. The Germans themselves didn't believe the airlift could be sustained in the kind of weather "when even the birds were walking," to quote an old airman's saying. Another factor in its success was the superb advance training of less experienced flight crews. While some of the pilots assigned to Vittles were airline-trained veterans from the old war-time ATC days, many were youngsters who received special instructions at a USAF school at Great Falls, Montana, where duplicates of the three Berlin air corridors were created, complete with approach path navigation aids and GCA radar. The newer pilots practiced until they could just about make GCA landings as routinely as the veterans. Yet even then, they were required to fly two airlift round-trips as copilots with veteran IPs (Instructor Pilots) before they flew regular missions on their own. Those IPs, almost to the man, had been airline-trained—primarily on instrument flying—during the war.

The flight plans for the Berlin missions had to be followed with absolutely no deviations allowed—there was no room for mavericks nor freethinkers in the Berlin Airlift. Claude Luisada, writing for the aviation/space encyclopedia *Above and Beyond,* provided this laconic description of the strict rules governing the airlift's daily flying activities:

"The lift system utilized the northern and southern air corridors for eastbound flights to Berlin, and the center corridor for west-bound flights. On a typical flight, the crew would board their C-54 at Rhein-Main Base. At a specified time, they would taxi behind other C-54s, each fully loaded with ten tons of cargo. Takeoff followed a split second schedule. Climb-out was toward a radio beacon which marked the beginning of the air corridor leading to West Berlin. This procedure required a set airspeed and rate-of-climb. All aircraft had assigned altitudes between 5000 feet and 7000 feet at 500-foot intervals. Airplanes at the same altitude were fifteen minutes apart. Every three minutes, aircraft were taking off or landing.

"The C-54 would reach its assigned altitude before reaching the corridor. Entering the twenty-mile-wide corridor, the airspeed was set at 170 mph, the rate which all aircraft maintained throughout their [eastbound] flights. In the vicinity of Berlin, radar would direct the flight to its final heading for the airport runway. As soon as the aircraft landed and was parked, unloading crews would swarm aboard and unload all cargo in less than thirty minutes. Flight crews were not permitted to leave the vicinity of their plane, since they were normally airborne for the return flight exactly thirty minutes after landing."

The ten tons each C-54 carried—20,000 pounds—was nearly two tons more than the airplane normally carried, but this was partially offset by the fact that the distance to be flown (it was 350 miles between Rhein-Main and Tempelhof) didn't require a full load of fuel. Each C-54 was allotted 1200 gallons of fuel. About 400 gallons were consumed on the flight from Rhein-Main at Frankfurt or Wiesbaden into Berlin and another 400 for the return trip; the remaining 400 gallons was the reserve that might be needed to reach an alternate field.

Adherence to a precise schedule was essential to prevent bottle-necks; a delay in only one landing unraveled the whole system, which at the height of the airlift was aimed at a landing every three minutes. A pilot who missed his approach had to return to base and literally "go to the end of the line" to start all over again. Technically, there were ceiling and visibility limits to bad weather landings, depending on the wind direction and the runway being used. Precision GCA was not available to pilots landing at Tempel-hof out of the east; all they got was a heading and general advice on correlating aircraft altitude with distance from the airport. For such nonprecision approaches the minimum ceiling was 400 feet with at least a mile visibility. Precision GCA allowed minimums of 200 feet and a half mile, but as the crews gained experience, landings with a ceiling of only 100 feet and quarter-mile visibility were not uncommon.

The best way to understand what the Berlin Airlift was like is to see it through the eyes of a typical pilot, like Bill Lafferty, who flew 190 missions from Frankfurt and Wiesbaden into Berlin before being transferred to the Strategic Air Command just before the blockade was lifted. Lafferty was a baby-faced nineteen-year-old from the little town of Centralia, Illinois, when he enlisted in the Air Force in 1944—"You're too damned young to do anything but fly," a recruiting officer told him.

He received AWTI-approved transport training and joined the 60th Troop Carrier Group at Wiesbaden as a first lieutenant and aircraft commander. On the morning of Sunday, June 26, 1948, he flew his regular mail run in a C-47 from Rhein-Main into Berlin via the central corridor which, at the time, because traffic was light, was used for both eastbound and westbound flights. He returned to Frankfurt in mid afternoon, figuring the day's work was over; there was a rule against flying the Berlin corridor at night, there were no overnight facilities at Tempelhof anyway, and it would be dark if he flew back to Berlin again. So he walked into base operations and cheerfully told the duty officer, "I'll go out again at first light."

"Wrong, Lieutenant. You're going now."

"You don't understand," Lafferty protested. "The rules . . ."

"*You* don't understand, Lafferty," the duty officer snapped. "You're going back to Berlin right now. Your aircraft's already being loaded."

So he flew to Berlin and was inquiring as to where he could spend the night when he was ordered right back to Wiesbaden and told to report to the group commander upon arrival. By the time he landed, he knew something must be up; the field was bulging at the seams with C-47s. He reported as ordered to the group commander, who smiled and shook his hand.

"Congratulations, Lieutenant."

"Sir? What for?"

"Son, you've just flown the first Berlin Airlift mission for the 60th Troop Carrier Group."

Lafferty looked at him blankly.

"You don't know what the hell I'm talking about, do you?"

"No, sir."

The colonel told him about the blockade, then picked up a phone and chewed the hide off some officer at Rhein-Main for not giving Lafferty an intelligence briefing. That chore finished, he turned back to the lieutenant.

"Do you understand why I'm so goddamned mad?"

"Yes, sir."

"Are you mad?"

"I am now," Lafferty muttered.

And that's how First Lieutenant William Lafferty, who eventually retired as a full colonel himself, began the most interesting few months of his flying career. He shifted over to C-54s as soon as they began arriving, flew the requisite two trips with an IP, and became an Skymaster commander himself. His record was virtually spotless—"virtually" because for the airlift pilots, most of them young and uninhibited, the only real sin was cracking up a valuable airplane.

Lafferty flew one mission in early December which happened to be on the same Saturday the annual Army-Navy football game was being played, and there was no way he was going to miss the action being broadcast on Armed Forces Radio. So he, his copilot, and the flight engineer, who also doubled as crew chief on every C-54, listened to the game while en route to Berlin. They became so involved with the radio play-by-play that they overflew Tempelhof and wound up 100 miles off course. Understandably embarrassed, Lafferty came down through the overcast to look around and discovered they were over a Russian fighter base inside the Soviet-occupied zone. He climbed right back into the overcast and finally got vectored back to the American zone.

"To this day," he admitted, "I can't remember who the hell won the game."

Harassment by Soviet fighters was sporadic, but scary when it did happen; the unarmed airlift planes flew unescorted, and the Russians actually shot down two British transports. Lafferty himself was fired on twice, but one of the most frequent methods of harassment was for a Yak fighter to approach a C-54 head-on in a game of aerial chicken.

"Of course you'd get the hell out of the way in a hurry," Lafferty related, "but we had a few guys who were tigers, and wouldn't take evasive action until the last possible second. After that happened a few times, the old man told us at debriefing: 'It's one thing to be brave and it's another thing to be stupid. For God's sake don't sit there until you get rammed.' "

A total of twenty-eight Americans and forty-seven British airmen lost their lives in crashes during the Berlin Airlift. Fatigue may well have been a factor in the accidents; what with some 400 airplanes making 700 flights a day into Berlin, the crews didn't get nearly enough rest and stress heightened in winter flying.

"Fatigue certainly entered into it," Lafferty agreed, "but another factor was trying to stretch the limits of the airplane, and there wasn't much margin for error. The GCA approach to one of the original Tempelhof runways took you smack over some tall apartment buildings, and when you cleared the last one you were only seventeen feet from the top of the roof. I saw one C-54 clip that roof with its landing gear. It ended up on its back, and although everyone walked away, it was the classic case of stretching your ability just a little bit too far.

"We never took off at maximum weight, always a couple of thousand pounds under. But because our fuel load was light, we always landed way over max. The book said you couldn't land on those steel mats or asphalt with an overweight airplane and stop in time. So we made a habit of touching down right at the end, hitting the brakes as soon as the main wheels touched, and then rotating the nose up until the tailskid hit the runway and slowed you down. It was tough on the airplane, but not as tough as running into something. I saw one C-54 land too fast and too far down. When the guy tried to make the turnoff the nose wheel collapsed. Nobody chewed you out for aborting a landing and going back to base, but tearing up an airplane brought you a lot of unwanted attention.

"A lot of pilots violated bad weather landing limits, especially when the new runway at Tempelhof opened with new high-intensity approach lights, and we'd land even with a hundred-foot ceiling just to get the job done. Normally in a C-54 you'd make a GCA approach at a hundred and thirty miles per hour indicated airspeed, with twenty-degree flaps. But on the airlift with those narrow corridors, because you had to keep from straying too wide, you'd approach a lot slower at a hundred and twenty, with flaps at thirty degrees. No sweat unless you had to abort, and then things got interesting. By the time you started to increase power to climb, you'd already lost a hundred feet of altitude and you needed another ten mph to get any rate of climb. If you lost an engine at that point, you had problems."

On really bad days, when the so-called ceiling went almost to the ground, only those pilots qualified as IPs were allowed to make landings, and it was necessary to reduce traffic volume to a landing every ten minutes instead of every three minutes. The usual schedule required each crew to fly two round-trips a day between Frankfurt or Wiesbaden and Berlin; the RAF pilots made three round-trips, but their route was an hour shorter each way. The pilots and flight engineers joined in the unloading process; off-loading ten tons of cargo within the mandatory thirty minute turnaround time was as difficult as making the flight itself—worse in a physical sense, and especially tough if the cargo happened to include coal. Many mechanics and loadmasters, after hosing down numerous aircraft interiors covered in black coal dust, developed skin sores to go with sore backs and aching muscles.

Lafferty and his two fellow crew members were helping to unload flour from a C-54 after one flight and noticed that the driver of the German truck waiting to receive part of the cargo was just sitting in his cab, idly observing the activity.

"The least the SOB can do is help us," Lafferty grumbled. He pulled the driver out of the truck and put him to work. The next day, Lafferty was informed that German truck drivers were strongly unionized, that their contract exempted them from unloading activities, and that if he ever did it again he'd need a good lawyer.

But that incident of noncooperation was a rare exception. The real reward for all the hardships, both in the air and on the ground, came from the looks of gratitude in the eyes of the German people, and their increasing if somewhat hesitant manifestations of friendship. There were no so-called "ugly Americans" in West Berlin, not among the pilots and ground crews of Operation Vittles. The Germans were grateful to the British, too, but they seemed to respond more openly to the informality of the American crews. William Manchester, in his history of 1932–1972 America (*The Glory and the Dream*), probably explained the difference better than anyone else with this unattributed quote:

"The British walk the earth as if they owned it; the Americans walk the earth as if they don't give a damn who owned it."

And Manchester also quoted CBS reporter Eric Sevareid's equally applicable description of the GIs who stormed through Germany as Nazi resistance collapsed:

"They had no sense of conquering a country; they were just after the Germans, and had to walk over this particular piece of the earth's surface to get at them."

The finest example of cementing German-American friendship during the airlift was set by a C-54 pilot named Gail Halvorsen, a rather shy young Mormon from Garland, Utah, who was haunted by the sight of German children in threadbare clothing, standing behind the perimeter fence at Tempelhof and watching, wide-eyed, at the planes landing and taking off. Lieutenant Halvorsen looked at their pale, pinched faces and wondered why they never begged for gum or candy, as he had seen so many children do during the war years, when he flew ATC transports to North Africa, Latin America, and Ascension Island.

He struck up a conversation with some of the older ones, who were learning English in school. They said they watched the planes all day, and on impulse he told them he'd be flying in there the next day and would drop gum and candy out of his plane if they promised to divide it equally with the younger kids.

"But how will we know which is your plane?' one asked.

"I'll waggle my wings. That's how you can tell."

It occurred to Halvorsen later that he had no idea how he was going to drop goodies out of an airplane without scattering them all over the landscape. Getting candy and gum was no problem; he could load up at the Rhein-Main PX. Then he came up with the idea of miniature parachutes to increase the drop accuracy. He happened to have a whole supply of handkerchiefs which he, his copilot, and his flight engineer—who were sworn to secrecy— fashioned into tiny parachutes.

The next day, as promised, he spotted the children lined up along the fence, waggled his wings, and dropped the "chutes" out the small exit normally used for ejecting emergency flares. That was the start of the "Candy Bombers" and an everlasting love affair between Gail Halvorsen and the children of West Berlin. The word spread until there were hundreds lining the perimeter fence awaiting the arrival of the American who began getting fan mail addressed to "Onkel Wackelfluegel" (Uncle Wiggly Wings) or "Der Schokoladen-flieger" (The Chocolate Flier).

Uncle Wiggly Wings continued his supposedly surreptitious bombing missions hoping nobody would catch him. But he was nailed after a bag full of Hershey bars nearly beaned a reporter, and summoned before higher authorities expecting to be court-martialed. Instead he was informed that General Tunner considered this the greatest idea since the light bulb and wanted more Candy Bombers than one lone first lieutenant; within days, scores of pilots were dropping improvised little parachutes out of C-54s, and Halvorsen's fame had spread not only throughout the city of West Berlin but the entire United States Air Force.

Every man who took part in the Berlin Airlift was a goodwill ambassador. In 1986, Lafferty went back to Germany on a vacation and discovered that time hadn't erased one vestige of gratitude among Germans who had lived through the blockade. "Even after almost forty years," he remarked, "if you said you flew the Berlin Airlift you were treated like visiting royalty. I remember flying over Berlin on good days and there'd be hundreds of Germans waving at the planes overhead. In January of '49, the mayor of West Berlin gave some of the airlift veterans special lighters and stickpins along with honorary memberships in what they called 'The Chimney Sweeps Club.' It may not sound like much, but those people stuck their necks out during the blockade, just as we did. Today, if you asked an American high school kid about the Berlin Airlift chances are you'll get just a blank stare. Ask almost any Berliner of any age, and you're more likely to get a big smile, and maybe a hug."

The Germans themselves supplied much of the labor needed to keep the runways at Tempelhof and Gatow under constant repair; the unending stream of heavily laden C-54s would tear up the steel landing mats in quick order. Teams of German laborers armed with wheelbarrows, shovels, asphalt, and fresh patching for torn mats, would follow in the wake of almost every landing, picking up loose debris and fixing any runway damage before the next C-54 arrived, only minutes later. To casual observers, they must have resembled circus workers cleaning up behind elephants lumbering down Main Street.

The new airfield at Tegel was built from scratch by 17,000 German civilians (many were ex-soldiers) working in three shifts eight hours a day for less than ten marks and one hot meal. The supreme irony was what they used for the foundation on which were laid the crushed stones, asphalt binding, and steel mats that formed the runway: pieces of bricks taken from the rubble of the buildings the Eighth Air Force and RAF had pulverized during the war.

LeMay left Operation Vittles late in 1948 to take over the newly created Strategic Air Command, and General Tunner kept the airlift machinery moving at full speed. Before departing Germany, however, LeMay insisted on flying several Vittles missions himself, including one coal delivery that promptly tagged Vittles with a new nickname: "LeMay's Coal and Fuel Company."

While the C-54 was the airlift's dominant airplane, newer transports made their debuts in the latter months. One was the huge Douglas C-74 Globemaster, forerunner of the later C-124 version. Its size earned it the nickname of "The Aluminum Overcast" and its two cockpit canopies earned it another nickname: "Bug Eyes." It was fast despite its bulk, cruising at more than 225 mph, and it could fly nonstop between its Mobile, Alabama, base and Rhein-Main. On the C-74's initial flight into Germany, it carried eighteen spare engines for C-54s that weighed more than 38,000 pounds. On another flight the plane hauled sixteen tons of coal into West Berlin.

Also making its initial appearance was the twin-engine Fairchild C-82, first of the "Flying Boxcars." Its rear clamshell cargo doors made loading heavy equipment easy, and the five assigned to the airlift often carried road-building machinery and bulldozers. The crews loved the C-82's roomy cockpit but not its single-engine performance. A friend let Bill Lafferty fly one once and Bill started to retard the throttle on one engine. The regular C-82 pilot grabbed his arm and stopped him.

"What the hell do you think you're doing, Bill?"

"I'm giving you single engine," Lafferty said. "I just want to see how she flies on one engine."

He received a very brief, excruciatingly blunt warning.

"Well, don't. Because she won't."

By the end of 1948, the airlift was delivering an average of 4500 tons a day, and in the first two months of the new year the daily average tonnage soared to 5500 tons. By mid April 1949, everyone knew the Berlin blockade had been licked; on one day alone, April 16, USAF and RAF transports flew nearly 13,000 tons of supplies into West Berlin. But there were indications as early as January that

Stalin was getting ready to admit defeat, conceding that the world's greatest land power had been thwarted by unarmed air power. Stalin, in a rare interview granted to an American reporter, allowed that he would "be willing to discuss peace with President Truman."

Russia officially lifted the Berlin blockade at 12:01 A.M., May 12, 1949, exactly 274 days after it began, but the airlift continued until sufficient supplies could be stockpiled, just in case the Soviets tried it again. The final airlift flight landed at 8:30 A.M. Berlin time, September 30, the last of 279,114 missions that had delivered more than 2.3 million tons of supplies, almost one ton for every person living in West Berlin; coal represented nearly seventy percent of the total tonnage.

It was an unparalleled triumph for air transport capability that cast large shadows of things to come; the Berlin Airlift helped prevent one war, but Korea, Vietnam, and the Gulf wars remained to be fought, and in these, the airlines would be even more active airlift allies.

Germany did not forget the professionalism of the American airmen whose skill helped save its western capital. When the German airline Lufthansa was allowed to resume commercial service in the early 1950s, it began rebuilding its war-shattered fleet with four Lockheed L-1049 Super Constellations to fly its international routes, and turned to a U.S. airline for help in crew training. It selected TWA, the largest Connie operator and also a carrier with considerable oceanic experience,

The first TWA contingent to reach Germany was headed by a burly check captain named Ernie Pretsch, who was not only of German ancestry, but actually looked like someone Central Casting would pick to play a Prussian general. He had close-cropped blondish hair, jug ears, and features that could have been hacked out of solid granite. He spoke fluent German and even his English carried a slight Teutonic accent.

For the training mission, Pretsch recruited only pilots who weren't deathly afraid of him, a policy that effectively eliminated about 99.5 percent of the TWA pilot corps. Hal Blackburn was among those who accepted Ernie's invitation, and a captain asked Blackie why he was going to Germany to work with the redoubtable Captain Pretsch, who reportedly would have scared Dracula.

"You must be nuts flying for that bastard," the pilot added. "I hear he's just taking his friends."

Blackburn nodded placidly. "And he's right—that's what I'd do."

The TWA pilots thoroughly enjoyed their assignment, so much so that some were suspected of prolonging the training more than necessary. A visiting TWA official asked an instructor how the Germans were doing.

"They're real sharp. Excellent pilots."

"Then I suppose you'll be releasing them for line duty soon."

The instructor looked horrified. "Oh, no. We're being very thorough, because they've got so much to learn."

In truth, some of them did. Many were rusty ex–Luftwaffe pilots who hadn't flown since the war ended and had little if any instrument experience. The younger ones had only a few hundred hours on small planes before they were turned over to TWA. They were scrupulously polite, respectful to the instructors, and almost pathetically eager to learn. The TWA pilots got used to having doors opened for them and even having their cigarettes lit. More important, the Americans began to respect them as professionals in attitude and steadily improving performance.

The early Lufthansa overseas flights took off with a TWA captain in command and Germans making up the rest of the flight crew. Hal Blackburn flew one such trip, from West Berlin to Hamburg, Paris, and across the South Atlantic to Natal. At one point, Blackburn suggested that the young copilot get some sleep on the next leg, with a relief pilot sitting in for him. The German refused.

"Captain," he explained soberly, "if I stay up here I might learn something."

Dick Beck, a TWA captain cast in the same practical jokester mold as American's Si Bittner, was taking a Lufthansa Connie into New York one night and let his German copilot make the landing. Beck had a pair of false teeth in his nav kit and when the Lufthansa pilot bounced a little hard on touchdown, Beck surreptitiously pulled out the teeth and held them accusingly in front of the startled young German.

"Can'th you make a dethent landing?" he lisped.

The Lufthansa pilot turned pale. "Oh, my God, sir, I'm sorry!" he gasped.

Beck confessed later that he felt sorry for the youngster. "If he hadn't had his seat harness fastened," he reminisced, "the poor guy would have stood up and saluted. Actually, they were excellent pilots and so polite we free spirits couldn't believe it. I'd stand there in operations, pull out a cigarette, and there'd be five Zippo lighters in front of my face."

Polite, yes. Disciplined, absolutely. Obsequious, no. By the time Lufthansa was able to take over its own training, it had a cadre of skilled airmen TWA or any other airline would have welcomed. But the Lufthansa experience, coming in the wake of the Berlin Airlift, demonstrated the respect even our wartime adversaries held toward U.S. airlines, their crews, their operating and maintenance procedures, and the airplanes they flew.

As soon as Japan was allowed to resume civil air operations, Japan Air Lines began operating American-built transports—its first new postwar airliner was the DC-6—and also hired American pilots as instructors and senior captains. When JAL inaugurated jet service between New York and Tokyo, the captain of the DC-8 was an American, and the airline went on to become one of Boeing's biggest customers; JAL, for example, has bought more 747s than any American or European carrier.

Italy's airline, Alitalia, didn't hire American flight crews but it started flying Douglas transports after the war and still operates a jet fleet that's predominantly American-made.

It must be admitted that in selling transport aircraft to former enemy nations, or any other country, the U.S. had a tremendous advantage and one that was the direct result of the use of airlift in World War II. America's only real transport airframe competitor after the war was Great Britain, which like the U.S. possessed several highly skilled, well-established aircraft and engine manufacturing concerns. But the British never had a chance to really compete, simply because their wartime design and production had concentrated exclusively on combat aircraft—fighters, light bombers, and two heavy bomber types.

In contrast, the U.S. designed and built transports as well as military planes throughout the war. After V-J Day, companies like Douglas, Lockheed, and Boeing were perfectly positioned to dominate the postwar market for new airliners; no one else had the design experience or an equally important asset: the priceless reputation so solidly earned by the wartime manufacturing/airline/

military coalition that not only created the first global airlift, but established its incredible potential.

The advantage this gave American aircraft companies also applied to the U.S. airlines that charged into a postwar international air travel market supposedly guided by the "Five Freedoms" first proposed by President Roosevelt even before the war ended. In 1944, FDR had instigated the first international civil air conference, held in Chicago; fifty-five friendly nations were invited and all but two showed up—the Russian delegation got halfway to Chicago and then, without explanation, turned around and went back to Moscow, while the Saudi Arabian representatives never even left home. No Axis country was invited, of course; in fact, FDR had privately voiced to Winston Churchill his conviction that after the war, Germany, Japan, and Italy shouldn't be allowed to fly anything bigger than a toy plane powered by a rubber band.

Roosevelt's Five Freedoms looked reasonable—on paper, anyway. They were:

1. The right to fly through another country's air space.
2. The right to land in a foreign country for technical purposes such as refueling, repairs, or in an emergency.
3. The right to carry traffic from a carrier's country to another country.
4. The right to pick up passengers in another country and fly them back to the airline's country.
5. The right to pick up passengers at a foreign airport and transport them to destinations beyond the carrier's home country.

The problem with the Five Freedoms was that they also could be interpreted as the Five Restrictions. Could a British airline, for example, land its passengers in New York and then fly a load of new passengers to Chicago? Could TWA discharge its passengers in Paris and then take a planeload of French tourists to Bordeaux? Absolutely not; such intrusion on domestic traffic would be called cabotage, a practice dating back to the 19th century, when merchant ships were allowed to carry traffic between two ports within the same foreign country. The Five Freedoms, simply by omission, placed limitations on international travel rights—practically anything not listed as a specific right was illegal.

Because the war was still in progress, the Chicago conference was inconclusive—more of a preliminary sounding board for various ideas and opinions than a we-must-act-now meeting. After six weeks, the delegates did approve the first two freedoms and also agreed to establish an international civil aviation organization that actually was aimed at blocking American domination of the postwar overseas travel market. There was great fear that the U.S., largely because it was the major supplier of aircraft, could call the competitive shots in everything from fares to scheduling.

If America in general was the free world's aviation bogeyman, carriers like TWA, Northwest, and American Overseas had one of their own: Juan Trippe and his "Chosen Instrument" plan for a single U.S. flag carrier on all international routes.

Roosevelt already had passed the word that he wanted no part of any "One Flag—One Carrier" policy for America's role in postwar international air travel. He especially sought competition in the North Atlantic, and FDR's idea—which later became a reality—was "area competition," which basically called for Pan Am to serve central Europe, American Overseas northern Europe, and TWA southern Europe. More specifically, Pan Am would fly to London and then across central Europe to Turkey and India; American Overseas would also operate to London and continue on to Scandinavia and northern Germany; TWA would serve Paris and beyond to Rome, Athens, Cairo, and Bombay.

Many observers thought Trippe had an inside track to kill the area competition proposal and win approval of his Chosen Instrument dream; his daughter was married to Undersecretary of State Edward Stettinius. But Trippe's son-in-law might as well have been plain Joe Smith, a plumber from Cleveland; Assistant Secretary of State Adolf Berle had been picked to head the American delegation at Chicago, apparently a deliberate move to counter Trippe's influence, and whatever future clout Trippe may have hoped the Stettinius relationship gave him turned out to be imaginary.

Pat Patterson's support for the Chosen Instrument at a 1944 congressional hearing preceding the Chicago conference also proved ineffectively fragile. Even Hal George, who sincerely admired United's president, ridiculed his claim that by 1955 not more than twenty-three planes would be needed to carry all the North Atlantic air traffic. George, reminding Congress that his ATC together with NATS had carried some 3 million wartime passengers, predicted that the size of postwar international air travel would "stagger the imagination." And Josh Lee of the Civil Aeronautics Board said that to accept Patterson's reasoning, "It would have been just as logical to have determined how many people crossed the American desert by stagecoach, projected the figure, and announced that this is the number of passengers who may be expected to cross the United States by rail."

Nor did Roosevelt's death in 1945 aid Pan Am's cause, for Harry Truman was not likely to mistreat Kansas City–based TWA. In the summer of 1945, the CAB approved FDR's zone plan subject to the outcome of bilateral negotiations between the U.S. and the individual nations involved. In 1946, the first such bilateral agreement was reached between the United States and Great Britain at a conference in Bermuda, and over the next half century these miniature air treaties would dictate who flew where, how often, and under what restrictions.

(There were a series of meetings on international air issues toward the close of the war, and Eddie Rickenbacker was invited to one in Havana, Cuba, as Eastern's representative. He was invited to speak at a civic luncheon prior to the conference's opening session, but just before he was introduced, word spread through the audience that President Roosevelt had just died. Unbelievably, Rickenbacker began his talk by remarking that this was the best news he had heard for a long time. He was immediately asked to leave Cuba and Eastern had to rush a vice president to Havana to replace him.)

The proposal the Dutch had made at Chicago for some kind of international air council bore early fruit with the establishment of the International Civil Air Organization (ICAO), with headquarters in Montreal, although ICAO developed into more of a technical organization than one concerned with airline economic and competitive issues. To this day it continues to promote numerous air safety programs, from navigation standards to security, and while it offers advice on bilateral agreements, it stays out of actual negotiations.

The gestation of another aviation organization took place in Chicago: the International Air Transport Association (IATA), which came into being late in 1945 and evolved into a powerful body that for years controlled international fares and just about everything else—including the size of airline sandwiches. What came to be known as the "Great Sandwich War of the North Atlantic" was indirectly fomented by none other than Juan Trippe, although he never intended to start an international dispute over airline food.

In 1948, Pan Am inaugurated tourist-class service between New York and San Juan, using sixty-four-passenger DC-4s and charging only $75 for a one-way ticket instead of the regular $133 fare. Traffic exploded, multiplying five times in only five months. Of the 5 million Puerto Ricans who migrated to the U.S. after the war, two-thirds of them arrived in New York via Pan Am.

His Chosen Instrument dream may have been demolished, but Trippe proved he still had both business savvy and influence. He ordered an improved version of the DC-6, the DC-6B (which some experts insist was the best piston-engine airliner ever built), into which he packed eighty-two seats and assigned the new planes to an all-tourist service across the Atlantic. His European competitors quickly copied the service after winning IATA approval for lower fares, but IATA also dictated limits on in-flight service: no free drinks, and only simple meals, such as cold sandwiches, could be offered.

SAS, the Scandinavian airline, took the sandwich rule as merely a general guideline, and began serving a tourist class feast that would have done justice to first class: open-face sandwiches smothered in anchovies, herring, and delectable cheeses. TWA led the screams of protest, filed a formal charge of unfair competition with IATA, and SAS had to pay a $25,000 fine—which, considering all the publicity the Great Sandwich War received, must have been worth every cent.

Coach and tourist service . . . economy fares . . . two-class airplanes . . . bilateral agreements . . . international civil aviation organizations . . . more and more flights in pressurized cabins above most weather . . . radar-guided landings . . . the salvation of a great city by 400 airplanes filled with life-preserving supplies and a combination of human courage and skill . . . daily transatlantic crossings over routes that the airlines and ATC had turned into routine aerial highways . . .

These were the postwar developments, all significant and some of major import, that had occurred in less than a decade and were molding aviation's fate. The shape of what lay ahead was still indistinct, uncertain, unsettled. Never quite congealing and compressing into an easily recognizable future, for aviation itself never stands still. One could guess, however . . .

A broad hint came July 27, 1949, in the sound of Britain's Comet jetliner making its first test flight.

An even broader hint was there if on that same day one could have looked over the shoulders of aeronautical engineers at Boeing and Douglas and grabbed a peek at the blueprints in front of them: the preliminary designs for the 707 and the DC-8.

A bright hint of greater air safety as Alaska Airlines, in September 1996, became the first carrier to test integration of the Global Positioning System (GPS) with Enhanced Ground Proximity Warning System technology, a combination assuring pinpoint landing guidance under virtually the worst weather and terrain conditions. Alaska committed $10 million to first equip twenty-five aircraft regularly operating in mountainous terrain with the new system, and American announced plans to install it in all of its 625 jets. That this major safety advance was tested and proved in the treacherous mountains around Juneau was poetic justice—aviation, so vital to the northernmost state in war and peace, had come a long way since the days of the pioneering bush pilots and the hazard-crammed ATC flights of WW II.

Military airlift was born, developed, and matured in a world war . . . honed over the skies of West Berlin to as near perfection as the technology of that era could achieve . . . and reinforced by confidence that in the jet age, the airlines of the United States would again be ready to help when needed.

It turned out they would be.

★ ★ EPILOGUE ★ ★
The Legacies

The Berlin Airlift was a postgraduate course in the application of air power to solve even the most difficult supply logistics. Yet when the outbreak of the Korean War confronted the U.S. with the task of supporting a supply line 10,000 miles long, it was almost as if the smashing of the blockade had never happened; as if the bitter lessons of complacent unpreparedness, so painfully learned in the early months of World War II, had been completely forgotten by everyone—presidents and politicians alike. There were only a few exceptions, and most of them were those who would have to win another war.

As of June 25, 1950—the day the North Koreans crossed the 38th parallel in a full-scale invasion of South Korea—MATS's Pacific Division could muster only sixty C-54s. Military airlift capability had been one of the chief victims of the nation's rapid demobilization and the corresponding slashing of military funding; not only was MATS short of airplanes, it was also so short of crews that its daily aircraft utilization rate had dwindled to only two and a half hours. The Air Force, through no fault of its own, was as ill-prepared to supply the Korean war theater as the Army was to fight in it.

It was *déjà vu* for the airlines, who might as well have entered a gigantic time warp that sent them back to December 1941, when they possessed the only equipment and manpower resources to launch a long-range airlift. Now they had to do it all over again; MATS needed at least seventy-five days in which to recall flight and ground crew reservists, retrain them, and reactivate transport aircraft that had been gathering dust for many months.

The civil carriers, scheduled and supplemental alike, pumped some sixty four-engine transports into a quickly improvised aerial bridge that stretched from the United States to Japan, where MATS aircraft took over; as with the Berlin Airlift, it was considered too risky for civil airliners to fly directly into combat areas. (This policy did not hold true in Vietnam, when airline military charters flew right into the war zone.)

Trans-Ocean, a supplemental carrier founded by former United pilot Orvis Nelson, flew the first Korean airlift mission for MATS: a DC-4 crammed with antitank bazooka rockets. Subsequently it assigned seven DC-4s to the airlift and hauled nearly fourteen percent of its total: 22,000 military passengers and nearly 10 million pounds of cargo on 673 flights between Travis Air Force Base, north of San Francisco, and Japan.

(Its small size notwithstanding, Trans-Ocean was an aggressive outfit whose pilots included the well-traveled Ernie Gann; after the war he had left American and the structured environment of a scheduled airline for the more informal atmosphere and fresh challenges of the nonskeds. It was on a Trans-Ocean DC-4 charter flight from Hawaii to California that Gann encountered a severe vibration problem, almost had to ditch before making it safely into San Francisco, and used the incident as the basis for his best-selling novel and subsequent film *The High and the Mighty*.)

Trans-Ocean and other carriers—United, Pan Am, and Northwest—were the major contributors among the scheduled airlines because they possessed the most transpacific experience; together they flew nearly 11,000 military contract missions between Travis and Japan in support of the Korean campaign. This represented only forty percent of the total number flown—MATS really got rolling after the seventy-five days of breathing room the airlines had provided—but that forty percent included nearly seven out of every ten passengers, more than half the total cargo, and seventy percent of the mail.

United's involvement began less than two weeks after the invasion, when General MacArthur informed Washington he needed 105 special technicians flown to Tokyo in a hurry. UAL pulled two DC-6s off their regular schedules, dispatched the planes to a dozen scattered airports where the various technicians were standing by, and the DC-6s delivered them to MacArthur less than twenty-five hours after leaving San Francisco. Over the next thirty-nine months, United's planes crossed the Pacific to Japan a thousand times, logging 13 million miles on Korean War charters.

Pan Am assigned eight DC-4s and two of its new Boeing Stratocruisers to the Korean airlift, and in not quite three and a half years carried more than 114,000 passengers and 31 million pounds of cargo and mail across the Pacific. Northwest completed 1380 Pacific crossings, totaling more than 13 million miles, carrying 40,000 troops and 12 million pounds of priority cargo.

The Korean "police action," which turned into a real war, motivated Congress to finally do something about the situation that had plagued Pan Am in the early days of World War II: the difficulties of insuring airline aircraft exposed to the increased risks that military airlift assignments involved. It passed an amendment to the old but still existing Civil Aviation Act of 1938 that authorized federal insurance in cases where commercial underwriters refused to provide coverage, or offered it at such expensive premiums that few carriers could afford them. The wisdom of this action would be demonstrated forty years later when, at the outbreak of the Gulf War, insurance companies either canceled hull coverage for airlines participating in the military airlift or drastically raised premiums on any civil airplane flying into the war region.

In 1951, with the Korean conflict still raging, the Pentagon and the Air Transport Association conceived a new and far more efficient method of utilizing airline aircraft and crews in a national emergency. MATS and the airlines agreed to create a Civil Reserve Air Fleet (CRAF), a plan which allocated the specific number and type of transport aircraft the military could call on *automatically and instantly*. Participating carriers submitted to MATS an annual summary of their operating costs for each type of pledged equipment, and if the airplanes flew military missions, compensation was set at actual operating costs plus a fixed markup.

CRAF was launched officially in 1952, but was never activated for Korea, nor was it used in Vietnam, simply because both conflicts involved gradual buildups of American forces; increasing utilization of airline equipment to operate the respective airlifts was correspondingly gradual. There was no general "fire alarm" call-up to the airlines because MATS's needs for airline help—except for the

Korean War's initial sixty-airplane influx—were relatively small at first.

CRAF was different; in effect, it constituted a kind of airlift national guard—a constant, in-readiness reserve of transports and crews in case a large air transport force was needed quickly, and the increasing emphasis was on big, long-range aircraft. Economy as well as efficiency was behind its creation; the Air Force was acquiring an adequate reserve fleet of fully manned transport aircraft readily available, with exact operating costs set in advance, and paid for only when needed. For the USAF this was infinitely more economical than having to buy, maintain, and operate the same size fleet on its own. CRAF, in fact, didn't become a real force-in-being until well into the jet age, when huge and enormously expensive airline "jumbos" like the 747, DC-10, and L-10ll were assigned to the reserve fleet.

Vietnam was a repeat performance of Korea—a kind of larger and distorted mirror image, because this most unpopular of all the wars America has ever fought lasted longer than anyone anticipated or wanted, and ended in defeat. It involved the first use of jet transports in a military airlift, most of them airline-operated. MATS itself changed its name during the war, becoming a full command designated as the Military Airlift Command, or MAC, as it still is known today.

Continental, Northwest, and World Airways, plus American and TWA, handled most of the military passenger flights as part of the Vietnam airlift. Pan Am and United flew them, too, but to a lesser extent; United's pilots took a dim view of the greeting they invariably received from air traffic controllers in the Saigon tower.

"Welcome to the Unfriendly Skies of Vietnam," almost every controller would chirp in a parody of the airline's famous advertising slogan.

Bob Prescott's Flying Tiger line, doing what came naturally to an airline whose original pilot nucleus had consisted of eighteen-to twenty-year-old airmen who had once flown the Hump for General Claire Chennault, contributed a large chunk of the cargo missions. Among the varied types of piston, turboprop, and jet aircraft these Hump veterans flew through the years was the Canadian-built CL-44, freighter version of the prop-jet Bristol Britannia airliner, which featured a "swing tail"—the hinged aft fuselage swung open to facilitate cargo pallet loading. Although designed primarily as a cargo transport, a number carried passenger seats that could be attached or removed depending on the airplane's mission. The CL-44s were widely used in the Vietnam airlift by Flying Tiger, Slick and Seaboard World.

George Knuckey, who later became a top economist for Alaska Airlines, served as the Flying Tiger station manager at the Saigon airfield and came to hold the ex-Hump pilots in awe.

"There wasn't very much they wouldn't do to complete an airlift assignment, and that included outright theft," Knuckey recalled.

Flying Tiger used to have a lot of trouble at Travis, where some Air Force officer would ramp-check a plane before it left and almost invariably find something missing, that hadn't been boarded at the airline's San Francisco home base. A navigator's kit would be absent. Or the airplane was minus a medical kit. Or half the meals that were supposed to have been boarded might be AWOL.

One day an Air Force inspector discovered there was no fire axe on the airplane and wouldn't let the Tiger CL-44 take off without one. So the captain, an ex-Hump pilot, walked over to one of his stewardesses, who was a youngster fresh out of training.

"Young lady, do you see the Slick CL-44 parked next to us?"

"Yes, sir."

"You know where we normally keep the fire axe on our airplane?"

"Sure, Captain, I learned that in school."

"Fine. Now you go over to that Slick CL-44 and in the same location you'll find *their* fire axe. Kindly remove it and bring it over to our airplane so we can get the hell out of here."

The CL-44's swing tail required that during the unloading process, weights had to be added to the nose to compensate for the release of the ten heavy cargo pallets the airplane carried; otherwise the nose would lift right off the ground. In 1964, as the airlift was gaining momentum, the military decided it didn't have the manpower to cope with the huge traffic volume generated at Saigon by airline transports. So unloading and loading operations were turned over to the native ground crews of Air Vietnam, and from that decision sprang an incident that would have been comic if it were not so tragic.

In came a cargo-crammed Tiger CL-44 and the Vietnamese ground crew began to unload. The first mistake was that nobody remembered to add the nose weights. The second mistake was committed by the cargo handlers; instead of unlocking and off-loading each pallet separately, they unlocked all ten simultaneously and began shoving them out.

"I couldn't believe what happened," Knuckey recounted. "The nose went up in the air at a thirty-five degree angle, and two or three of the handlers inside the cabin were tossed out of the plane like bullets out of a rifle. A couple of pallets followed and crushed them to death."

Knuckey also remembered that the shortage of ground crews resulted in enormous waste.

"The airlines were unloading so much stuff at Saigon, for about five hundred yards in front of the terminal building it was double and triple deep in pallets. Once I saw hundreds of IBM electric typewriters there, worth about eight or nine hundred dollars apiece; they had been monsooned on for a month. I've never witnessed such waste in my life. There must have been five or six hundred pallets out there and there just wasn't enough manpower or forklifts to move them.

"At one stage, just before I left Flying Tiger, we had eight airplanes, mostly DC-8s, arrive inside an hour. Even at the best of times, the Saigon ramp could accommodate about four aircraft. At one point there were two DC8s parked nose to nose and we didn't know how we were going to get them out. We couldn't even scrounge up a tow truck to back one of them up. It all started out about seven o'clock one morning, it was absolute chaos, and I was the only ramp agent on duty. One of the outbound flights was a passenger charter and these were always much more labor-intensive, much worse than the cargo loading and unloading—it was a mess."

But, Knuckey added, "As an airline operation it was run pretty smoothly except for the congestion problems. All the airline reps in Saigon formed a big, happy family. If Bob Six, Bob Prescott, or any other carrier president came over on a visit, the reps from the other airlines would play hosts at a dinner. Spare parts interchange was an accepted practice. It was as though we were one airline. If a Flying Tiger airplane needed a replacement part in a hurry and we didn't have one in stock, we could always borrow one from World or Continental or any other carrier—we even got some cooperation from Pan Am, which wasn't exactly known for such generosity."

One of the more unlikely participants in the Vietnam airlift, unlikely considering its status as a strictly regional carrier, was Alaska Airlines. Well, perhaps not *that* unlikely, for Alaska had a proud and also unusual emergency airlift heritage despite its predominantly West Coast–Alaska route system. Its DC-4s (actually surplus C-54s) had flown eighty-seven trips across the Atlantic in the Berlin airlift, carrying cargo and military personnel to Munich, Frankfurt, and Wiesbaden, and returning with servicemen's dependants—the latter including eleven loads of German war brides who had married American GIs.

Alaska's most unique aerial mission, however, was a nonmilitary effort that began in 1948, when the new state of Israel was born. The American Joint Distribution Committee, seeking to bring Jews from all over the world to the new nation, was particularly anxious to settle Yemenite Jews there; the Yemenites were one of the original and fabled lost tribes of Israel. The committee couldn't arrange sea transportation from Yemen's city of Aden in Africa, because the Arabs wouldn't allow any ship carrying Jews through the Red Sea and the Gulf of Aquaba; bringing them by air was the only solution.

Alaska Airlines was not an obvious candidate for an airlift between Africa and Palestine, and exactly how it became involved seems to be a minor mystery. When author Archie Satterfield was researching company historical files for his *Story of Alaska Airlines,* he discovered that the whole episode of what became known as "Operation Magic Carpet" was covered by only two brief sentences in the minutes of a board of directors' meeting.

"When an accountant went through the airline's records a short time after the event," Satterfield wrote, "the pages relating to this charter work had been torn out." The author believed that James Wooten, Alaska's president at the time, committed the airline without bothering to notify his directors, and kept it from these nominal superiors until the contract had been signed. As it turned out, however, Operation Magic Carpet was unexpectedly successful. Utilizing a C-46 and a pair of DC-4s, the latter reconfigured to carry 120 people by installing wooden benches with seatbelts, Alaska flew some 40,000 Yemenite refugees to their new country—about 39,000 more than Wooten had originally expected to carry. Operation Magic Carpet itself became an episode in Leon Uris's best-selling novel *Exodus.*

The airline's military missions included flying drilling rigs, prefabricated buildings, and other equipment to the Navy's northern-most oil reserve fields on Alaska's North Slope—about as cold, desolate, and uninviting an area as anyone could imagine. The pilots used C-46s, a DC-4, and a ski-equipped DC-3, but the principal aircraft employed was Lockheed's reliable and versatile C-130 prop-jet Hercules, originally designed for the Air Force. Its propellers were hooked to four Allison jet engines and Alaska operated six of them, known as the L-382 in this civilian cargo version. They could land virtually anywhere, including the many frozen lakes that served as landing fields because not much else was available. One North Slope site that passed as an "airport" had a runway with a fourteen percent grade. Winter operations were reminiscent of ATC's World War II Alaskan difficulties—instruments froze, cabin heaters worked only intermittently, and it took two gasoline heaters hooked together to preheat the engines before taking off.

Alaska had another Navy contract that involved flying almost to the North Pole, carrying supplies to a scientific geological and seismographic expedition based on a frozen strip of Arctic real estate known as Ice Island. It was a challenging mission because, as Captain Warren Metzger observed, "the island kept moving, which made it interesting to our navigators."

Under a MATS contract of the early 1960s, Alaska operated a daily flight carrying military passengers between McChord Air Force Base near Seattle and Elmendorf AFB in Alaska, using the only four-engine jet transport it currently owned: a Convair 880. As soon as the round-trip was completed, the Convair was dispatched back to Anchorage on its single daily regular passenger flight. The four engines on that lone 880 apparently convinced someone in the airline's marketing department that Alaska could advertise "four jets daily to Alaska."

(Such imaginative advertising didn't surprise anyone at Alaska, because few things ever surprised anyone at this history-rich carrier. Alaska was the only airline in the history of aviation to have one of its airplanes collide with a fish at an altitude of 300 feet. The pilot's radio message—"a fish just hit my cockpit windshield"—was initially attributed to hallucinations, until the captain explained later what happened. A fast-climbing eagle was clutching a salmon it had just plucked from the water, saw the airliner coming toward it, and dropped the fish in panic.)

That Alaska 880 was a rather plush airplane well-admired by

military and civilian passengers alike; it featured a stand-up bar that served only draft beer. The mechanics were less enamored of the aircraft, however. They referred to the Convair as "Old Smoky" because on every takeoff four thick, black trails of smoke would spurt from the engines.

Alaska was short of funds in the '60s, and on one of the earliest 880 military charters, the cabin crew discovered not enough silverware had been purchased to serve dinner to all ninety-six passengers. So the flight attendants improvised; they served the forward half of the airplane first, sneaked the used silverware into the bathrooms, where soiled forks, knives, and spoons were washed, and then put on the meal trays that went to the passengers in the rear section.

Alaska had been the first U.S. carrier to operate the civil version of the C-130, and its experience with this airlift workhorse was instrumental in Alaska's Vietnam participation; there were several airports in Vietnam closed to 707s, DC-8s, and even CL-44s, but a Hercules could go almost anywhere. Alaska's cost-plus-fixed-fee MATS contract had a little higher profit margin than anyone else's because the C-130s had the lowest operating costs of any airplane serving the Vietnam airlift.

Even this advantage, however, didn't erase what was then the airline's Murphy's Law reputation. Somehow, it had neglected to obtain diplomatic authority to land in Vietnam. Its first MATS flight came into Saigon, unloaded, and took off again before anyone could challenge its legality. But when the second C-130 landed, its crew was arrested and threatened with imprisonment. Fortunately, George Knuckey of Flying Tiger had enough local connections to get the crew released and arrange the proper authority; Alaska later hired him.

Another Vietnam veteran who eventually climbed high up Alaska's management ladder was a C-130 navigator named Pat Glenn, a youngster fresh out of the Air Force. His was one of those countless Horatio Alger stories so typical of the airline industry: years later he retired from Alaska as executive vice president and chief operating officer.

"I'll never forgot those Vietnam days," he reminisced. "Nobody liked to land at night, because you could see the tracer fire below so plainly. Of course they were shooting in the daytime, too, but at least you couldn't see those tracers. We always stopped in Japan on the way home and loaded up the C-130s with Hibachi cooking pots and Honda motorcycles. We wouldn't take off without those pots, and I don't think there was an Alaska Airlines employee who didn't own a Hibachi."

(Flying Tiger's Vietnam crews actually started the voluminous transporting of Hibachi pots, but had to stop the practice when local Hibachi retail dealers in the airline's Los Angeles home base protested to the Japanese manufacturer.)

Alaska was one of the few carriers that didn't carry passengers in and out of Vietnam, and in that respect their crews were lucky. Most memories of the airline cabin attendants who volunteered to work MATS or the later MAC flights are sad and poignant, and that applied to every participating carrier, whether scheduled or supplemental. They all witnessed too many scared young soldiers reluctantly on their way to Vietnam, and they also saw them on their way back—often disillusioned, bitter, and sometimes maimed for life psychologically as well as physically.

The trips were bid mostly by experienced senior flight attendants like TWA's Ida Staggers, whose airline career had begun on DC-2s and DC-3s and who didn't quit flying until 1972, when she reached the mandatory retirement age of sixty. The MATS/MAC flights were her last assignment before retiring; the troops got to calling her "Aunt Ida."

"I bid the trips, though sometimes I wondered why," she once admitted. "We were so loving to those kids, and I guess it was right that we were, if only to make their lives a little bit happier, because they didn't know what they were going into. We were their mothers for just a little while, maybe for some of us even their grandmothers. One thing I refused to do was give them my address. It would have torn me up to hear from them. One sweet, wonderful kid conned me into it and I got two heartrending letters from him after he had gone into combat. I never did it again."

One of her fellow hostesses, Marie Escarzega, remembered meeting a TWA 707 that had come into Okinawa for a cabin crew change on a MAC flight from Vietnam; Ida, the senior hostess aboard, had bid a ten day trip over Christmas and New Year's. She laughingly told Marie and the other hostesses, "Now don't you girls take down my holiday decorations."

Marie thought sourly, what decorations, and who cares about decorations? She was tired and, being so far away from home during

the holidays, feeling sorry for herself. But she boarded the 707—
and blinked in surprise.

"The sadness left my heart," she recalled. "I had tears in my
eyes, but from shame, not sorrow. Ida had brought Christmas to
that drab, blue-gray, six-abreast, one-hundred-and-sixty-five-seat 707
interior. There were wreaths on the cockpit and lavatory doors,
candy canes above every seat, and on the forward bulkhead a big
sign reading MERRY XMAS FROM YOUR TWA CREW. It was signed by
everyone working Ida's flight, and I found out later she had paid
for all the decorations and candy herself."

That was Ida Staggers, personifying the profession of flight attendant. She was about forty years older than the 707 she had decorated, but those decorations had included two special items that
were unseen but felt: compassion and sentiment.

TWA's military charters were typical of those flown by all the
carriers taking part in the Vietnam airlift. Most were operated out
of Travis AFB near San Francisco or McGuire AFB in New Jersey
via Travis. A 707 or DC-8 would embark some 165 troops at Travis,
and usually land at Bien Hoa, Vietnam, thirty-five hours later, after
refueling stops at Honolulu and Okinawa. In Honolulu, for carriers
that didn't serve Hawaii regularly, much of the necessary maintenance along with provisioning was turned over to Aloha Airlines.
In Vietnam, turnaround time was approximately one hour—sixty
minutes in which to refuel, usually board 165 homeward-bound
soldiers, and take off again. Airline crews were not allowed to
deplane in Vietnam; crew changes were made in Okinawa. (And
by unwritten, unofficial agreement, no carrier ever served rice on
an eastbound flight.)

The airlines did their best to add little touches of extra service
on the Vietnam-bound flights, such as making up goodie bags filled
with toothpaste, soap, postcards, and cigarettes. Many planes hauled
care packages from home, while suppliers of in-flight movies
donated films for many MAC/airline aircraft equipped to show
movies. One of the most precious commodities any incoming flight
could bring was fresh milk, so scarce that Americans working in
Saigon looked on it as an absolute delicacy. Also welcome were
box lunches, especially when they included fried chicken.

There wasn't much chance for soldiers to reciprocate for little
acts of kindness and special attention, but they tried. One TWA
hostess had a sash with some 200 military unit badges presented

to her by servicemen returning from Vietnam. Another ended up with a dress on which she had pinned eleven pounds of insignia GIs had given her.

Even with the long on-duty time a thirty-five-hour trip entailed, the carriers never lacked for volunteers. American, for instance, had 725 flight attendants bidding for 142 positions. All airline pilots and cabin crews working MAC flights were required to wear identification tags in case an airplane was forced to land in a combat zone and they were taken prisoner. Nor were they that far away from the fighting on more than one occasion, as American flight attendant Mary White recalled:

"Almost always, our turnaround would leave late at night, returning to Okinawa in the early hours. The reason for that was that we would not be as much of a visible target at night. We could occasionally see the 'fireworks' down below, and sometimes the runways would be shelled. It was almost an unreal situation, because we never really saw the horror of the war. We only saw the thousands of young men we would drop off and only pray that we could bring them home. Many that we did bring home would never be the same again."

Gwen Mahler, a former TWA hostess who produced two histories of TWA and American flight attendants, summed up the Vietnam-MAC experience for all carriers in these heartfelt words:

"Those who served these flights had to pay a price. The sadness of delivering so many boys into a war zone was lost on no one."

World Airways operated military flights between Okinawa and Denang, Vietnam, using 727s. Its feisty and volatile president, Ed Daly, was aboard the last flight out of Denang as Vietcong troops neared the airport. Panic-stricken Vietnamese soldiers trying to flee south tried to mob the plane before it took off. A few started to storm the 727's rear ventral staircase, where Daly was standing, firing at them with a revolver. Two or three were still trying in vain to hang on to the edge of the half open stairwell as the jet left the ground.

The Vietnam airlift lasted from 1969 to the spring of 1973, during which time MAC itself took on the name it still carries today, and proved to be the last major conflict in which the CRAF sat offstage waiting for its cue. An airlift that fell far short of an all-out effort occurred in the fall of 1973, when Syria and Egypt attacked Israel in an attempt to regain territory lost in the Six-Day War of

1967. President Nixon, fearing Israel might be overrun, ordered an emergency airlift that was hamstrung by several allies who refused to let MAC planes land on their soil to refuel; helping Israel, they were convinced, would invite retaliation by oil-producing Arab nations. The Israelis managed to hold their own and force an uneasy truce, yet MAC's lack of heavy, long-range transports in significant strength (there weren't many jumbo jets around in 1973) limited U.S. aid; the one-month war ended before airline help was needed, but the importance of a large civil transport airlift backup force was not lost on American military planners, nor could they ignore the sword of Damocles that hung over the Western world and Japan in the form of their reliance on Arab oil.

The absolute need for military airlift capability was underlined again in 1982, when Great Britain went to war against Argentina over the Falkland Islands and faced the problem of supplying a combat zone 8000 miles away with a sadly inadequate air transport fleet. Once the U.S. decided to support the British, one of its most important contributions consisted of flying heavily loaded Air Force cargo planes secretly to Ascension Island in the Azores, the closest staging point to the Falklands, where crucial supplies—including Sidewinder and Shrike missiles, fuel, communications equipment, and ammunition—could be transferred to British vessels.

Through the years, much of CRAF's composition changed with the introduction of new and bigger jetliner models into air carrier fleets. The Air Force saw them not merely as far more efficient, longer-legged transports, but as an emergency airlift capability it could not otherwise have afforded. MAC itself was gradually acquiring its own fleet of transports designed specifically for airlift duty: first, the double-decked Douglas C-124 Globemaster introduced in the 1950s, successor to the earlier model C-74 that took part in the Berlin Airlift. The C-124 was used extensively in Korea, and was capable of carrying a 70,000-pound payload including light tanks or 200 fully equipped troops. Then came Lockheed's justifiably famous C-130, still in wide use throughout the world; it might even be called the DC-3 of second-generation military cargo airplanes. In the 1982 battle for the Falklands, it was a rather ironic compliment to Lockheed's engineers that the C-130 served as the primary military transport for both the Royal Air Force and its Argentine foe.

The Hercules was followed by two more Lockheed designs: the

larger C-141 Starlifter, MAC's first big all-jet transport, and the mammoth C-5A Galaxy, so enormous it would have required only seventeen C-5As to carry the same tonnage flown by the 308 C-54s that served the Berlin Airlift. Boeing's KC-135, the military version of the 707, was used extensively as a refueling tanker and also served as a transport. The most recent addition to MAC was the huge and versatile McDonnell Douglas C-17, which entered Air Force service after the Gulf War.

Billions were spent on the acquisition of such aircraft as the Galaxy and C-17, known as "battlefield airlift" transports, because they could land or take off using virtually any kind of field. These and the earlier C-130s and C-141s constituted MAC's so-called "organic" fleet of specialized transports, adequate under normal circumstances but still numerically insufficient to provide maximum airlift capacity in a major crisis that may occur thousands of miles from the United States and require a full-scale airlift involving thousands of troops and tons of equipment within forty-eight hours. That is exactly what CRAF provided: maximum airlift capability on demand.

Costly, yes, but cheaper than buying the equivalent of that capability in the form of new airplanes. In 1986, the Air Force spent about $600 million on what it called the CRAF Enhancement Program, much of the money going toward modifying nineteen conventional Pan Am 747s assigned to CRAF into airplanes that could be converted from passenger airliners into military cargo planes in not more than two days. The modification was no mere removal of passenger seats; the cabin floor of each airplane had to be beefed up, a big rear cargo door installed, and the entire electrical system reworked. The changes added 11,000 pounds to the 747's weight, which meant all nineteen CRAF airplanes would cost Pan Am more to operate as purely passenger aircraft. Part of the program funding went to the airline to compensate for those additional operating expenses, and each conversion cost more than $25 million. But the Air Force spent far less on the conversions than it would have had to pay for nineteen brand-new 747s specifically designed and built as military freighters, at an estimated price of $120 million per airplane. A single C-17 costs the Air Force $174 million.

The roster of airlines participating in CRAF was subject to frequent revisions along with the number and types of aircraft each airline pledged to the program. Both scheduled and supplemental carriers joined, enticed by an Air Force promise that only those airlines enlisting in CRAF would be eligible for future MAC contracts. The size of airline participants varied, too, ranging from the big airlift veterans like American, Northwest, and United, to smaller carriers that hadn't existed in the days of the Air Transport Command.

Even a few strictly regional airlines joined CRAF. Typical was Aloha, which started interisland service in 1946 under the grandiose name of Trans-Pacific with a one-airplane "fleet." It consisted of a single war surplus C-47—actually an ex-Navy R-4D which had been used as a VIP transport during the war. This function had prompted the Navy to put upholstering on the normally rock-hard bucket seats, and Aloha—which at the time couldn't afford to convert the airplane into a legitimate airliner—operated it with this unique kind of interior until its finances improved. Aloha (or TPA) paid less than $75,000 for its first three airplanes, all used R-4Ds; this was $25,000 less than the price of a single brand-new DC-3 before the war.

Throughout the 1980s, Aloha flew personnel between Honolulu and a huge military training base on the main island of Hawaii, and operated other military charters between Hawaii and Johnston Island, although the airline finally decided to drop out of CRAF; its all-737 jetliner fleet, perfect for Aloha's interisland route system, lacked the long-range CRAF aircraft MAC required.

Hawaiian Airlines, which started out as Aloha's bitter competitor for interisland traffic, was actually much older than its rival; it was launched as Inter-Island Airways in 1929, with a few eight-passenger Sikorsky S-38 seaplanes, and became a long-range carrier in 1983, when it inaugurated DC-8 service to California. Its military airlift role, which began in 1958 with a MATS contract under which it flew more than 4000 passengers between San Francisco and Japan, thus expanded dramatically. During the Gulf War, Hawaiian—which already had achieved a perfect safety record spanning more than sixty-five years—completed an impressive 231 CRAF missions, including a number that marked the final flights for its remaining DC-8s.

In the late 1980s, MAC itself formed a "subsidiary airline"— the Air Mobility Command, which combined MAC's own long-range heavy transports with those in the CRAF fleet, a strategic move with the Middle East in mind as the likeliest location on the planet for a potentially explosive situation that might involve military action. The organization of the AMC/CRAF duo was accompanied by a decision to activate the latter in three successive stages as needed: As of the spring of 1990, Stage 1 called for activation of at least 41 long-range airline freighters and passenger transports; Stage 2 added another 140 airplanes, and under a fully implemented Stage 3, CRAF's commitment would involve another 325 aircraft, for a total of 506.

On August 1, 1990, the day Saddam Hussein sent the Iraqi army across the border of tiny Kawait and defied the rest of the world to do anything about it, MAC and the CRAF were ready. On August 6, the following transmission from the Military Airlift Command to all CRAF members flashed over ARINC (Aeronautical Radio, Inc.), a communications system serving commercial air carriers:

> CRAF STAGE 1 ACTIVATION NOTIFICATION. THIS IS NOT AN EXERCISE. THE COMMANDER IN CHIEF OF MILITARY AIRLIFT COMMAND HAS DETERMINED THE UNITED STATES HAS SUBSTANTIALLY EXPANDED PEACETIME MILITARY AIRLIFT REQUIREMENTS. HE HAS THEREFORE ACTIVATED STAGE 1, EFFECTIVE 0001Z, 18 AUG 90. THE GOVERNMENT MAY EXERCISE ITS OPTION TO INCREASE THE SERVICES TO BE PERFORMED UNDER YOUR AIRLIFT SERVICES CONTRACT TO THE FULL CAPACITY OF THE AIRCRAFT VOLUNTEERED TO CRAF STAGE 1. CURRENTLY WE DO NOT HAVE A REQUIREMENT FOR ALL OF STAGE 1, AND THEREFORE ANTICIPATE A SELECTIVE UTILIZATION OF STAGE 1. SPECIFIC MISSION SCHEDULES WILL BE SENT AT LEAST 24 HOURS PRIOR TO MISSION ONLOAD TIME . . . CRITICAL: VERIFY RECEIPT OF THIS MESSAGE. THEN IMMEDIATELY PASS TO YOUR CHIEF OPERATING OFFICER AND CIVIL RESERVE AIR FLEET MOBILIZATION REPRESENTATIVE. RESPOND VIA AIRING CIRCUIT . . .

Thus was launched the airlift that supported first the defensive deployment known as Desert Shield, and subsequently the Desert Storm offensive that kicked the Iraqis out of Kuwait and savaged Saddam Hussein's army until its agreement to a cease-fire. The Gulf crisis lasted five months, but actual combat operations were over in only 100 days. So fast and overwhelming was the coalition victory that only CRAF Stages 1 and 2 were activated (the latter on January 10, 1991), but the combination of MAC aircraft and those two stages of CRAF transports produced in six months the same size of troop buildup that had taken four years in Vietnam.

A total of eleven scheduled passenger airlines, Federal Express, UPS, and Emery—the three "overnight delivery" specialists—and thirteen supplemental carriers took part in the Gulf War airlift. They flew more than 5300 missions, including 100 even before CRAF was activated, carried sixty-four percent of the troops and just under twenty-seven percent of the war cargo, while flying Gulf War missions that took them thousands of miles from their normal operating areas. FedEx, UPS, and Emery alone completed nearly 900 flights to Saudi Arabia.

Air travelers used to patronizing familiar scheduled carriers might not have recognized the names of the supplemental airlines that sent plane after plane winging toward Saudi Arabia: Airlines such as Connie Kaletta, Evergreen, World, Southern Air, Tower, Buffalo Air, Arrow, Florida West, Rich International, Trans Continental, and Rosenbaum.

Heading the supplemental contributors was American Trans-Air, whose Lockheed L-10lls completed 494 Gulf troop charters, second only to the 605 passenger and cargo flights flown by Federal Express. ATA exemplified the modern efficiency, maturity, and valuable contributions of these once-maligned carriers formerly known as nonskeds.

Indianapolis-based ATA was founded in 1973 by J. George Mikelsons, a Latvian immigrant and the son of a concert violinist who came to the U.S. in 1960 when he was hired by the Indianapolis Symphony Orchestra. Mikelsons himself started out as a pilot for a local travel club before starting his own travel club, called Ambassadair, with a single jetliner: a former Eastern Air Lines Boeing 720. He would have been very much at home among Alaska's one-man-airline bush pilots like Bob Reeve; Mikelsons not only captained the 720 on charters, but his wife served as the senior flight attendant, and the two of them drove passengers to the Indianapolis airport on the travel club's bus.

American Trans-Air was launched as Ambassadair's airline subsidiary and today ranks as the largest charter airline in North America, with 5000 employees and a fleet of almost fifty jetliners, including Lockheed 1011s and Boeing 757s, that carries some 5 million passengers a year. ATA expanded into scheduled operations in 1983, and now serves more than twenty cities on a route system that includes seven mainland states plus Mexico, the Bahamas, Hawaii, and Puerto Rico. After the Gulf War, American Trans-Air donated the services of an L-1011 and its crew to carry relief supplies to displaced Kurds. Three years later ATA, although it was only one of thirteen participating scheduled and supplemental carriers, flew more than one-third of the "Project Restore Hope" missions to war-ravaged Somalia.

Time also changed the military airlift role of airlines like Delta, a carrier considered minor league in World War II, when it operated only domestic military cargo flights, but whose long-range jets flew a number of CRAF missions in the Gulf War. Delta and its sister airlines also contributed hundreds of reservist employees recalled to service when Saddam threatened to stage "the mother of all battles."

(They included, incidentally, a 727 second officer from Alaska Airlines named Michelle Olczvanowska, who went to the flight decks of C-141s as a first lieutenant. She typified the women on active air transport duty during the Gulf War who were carrying on an airlift tradition of their own: that of World War II's Women's Auxiliary Ferry Squadron (WAFS) and Women's Air Force Service Pilots (WASP), whose gutsy personnel ferried hundreds of combat aircraft into the war zones as part of the Air Transport Command—three decades before the U.S. airlines began hiring women as pilots.)

The drama of America's gigantic aerial bridge to the Persian Gulf, unprecedented in sheer speed and capacity, was best described by a man with eyewitness status and a lot at stake in the airlift's outcome: the commander-in-chief of Desert Storm, General Norman Schwartzkopf. In his autobiography, *It Doesn't Take a Hero* (Bantam Books), Schwartzkopf writes:

"I went out to the air base at Dhahran, which was serving as the main entry point for U.S. Army troops. Elements of the 82nd Airborne Division, the 101st Air Assault Division, and the 24th Mechanized Infantry Division were streaming in aboard civilian airliners on loan to the Pentagon.

"The Saudis had practically vacated the base to make room for our operation. I looked up and could see—stretching way out into the distance—at least a half dozen large aircraft stacked up in holding patterns awaiting their turn to land. I looked out along the runways at eight or ten mammoth transport planes, their noses and tail doors yawning open, disgorging all kinds of gear, from attack helicopters to crates of rations. Near where I stood, a Northwest Airlines 747 had pulled up, and I watched soldiers from the

24th Mechanized Infantry Division tumbling out into the 130-degree heat. They were shouldering heavy packs and clutching their weapons and the water bottles that had just been handed to them. Reception officers stood by and singled out the officers and NCOs, who were sent to be briefed, while the soldiers fell out of line and made their way to the large reception tents at the edge of the runway apron . . .''

What this fighting general had just witnessed was global airlift, come of age.

What was transpiring before his eyes was the ultimate fulfillment of Edgar Gorrell's pledge to Franklin Roosevelt: *The nation can depend on its airlines when the chips are down.*

What Schwartzkopf had just seen was the legacy of a tradition born fifty years earlier, when an obscure airline operations planner named Rosie Stallter and five assistants went into the basement of his home to work out the first real air carrier mobilization plan.

What was occurring on that dusty Saudi Arabian airfield was the culmination of a half century of military airlift progress that had matured through three wars and the incredible defeat of the Berlin blockade.

In every giant transport and in every skilled crew member landing in Saudi Arabia, airline and military alike, were the genes of their gallant predecessors, both men and machines. These CRAF and MAC crews and their winged goliaths were the inheritors of what the flight and ground crews of the old Air Transport Command and the Naval Air Transport Service had bequeathed them: the proud traditions, the exacting standards, the pioneering precedents those military and airline comrades had established in a long-ago era.

Edgar Staley Gorrell would have been proud.

The Gulf War was history when, in spring 1992, the Pentagon announced that airline pilots and ground personnel who had served overseas with ATC and NATS between December 14, 1941, and August 14, 1945, were considered to have been on active duty with the armed forces, and therefore eligible for Veterans Administration benefits.

The Little Colonel would have been even prouder.

Acknowledgments

I doubt whether any author, especially in a nonfiction book that by its very nature must involve considerable research, historical perspective by numerous sources, and many personal recollections, can fly solo.

When the Airlines Went to War was no exception; I could not have produced it without the encouragement and aid of people who shared my belief that the airlines' role in World War II and the further development of global airlift as a vital component of national defense have been sadly neglected subjects almost totally ignored by too many historians. The number of World War II histories and biographies that hardly mention or in some cases don't even devote a single word to the roles of the Air Transport Command or the Naval Air Transport Service is surprising.

I find it hard to do justice to the enormous debt I owe R. Dixon Speas, president of PRC Aviation and an influential airline industry figure since the days of the DC-3. Only his faith in and persistent support of this project, from gestation to birth, made its fruition possible.

I must acknowledge the contributions of Carol Hallet, president of the Air Transport Association of America; like Dixon she, too, believed this was a book that had to be written. Equally helpful and supportive was that grand patriarch of air safety, Jerry Lederer, who provided essential background on the development of the airlines' wartime training schools which he helped establish.

I also am indebted to the chief executives of the following airlines whose encouragement and help took many shapes and forms even though several represented carriers that did not even exist in World War II: Alaska, Aloha, American, American Trans Air, Continental, Delta, Emery, Federal Express, Hawaiian, Northwest Orient, Reeve Aleutian, TWA, United, and US Airways.

For special interviews, my profound gratitude goes to retired Air Force Colonel Bill Lafferty who provided valuable background on the Berlin Airlift, and Alaska Airlines retirees Captain Warren Metzger, Pat Glenn, George Knuckey, and "Stub" Kingsolver.

As I've indicated in this book's bibliography, there were scores of other airline officials and wartime airlift veterans, who were interviewed for my previous airline histories and whose invaluable contributions were acknowledged in those works. I renew my debt of gratitude to them all.

The following additional aviation industry organizations and personnel were of immense research help, including obtaining requested (and often rare) photographs:

Air Transport Association—Librarian Marion Mistrik (with extra thanks for essential biographical material on Edgar Gorrell).

Alaska Airlines—Lou Cancelmi, assistant vice president corporate communications, and Ron Suttell.

Aloha Airlines—Stephanie Ackerman, staff vice president corporate communications; Julie King and Jim King.

American Airlines—C.R. Smith Museum—Collections curator Shannon Risk.

American Trans-Air—William Doherty, Jr., director of Military & Governmental Affairs.

The Boeing Company—Michael Lombardi.

Continental Airlines—Ray Scippa.

Delta Air Transport Heritage Museum—Collections curator Carrie Taylor.

Federal Express—Patrick Melancon.

Hawaiian Airlines—Keoni Wagner, Senior Director, corporate communications.

Lockheed-Martin Tactical Aircraft Systems—Mike Moore.

McDonnell Douglas Aircraft Division—Don Hanson and Doug Jacobsen.

Pima Air & Space Museum—Assistant director Tom Swanton; Kirsten Tedesco and Scott Thompson.

United Airlines—Barbara Hanson.

US Airways—Corporation communications vice president Paul Turk, and Pat Crigler.

My old and treasured friend Jim Greenwood, fellow aviation author and "bird-loving" compatriot, warrants a medal for all the aid he gave me in solving various research problems.

Ditto Kathy Stogsdill, PRC Aviation administrative assistant; among her many contributions was a sense of humor that helped me over more than one rough spot.

Many thanks to Jon Proctor, senior editor of *Airliners* magazine and a gifted scribe in his own right; the same accolade to John Wegg, editor-in-chief of *Airways International* magazine; retired Captain Charles McNab, editor of *TARPA Topics,* publication of retired TWA pilots; Ed Betts, retired captain and unofficial TWA historian, and Margie Gerwirtz, secretary of the Wings Club of New York.

My heartfelt gratitude to Walter Zacharius, Kensington Publishing's president and board chairman; Kensington editor Karen Haas, and my agent Aaron Priest. You all made possible fulfillment of a long-time hope that someday this story would be told.

Robert J. Serling
Tucson, Arizona
April, 1997

Bibliography

In researching the story of the U.S. airlines in World War II, I relied in part on material, including personal interviews, from my own published histories of American, TWA, Eastern, Continental, and Western airlines. The interviewees included approximately forty former airline pilots who flew for the wartime Air Transport Command and Naval Air Transport Service, as well as such ground personnel as mechanics, route planners, dispatchers, and navigators. Those five books are:

Maverick, *the Story of Bob Six and Continental Airlines,* Doubleday, 1974.
The Only Way to Fly, the Story of Western Airlines, Doubleday, 1976.
From the Captain to the Colonel, An Informal History of Eastern Airlines, The Dial Press, 1980.
Howard Hughes' Airline, An Informal History of TWA, St. Martin's/ Marek, 1983.
Eagle, the Story of American Airlines, St. Martin's/Marek, 1985.

Other reference books:

Arnold, H.H. *Global Mission,* Harper, 1949.
Baptie, Charles. *Capital Airlines,* Baptie Studios, 1984.
Bean, Barbara. *Of Magic Sails,* Graphic Alliance, 1975.
Bender, Marylin and Altschul, Selig. *The Chosen Instrument,* Simon & Schuster, 1982.

Borman, Frank. *Countdown,* Morrow, 1988.

Brinkley, David. *Washington Goes to War,* Ballantine, 1989.

Cearly, George Jr. *Braniff, an Illustrated History,* Airline Historical Publishing, 1980.

Cohen, Stan. *Hawaiian Airlines,* Pictorial Histories Publishing, 1986.

Collier, Richard. *Bridge Across the Sky,* McGraw-Hill, 1978.

Daley, Robert. *An American Saga,* Random House, 1980.

Davies, R.E.G. *Airlines of the United States Since 1914,* Putnam, 1972.

Follett, Ken. *Night Overwater,* Signet, 1991.

Gann, Ernest. *A Hostage to Fortune,* Knopf, 1978. *Island in the Sky,* Bantam edition, 1990. *Fate Is the Hunter,* Simon & Schuster, 1961. *Ernest K. Gann's Flying Circus,* Macmillan, 1974.

Glines, Carroll & Moseley, Wendell. *The DC-3,* Lippincott, 1966.

Gunston, Bill. *Illustrated Encyclopedia of Propeller Airplanes,* Exeter Books, 1980.

Haggarty, James. *Aviation's Uncle Sam,* Aero Publishers, 1974.

Harris, Walter. *Gable and Lombard,* Simon & Schuster, 1974.

Hopkins, George. *Flying the Line,* Air Line Pilots Association, 1982.

Ingells, Doug. *The Plane That Changed the World,* Aero Publishers, 1966. *The Lockheed Story,* Aero Publishers, 1973. *The McDonnell Douglas Story,* Aero Publishers, 1979.

Jablonski, Edward. *Seawings,* Doubleday, 1972.

Kanin, Garson. *Hollywood,* Viking, 1974.

Kelly, Charles Jr. *The Sky's the Limit,* Coward-McCann, 1963.

King, Jack. *Wings of Man,* Aviation Book Co., 1981.

LeMay, Curtis (with McKinley Kantor). *Mission With LeMay,* Doubleday, 1965.

Lewis, Ralph. *Dead Reckoning,* Paladwr Press, 1994.

Lewis, W. David (with Wesley Newton). *Delta, the History of an Airline,* University of Georgia Press, 1979. (with William Trimble). *The Airway to Everywhere, a History of All-American Aviation,* University of Pittsburgh Press, 1988.

Mahler, Gwen. *Wings of Excellence,* Walsworth Publishing, 1993.

Manchester, William. *The Glory and the Dream,* Bantam/Little Brown 1973.

Mills, Stephen. *More Than Meets the Sky,* Superior Publishing, 1972.

Morison, Samuel Eliot. *The Two-Ocean Navy,* Little, Brown, 1963.

Morris, James. *History of the U.S. Navy,* Longmeadow Press, 1993.

Mudge, Robert. *Adventures of a Yellowbird,* Branden Press, 1969.

Murchie, Guy. *The World Aloft,* Houghton Mifflin, 1954.

Potter, Jean. *The Flying North,* Macmillan, 1965.

Proctor, Jon. *Convair 880 & 990,* World Transport Press, 1996.

Reichers, Lou. *The Flying Years,* Henry Holt, 1956.

Rickenbacker, Edward. *Rickenbacker,* Prentice-Hall, 1967. *Seven Came Back,* Doubleday, 1943.

Sakai, Saburo (with Martin Caiden). *Samurai,* Dutton, 1957.

Satterfield, Archie. *The Story of Alaska Airlines,* Alaska Northwest Publishing, 1982.

Schwartzkopf, Norman (with Peter Petre). *It Doesn't Take a Hero,* Bantam, 1992.

Sigafoos, Robert. *Absolutely Positively Overnight,* St. Luke's Press, 1983.

Solberg, Carl. *Conquest of the Skies,* Little, Brown, 1979.

Spight, Edwin and Jeanne. *Eagles of the Pacific,* Historical Aviation Album, 1980.

Steele, Donna (with Gwen Mahler). *Wings of Pride,* Walsworth Publishing, 1993.

Sterling, Christopher. *Commercial Air Transport Books—An Anotated Bibliography,* Paladwr Press, 1996.

Taylor, Frank. *High Horizons,* McGraw Hill, 1962.

Thorne, Bliss. *The Hump,* Lippincott, 1965.

Tunner, William. *Over the Hump,* Duell, Sloan & Pearce, 1964.

Turner, P. St. John. *Pictorial History of Pan American World Airways,* Ian Allan Ltd., 1973.

Whitehouse, Arch. *The Sky's the Limit,* Macmillan, 1971.

Wighton, Don. *From Jenny to Jet,* Floyd Clymer Publishing, 1963.

Williams, Brad. *Anatomy of an Airline,* Doubleday, 1970.

Wood, Bill. *50 Years of Aloha,* Aloha Airlines, 1996.

Zicree, Marc. *The Twilight Zone Companion,* Bantam, 1982.

PERIODICALS

Above and Beyond, the Encyclopedia of Aviation and Space Science, Volume 2: "The Berlin Airlift," by Claude Luisada.

The Air Line Pilot, September 1978: "Airlift Anniversary."

The Air Line Pilot, June/July 1995: "WW II 'Hangar Flying'," by Captain Kevin Garrison.

Airline Quarterly, Summer 1977: "MAC, the Military Airline," by Donald Sims.

Airliners, July/August 1996: "The Last Passenger Electras Earn Their Keep," by Henry Tenby.

Airliners, July/August 1996: "The Last Ridge Before Washington," by Russell Ferris.

Airways, January/February 1991: "American Trans Air—On Vacation for 22 Years," by Phil Brooks.

Airways, September/October 1996: "Hawaiian Says 'Aloha' to a New Era," by Michael Bitsoff.

Avmark Aviation Economist, August 1990: anonymous article on CRAF.

Defense Transportation Journal, Operation Desert Shield/Desert Storm Special Edition, June 1991.

Published for the Department of Defense Policy Board on Federal Aviation, 1991: "The Civil Reserve Air Fleet," by Ronald Priddy.

Journal of Commerce, May 2, 1995: "Civilian Airlift in the Military."

Journal of the American Aviation Historical Society, Fall 1989: "The Berlin Airlift," by Arthur Pearcy, Jr.

TARPA TOPICS, Journal of the Active Retired Pilots Association of TWA, February 1994: "The ICD," by Ed Betts.

TARPA TOPICS, August 1994: "The Boeing Strats," by Ed Betts.